In memory of our beloved Aharon (Ahrala) Katz, who died in devotion to his country and people.

> Be of the disciples of Aaron, loving peace and pursuing peace; be one who loves his fellow men and draws them near to the Torah. (*Ethics of the Fathers* 1:13)

A Living Covenant

A LIVING COVENANT

The Innovative Spirit in Traditional Judaism

David Hartman

JEWISH LIGHTS Publishing
Woodstock, Vermont

Library of Congress Cataloging-in-Publication Data

The Cataloging-in-Publication Data for the hardcover edition of this book
is as follows:
    Hartman, David.
      A living covenant.
      Includes index.
      1. Covenants (Jewish theology)—History of doctrines. 2.
Prayer (Judaism)
      3. Judaism—Essence, genius, nature. I. Title
      BM612.5.H37   1985   296.3   85–10125
      ISBN 1-58023-011-3

First Paperback Edition
10 9 8 7 6 5 4 3 2 1

Credits
The author is grateful to the following publishers for permission to
quote:
University of Chicago Press, from Schlomo Pines, trans., *Guide of the
Perplexed*; Yale University Press, from Isadore Twersky, trans.,
Introduction to the Code of Maimonides (Mishneh Torah); from Joseph
B. Soloveitchik, *Halakhic Man*, Lawrence Kaplan, trans., copyright by
and used through the courtesy of The Jewish Publication Society of
America; Human Sciences Press, from Soloveitchik, "The Lonely Man of
Faith"; from translation of the Babylonian Talmud, reprinted with per-
mission of The Soncino Press Limited, London; Boys Town Jerusalem
Publishers, from Moses Hyamson, trans., *Mishneh Torah*; from
Yeshayahu Leibowitz, *Yahadut, am yehudi u-medinat Yisrael*, copyright
© by Schocken Publishing House, Ltd., Tel Aviv, Israel.

Published by Jewish Lights Publishing
A Division of LongHill Partners Inc.
P.O. Box 237
Sunset Farm Offices, Route 4
Woodstock, VT 05091

Contents

Acknowledgments   ix

Introduction   1

Part One   THE HUMAN BEING IN JUDAISM

   1. Fundamentals of a Covenantal Anthropology   21

   2. Assertion Versus Submission: The Tension
      Within Judaism   42

   3. "Halakhic Man": Soloveitchik's Synthesis   60

   4. Ethics and *Halakhah*   89

   5. Human Beings in the Presence of God   109

   6. The Spirit of Judaic Prayer   131

      Appendix: Halakhic Critique of Soloveitchik's
                    Approach to Prayer   150

   7. Individual and Community in Prayer   160

**Part Two THE COVENANT AND THE LIVING
          GOD OF HISTORY**

  8. Rabbinic Responses to Suffering   183

  9. The Rabbinic Renewal of the Covenant   204

10. Two Competing Covenantal Paradigms   229

11. The Celebration of Finitude   256

12. The Third Jewish Commonwealth   278

      Postscript   300

      Notes   305

      General Index   333

      Index of Jewish Sources   337

Acknowledgments

THIS WORK HAS BEEN GERMINATING for over twenty-five years. To acknowledge all those who have been helpful in extending my spiritual horizons would be impossible. The process began while I was still a rabbi in North America. The questions and concerns of a community that experienced modernity in all of its forms yet sought anchorage in the Jewish halakhic tradition were a challenge I could not ignore, and served as an important catalyst for my earliest thinking about Judaism.

Nor could the work have been completed had I not had the privilege of participating in the rebirth of the Jewish people in Israel, with its joys and sufferings, its hopes and disappointments. The knowledge that I can no longer speak of Judaism from the framework of a pulpit, but must enter into the total living experience of a nation and attempt to make sense of how Judaic spirituality can live in this new society, has been central to my work as a Jewish philosopher.

In the Israeli context, Jewish ideas may touch on life and death issues. The way one does Jewish theology and religious anthropology may decide the future existence of one's own children and grandchildren. To philosophize in this context is both a privilege and an awesome responsibility. How does one express gratitude to a people that had the courage to expose their religion to the severe test of a total Jewish society? Without that courage, I doubt if I would have felt the urgency to provide new directions for Judaism as a living covenant.

Among specific individuals who have helped me, Shlomo Pines, one of the world's greatest authorities on Maimonides, has been both a source of support and a constant challenge in my attempt to bring Maimonides into the contemporary philosophical discussion. So much of my thinking on Maimonides has emerged from the long hours of discussion over the past eighteen years with Professor Pines. His openness to new possibilities in appreciating Maimonides is a testimony to how scholarship and philosophy can merge.

The manuscript was read carefully by the senior research fellows of the Shalom Hartman Institute, who explored, criticized, and challenged every line. To live in their midst is to live within a community of keen talmudic and philosophic minds who unite commitment and concern for the quality of Jewish life in Israeli society with a profound grasp of philosophy and *halakhah*. I have learned a great deal from them. I cannot imagine what this book would have been like had it not gone through the intellectual furnace of their criticism. I am particularly grateful to David Dishon and Noam Zion, who paid special attention to the internal structure of this work.

In my philosophical inquiry, I have benefited from discussions with Warren Harvey, Larry Kaplan, Sanford Levinson, Avishai Margalit, Sidney Morgenbesser, Richard Popkin, Joseph Raz, Nathan Rotenstreich, Michael Sandel, Charles Taylor, and Michael Walzer. Moshe Greenberg and Yochanan Muffs have influenced my perception of the wide range of theological and anthropological motifs present in the Bible. Moshe Idel read the entire manuscript and was helpful in the chapter on Maimonides and Nachmanides.

Emanuel Green's insights into Judaism and the human condition have contributed greatly to my attempt to keep Judaism in touch with reality.

Paul van Buren and the Christian theologians who participated in the Contemporary Theology Seminar of the Shalom Hartman Institute suggested important ways of making the book more intelligible to those who are not at home in the Jewish halakhic tradition.

I have been fortunate to have two fine editors in Jerusalem, Malcolm Lowe and Arnold Schwartz. Both have carefully worked with me over the multiple drafts of this work. The style, rigor, and coherence of the argument have benefited immensely from their devoted efforts. Ruth Sherer, my secretary, has typed and retyped the manuscript many times. Her patience is endless, and her devotion is deeply appreciated.

It was also fortunate that Laura Wolff of The Free Press was the editor who took the manuscript under her wing. Her suggestions added to the clarity and tightness of the argument.

The writing of this work was made possible by the continuous concern and support of the leadership of our institute—Sol Lederman, Bob Kogod, and Tom Taras—and the devotion of the board and many friends of the institute. Their friendship and encouragement through the writing of this book were of great importance to me.

This work has been written in memory of my beloved son-in-law, Aharon (Ahrala) Katz, who was killed in the tragic Lebanese war. Born in Ranana, Israel, to Michael and Tziporah Katz, he attended Midrashat Noam, excelled in the sciences, and was a brilliant student of Talmud when, at the age of eighteen, he gave up a promising intellectual career to enter the Israeli Air Force. He believed that the "commandment of the hour" was to provide for the security of his people. He served with great distinction in the Israeli Air Forces for fourteen years, being decorated with the highest medal for his efforts in the Yom Kippur war. Gentleness and courage merged in his soul. I have never met another human being who cared so much for human life and was so able to rejoice at the well-being of others. His joy at our Shabbat table was contagious. He had an amazing capacity for empathy and self-transcendence. Aharon taught us that strength and bravery can grow in the soul of a human being filled with tenderness and love. He was genuinely a man of faith. His love for his children, Yishai and Amitai, his joyful delight at their growth, his love for my daughter, Devorah, were a privilege to behold and to share. His deep faith in Torah and in the significance of our national renaissance refuses to leave me and often prevents me from sinking into despair and disillusionment. He became my son-in-law in marrying my daughter, but truly he was my teacher who helped me to appreciate the vitality and latent spiritual powers present in Israeli society. This work was written in his memory and hopefully mirrors his belief in the new possibilities for the future.

My family's love and concern during our great bereavement, the strength that one draws from living with honest people, and the support of their love through the most agonizing period of my life are something for which I am eternally grateful.

Introduction

ONE OF THE CENTRAL critiques of Judaism found in Western thought has focused upon its alleged excessive concern with the law.[1] Judaism has been accused of "legalism," meaning a concern with externals and lack of inward passion. It has been identified with formalism and soulless regimentation. Its supposed behavioral conformism is said to have reduced the spiritual life of the individual and the passion for God to minor and insignificant roles.

This characterization of Judaism grows from a kind of theological critique that contrasts the God of love with the God of justice, grace with law, and deplores the sense of guilt that accompanies a spiritual life which focuses upon accepting the yoke of the commandments.[2] Spinoza wrote in the spirit of this critique when he distinguished between a religion characterized by emphasis on ceremonial law and external obedience and a religion of inwardness and piety. Since, argued Spinoza, Mosaic law had no inherent spiritual significance outside of a political commonwealth, the Torah was adhered to in exile "more with a view of opposing the Christians than of pleasing God." According to Spinoza, the image of a person committed to the Torah who builds one's life around the normative guidelines of Judaism reflected a slavish orientation to life.[3]

This then was the object of the ceremonial law, that men should do
nothing of their own free will but should always act under external authority, and should continually confess by their actions the thought that
they were not their own masters, but were entirely under the control of
others. (*Tractatus* 5)

Modern critiques of religion focus less on the epistemological con-
flicts between science and religion than on the negative influences of
religious faith on the shaping of character. A basic presupposition of
these critiques is that in order to reinforce belief in human initiative, it
is necessary to uproot commitment to religious outlooks that engender
passivity and feelings of self-negation. The revolt is not so much against
God per se as against a religious anthropology which offends against a
Zeitgeist that celebrates the unfolding of human powers and creative
potential. Scientific and technological advances in the nineteenth and
twentieth centuries confirm the need for a modern conception of the
human being that strengthens belief in human adequacy and in the
ability to bear responsibility for history. The main aim of such philosophical anthropologies is to counteract all ideologies that undermine
belief in the human individual as a responsible agent fully capable of
transforming the physical and social environment.

Karl Marx attacked religion for fostering belief in the inalterability
of the social-political status quo and therefore called religion "the opium
of the people." Indeed, belief in an omnipotent, benevolent Lord of
History can induce feelings of human impotence and resignation in the
face of injustice and exploitation. One can tolerate a state of affairs in
which the wicked prosper and the righteous suffer if one's worldview
fully accepts Rabbi Jacob's description: "This world is like a vestibule
leading to the world to come; prepare yourself in the vestibule that you
may enter the banquet hall" (*Pirkei Avot* 4:16). One can endure suffering
in this world if one accepts the popular rabbinic view that God metes
out punishment to the righteous in this world so that rewards alone
will await them in the world to come. One possible result of all such
rationalizations of evil in this world is resignation to the morally arbitrary vicissitudes of history and an attitude of postponing gratification
to a state of existence beyond the here and now. Present history ceases
to be the domain wherein human happiness and aspirations may be
realized.

Among the many elements in traditional Judaism, there are indeed
some which suggest that rabbinic Jews are psychologically repressed and
inhibited, that they are never wholly spontaneous and unguarded, that
they lack courage, self-confidence, and faith in their ability to affect the

external world significantly. The distaste for and rejection of traditional Judaism by the early pioneers in Israel was not primarily due to
intellectual discomfort with the notion of God but much more due to
feelings of revulsion for the passive, emasculated human type associated
with a life disciplined by traditional *halakhah*.[4] The picture of the talmudic student of eastern Europe, whose courage and daring were expressed in a commitment to learning, offered no inspiration to politically
active Jews who in the real world could not defeat their enemies with
clever arguments based on rabbinic texts. The rabbinic tradition's ideal-
ization of the study of the Torah, and its emphasis on the scholar (*talmid
hakham*) as the ideal human type, had no attraction for those political
movements which sought to transform the Jewish community and turn
it once again into an autonomous nation with a full social and economic
life.

In contrast to the above characterization of the Torah and Judaic
spirituality, this book attempts to characterize Judaism in terms of a
covenantal anthropology that encourages human initiative and freedom
and that is predicated on belief in human adequacy. I argue that a covenantal vision of life, with *mitzvah* (divine commandment) as the central
organizing principle in the relationship between Jews and God, liberates
both the intellect and the moral will. I seek to show that a tradition
mediated by the Sinai covenant can encourage the development of a
human being who is not afraid to assume responsibility for the ongoing
drama of Jewish history. Passive resignation is seen not to be an essential
trait of one whose relationship to God is mediated by the hearing of
mitzvot.

In this work I do not argue against the viability of secular humanism.
Nor do I claim that a system of ethics must be founded on the authority
of divine revelation. Nor is the viability of Judaism established through
a critique of other faith postures. The discussion of Judaism is always
internal to Jewish experience and in no way pretends to show how Judaism or the Jewish people are unique or superior to other faith communities.

I argue strongly for the significance of Jewish particularity, not for its
uniqueness. The covenantal election of Israel at Sinai, which is a central
theme in this work, should not be understood as implying a metaphysical claim regarding the ontological uniqueness of the Jewish people. I do not subscribe to the view that a serious commitment to the
God of Israel and Torah requires one to believe that the Jewish people
mediate the only authentic way for the worship of God. I make no
claims regarding all the non-Judaic ways of giving meaning and signifi-

cance to human life. The range of my philosophizing about Judaism does not go beyond the range of my limited, particular experience as a Jew. Judaism does not provide me with an anchor point beyond a particular community and its history. The Jewish tradition and the Jewish people mediate for me the dignity and humility that comes from the full acceptance of particularity and human limitation. I only explicate a way in which the tradition can encourage a spiritual direction through its emphasis on the covenantal relationship of Israel with God.

Covenantal Metaphors

The covenantal anthropology suggested in this work places the individual Jew firmly inside the framework of a community. Since the covenant is made with the people as a whole and not with Jews as individuals, the ample scope that it gives to individual spiritual self-realization cannot exist in isolation from a communal political consciousness. The covenantal mode of spiritual life challenges the individual to live with the tension between the dignity of the autonomous self and unswerving commitment to the community.

Although my conception of the Sinai covenant has its precedents in the Judaic tradition, it is not the only one found there. Both that tradition and modern scholarship have used many models and metaphors to explicate the covenantal relationship between God and Israel.[5] One such model is the ancient vassal treaties in which the king promised to provide for the needs of his subjects and to protect them from enemies, while they in turn promised him their allegiance. Many scholars take this to be the model for the biblical notion of the covenant. A somewhat similar notion is found in the *Mekhilta* (*ba-hodesh* 5), where God's authority to legislate for the Israelites is based upon the fact that He redeemed them from Egypt and provided for their needs in the desert. They are bound to Him because of what He has done for them. The Bible's reiterated statement "I am the Lord, your God, who brought you out of the land of Egypt" is the ground for their obligation to obey the *mitzvot*. God's protecting love and His ability to defeat the enemies of the Israelites establish His right to demand the allegiance of this community. The right has to be earned, and it is earned when the would-be king can demonstrate his power to benefit his prospective subjects. On this model, the Exodus from Egypt was an essential precondition without which God would not have had the right to lay down the commandments specified in the Sinai covenant.

My understanding of the covenant is radically different, since it presupposes that God *invited* the Israelites to participate in the drama of building His kingdom in history. It is more in keeping with another rabbinic *midrash* (also *ba-hodesh* 5), according to which the Torah was offered to all the nations, but only Israel agreed to accept it. The community accepts the *mitzvot* both because it loves God and because it appreciates the significance of the way of life charted out by the *mitzvot*. God has the community's allegiance because the *mitzvot* give meaning to its relationship with God and to its existence in the world. The *mitzvot* are not perceived as the price exacted by God at Sinai for services rendered, not as quid pro quo, but as a gift of God's love. The community's covenantal commitment is independent of its rescue from slavery. Nor does it depend on the promise of future rewards or the threat of future punishments. The commitment springs from love of God and willing acceptance of His gift of the *mitzvot*.

Because the covenantal relationship is one of love, I find that it is less well expressed by the metaphor of kingship than by another biblical metaphor: that of *husband and wife*. Marriage is an invitation to enter a relationship that is close and intimate but that does not abolish the individuality of either partner. The commitment to respond to the feelings and needs of the other is so strong that the other becomes a part of one's own self-definition, yet the same commitment implies that the other is recognized as an individual with a will distinct from one's own. The self remains autonomous, but it is an autonomy in which the relational framework is fundamental to one's self-understanding. The covenantal relationship involves a similar fusion of relational self-understanding and autonomy. The love of the covenantal community for God is such that its members do not act with an isolated consciousness. Their self-definition includes their relationship to God, both as a community and as individuals, and they act in the world always in the presence of God. But their covenantal relationship is not a mystical union with God in which their individual self-consciousness has vanished. The covenant invites responsibility and the acceptance of one's otherness from God. The covenant is not grounded in the necessity of God's redeeming us from our finite human condition. It is always a relationship with Another and never a union that liberates the self from the problematics of human freedom.

The metaphor of God as *teacher* and human beings as His pupils, a metaphor that gains prominence in the rabbinic period, is also an apt means of describing the covenantal relationship.[6] God as teacher encourages His pupils to think for themselves and assume intellectual responsibility for the way Torah is to be understood and practiced. The fact that the rabbis not only declared that the age of prophecy had ended, but insisted also that the talmudic sage ranked higher than the prophet, seems to suggest that the community has a higher appreciation of its covenantal relationship to God when it sees Him as its teacher than when it sees Him as an authoritarian voice dictating His will through the prophets.

Unlike the metaphors of God as king and father, the metaphors of God as the loving husband and the devoted teacher do not require reward and punishment to play a significant role in the convenantal relationship. They are not frameworks of absolute power of one covenantal partner over the other, but frameworks in which the integrity of both partners is recognized and the human partner is enabled to feel personal dignity and to develop capabilities of responsibility. These are the metaphors that illustrate my understanding of the Sinai covenant as mediated by the talmudic tradition.

The Primacy of the Talmud

In order to do justice to the way Jews have understood their own covenantal relationship with God, it is essential to go to the Talmud and not only to the Bible. For many centuries, committed halakhic Jews have viewed the oral Torah (the legal tradition recorded in the Talmud) as no less valid than the written Torah (the Five Books of Moses). It was commonly claimed that both the written and oral traditions were communicated at Mount Sinai. According to the Talmud (*Gittin* 60b), Rabbi Johanan even maintained that "the Holy One, blessed be He, made a covenant with Israel only for the sake of that which was said by mouth, as it says [literally]: 'For by the mouth of these words have I made a covenant with you and with Israel' [Exod. 34:27]."

How can Rabbi Johanan give greater weight to reasoned halakhic discussions between human beings than to the word of God spoken directly to the prophet? What one finds in studying a page of Talmud, after all, are arguments between different teachers over the way Jewish law and God should be understood. No rabbinic teacher begins his statement with "Thus says the Lord." One does not hear the religious pathos of Jeremiah's "The word of God burns in me, how can I be silent?" Unlike the Bible, the Talmud makes the rarest mention of direct intervention by God in contemporary events. God in the Bible is at the center of the stage on which the drama of the Jewish people takes place.

He guides, He punishes, He responds. He speaks to Israel through His chosen elect. In the Talmud, it is the community, through its teachers, that is ostensibly at the center of the drama. Yet, despite the fact that there is no claim to direct revelation, the reader who penetrates beneath the surface of talmudic discussions increasingly realizes how deeply God is present and involved in every page of the Talmud.

Halakhic scholars who devote their life to the study of the tradition show the Judaic community how it is to understand what God requires of Israel. The Talmud teaches us that one need not be a prophet in order to chart a path in the service of God. One does not have to adopt Buber's notion of ongoing revelation in order to make contact with the God of Israel. Revelation finds its continuation in the rabbinic application of human wisdom. The halakhic tradition shows us how finite human beings employing their limited rational capacities, rather than God-inspired prophets, can reliably mediate the eternal demands of the God of Israel.

When Christian ministers ask me at what age or on what occasion I received my calling as a rabbi, I often find myself hesitating over how to respond. If I answer that it began when I entered *yeshivah* at age five to study Bible and Talmud, they might believe that I am likening myself to Jeremiah, who received his prophetic calling as a child. If I tell them that I never received a calling but was ordained after my teachers concluded that I was intellectually capable of rendering competent decisions regarding what is prohibited and permitted by Jewish law, they might be shocked at meeting a modern version of a Pharisee. They could perhaps find confirmation for the allegation that legalism had replaced the living guidance of God. How could I, they might wonder, preach the word of the Torah without first experiencing God's direct active guidance in my life? How dare I assume responsibility to mediate the living word of the God of Israel without being assured that I was called upon by God to undertake this sacred mission? Yet, as a traditional halakhic Jew, I know that a rabbi is a teacher whose spiritual role is premised on possession of an intelligent understanding of the Jewish tradition and a commitment to the Jewish people. A direct call from God is not required to legitimize activity as a rabbi in Israel.

At the assembly celebrating our ordination, my teacher, Rabbi Soloveitchik, spoke not of God's calling, but of our awesome responsibility to the many generations of Jews who devoted their lives to Torah. In my years of study at Orthodox *yeshivot*, I learned that one cannot talk about the God of Israel in isolation from the living tradition that mediates His words for the covenantal community. One is asked to imagine oneself standing at the founding moment of Sinai, but to do so in the company of the many teachers who reinterpreted, expanded, and gave new directions to Torah. A covenantal Jew always listens to Torah within the context of the tradition.

In Soloveitchik's classes on Talmud, no sharp distinctions were drawn between the written law and the oral law. The Book of Exodus, the talmudic tractate *Berakhot*, Maimonides' *Mishneh Torah*, the writings of Soloveitchik's grandfather, Reb Hayyim of Brisk—each of these texts was studied with the same devotion, love, and seriousness; each was. approached with uncompromising intellectual honesty. The entire halakhic corpus was considered to be Torah. From my many years of Talmud study, I learned that one can sense the living God of revelation not only in reflection upon the words of the prophets or the authoritative teaching of rabbinic scholars in the talmudic era, but equally in the writings of any committed and learned covenantal teacher. A careful study of rabbinic interpretations and *responsa* would reveal that it is a near-impossible task to define the limits of interpretative freedom found in the tradition. As the historian Jacob Katz once remarked to me, the limits are simply what the community is in fact prepared to accept as Torah.

Torah, therefore, should not be understood as a complete, finished system. Belief in the giving of the Torah at Sinai does not necessarily imply that the full truth has already been given and that our task is only to unfold what was already present in the fullness of the founding moment of revelation.[7] Sinai gave the community a direction, an arrow pointing toward a future filled with many surprises. *Halakhah*, which literally means "walking," is like a road that has not been fully paved and completed. The Sinai moment of revelation, as mediated by the ongoing discussion in the tradition, invites one and all to acquire the competence to explore the terrain and extend the road. It does not require passive obedience and submission to the wisdom of the past.

"My God and the God of My Father"

Traditional Judaism has always contained a vital dialectic between "This is my God and I will adore Him" and "The God of my father, and I will exalt Him" (Exod. 15:2). Loyalty to the God about Whom our fathers told us does not exclude the discovery of new insights and experiences that lead one to say, "This is *my* God." The past does not exhaust all that is possible within one's covenantal relationship with God. When

Moses asks God how he should announce God's "name" to the community, he is told to say that he was sent by the God of Abraham, Isaac, and Jacob, but also to say that " 'I will be' has sent me" (Exod. 3:14–15). He is not only the God Who was experienced by Abraham, Isaac, and Jacob, but is also the God Who is worshiped through the new possibilities that the future may uncover: "I will be what I will be."[8] One loyal to Sinai does not only look backward.

As understood by the Judaic tradition, the Sinai covenant was not perceived as one moment in history. The tradition calls upon the community to renew the covenant in each generation. As the rabbis teach, one must live by the Torah as if it had been given in one's own time. Covenantal renewal imparts contemporaneousness and immediacy to the experience of studying and living by the Torah. The word of God, mediated through the prophets and filtered and expanded by generations of halakhic teachers, must be heard ever anew as one brings today's historical context into the process of covenantal renewal. I take this to imply that one should not be paralyzed by feelings of inadequacy in contrast to those previous generations. No generation in covenantal history can account itself closer to God merely because it is closer to the time of Moses, if a generation's spiritual health is measured by its ability to renew the covenant and reapply the Torah in its own time. The Talmud contradicts the idea that "later" means "spiritually inferior" when it insists that the rabbinic sage is superior to the prophet.

To accord the Talmud equal status with the Bible is to augment revelation not merely with a particular body of literature or school of teachers but with a method of interpretation that emphasizes the open-ended possibilities of learning from the received word. The covenant as reflected in the creative talmudic style of interpretation enables Jews to feel free to apply their own human reason to the understanding and application of Torah. The existence of this intellectual freedom refutes Spinoza's claim that the halakhic tradition must foster a docile personality. Spinoza in his *Tractatus* could not understand how Maimonides integrated the philosophical teachings of Aristotle into his interpretation of the Bible. How dare Maimonides identify the physics of Aristotle with the creation story of Genesis? How could Maimonides be so naive as to claim that the prophets were philosophers? For Spinoza, Maimonides' *Guide of the Perplexed* is an intellectually mistaken enterprise and a misrepresentation of the Judaic tradition because it attempts to bring the teachings of Aristotle and Plato into dialogue with those of Moses, Isaiah, and Rabbi Akiva.[9] The mistake was made not by Maimonides but by Spinoza: he forgot that for a loyal Jew, the meaning of the Torah is defined by the living tradition of rabbinic teachers. If the Torah is merely an ancient Near Eastern text describing the customs of a vanished form of society, then Aristotle and the prophets must dwell apart. But if the Torah cannot be separated from an ever-developing tradition of interpretation, then Aristotle and the prophets can come and sit in the same talmudic classroom. Just because Maimonides was a master talmudist, he was able to create a synthesis between Aristotle and Judaism. He, unlike Spinoza, understood the significance of Rabbi Johanan's claim that the covenant with the Jewish people was made for the sake of the oral tradition.[10]

It is this epistemological understanding of the central place given to tradition that shapes the direction of this book. I philosophize within a tradition in which human teachers mediate my covenantal relationship with the God of Israel. Although to "do" Jewish philosophy, as I understand it, does not mean to seek legitimization for whatever one says from recognized authoritative teachings or teachers of the tradition, it does mean that the direction that I have chosen would not have been possible, had I not heard the way autonomous human reason was expressed within the tradition.

As the reader will discover, there are above all three Jewish philosophers in the tradition who have stimulated my own thought, whether by way of agreement or disagreement. First and foremost is Maimonides. He is the major paradigm for how I feel that Jewish philosophy can be done today. This is partly because of specific Maimonidean doctrines that I find still highly relevant, such as his demythologization of Jewish messianism and his emphasis on love of God as the goal of *halakhah*, but also because his ability to integrate *halakhah* with Aristotelian physics and ethics can teach us how to set about the corresponding tasks in an era when philosophers and scientists have moved far away from Aristotle. Although this book owes much to the spirit of Maimonides, I have not sought to find everywhere a position that is in some sense "authentically Maimonidean." As I have mentioned, it is not formal legitimization that I seek from the past, but direction for participating in what I believe to be an ongoing conversation that began at Sinai.[11]

The other two Jewish philosophers with whom I have an ongoing discussion belong to our era. They are Joseph Soloveitchik, for many years my teacher, and Yeshayahu Leibowitz, whom I have met constantly in Israel. Both of them find a major inspiration in Maimonides, though it leads them in other directions than my own. Like Maimonides, they exemplify for me how a deep commitment to the *halakhah* can go together with a readiness to hear significant voices from outside one's own tradition. Soloveitchik, who sensed that Kierkegaard and Rudolph Otto had given expression to new depths of religious experience, is able to interpret the biblical story of creation within the categories of modern existentialism. Leibowitz, who responded to the conception of human autonomy and freedom developed by Kant, who appreciated the significance of modern empiricism and positivism, understands the covenant in a way that frees him from having to make factual claims that can in no way be substantiated by what he understands to be truth. Maimonides listens to Moses through the filter of Aristotle, Leibowitz through Kant, Soloveitchik through the depths of existential dialectic theology. All three demonstrate that loyalty to the tradition need not make one blind to the new spiritual and intellectual opportunities that successive ages in history make possible.

It would be improper to conclude this introduction without emphasizing that the halakhic community also contains voices that are antithetic to new opportunities and constant renewal. There is a very serious traditional orientation to the covenant that points in the direction opposite to the one that I am suggesting in this work. It is an orientation that, were it the only one in the tradition, would lend substance to Spinoza's characterization of Judaism. This orientation claims that the closer one is to Sinai, the more truly one can understand the meaning of Torah and live authentically with God. The further one gets away from Sinai, the more one must be obedient and reverential to those earlier generations, who mediate in a more authentic way the living word of Torah. From this perspective, the present can find legitimacy only through the authentication of the past. The experience and thought that the modern world makes possible cannot enter into the Jewish experience until one can show that the past has legitimated and authenticated such modes of experience and comprehension. Jews encounter the world from the perspective of a total system that defines how they should think and experience. They walk on a road that has in all important respects been fully laid out and paved. *Halakhah* is identified with the code of the *Shulhan Arukh*, literally a "set table." A Jew of our generation has no great need for autonomous reason and an autonomous moral sense. Justice is what the tradition says is justice. Morality does not derive from one's own intuitive moral sense, but is reflected in the authoritative teachings of the past.

Tradition and Experience

As I have explained, I believe that such orientation is contrary to the primacy given to the Talmud in the Jewish tradition. But this is not my only reason for rejecting it. My rejection also stems from personal experiences that have demonstrated more than sufficiently that there are many things in this world whose legitimacy and significance have to be acknowledged by halakhic Jews, even if the tradition has nothing explicitly to say about them. These experiences fall into four main categories.

First, there were the experiences of growing up in the pluralistic society of the United States, where from an early age I had every opportunity to appreciate many cultures and faith postures. Just playing basketball brought me into human contact with blacks and whites, with Greeks, Italians, and Irish, with Catholics and Protestants. The exclusively Jewish world of the *yeshivah* did not isolate me from the rich mosaic of humanity in the surrounding streets of Brownsville, my neighborhood in Brooklyn, New York.

Second, those early experiences were given profound intellectual and philosophical support in the years of my graduate study at Fordham University. Living with the Jesuits, sensing the intellectual and spiritual integrity of my teachers, observing how our different faiths were reciprocally enriched through our encounters—these were experiences that I could not ignore in developing my own appreciation of what it is to stand as a covenantal Jew before God. Above all, I was blessed to have a great philosophy teacher, Robert C. Pollock of blessed memory, who remains a permanent influence on my thinking.

A third result of the American experience, with its openness to modern philosophical currents, was to show me that people can live a significant human life without making a commitment to a personal God. Secular humanism had to be recognized as a vital possible orientation of human beings to the world, even if it was not a live option for me. I learned not to claim that one must be religious in order to be ethical. What I learned in America, in these various ways, can be summed up in my resolution to speak only of the value of Jewish particularity, never to make claims to know a Jewish uniqueness that demonstrates an absolute superiority of Judaism to all other ways of life.

Last come all the experiences connected with life in Israeli society. In coming to live in Israel, I chose to make the renewal of Jewish political independence into a normative framework influencing my appreciation of how Judaism is to develop in the modern world.

Although those different kinds of experience influenced my choice to see *halakhah* as an open-ended range of possibilities, this was not an inevitable consequence. There are Jewish religious thinkers in the United States who had experiences similar to mine, yet their understanding of

Judaism was unaffected. They continued to perceive the system as complete; countervailing evidence was set aside. They knew of those other features of human life, but did not feel called to reshape anything in their received tradition so as to incorporate or respond to them. Similarly, there are many religious Jews living in Israel who deny that the existence of the state of Israel has any normative implications for Judaism. My philosophical appreciation of Judaism is shaped by the opposite attitude: one that allows the present to surface in its fullness, without prior legitimization by the past, and provide an orienting framework for living with tradition.

Outline of the Book

To conclude, I shall outline the course of my argument. In the first chapter, I explore the idea of human adequacy as it appears in the biblical theme of the covenant and especially as it is reflected by the intellectual freedom of the talmudic rabbis. Their bold interpretations of Torah belie any suggestion that they had obedient personalities which made them submit to a fixed legal system and renounce personal involvement in molding their own way of life. The neutralizing of direct dependence upon revelation has for me serious religious and anthropological consequences, which I develop in this chapter.

My approach to the rabbinic tradition, it must be emphasized, is selective and conceptual. It is in no way an attempt at historical analysis. It is totally thematic and related to my philosophical concern with trying to locate specific tendencies or possibilities within the rabbinic tradition that could be supportive of a covenantal religious anthropology capable of participating adequately in the challenges of modernity.

In chapter 2, I correct what could be a misunderstanding of my argument about the rabbinic encouragement of human adequacy and critical reflection. It would be a mistake to imagine that the talmudic tradition points exclusively in that direction. The tradition does contain a theme of human initiative and autonomy, but also a hardly less emphatic theme of resignation and submission to the inscrutable will of God. I show that the tension between self-assertion and submission can be found in nearly all aspects of the rabbinic tradition. Terror and feelings of human insignificance before God appear together with a Promethean spirit in which halakhic teachers assert their intellectual strength and moral adequacy to define the directions of the covenant. I do not attempt in the first two chapters to propose any resolution of the tension or to identify a dominant thrust in the rabbinic tradition. I seek only to demonstrate a polar tension within the rabbinic halakhic spirit.

The next three chapters deal with modern responses to that polar tension. Chapter 3 shows how Soloveitchik has tried to create a dialectical synthesis in which both the assertive and submissive dimensions are necessary for the building of an integrated religious personality. He argues, however, that the supreme Judaic religious pathos is embodied in the mode of voluntary submission and self-negation, as exemplified in Abraham's willingness to sacrifice Isaac (the Akedah).

In chapter 4, I take issue with Soloveitchik's identification of religious intensity with the mode of defeat and resignation. The starting point for my argument is the religious anthropology of Maimonides, in which human reason is given the highest function for the development of religious passion. The covenant that invites mutuality cannot be characterized by an acceptance of defeat in which our rational and ethical senses are violated. The ethical is constitutive of a covenantal conscience and must enter into the manner in which *halakhah* is to be applied.

Chapter 5 introduces the thinking of Leibowitz, who believes that Maimonidean anthropology is best understood within the framewok of successive stages of worship. The initial anthropocentric stage must ultimately be transcended as one reaches the highest point of Judaic spiritual life. When Maimonides argues that all the *mitzvot* have purposes that can be understood in terms of human well-being, he is merely describing that first stage, according to Leibowitz. Ultimately, Maimonides leads Jews to the theocentric passion in which they perform *mitzvot* purely out of the will to serve God, irrespective of human concerns. My argument with Leibowitz reflects the fundamental difference between our appreciations of Maimonides. I believe that the covenantal spirit of mutuality between God and the Jew is never violated by Maimonides.

In Leibowitz's approach, the model of the Kantian spirit of autonomy best explains commitment to the life of *mitzvah*. Human needs and individual self-realization have no religious significance in the decision to worship God through the *halakhah*. For myself, it is the Maimonidean-Aristotelian spirit that guides my approach to the *mitzvot*. For Maimonides, *mitzvot* are essentially related to the well-being of the community and the building of a healthy moral character. The covenantal relationship to God rests not upon the pure act of will, but on the unfolding of a total human personality in the presence of God.

The covenant is not a purely legal obligation; it is a total relationship.

The logic of a legal system cannot do full justice to the relational framework of the covenant built upon the metaphors of God as lover and teacher. For Leibowitz, the focus of Judaism is exhausted by the subjective commitment. For me, the covenant demands that the relational matrix define the understanding of halakhic commitment.

Chapters 6 and 7 show how our respective anthropologies—Soloveitchik's, Leibowitz's, and mine—find expression in the life of prayer. Chapter 6 discusses Soloveitchik's dialectical anthropology as reflected in his approaches to prayer, and chapter 7 shows how Leibowitz makes sense of the routinization and ritualization of halakhic prayer in light of his theocentric focus.

For Soloveitchik, prayer expresses the mood of self-sacrifice that is essential to the life of worship. Petitional prayer teaches the worshiper to understand the religious importance of dependency upon God. In petitional prayer, one brings to consciousness the importance of giving up all sense of human adequacy and dignity before the overwhelming presence of God. Human assertion and creativity and the halakhic concern with active human responsibility are legitimate only after the mood of resignation and total reliance on grace is expressed in petitional prayer.

For Leibowitz, Judaic prayer is significant only as a response to *mitzvah*. Jews pray because they are commanded to pray and not because of any human need. Prayer is not a beseeching of God's mercy but the fulfillment of a commandment. Institutional prayer, as it developed through the exacting requirements of *halakhah*, is the archetypal *mitzvah* in that it reflects how individuality and human self-realization have no significance in the life of worship.

I argue that petitional prayer expresses the dignity the covenantal *mitzvot* give to Judaic religious consciousness. Petitional prayer is seen not as self-sacrifice or as mere obedience to *halakhah*, but as a way of expressing before God the problems of our human situation. Judaic prayer confirms the covenantal sense of being accepted as a full human being before God. Covenantal Jews are not embarrassed to talk about their communal and personal needs in the presence of God. In contrast to Leibowitz, I argue that halakhic prayer does not neutralize the spontaneous feelings of the worshiper. Rather, it allows for the integration of individual self-realization with commitment to community, of spontaneity with obligation.

Part Two shifts the focus from the human to the divine partner in the covenant. Covenantal consciousness is fundamentally relational in its self-understanding. There is no autonomy in the sense of Kant, nor is there a longing for stoic self-sufficiency. The consciousness of existing in relationship to God permeates the Judaic perception of every aspect of reality. How God is perceived to respond to the human partner in the relationship is therefore crucial for the covenantal Jew's sense of dignity and worth. From biblical times to the present, Jews have constantly asked themselves whether their experience as individuals and as a community confirms their belief that they are objects of God's covenantal love and concern.

The greatest challenge to that perception has always been the experience of inexplicable suffering and tragedy, be it the suffering expressed by the psalmist or the sufferings of our people in modern times. This part of the book examines different ways of viewing the issue in a covenantal perspective. In chapters 8 and 9, I show how the rabbinic tradition dealt with the issue of suffering and how it began slowly to minimize the biblical tendency to see in the material conditions of the nation God's immediate response to its behavior. I show that the rabbinic tradition does not offer a consistent theodicy, but rather various modes of response to suffering that enable the mitzvot to continue to play a vital role in the religious life of the community. The rabbis did not overthrow the biblical perception of the covenant, but channeled covenantal consciousness in new directions. They suggested ways of appreciating God's power in history that do not necessarily make the exile and suffering of Israel an expression of God's rejection or punishment for sin. The important conceptions of "The world pursues its normal course" and "The reward of mitzvah is mitzvah" began to enter into the covenantal Jew's perception of God's relationship to history. God's power may also be discerned in His silent and patient waiting for the wicked to change their ways or bring about their own destruction.

The rabbinic tradition provides the starting point for my own rethinking of how one can make sense of the covenantal presence of God in the life of the individual and the community. Chapter 10 focuses on how "The world pursues its normal course" is elaborated in Maimonides' perception of history and messianism. Maimonides was that master halakhic thinker who, more than any other, moved away from the literal understanding of the Bible's perception of God's relationship to history. This chapter indicates that Maimonides may serve as a foundation for a more radical neutralization of the biblical view of events in nature and history as the carriers of God's personal will. The chapter contrasts two Judaic paradigms for understanding history and divine providence. In one, which can be discerned in Maimonides, miracle is given minimal significances and the Sinai revelation becomes understood as a founding moment rather than the controlling perception for the ongoing covenantal drama. The contrary position is that of Nachmanides, whose perception of history and the world of nature is infused with the belief that God's spontaneous will operates constantly in the conditions of the covenantal community.

In chapter 11, I argue that we do not have to seek a personal manifestation of God in the events of nature or history. Suffering and human tragedy are not signs of divine rejection or punishment. God's providential concern is manifested in the guidance provided by the Torah. God is present as a personal reality through the hearing of *mitzvot*. Commitment to the Sinai covenant does not require that one believe in the ultimate redemption of history.

The covenant of Sinai points to the ever-renewed possibility of beginning the spiritual process. It does not give one certainty regarding the ultimate direction of history. *Mitzvot* are significant not because they point to or make possible a future redemption, but for the quality of life they make possible in the present. Human finitude and the sense of being a creature separate from God remain permanent features of the religious life. Faith does not give one an anchor point through which one transcends the finite human situation.

The concluding chapter applies this covenantal perception of history to the new challenges posed by the birth of the third Jewish commonwealth. Here I show that it is possible to attach profound religious significance to the creation of the state of Israel even if one refrains from making a judgment on how God acts in history. One can religiously celebrate the rebirth of Israel without being forced to make the claim that in Auschwitz God either withdrew or punished the community.

Israel is significant from a covenantal perspective because it provides the Jewish world with a complex social and political framework within which one can evaluate the different claims made regarding Jews and Judaism. Israel widens the range of covenantal responsibility and provides greater opportunities to test the viability of Judaism as a way of life. Israel as the focal point for the ingathering of the Jewish people provides a new moral and religious agenda for the Jewish world.

The breakdown of halakhic authority, the loss of a shared value framework for translating our historical consciousness into present experiences, is one of the most significant challenges to which Jewish philosophical though must address itself in the modern world. Can Jewish monotheism admit the legitimacy of religious pluralism? Can covenantal Judaism accommodate the various options through which Jews have chosen to give meaning to their existence?

My book does not attempt to work out the way in which ethics can control halakhic development, nor does it try to establish the limits of tolerance and pluralism. Nevertheless, it provides a framework and a religious sensibility from which to begin to chart a new direction for Judaism so that it might become a living possibility for a Jew who takes the modern world with radical seriousness.

Pluralism requires an epistemological framework that limits the claims of revelation. It requires a political philosophy in which the unity of God does not imply one universal way for all humankind. However, before epistemological and political theory can chart new directions for Judaism, we need a conceptual framework in which covenantal consciousness is permeated by a religious sensibility that celebrates finitude and creatureliness as permanent features of covenantal life. A human sensibility that is open to and appreciative of the possibilities of pluralism is the foundation from which one can build a new epistemological understanding of revelation and *halakhah*.

PART ONE

The Human Being
in
Judaism

1

Fundamentals
of a Covenantal
Anthropology

THIS CHAPTER presents the foundations of my covenantal anthropology of Judaism. My analysis of the covenant will begin with an explanation of how the notions of divine self-limitation and human freedom and responsibility are reflected in the biblical account of creation and in the covenants of Noah, Abraham, and Sinai. I shall then indicate how the talmudic tradition unfolds new spiritual dimensions of autonomy for covenantal Jews.

The Implications of Creation

The opening chapters of the Book of Genesis are not concerned only with cosmogony. The language and details of the biblical account of creation go beyond imparting information about how the universe came into being. The rabbinic tradition was awake to this fact and did not hesitate to scrutinize the biblical text in search of normative implications. Rabbi Isaac's question regarding the very first verse of the Bible—"Why did the Torah begin with an account of creation and not with the first commandment addressed to Israel?" (*Tanhuma*, Gen. 1:11)—reflects the overriding rabbinic concern with eliciting normative mean-

ing from biblical passages that seem at first sight to be merely descriptive
of events.[1]

The account of creation in Genesis admittedly does not involve a
covenant with any human being or with any particular historical people. Nevertheless, implicit in the account are important concepts required for later biblical accounts of covenantal relationships with God.
They are (1) the freedom of God, (2) the human accountability that
derives from human freedom and divine self-limitation, and (3) the interdependence of God and humans in history.

First, creation reflects the freedom of God. As noted by many biblical
scholars, the Bible lacks an account of the coming into being of God
(theogony) and differs from other Near Eastern religious traditions by
conceiving of God as being prior to and independent of creation.[2] God
is neither created nor formed and thus is not limited by any cosmic
primal power. God—empirically and logically—precedes the universe;
He alone creates.

This aspect of creation is logically connected to the notions of revelation and the covenant. For Maimonides, creation presupposes a
metaphysics of divine will, that is, God's freedom to act in response to
particular historical circumstances and to intervene actively in the established course of nature and history. The notion of creation is incompatible with the metaphysical constraints of eternal necessity that are
found in Aristotelian philosophy. The first mention of God in the Bible
points to the wonder of divine freedom and spontaneity. The universe
came into being at a moment when God chose to express His free will.
With this, He revealed His independence and freedom, which constitute
logical presuppositions for His entering into a covenant with human
beings.

Maimonides accordingly regarded creation as a necessary belief without which the covenant at Sinai would be philosophically indefensible.
In contrast to an Aristotelian cosmology of eternal necessity, creation
implies a notion of divine will that allows for God's spontaneous action
at particular moments of time.[3]

> Know that with a belief in the creation of the world in time, all the
> miracles become possible and the [giving of the] law [at Sinai] becomes
> possible, and all questions that may be asked on this subject vanish.
> Thus it might be said: why did God give prophetic revelation to this
> one and not to that? Why did God give this law to this particular nation,
> and why did He not legislate to the others? Why did He legislate at this
> particular time and why did He not legislate before or after? Why did
> He impose these commandments and these prohibitions? . . . If this were

said, the answer to all these questions would be that it would be said: He wanted it this way; or His wisdom required it this way. And just as He brought the world into existence, having the form it has, when He wanted to, without our knowing His will with regard to this or in what respect there was wisdom in His particularizing the forms of the world and the time of its creation—in the same way we do not know His will or the exigency of His wisdom that caused all the matters, about which questions have been posed above, to be particularized. If, however, someone says that the world is as it is in virtue of necessity, it would be a necessary obligation to ask all those questions. . . . (*Guide* 2:25)

Second, the biblical account of creation also dramatically conveys information about humanity. The nature of man and woman is initially described as being similar to that of God: "And God created man in His image, in the image of God He created him, male and female He created them" (Gen. 1:27). One may understand the concept *tzelem elohim* (image of God) as indicating the similarity between human beings and God with respect to freedom and spontaneity. Just as God is characterized as being free by virtue of will, so too are humans set apart from other creatures by virtue of freedom of choice and the capacity for deliberation and reasoned decision making.

As a result of human freedom and reason, human beings are singled out by being assigned norms. Unlike the rest of creation, they are addressed directly by God: "God blessed them and God said to them, 'Be fruitful and multiply, fill the earth and master it; and rule the fish of the sea, the birds of the sky, and all the living things that creep on earth. . . . ' " (Gen. 1:28). The continuity of life through procreation ceases to be an expression of divine grace alone, whereby God creates natural conditions for the perpetuation of natural species. Since human beings can choose *not* to procreate, in the human domain "Be fruitful and multiply" becomes the content of a divine norm.[4] Humans not only experience the bountiful blessings of divine grace in nature; they also stand over and above nature by virtue of their ability to weigh their actions conscientiously and to act on the basis of values and normative considerations. "Be fruitful and multiply" obligates them to transform what would otherwise be regarded as a purely biological instinct into a normative performance. The fact that the content of this norm pertains to human sexuality expresses the unique ontological status of the human being as one who can transcend natural necessity and act within a context of freedom.

The consequences of human freedom are dramatically described in the stories immediately following the biblical account of creation. The violation of God's command not to eat of the tree of knowledge is the first in a series of events where man and woman say no to God. God's creation of nature is the work of the solitary Artist who expresses Himself by producing a universe according to His will, but the creation of the human species introduces freedom into creation. The term "law" has a more rigorous significance in expressions such as "the laws of nature" than it has when applied to the laws—be they called natural or conventional—by which human beings are expected to regulate their conduct. Laws of nature are universal statements of the regularities observed in nature. Unlike laws addressed to humans, they may not be broken or violated. A human being, however, may deliberate and choose whether to comply with norms. Only laws addressed to humans have normative force.

By virtue of possessing freedom, a human being not only stands apart from nature, but stands over and against God as an "other." Whereas the natural world may be regarded as an extension of God programmed to reflect His will, a human being may confront God as an independent other. The creation of a being capable of saying no to divine commands is the supreme expression of divine love, insofar as God makes room for humans as independent, free creatures. The mystery of God's love for them is expressed in this act of divine self-limitation. God limits His power so as to permit human development within the context of freedom.

The Torah does not describe the principle of divine self-limitation in the esoteric language of the Kabbalah as the ontological mystery of the *Ein-sof* (Infinite) making room for finitude.[5] The biblical drama is formulated in historical-relational rather than in cosmological-mystical terms. Accordingly, divine self-limitation need not be understood only in terms of the cosmological mystery of *tzimtzum* (contraction) of Lurianic Kabbalism, but may also be understood in terms of a parent's loving decision to limit his or her intervention in a child's behavior so as to allow for the growth of the child's sense of personal dignity and self-worth. Love for one's child often demands self-restraint even in the face of failure and errors in judgment. Aside from the issue of moral or legal rights, noninterference is often a requirement of love and concern.

Self-restraint by the stronger partner is a necessary component of relationships that respect and seek to enhance the sense of worth and dignity of the weaker partner. Covenantal theology differs from the quest for mystic union insofar as the former retains the notion of human independence whereas the latter focuses primarily on the perfection of the Infinite and seeks to overcome individual self-consciousness by absorption into the Infinite. Covenantal relatedness presupposes the integrity of the other; it makes sense to speak of a covenant between two parties only if there is mutual commitment, regardless of the relative power of the covenantal partners or the conditions of the covenant. Though covenantal relatedness does not imply the equality of the parties to the covenant in all respects, it does presuppose mutual recognition of the separate existence and rights of the parties involved.

The theophany marking the inception of the covenant at Sinai is devoid of descriptions of loss of self, or of absorption into and identification with the Infinite. God addresses the people and enjoins norms. However one explains the divine voice that Israel heard (Deut. 4:12), the description of the mode of revelation in terms of Israel's hearing God's speech presupposes two separate identities—God and Israel. The theophany at Sinai is not the result of otherworldly contemplation or of ecstatic identification with the Ground of Being. God elects Israel for a historical task, that is, to become a holy nation. This holiness is not otherworldly, but entails the establishment of a society that embodies the normative content of revelation. The normative-historical framework of Judaic thought presupposes human separateness and moral accountability. Halakhic Jews typically act with dignity and self-awareness before God and do not aspire to be absorbed by a divine reality that redeems them from human finitude.[6]

Third, the biblical story in Genesis serves as a framework for the covenant at Sinai by suggesting that the realization of God's design for history, as opposed to His design for nature, involves human beings. The notion of divine-human interdependence provides a rationale for the covenant consummated between God and Israel at Sinai.[7] The biblical chronicle of God's "failures" in His plans for humanity supports the view that according to the biblical conception of history, God does not act in history by fiat alone. God is not the sole agent in history manipulating events to His satisfaction and according to His grand design. Though theologians may have difficulty accounting for the repeated failures of God's expectations in history, the fact is that the Bible depicts divine frustration and rage when God, the Lord of History, is confronted with human recalcitrance.

In *The Guide of the Perplexed* (3:32), Maimonides states categorically that "God does not change at all the nature of human individuals by means of miracles." He argues that this does not imply that God cannot do so, nor that it would be difficult for Him, but simply that "according to the foundations of the law, of the Torah, He has never willed to do it, nor shall He ever will it." Were this not the case, argues Maimonides, the giving of the Torah—that is, the covenant—and the sending of the prophets to exhort the people to do *teshuvah* (repentance) would be pointless. In other words, the Sinai revelation presupposes that history is not governed exclusively by unilateral divine power. The giving of the law indicates that the omnipotent Lord of History does not program the human individual to become a puppet who cannot but obey the will of God. The promise that the covenant of *mitzvah* shall be eternal is tantamount to God's promising to respect the inviolability of human freedom.

Genesis chronicles a series of divine schemes and failures that led up to the Sinai covenant. Although God surrounded man and woman with idyllic conditions in the Garden of Eden and expected that they would reflect the divine image, He quickly "learned" that the price of human freedom was human rebellion and failure. God's spontaneous expression of delight with His creation was tempered when human beings defied His commands, challenged His authority, and became corrupt. God's delight turned to anger, rage, and frustration with them, culminating in the Flood. "And the Lord regretted that He had made man on earth, and His heart was saddened. The Lord said: 'I will blot out from the earth the men whom I created—men together with beasts, creeping things, and birds of the sky; for I regret that I made them.' But Noah found favor with the Lord" (Gen. 6:6–8).

God's repeated confrontation with human corruption and His experimentation with new ways of relating to human beings in history are the consequences of His allowing for human freedom. God's reliance on humans to embody His designs and expectations in history results from His uncompromising commitment to safeguard human freedom and integrity.

In Midrashic exegesis of Genesis, the rabbis noted the absence of the sentence "And God saw that it was good" immediately following the creation of humankind. The biblical statement "And God saw all that He had made and found it very good" (at the end of the sixth day of creation) refers to all of creation ("*all* that He had made") and not specifically to the creation of the human species. The judgment that this last creation was good (where "good" implies the realization of the Creator's intention) cannot be made by God alone, but ultimately depends upon human beings themselves.

The conceptual background for the Sinai covenant is thus implicit in these three main elements of the creation story: (1) the freedom and spontaneity of God; (2) human freedom, the self-limitation of God, and acknowledgment of the integrity of the human "other"; and (3) God's interaction with humans in history and His choice to involve them in determining the course of their history.

The Covenants with Noah and Abraham

While the Sinai covenant usually serves as the paradigm case of a covenantal relationship between God and human beings, two covenants preceded Sinai: the covenant with Noah and the covenant with Abraham. I shall not attempt an exhaustive comparative analysis of Noah and Abraham, but merely indicate salient characteristics of their respective covenants with God and explain how each exemplifies essential elements of covenantal theology.[8]

The term *brit* (covenant) is used with regard to both covenants (Gen. 9:8–17; 17:1–14), but there are important differences. In the Bible, a covenant is an agreement offered by a stronger party (such as a king) to a weaker party. Sometimes the offer is an unconditional promise on the part of the stronger party; sometimes the promise is conditional upon an act or acts of the weaker party. The covenant with Noah is of the first kind; that with Abraham is conditional upon the act of circumcision. A second difference is that the covenant with Noah lacks the singling-out quality of intense relationships. God announces the covenant to Noah, but on closer examination the covenant appears to be addressed to all of nature. Noah's presence appears to be relevant solely by virtue of his being a member of the class of "living things on earth."[9]

> I now establish My covenant with you and your offspring to come, and with every living thing that is with you—birds, cattle and every wild beast as well—all that have come out of the ark, every thing on earth. I will maintain My covenant with you; never again shall all flesh be cut off by the waters of a flood and never again shall there be a flood to destroy the earth. (Gen. 9:9–11)*

The significance of this covenant may be analyzed in terms of what it indicates about God. God's response in bringing about the Flood is like that of the creative artist who rips up works of his hand that fall short of his artistic standards. God lashes out in anger and frustration and destroys almost all of life because of human wickedness. After the

---

*The quotations from the Bible and the Mishnah are from various translations and often have been checked and modified by the author.

Flood, however, God announces that He will never again wreak such destruction in response to human evil.

> Then Noah built an altar to the Lord and, taking of every clean animal and of every clean bird, he offered burnt offerings on the altar. The Lord smelled the pleasing odor and the Lord said to Himself: "Never again will I destroy the earth because of man, since the devisings of man's mind are evil from his youth; nor will I ever again destroy every living being as I have done." (Gen. 8:20–21)

God separates His responsibility for creation from His response to the moral condition of humankind. Prior to the Flood, all of nature was doomed to destruction because God "regretted that He had made man on earth"; human corruption was sufficient reason to justify the destruction of all living things. After the Flood, however, God proclaims His awareness that although human beings are created in His image, they do not automatically embody all that God wishes them to be. God's reflections on them are, as it were, similar to a parent's realization that his child is not his mirror image but is a separate being with limitations, weaknesses, and an independent will. The child may come from the parent, but it is nevertheless separate and independent. The newly felt distance between God and humans is expressed after the flood by God's covenant not to destroy nature as a result of what humans, created in the image of God, will do. This distancing of humans from God and God's realistic assessment of their propensity to evil are necessary stages of the process leading to the covenantal mutuality represented by the giving of the law at Sinai, which charges a particular human community with responsibility for its own spiritual growth.

Notwithstanding the importance of the differences already noted, the crucial difference between the covenants with Noah and Abraham involves the relative importance of these two figures in their respective covenants. Abraham emerges as a protagonist in the drama of human history—a worthy partner of the Lord of History. For instance, God decides that Abraham should be informed of His intention to destroy Sodom.

> Now the Lord said, "Shall I hide from Abraham what I am about to do, since Abraham is to become a great and populous nation and all the nations of the earth are to bless themselves by him? For I have singled him out. . . . " (Gen. 18:17–19)

An argument ensues in which Abraham obtains a promise from God that Sodom will be spared if ten righteous men can be found within it (Gen. 18:23–32).

Abraham is God's beloved friend, in whom He feels obliged, as it were, to confide His plan to destroy Sodom. The rhetorical question "Shall I hide from Abraham what I am about to do?" indicates the responsibilities that God has assumed toward human beings as a result of His decision to participate in a covenantal relationship with Abraham and his descendants.

> Rabbi Samuel ben Nahman said: "It may be compared to a king who had an adviser without whose consent he did nothing. On one occasion, however, he wished to do something without his consent, whereupon he observed: 'Surely I made him my adviser for no other reason than that I should do nothing without his consent.' " . . . The rabbis said: "I have already called him [Abraham] their father, as it says, 'For the father of a multitude of nations have I made thee' [Gen. 17:5]: does one judge the son without the father's knowledge?" (*Genesis Rabbah* 49:2)

Noah does not inhibit or impose restrictions on God's actions. The Creator, who has not yet established a covenant with human beings, can unilaterally decide to destroy nature without having to justify or explain His plan to anyone. The God of nature acts alone. The God of covenantal history, however, acts within a relational context. He must weigh his actions, as it were, in the light of how they affect His covenantal partners, in this case Abraham and his descendants.

A *midrash* elaborates on the expression "the God of the earth" in Abraham's statement to his servant Eliezer, "Put your hand under my thigh and I will make you swear by the Lord, the God of heaven and the God of the earth" (Gen. 24:2–3), as follows:

> Until Abraham our father came into the world, God, as it were, was king of heaven alone, as it is said: "The Lord, the God of heaven who took me from my father's house . . . " [Gen. 24:7], but when Abraham our father came into the world, he anointed Him king of heaven and of the earth, as it is said: "and I will make you swear by the Lord, the God of heaven and the God of the earth." (*Sifre, ha'azinu* 313)

Abraham represents the shift from God the solitary Creator of Nature to God the self-limiting covenantal Lord of History. Abraham is not simply an instrument of the omnipotent Master of Nature; he stands over and against God as an other; his importance as a historical figure is marked by divine self-limitation, that is, by God's becoming the "God of the earth" only through the efforts of Abraham.

Another indication that, whereas Noah was incidental to his covenant with God, Abraham was a full-fledged partner, is that Abraham's spiritual stature dwarfs Noah, who emerges as a passive, nonheroic character noteworthy only by virtue of his being saved from the Flood.

"Noah walked with God" [Gen. 6:9]. Rabbi Judah said: "This may be compared to a king who had two sons, one grown up and the other a child. To the child he said, 'Walk *with* me,' but to the adult, 'Walk *before* me.' Similarly, to Abraham, whose moral strength was great, [He said,] 'Walk before Me' [Gen. 17:1]; of Noah, whose strength was feeble, [it says,] 'Noah walked with God.' " (*Gen. Rab.* 30:10)

The Midrashic comparison of Abraham and Noah in terms of the difference between a responsible, mature person and a child in need of parental support and guidance may explain why Abraham was singled out and deemed worthy of being a covenantal partner. The two verses brought by the author of the *midrash* to support his comparison merely serve as a literary device for dramatizing differences that a careful reading of the biblical text reveals. Like Noah, Abraham is told of an impending disaster that God is going to bring about. Unlike Noah, who silently listens to God's plan to "put an end to all flesh" and who unquestioningly complies with God's command to prepare an ark to save himself, his family, and a specified number of animals, Abraham, when informed of God's intention to deal with the sins of Sodom and Gomorrah, argues with God.

Will You sweep away the innocent along with the guilty? What if there should be fifty innocent within the city; will You then wipe out the place and not forgive it for the sake of the innocent fifty who are in it? Far be it from You to do such a thing to bring death upon the innocent as well as the guilty, so that innocent and guilty fare alike. Far be it from You! Shall not the Judge of all the earth deal justly? (Gen. 18:13–25)

Noah's utter silence and acquiescence in God's plan to destroy all of life stand in sharp contrast to Abraham's heroic confrontation with God. Noah is not portrayed as a person actively responsible for the fate of others. He "walks with God"; that is, he agrees to be led. There are numerous *midrashim* that indicate that God's picking Noah to survive the flood was not based on great personal merit. Although some rabbis interpret the verse "Noah was a righteous man; he was blameless in his generation" (Gen. 6:9) as indicating Noah's unqualified righteousness, other rabbis consider the phrase "in his generation" to be a qualification: "Were he [Noah] to have lived in Abraham's generation, he would have been entirely unnoteworthy" (*Gen. Rab.* 30:9). Noah never achieves the stature of a responsible covenantal man. He responds; he never initiates.

"Noah, with his sons, his wife and his sons' wives, went into the ark because of the waters of the Flood" [Gen. 7:7]. Rabbi Johanan said: "He lacked faith: had not the water reached his ankles he would not have entered the ark." (*Gen. Rab.* 32:6)

By contrast, Abraham walks before God. He challenges God by appealing to universal moral principles. He is fully awake to his responsibility for others and confronts God on their behalf. Noah was not weaned from childlike dependency on his Creator and could not stand in moral confrontation with God.

According to rabbinic characterizations, Abraham stands out as a socially concerned and compassionate person. A *midrash* has it that when God appeared to Abraham by the terebinths of Mamre (Gen. 18:1–4), Abraham interrupted the encounter to attend to three passing travelers. The *midrash* portrays Abraham as asking God to wait while he welcomes his guests. Rabbi Judah, in the name of Rav, explains Abraham's action by asserting:

> Hospitality to wayfarers is greater than welcoming the *shekhinah* [the presence of God]; for it is written: "He said, 'My Lord, if it please you, do not go on past,' etc." [Gen. 18:3]. (*Shabbat* 127a)

The *midrash* should be read not as indicating that there is a conflict between respect for God and compassion for human beings, but rather as a statement that anyone who loves God as Abraham does knows that in welcoming the stranger he welcomes the *shekhinah*. Abraham's apparent obsession with caring for the needs of passing travelers is more than an interesting aspect of Middle Eastern hospitality to strangers. It indicates the essential connection between covenantal consciousness and involvement with and responsibility for others. One may not commune with God of the covenant if one is not responsive to the social, economic, and political needs of human beings.

Abraham is therefore closer to being an archetype of a covenantal man than Noah. Abraham is singled out; his covenant is symbolized and consummated in his own flesh (circumcision), whereas the covenant with Noah is universal and nonspecific; its sign is the rainbow in the sky (Gen. 9:16–17).

Despite the singling out of Abraham and his descendants, Abraham's covenant has universal implications. As understood by the *halakhah*, Abraham's covenant signifies rejection of the idea that covenantal faith commitments are defined by racial and biological conditions. The predominance of norms over biology and race is evident in the halakhic ruling that a convert who enters the covenant, of whatever sociocultural or racial background, may refer to Abraham as his or her father. The convert, like any Jew born of Jewish parents, may, in prayer, address God as "our God and God of our fathers, the God of Abraham, the God of Isaac." In singling out Abraham, God made covenantal religion accessible to all. Abraham is the father of any person who seeks to emulate his way of life and to practice its values, norms, and beliefs.[10]

Abraham is the historical iconoclast who broke blood and cultural ties by leaving his home in Mesopotamia and entering into a covenant with God whose concrete sign—circumcision—signified to later generations that commitment to particular norms and values must define a person's identity. The ritual of circumcision performed on the organ of procreation may symbolize Judaism's rejection of racism as the ground of covenantal consciousness. Jewish parents are not only related to their children biologically, but must also participate with them in the larger covenantal normative family of Israel.

The Expansion of Human Adequacy Through Learning

In the Bible, the call to activism and responsibility is expressed by the prophetic challenge: "He has told you, O man, what is good, and what the Lord requires of you: Only to do justice, and to love goodness and to walk humbly with your God" (Mic. 6:8). In rabbinic Judaism, feelings of adequacy find expression not only with regard to moral practice, but also with regard to intellectual creativity. Whereas the Bible liberates the moral will, the Talmud liberates the intellect. In the Bible, God limits His power in history in order to activate the will to moral action; in the Talmud, human independence is expanded to include the intellect. God's self-limiting love for human beings is expressed in His entrusting the elaboration and expansion of the Torah to rabbinic scholars.

There is a well-known aggadic story involving a dispute among talmudic sages concerning the ritual status of the "oven of Aknai." Rabbi Eliezer declared it ritually pure; the sages argued that it was impure. After failing to convince the sages through rational arguments, Rabbi Eliezer then invoked supernatural miracles to convince his colleagues that he was right.

> On that day Rabbi Eliezer brought forward every imaginable argument, but they did not accept them. Said he to them: "If the law is as I say, let this carob tree prove it!" Thereupon the carob tree was torn a hundred cubits out of its place—others say, four hundred cubits. "No proof can be brought from a carob tree," they retorted. Again he said to them: "If the law is as I say, let the stream of water prove it!" Whereupon the

stream of water flowed backward. "No proof can be brought from a stream of water," they rejoined. Again he argued: "If the law is as I say, let the walls of the schoolhouse prove it." Whereupon the walls inclined to fall. But Rabbi Joshua rebuked them, saying: "When scholars are engaged in a halakhic dispute, what have you to interfere?" Hence they did not fall in honor of Rabbi Eliezer; and they are still standing thus inclined. (*Bava Metzia* 59b)

Seeing that the sages were not moved to accept his position as a result of the miraculous "hints" of divine support, Rabbi Eliezer tried to present what might be considered the final blow in any argument concerning the interpretation of the Torah: he appealed directly to God to confirm his view.

Again he said to them: "If the law is as I say, let it be proved from heaven!" Whereupon a heavenly voice cried out: "Why do you dispute with Rabbi Eliezer, seeing that in all matters the law is as he says!" But Rabbi Joshua arose and exclaimed: "It is not in heaven" [Deut. 30:12]. What did he mean by this? Said Rabbi Jeremiah: "That the Torah had already been given at Mount Sinai; we pay no attention to a heavenly voice, because Thou has long since written in the Torah at Mount Sinai, 'After the majority must one incline' " [Exod. 23:2]. Rabbi Nathan met Elijah and asked him: "What did the Holy One, blessed be He, do at that moment?" He replied: "He laughed, saying: 'My sons have defeated me, My sons have defeated Me.' " (Ibid.)

This rich *midrash* can be interpreted in many different ways. But it decidedly favors the orderly procedures of legal adjudication above the nonrational intrusions of miracles and heavenly voices in the academies of Torah study. Allowing for such supernatural intrusions would undermine the central role of study and rational debate in the development and elaboration of the law. Apart from the social and institutional justifications for rejecting supernatural intrusions, one may understand this text in the light of the covenantal emphasis on human responsibility.

God's defeat—"He laughed, saying: 'My sons have defeated Me, My sons have defeated Me' "—signifies God's self-limiting love for the sake of making His human covenantal partners responsible for intellectually developing the Torah. "The Torah is not in heaven" captures the feeling of intellectual competence of talmudic rabbis who no longer require prophecy or divine intervention by signs and wonders in order to discover how to apply the living word of God.[11] For serious rabbinic scholars, extrarational miraculous signs are unnecessary in order to confirm the validity and cogency of a legal argument.

There is a classic talmudic text that clearly implies that, from the death of Moses onward, the role of prophets and the appeal to revelation became irrelevant to problems of ascertaining the correct understanding of the Torah. The Talmud states that many laws were forgotten during the period of mourning for Moses. The principle "It is not in heaven" was repeatedly invoked in order to show that revelation was no longer available as a way to rediscover those forgotten laws.

> Rav Judah reported in the name of Samuel: "Three thousand traditional laws were forgotten during the period of mourning for Moses. They said to Joshua: 'Ask'; he replied: 'It is not in heaven' " [Deut. 30:12]. (*Temurah* 16a)

After listing several incidents where Pinhas and Joshua sought in vain to rediscover forgotten laws by appealing directly to God, the Talmud (ibid.) asserts in the name of Rabbi Abbuha that even though thousands of legal teachings were forgotten during the period of mourning for Moses, "Othniel, the son of Kenaz, restored [these forgotten teachings] as a result of his dialectics." Human beings can, through their own reasoning, compensate for the absence of God's active involvement in revealing the Torah. When God exercises self-restraint—"It is not in heaven"—students of the Torah are called upon to exercise human initiative and creativity. They must restore the forgotten word of God through the power of study. Learning and not only direct revelation mediates the word of God.

The absence of revelation is not a tragedy as long as there exist scholars who, by their intellectual efforts, can restore the full content and scope of the Torah. What is more, greater credibility is granted to scholars whose authority is based on their own intellectual competence than to prophets who are the mouthpiece of God.

> They [the scribes and the prophets] are like two agents whom a king sent to a province. With regard to one, he wrote: "If he shows you my signature and seal, trust him, but otherwise do not trust him." With regard to the other, he wrote: "Even if he does not show you my signature and seal, trust him." So of the words of prophecy, it is written: "If there arises in the midst of you a prophet . . . and he gives you a sign" [Deut. 13:2]; but of the words of the scribes it is written: "According to the law which they shall teach you" [Deut. 17:11]. (*Song of Songs Rabbah* 1:2)

The prophet—the paradigmatic mediator between God and human beings in the case of the written Torah—appeals to direct revelation; he addresses the community in the name of God, and his legitimacy is conditional on his ability to produce proof of his direct contact with

God (signs and miracles being the signature and seal of God). The scribes and scholars who produce the talmudic tradition gain authority by virtue of the "law which they teach," that is, intellectual competence to reason and argue cogently about the law.[12]

The intellectual freedom to go beyond the strict literal meaning of the biblical text, and to develop a viable legal system by reasoning and the application of hermeneutic principles, expresses the intellectual autonomy of the student to create and innovate and not simply to accept the past blindly. When students feel sufficiently confident to interpret the implications of what they have received from their prophets, when they are not overwhelmed by their teachers' superiority and do not simply repeat their lessons verbatim, when the content of revelation develops into an ever-expanding corpus of law and commentary, only then do covenantal Jews reveal their maturity and full partnership with God.

> Once I was on a journey, and I came upon a man who went at me after the way of heretics. Now, he accepted the written, but not the oral law. He said to me: "The written law was given us from Mount Sinai; the oral law was not given us from Mount Sinai." I said to him: "But were not both the written and the oral law spoken by the Omnipresent? Then what difference is there between the written and the oral law? To what can this be compared? To a king of flesh and blood who had two servants, and loved them both with a perfect love; and he gave them each a measure of wheat, and each a bundle of flax. The wise servant, what did he do? He took the flax and spun a cloth. Then he took the wheat and made flour. The flour he cleansed, and ground, and kneaded, and baked and set on top of the table. Then he spread the cloth over it, and left it so until the king should come. But the foolish servant did nothing at all. After some days, the king returned from a journey and came into his house and said to them: My sons, bring me what I gave you. One servant showed the wheaten bread on the table with a cloth spread over it, and the other servant showed the wheat still in the box, with a bundle of flax upon it. Alas for his shame, alas for his disgrace! Now, when the Holy One, blessed be He, gave the Torah to Israel, he gave it only in the form of wheat, for us to extract flour from it, and flax, to extract a garment." (*Seder Eliyahu Zuta* 2)

According to rabbinic Judaism, revelation was composed of layers upon layers of meaning. Talmud and Midrash are expositions of the divine covenantal word from within the limits of its literal confinement. The rabbis and their descendants ignited such explosions of meaning by subjecting the text to creative analysis and interpretation. With the

development of the oral tradition, Israel became a partner in the development of revelation; revelation ceased being the divine Word completely given at Sinai and became an open-ended Word creatively
elaborated by countless generations of students.

> Mikrah [scripture], mishnah, halakhot, toseftot, aggadot, and even what an
> accomplished student shall in the future say before his teacher—all these
> were communicated to Moses at Sinai. (Leviticus Rabbah 22:1)

The revelation at Sinai embraced both what was explicit and what
future generations would consider to be implicit in the Torah given to
Moses at Sinai. As the following midrash dramatically indicates, the Torah communicated to Moses at Sinai transcends what was literally given
at Sinai:

> Rav Judah said in the name of Rav: "When Moses ascended on high,
> he found the Holy One, blessed be He, engaged in affixing coronets to
> the letters [of the Torah]. Said Moses, 'Lord of the Universe, who com-
> pels Thee to do that?' He answered, 'There will arise a man, at the end
> of many generations, Akiva ben Joseph by name, who will spin out of
> each tittle heaps and heaps of laws.' 'Lord of the Universe,' said Moses,
> 'permit me to see him.' He replied, 'Turn you round.' Moses went and
> sat down at the end of the eighth row [and listened to the discourses
> upon the law]. Not being able to follow their arguments, he was ill at
> ease, but when they came to a certain subject and the disciples said to
> the master, 'Whence do you know it?' and the latter replied, 'It is a law
> given to Moses at Sinai,' he was comforted." (Menaḥot 29b)

Although based on divine revelation, the Torah became inseparable
from the vast body of material generated by talmudic interpretation.
The rabbinic scholar rather than the prophet became the mediator of
the Torah; his intellectual skills of analysis and interpretation elevated
him to an unprecedented position of importance in determining the
content of revelation.

The Talmud relates the story of a dispute in the Heavenly Academy
concerning a case of ritual impurity (Bava Metzia 86a). After considering
the pros and cons of the case, God declared that the individual in question was ritually pure, whereas the entire Heavenly Academy maintained that he was impure. "Who should decide?" asked the members
of the Academy. "Rabbah bar Nahmani," was their answer, because he
was considered to be an expert in the laws of purity. The Heavenly
Court—including God Himself—would defer to the opinion of this talmudic scholar. And even though Rabbah bar Nahmani agreed with
God's view, Maimonides, in the Mishneh Torah (Hilkhot Tumat Tzara'at

2:9), decided the law according to the teachers who disagree with both God and Rabbah bar Nahmani.

The role of the rabbinic scholar in determining law supersedes the craving for the authoritative stamp of revelation. Through his ingenious methods of interpretation, the scholar becomes, as it were, the master of the text. The Talmud derides those who pay greater respect to the Torah scroll than to its rabbinic interpreters, citing a typical example of rabbinic exegesis that indicates the authority of the interpreter over the text. Although the Torah specifies up to forty lashes as punishment for certain transgressions, the rabbis, through interpretation, reduced the number of lashes to thirty-nine. This example of the power of the sage to determine how the Torah was to be applied prompted Rava to say:

> How dull-witted are those people who stand up [in deference] to the scroll of the Torah, but do not stand up [in deference] to a great personage, because while in the Torah scroll forty lashes are prescribed, the rabbis come and [by interpretation] reduce them by one. (*Makkot* 22b)

One remains on the spiritual level of Noah and simply "walks with God" if one feels inexorably bound to the literal word and permanently in need of revelation. In creative interpretation and commentary, rabbinic scholars "walk before God" in the spirit of Abraham. The more students overcome passivity, transcend learning the tradition by rote, and feel adequate to uncover the spirit and the aim of revelation, the more they fulfill the covenantal mission of Abraham and Israel. The biblical worldview, which directs Jews to assume moral responsibility for the community, finds a correlate in the Talmud, where they are declared intellectually adequate to assume responsibility for the application and development of the Torah.

The Talmud contains a strange and fascinating paradox. On the one hand, there is unconditional acceptance of revelation. Anyone who claimed that Moses inserted one sentence in the Torah on his own and not because of revelation was to be considered a heretic.[13] For the Talmud, no autonomous human authority can set aside the divine revelation embodied in the written Torah. On the other hand, it is clear to anyone familiar with the Talmud that rabbinic teachers exhibit enormous interpretive freedom and mastery over the revealed text. God, the majestic source of all wisdom and authority, is nonetheless depicted as participating in learned discussions with His "associates"—rabbinic scholars. He argues, presents learned opinions, but in the end must sub-

mit to the procedural rules of human academies of learning. The Torah
is from God; its living application is determined by human beings.

The spirit of intellectual autonomy can be further illustrated by the
frequent reference to God as the paradigm of the respect one ought to
show to teachers of the Torah. It is fascinating to note that the Talmud
felt the need to restrict the honor shown to the teacher so that it did
not exceed that shown to God: "A scholar may rise before his master
only morning and evening, that his glory may not exceed the glory of
heaven" (since one rises only twice a day in God's honor).

The Talmud records a serious controversy indicating that the legitimacy of comparing the respect due the scholar with the awe and respect
due God was not arrived at lightly.

> Simeon Imsoni—others say Nehemiah Imsoni—interpreted every *et* [the
> accusative particle] in the Torah; but when he came to "You shall fear
> *et* the Lord your God," he desisted. Said his disciples to him: "Master,
> what is to happen with all the *ets* which you have interpreted?" "Just as
> I received reward for interpreting," he replied, "so will I receive reward
> for desisting." Subsequently, Rabbi Akiva came and taught: " 'You shall
> fear *et* the Lord your God' is to include scholars." (*Pesahim* 22b; *Kiddushin*
> 57a)

Out of concern for the unique respect befitting God, Imsoni was prepared to risk undermining his system of interpretation. Rabbi Akiva,
the pillar of the oral law and master of the method of deriving the law
from skillful interpretation of the Torah text, saved it by his boldness
in comparing respect for the interpreter of the Torah with respect for
its Author. Rabbi Akiva embodies the dynamic tension between ascribing ultimate authority to every word, letter, and scribal form of the
Torah and freeing the scholar to offer bold creative interpretations that
even Moses could not fully comprehend.

Rabbi Akiva, who expanded the range of rabbinic interpretation of
the biblical text to an unprecedented extent, whose bold teaching in
the academy of learning, according to the Midrash, perplexed the
prophet Moses, and who dared compare reverence for the rabbinic
scholar with reverence for God, is the very same person who in his
death exemplified unqualified love of God. When asked by his students
why he defied the Roman government's ban on the study and practice
of Torah and thereby risked his life, his answer was: "If this is our condition when we sit and study Torah, of which it is written, 'For that is
your life and length of days' [Deut. 30:20], then if we neglect it, how

much worse off shall we be?" For his defiance he was condemned to death.

> When Rabbi Akiva was led out to execution, it was the hour for the recital of the Shema, and while they combed his flesh with iron combs, he was accepting the kingship of heaven [reciting the Shema]. His disciples said to him: "Our teacher, even to this point?" He said to them: "All my days I have been troubled by this verse, 'You shall love the Lord your God with all your soul,' [which I interpret] even if He takes your soul. I said: 'When shall I have the opportunity of fulfilling this?' Now that I have the opportunity, shall I not fulfill it?" He prolonged the word "one" [in the Shema] until he expired while saying it. (*Berakhot* 61b)

Rabbi Akiva's radical commitment to love of God, which he placed above the value of life itself, should be understood together with his equally radical appreciation of the far-reaching role of the rabbinic scholar in interpreting and expanding the Torah. The rabbinic Jew, as exemplified by Rabbi Akiva, does not view absolute loyalty to God and intellectual freedom as being mutually exclusive. The covenantal principle of Sinai, which joined the categorical authority of revelation to human moral freedom and responsibility, is expanded in the rabbinic tradition to include both the extension of God's revelatory authority over all aspects of life and the intellectual autonomy and dignity of the student of the Torah.

The wide-ranging intellectual and legislative creativity of rabbinic teachers is not a Promethean rebellion against an authoritarian God, as Fromm would have it.[14] As I have shown, acknowledging God to be the sole creator of the universe and the source of all wisdom does not function psychologically as an inhibiting and repressive influence on human intellectual and moral activity. But equally, one should not confuse a halakhic anthropology with modern humanistic attempts at equating the Infinite with the unlimited human possibilities for growth. Rabbinic faith in human initiative is not based on a naive belief in human perfectibility and goodness. For halakhic Jews, human independence and freedom result from the gift of divine self-limitation; the expansion of human responsibility develops within a covenantal, relational framework. Rather than feel guilt for human creativity, which is said by Fromm to be a feature of authoritarian religion, halakhic Jews can feel greater divine confirmation the more they expand the limits of their responsibility within the community. One whose passion for God is expressed in the fulfillment of the commandments can never accept a theology that leads to resignation, passivity, or mystic quietude. As Urbach has observed, mystic withdrawal was never a living religious option for the talmudic rabbis.

> Their eyes and their hearts were turned Heavenward, yet one type was not to be found among them—not even among those who occupied themselves with the "Work of the Chariot" and the "Work of Crea-tion"—namely the mystic who seeks to liberate himself from his ego, and in doing so is preoccupied with himself alone. They saw their mission in work here in the world below. . . . The vast majority of them recognized the complexities of life with its travail and joy, its happiness and tragedy, and this life served them also as a touchstone for their beliefs and con-cepts.[15]

Nor should the halakhic Jew's legislative and interpretive independence be identified with Kantian autonomy.[16] Rabbinic acknowledgment of the inviolable content of revelation ("heteronomy") did not inhibit the intellectual freedom of Jews to interpret and apply the law in ways that not only extended beyond the literal constraints of biblical revelation, but also often made the text appear subservient to its commentators. The autonomy of rabbinic Judaism was expressed within a framework of divine authority rooted in the revelation at Sinai. As talmudic Judaism indicates, the model of the prophet who directly mediates between God and human beings (the heteronomous spirit) is not the only way of dramatically capturing the experience of God's commanding presence. The living word of God can be mediated through the application of human reason (the autonomous spirit) to the revealed norms of Torah. This is the essence of the dialectical vitality of talmudic Judaism.

The transition from literalism (the heteronomous spirit) to the intellectual interpretive freedom (the autonomous spirit) of the talmudic sages may be compared in certain respects to changing patterns of response in interpersonal relationships. Contrary to what one may believe initially, structured frameworks allow for the growth of spontaneity, flexibility, and a relaxed psychological atmosphere in interpersonal relationships. In the early period of a newly formed relationship, explicit rules defining mutual expectations often alleviate uncertainty and anxiety. A person feels protected from the threat of unpredictable responses by adopting a literal and fundamentalist approach to the rules governing "human covenants." It is only after a relationship has been ongoing for a long period of time, and many joys and hardships have been shared, that one becomes sensitive to the "other" even without explicit verbal communication. The ability to focus on the "spirit" rather than on the "letter" is a precious gift born of mature, sustained relationships.

The intellectual-cultural climate of the rabbinic oral law tradition is analogous, in many ways, to this aspect of interpersonal relationships. In a tradition that no longer feels threatened by the seductive power of paganism, that has withstood repeated attempts to break Israel's loyalty to the Torah and to God, and that produces teachers prepared to accept suffering with the joy born of passionate love of God—in such a tradition one may feel sufficiently confident to allow human beings the freedom to interpret the letter of the law and define the spirit and intention of the revealed word of God.

The playful imaginative associations of the Midrashic writers and the boldness of interpretation of the talmudic jurists testify to the internalization of the norms of the Sinai covenant and to the security and ease of a deep and mature love relationship with God. Intensive study and analysis of the Torah over long periods of time encourage a sense of intellectual autonomy. Accomplished students of the Torah feel confident that their creative interpretation of the law is an integral part of God's original revelation. For the covenantal Jew, whose religious life centers around *mitzvah* (divine commandment), attentive listening and innovative interpretation are not antithetical intellectual postures. Torah sages are very careful readers. Their unqualified respect and love for the literal meaning of each word of the Torah is, paradoxically, what accounts for their enormous confidence in delving below the surface and addressing themselves to the undisclosed spirit and intention of the Word.

Through their active expansion of the Torah and their passionate commitment to create a culture where study of the Torah becomes a cardinal norm of the community, talmudic teachers are the faithful disciples of Jeremiah, who dreamed of a time when the Torah would be written on the human heart. We can paraphrase the quotation given earlier and say: How foolish are people who stand up in deference to a Torah written on parchment but do not stand up in deference to a scholar who has Torah written on his heart. Although Jeremiah and Ezekiel spoke as if God alone would write the Torah on human hearts, those who believe in the eternal validity of the covenant grounded in *mitzvah* know that not only God but also human beings must assume responsibility to create a culture that embodies the prophetic promise that "all of them, from the least of them to the greatest" will participate in the joy of knowledge of God.

2

Assertion Versus Submission: The Tension Within Judaism

CHAPTER 1 SOUGHT to delineate a possible religious anthropology of Judaism by drawing upon features of the Judaic tradition that encourage observant Jews to manifest a sense of adequacy, dignity, and initiative in their covenantal relationship with God. I would not wish, however, to give the impression that this was the only way in which Jews traditionally experienced God. On the contrary, the God of the covenant was also experienced in ways that inspired awe, silence, and even resignation. Much of this book will be devoted to exploring the interaction of these two traditional Judaic themes: the theme of human adequacy and dignity in partnership with God and the theme of human terror and submission when faced with the all-demanding might of God. This chapter will make a start by discussing some striking examples of how the two themes contrast with each other in classic Judaic sources.

For the purpose of the discussion, it will be useful to distinguish between a milder and a more acute form of the contrast. The milder form is when human beings encounter the awesome majesty of God in a way that is certainly distinct from the spirit of covenantal moral boldness and intellectual autonomy but does not impair or undermine that spirit. Examples will be given later. The more acute form is when the experience of God is so overwhelming and incomprehensible that it threatens or crushes the covenantal spirit. This occurs when human beings are forced to submit in terror and resignation before a God Whose ways are unfathomable, Who allows horrible events to occur in which it is impossible for human beings to see any purpose or justice. Such events undermine covenantal mutuality, since they suggest that God reserves the right to act unilaterally in disregard of the spirit of the covenant whenever it suits Him. The motif of the incomprehensibility of what happens "under the sun" is of course particularly strong in Ecclesiastes. It will be more instructive, however, to see how helpless resignation manifests itself even in those very passages of biblical and rabbinic literature that most emphasize the autonomy and responsibility of the human covenantal partner.

Terror and Submissiveness Before God

Earlier, Abraham was described—according with rabbinic tradition—as a paradigm of the adequacy and dignity conferred upon a human being through a covenant with God. When God decides to destroy Sodom and Gomorrah, it occurs to Him that He should first state His intentions to Abraham, since this was the man through whom He had promised to bless all nations of the earth (Gen. 18:17–19). Abraham is confident enough in his role as God's consultant to bargain over the fate of the threatened cities, lecturing God on the moral significance of not "slaying the righteous with the wicked" (Gen. 18:25). Yet only a few chapters later in Genesis we find Abraham offering no protest whatsoever when God proposes a step that is prima facie a far greater violation of the covenantal promises, indeed one that implies the total abolition of the covenant. This is the story of the Akedah: the demand of God that Abraham sacrifice Isaac, the only son of his wife, Sarah, born in her old age when she could no longer expect offspring. Without an heir, what meaning could Abraham see in God's promises that "I will make of you a great nation" and "to your descendants I will give this land" (Gen. 12:2,7)? Nonetheless, Abraham obediently set off for the land of Moriah as instructed, taking Isaac and a bundle of wood.

We are not only amazed at the unintelligible demand of God, but dumbfounded when covenantal Abraham, who had so boldly stood before God and argued for justice, now submits unquestioningly and is ready to give up everything that has been solemnly promised to him. What can explain this unconditional obedience to divine authority? Had Abraham forgotten what he himself had understood to be possible in the case of Sodom and Gomorrah? How can he walk with Isaac to the altar and still retain covenantal dignity and adequacy in any sense intelligible to us? He, the example of the man who "walks before God" and engages in moral struggle with God, becomes suddenly like Noah, the man who "walked with God" and offered no objection when God announced the destruction of the world. Regardless of the "happy ending" of the story, the whole drama of Abraham's willingness to offer his son as a sacrifice and to submit to God's arbitrary command suggests the basic unintelligibility and mystery of God's actions and reflects the religious tendency to accept them totally, irrespective of whether they clash with all that human beings value.[1]

The Akedah threatens covenantal adequacy because it seems to exclude ethics from religious consciousness. Can we speak seriously of the category of the ethical in Judaism and yet allow for the possibility of God's intrusion into human life in a way that can destroy everything to which we can ascribe any value? For Leibowitz, the Akedah shows that any talk about the ethics of Judaism absolutely misses the point.

In later chapters, I shall take up Leibowitz's contention and consider the relationship between revelation and action and the meaning of religious ethics within Judaism. What concerns me here is the fact that both the Sodom episode and the Akedah are compatible with Abraham's religious consciousness. He reflects a paradox within the biblical drama: God appears to invite our rational comprehension, speaks in a language that we can understand, invites human beings to participate with Him in establishing His kingdom in history; His normative laws contain ethical principles, His *mitzvot* suggest human well-being, yet His behavior can also suggest a notion of divinity that borders on the demonic. Whereas the Akedah at least has a "happy ending" in which Isaac does not die, there are subsequent biblical episodes in which God strikes people down, sometimes individually and sometimes on a massive scale, for reasons that seem to be quite trivial, for what may be at most innocent mistakes.

> Now Nadav and Avihu, the sons of Aaron, took their respective firepans, and after putting fire in them, placed incense on it and offered strange fire before the Lord, which He had not commanded them. And fire came out from the presence of the Lord and consumed them, and they died before the Lord. . . . Then Moses said to Aaron and to his [remaining] sons Eleazar and Ithamar: "Do not unbind your hair nor tear your clothes, so that you may not die, and that He may not become wrathful against all the congregation. . . . " (Lev. 10:1–2, 6)

And [the Lord] struck down the men of Beit Shemesh because they had looked into the ark of the Lord, striking down of the people 50,070 men, and the people mourned because the Lord had struck the people with a great slaughter. (1 Sam. 6:19)

But when they came to the threshing floor of Nakhon, Uzzah reached out toward the ark of the Lord and took hold of it, for the oxen nearly upset it. And the anger of the Lord burned against Uzzah, and God struck him down there for his error and he died there by the ark of God. (2 Sam. 6:6)

These are three biblical examples of a destructive force bursting into people's lives; their reaction is to accept it unquestioningly as the act of their God.[2] In the first story, two sons of Aaron bring an innocuous, spontaneous gift to God, for which misdemeanor they are immediately consumed by fire. The story exemplifies the unexpected devouring tragedies of human life, which are experienced as just punishment on the part of God. One is stunned by the disproportion between offense and punishment, by the prohibition on mourning that Moses imposes upon the bereaved next of kin, and most of all by Aaron's readiness to remain silent before what has the appearance of an arbitrary demonic force. Aaron, who has been designated the mediator who brings atonement for Israel, becomes a victim of the numinous mystery enveloping the sanctuary where atonement was to be sought. In the second story, thousands die on account of the curiosity of a few members of their community. In the third, a man who instinctively seeks to preserve the ark from being damaged is killed on the spot. In no case does the punishment fit the crime, even if there is any crime. These are not stories that mediate a covenantal God Who invites human beings to join Him in building a just kingdom. They rather suggest that people who dare to have dealings with God should realize that they are entering a minefield where at any moment they may be blown up.

It should be understood that we are *not* dealing here with the claim that God transcends the intelligible or the ethical, nor with the claim that there is an infinite power and mystery to God's plenitude that goes beyond the human community. Such claims do not make covenantal consciousness impossible; they do not in themselves imply that God will fail to adhere strictly to any covenant between Himself and human beings. What does threaten covenantal consciousness in those biblical stories is the feeling that in God we encounter a furious irrational Force Whose unpredictability makes it impossible for us to rely on His commitments to us, Whose impatience constantly threatens us with destruction for unwittingly infringing our commitments to Him. Better not to have any mutual commitments, we may feel, than to have commitments that prove ineffective in our greatest moments of need, but threaten us in our slightest moments of misjudgment.

The Rabbinic Appreciation of the Paradox

In rabbinic literature, God's sudden fury manifests itself more rarely. Nonetheless, we continue to find the theme of God's unpredictability, of our inability to comprehend from any ethical viewpoint events that He allows to take place on earth. The theme is hardly less conspicuous there than in the Bible, though it may express itself in different forms. As in the Bible, moreover, it can manifest itself in those very passages that otherwise seem to emphasize human adequacy most.

The story of Moses in the academy of Akiva, quoted in chapter 1, is a case in point. The discussion between Akiva and his pupils is so profound that Moses is at a loss to make sense of it, although they claim to be propounding laws that were given to Moses at Sinai. The story obviously reflects the innovative dignity and creative freedom of the rabbis: human beings are empowered and adequate to develop the potential in the revealed word of God. But let us examine the end of the story.

> [Moses] returned to the Holy One, blessed be He, and said: "Lord of the Universe, Thou hast such a man [as Akiva] and Thou givest the Torah by me?" He replied: "Be silent, for such is My decree." Then said Moses: "Lord of the Universe, Thou hast shown me his Torah, show me his reward." "Turn round," said He; and Moses turned round and saw them weighing out his flesh at the marketstalls. "Lord of the Universe," cried Moses, "such Torah and such a reward?" He replied, "Be silent, for such is My decree." (*Menahot* 29b)

What a horrifying contrast between the beginning and the end of the story! At the beginning, Akiva is the supreme teacher fully in control of the content of revelation. He vastly expands the range of Torah learning by employing daring methods of interpretation, inferring hidden meanings even from details of the shapes of letters. Akiva's brilliance supplies the need for cognitive enrichment of the Torah. Moses feels overshadowed by "such a man"; as a humble student in Akiva's academy, he is comforted to hear a mere mention of his own name. Then we switch to the end of the story: the great Akiva has suffered martyrdom under the Romans, and his butchered flesh is being sold in the market. What a gap between Torah learning and the living experience of history! What a gap between the soaring freedom of a man in the academy of learning and the degradation of the same man in political reality! What a gap between Moses humbly admiring the creative dignity of Akiva and the vendors treating Akiva's flesh like dogmeat! Moses cries out to God: "How can the manner of Akiva's death be reconciled with his Torah brilliance? What has happened to the covenant that led me to expect a unity between one's attachment to the Torah and one's condition in the world?" The answer given by God—"Be silent, for such is My decree"—is crushing for any human sense of adequacy and dignity. To Moses, history has become unintelligible. Moses, who spent forty years explaining God's intentions to the Israelite community, has to stand silent before the incomprehensibility of God's decrees.

Had the story ended with the death of Akiva, one might have thought that the author of the *midrash* meant to portray that death as a tragic mishap. One might have taken him to mean, say, that since God has granted responsibility to human beings to conduct their affairs, He cannot be constantly intervening to produce "happy endings." But the author concludes, instead, with God saying: "Be silent, for such is My decree. If you ask why such a scholar receives such a reward, it is because you cannot know My plan in history." The people of the covenant are encouraged to be bold when they encounter God's word in the Torah. They are told to submit silently when they are confronted with the unintelligibility of God's plan in history. They have to accept that in the eyes of God, Who grants the Torah to His people as an expression of His love and concern, Akiva's body being sold off like the carcass of an animal is compatible with Akiva's outstanding ability to interpret God's covenantal word. Human beings are dignified and creative, yet are subjected to cruelty and degradation, and both aspects of the human condition are part of the divine purpose. Through the Torah, God invites us to learn His will, but He bids us be silent at its incomprehensibility.

A similar mixture of the two themes is found in the story of Rabbi Eliezer and the "oven of Aknai," also discussed in chapter 1. When Rabbi Eliezer defied the juridical framework of the Sanhedrin by appealing to miracles and a heavenly voice, the heavenly court was on his side, but his opinion was rejected because the Torah "is not in heaven" (Deut. 30:12) and "after the majority must one incline" (Exod. 23:2). The ordered framework of majority rule must prevail if Judaic law is to develop as a coherent rational system whereby human beings fulfill their responsibility of implementing God's revelation. Obvious in this story is the spirit of covenantal adequacy and confidence, the banishing of nonrational intrusions into the ordered rational world of talmudic study. The authenticity of this spirit is confirmed by God's laughing over His own defeat, over the success of His sons in asserting that right to decide for themselves which He had guaranteed to them.

That, however, was not the end of the story, but rather only the first episode in it. Emboldened by their victory, Rabbi Eliezer's opponents had him excommunicated for defying the authority of the majority.

> On that day, all objects which Rabbi Eliezer had declared clean were brought and burned in fire. Then they took a vote and excommunicated him. They said: "Who shall go and inform him?" "I will go," answered Rabbi Akiva, "lest an unsuitable person go and inform him, and thus destroy the whole world." What did Rabbi Akiva do? He donned black garments and wrapped himself in black, and sat at a distance of four cubits from him. "Akiva," said Rabbi Eliezer to him, "what has particularly happened today?" "Master," he replied, "it appears to me that your companions hold aloof from you." Thereupon he too rent his garments, put off his shoes, removed [his seat] and sat on the earth, while tears streamed from his eyes. The world was then smitten: a third of the olive crop, a third of the wheat, and a third of the barley crop. Some say the dough in women's hands swelled up. (*Bava Metzia* 59b)

The majority has the right to rule, but it cannot always exert that right with impunity. Human justice is autonomous from divine justice, but woe betide the human judges if they imagine that divine justice is no longer concerned with their actions. When the court decided a question of ritual purity, God laughingly accepted His defeat, but when it went on to victimize Rabbi Eliezer, His anger was aroused. The leader of Rabbi Eliezer's opponents, Rabbi Gamaliel, narrowly escaped with his life.

> Great was the calamity that befell that day, for everything at which Rabbi Eliezer cast his eyes was burned up. Rabbi Gamaliel too was traveling in a ship, when a huge wave arose to drown him. "It appears to me," he reflected, "that this is on account of none other but Rabbi Eliezer ben Hyrcanus." Thereupon he arose and exclaimed: "Sovereign of the Universe! Thou knowest full well that I have not acted for my honor, nor for the honor of my paternal house, but for Thine, so that strife may not multiply in Israel." At that the raging sea subsided. (Ibid.)

Rabbi Gamaliel managed to appease the raging anger of God by insisting that the motivation of his legal proceedings against Rabbi Eliezer was pure: he had been motivated not by spite, but by a desire to uphold God's honor by not allowing God's covenantal people to become rent by civil strife. Rabbi Gamaliel was saved for the moment, but not for long. His protestations of good intention were enough to stay God's hands, but only because Rabbi Eliezer had not yet turned to God in prayer over his harsh treatment.

> Ima Shalom was Rabbi Eliezer's wife and sister to Rabbi Gamaliel. From the time of this incident onward, she did not permit him to fall on his face [and pour out his feelings in supplication to God]. Now, a certain day happened to be [as she thought] New Moon [when no time was allotted to private supplications], but she had supposed a month of thirty days to be one of twenty-nine days. Others say: a poor man came and stood at the door and she took out some bread to him. [Either way, she failed to maintain her watch over her husband and] she found him fallen on his face. "Arise," she cried out to him, "for you have slain my brother." In the meanwhile, an announcement was made from the house of Rabban Gamaliel that he had died. "How do you know [that my prayer led to his death]?" he asked her. "I have this tradition from my father's house: all gates are locked excepting the gates of wounded feelings." (Ibid.)

Up to this last episode, it was possible to understand the story in terms of the gap between human justice and divine justice. The furious intervention of divine justice—blighted crops and sudden death—makes human adequacy and autonomy acutely problematic, but at least it is intelligible: the victimization of Rabbi Eliezer, over and above the rejection of his views, may also seem to offend our sense of natural justice. But a sensitive reading of the end of the story detects that here the divine judgment becomes unintelligible. It appears that Rabbi Eliezer did not wish the death of Rabbi Gamaliel; he did not realize that God would respond to his supplication in that way. When he turns to God in his misery, the result is an increase in his misfortune. According to one version of events reported, moreover, it was the arrival of a poor man asking for food that brought about Ima Shalom's momentary absence from her husband's presence. She was distracted by her own compassion and by her readiness to fulfill the *mitzvah* of giving to the poor. Her struggle to keep her brother alive is defeated by her loyalty to God's covenantal *mitzvah*. God, as it were, deceived her by turning the compassionate law concerning the poor into a means of bringing about her brother's death. What could be a more cynical insinuation about God's methods of getting His own way in history?

As a third example from rabbinic literature, we shall look at two contrasting approaches to the question of whether human beings can

mitigate a divine sentence of death. In one talmudic discussion we find
an almost arrogant assertion of the right of the rabbis to avert divine
punishment; in another, by contrast, our qualms over the divine command to slaughter a whole nation are rudely suppressed in the spirit of
"Be silent, for such is My decree."

The former passage concerns the punishment of karet, of being "cut
off from the people," that is, a decision by God to shorten someone's
life because he or she has committed a transgression for which no punishment by human courts has been instituted. The transgressions concerned are listed in the Torah. The rabbis decided that anyone who had
committed one of those transgressions should be flogged, so as to avert
the more severe divine punishment. Once a human court had applied
a suitable punishment for those transgressions, the rabbis argued, the
transgressor's status as a member of the community would have been
restored and God would no longer be able to apply the punishment of
karet.

> All who have incurred karet, on being flogged obtain remission from
> their punishment of karet; for it is said, "Forty he shall have him beaten,
> he shall not exceed . . . lest your brother be dishonored before your eyes"
> [Deut. 25:3], which shows that on having received the flogging he is
> [again considered] "your brother." (Makkot 3:15)

In its discussion of this argument, the Talmud reports a conversation
between Rabbi Joseph and Abbaye. The former expressed doubt
whether flogging could avert karet, asking rhetorically who had gone
up to heaven to check that the divine punishment had indeed been
rescinded. Abbaye replied by citing Rabbi Joshua ben Levi's dictum that
three enactments that had been made by a human court were subsequently confirmed by the heavenly court: the institution of the festival
of Purim, greeting people in the name of God, and the decision that
the Levites' tithe should be brought to the temple and given as well to
the priests. Who had gone up to heaven in these cases? The heavenly
confirmation of the enactments had been inferred by Rabbi Joshua ben
Levi through interpreting biblical texts. Similarly in the present case,
claimed Abbaye: by interpreting the Bible, Rabbi Hananiah ben Gamaliel and others had shown that flogging would avert the divine punishment of karet.

These arguments presuppose that we can understand God, that we
may even be so bold as to define, in certain circumstances, the way He
will or possibly must act. It is enough to peruse the biblical texts and
interpret them skillfully. Revelation does not have to be a sudden in-

trusion of God into history. We are not restricted to Buber's under-standing of revelation as a spontaneous breaking forth of the eternal Thou before us in unexpected moments. For the rabbinic mind, reve-lation lives on in the cognitive discipline of the scholar who meditates upon the sacred texts and seeks a consensus on their implications with his colleagues. These scholars even decide what are to be the sacred texts that form their starting point: they can assign the same status to the Book of Esther as to the word of God spoken to Moses. Purim, like Passover, celebrates the rescue of the community from the threat of ex-tinction. But the Book of Esther, in sharp contrast with Exodus, appears to make no mention of God speaking or acting. Nonetheless, not only was Esther appointed to be read annually during the celebration of Purim, but Rabbi Joshua ben Levi interpreted a verse of this very book to show that the heavenly court had ratified the custom concerned.

> "They confirmed and they assumed, the Jews, upon themselves and upon their seed . . . " [Esther 9:27]. "They confirmed" above what "they as-sumed upon themselves" below. (*Makkot* 23b)

The full and total self-confidence as to what God requires of human beings grows from knowledge of and devotion to the text of the Torah. Just as the rabbis are competent to introduce new legislation defining how the community is to behave, so too can they define how God will act with the sinner. The intellectual mastery of the word of God in the Torah is all the scholar requires to understand and define how both members of the covenant, God and the community of Israel, are to behave.

What boldness, approaching arrogance, characterized the talmudic sages in this case! And what a contrast with the reaction of the Talmud elsewhere to the story of Saul and the Amalekites! As the Bible relates, Saul was ordered by God through Samuel to slaughter the Amalekites down to the last person and the last domestic animal. When Saul failed to carry out this order to the letter, Samuel informed him that he had definitively lost the favor of God (1 Sam. 15:1-35). The rabbis evidently felt uncomfortable about this story. As if to caricature their own style of biblical interpretation, they depict Saul trying to respond as a skillful halakhist.

> Rabbi Mani said: " . . . When the Holy One, blessed be He, said to Saul, 'Now go and smite Amalek' [1 Sam. 15:3], he said: 'If on account of one person the Torah said "Perform the ceremony of the heifer whose neck is to be broken" [Deut. 21:1-9], how much more [ought consideration to be given] to all these persons. And if human beings sinned, what has

the cattle committed? And if the adults have sinned, what have the little ones done?' A divine voice came forth and said: 'Be not righteous overmuch [and do not be overly wise; why should you ruin yourself?]' [Eccles. 7:16]. And when Saul said to Doeg, 'Turn and fall upon the priests' [1 Sam. 22:18], a heavenly voice came forth to say: 'Be not wicked overmuch [and do not be a fool; why should you die before your time?]' [Eccles. 7:17]." (*Yoma* 22b)

In this story, Saul is presented as offering two kinds of objection. One appeals to the Torah: if a person is found murdered in the open countryside, the elders of the nearest town have to perform an elaborate ceremony, which involves breaking the neck of a heifer, in order to proclaim that their town is innocent of the murder. If God requires us to show so much concern over the death of one person, how much more so when an entire nation is involved? The second objection recalls the one put forward to God by Abraham in the case of Sodom and Gomorrah: shall the innocent be swept away with the guilty? But whereas God took the objection seriously when it came from Abraham, Saul is curtly told, "Be not righteous overmuch." Saul's attempt to be a halakhist is rejected by a heavenly voice—the kind of divine response that had not deterred the rabbis in the case of the "oven of Aknai."

The story ends by reminding us that Saul later killed some priests out of spite against David, as if to say: who was Saul to raise moral objections against slaughtering the Amalekites? But this is an argument *ad hominem*; the substance of Saul's objections is not affected by it. In Saul's case, God chose not to laugh and admit, "My sons have defeated me," but to insist: "Be silent, for such is my decree." Or, in another version of the heavenly voice heard by Saul: "Be not righteous overmuch, *more than your Creator!*" (*Midrash Rabbah* on Eccles. 7:16).

The Dialectic Within Prayer

The terror induced by the inscrutable will of God can reduce any human moral concerns to naught. Yet this same mysterious God calls upon human beings to participate in a religious drama that requires them to develop their powers of reason and sense of morality. It seems that the Bible and the Talmud seek to ensure that the two themes intertwine. They deliberately introduce the one where we might expect to find only the other. As we have seen, situations that initially appear to exemplify human adequacy may end with an invasion of crushing divine power.

But the classic sources of Judaism also contain converse examples: situations in which terror before God seems natural, but then an element of human adequacy is brought in and emphasized.

Examples of the converse case are the rabbinic discussions of prayer and the days of penitence between Rosh ha-Shanah and Yom Kippur. These are situations in which awe before God's majesty and power is in order. Moreover, feelings of awe and trepidation do not then contradict the covenantal spirit, even though they do not exemplify that spirit.

> One should not stand up to say [the daily] prayers except in a reverent frame of mind. The pious men of old used to wait an hour before praying in order that they might concentrate their thoughts upon their Father in heaven. Even if a king greets him [while praying], he should not answer him. Even if a snake is wound round his heel, he should not break off. (*Berakhot* 5:1)

These instructions reflect the awesome dimension of the prayer experience. Reverence is demanded when we stand up to address the supreme King of Kings. It is not too much to spend an hour in order to reach a sufficiently humble frame of mind before beginning to pray.

It is not accidental, however, that the Talmud found it necessary to record in this very context that there are occasions when a totally different religious posture of prayer may be acceptable to God, even requisite for His purposes. Prayer may embody not only humility and awe, but also an assertion of the rights conferred by God upon human beings through the covenant and through the Torah. Prayer may become nonapologetic, even aggressive and defiant. Among the Talmud's paradigms are Hannah and Moses.

> "If Thou wilt indeed look" [1 Sam. 1:11]. Rabbi Eleazar said: "Hannah said before the Holy One, blessed be He: 'Sovereign of the Universe, if Thou wilt look, it is well, and if Thou wilt not look, I will go and shut myself up with someone else in the knowledge of my husband Elkanah. And as I shall have been alone [with a man other than my husband], they will make me drink the water of the suspected wife, and Thou canst not falsify Thy law, which says: "She shall be cleared and shall conceive seed" [Num. 5:28].' " (*Berakhot* 31b)

The laws that God gave to His covenantal people contain divine promises as well as threats of punishment. This provides Hannah with a way of forcing God's hand and obliging Him to grant her children even against His intention. She threatens to create the legal situation in which she will be a wife suspected of adultery who has to undergo the test of drinking the bitter water. Since the Torah says that the innocent wife who undergoes the test will both be cleared *and* conceive seed, God will be obliged to allow her a child, for otherwise He would be breaking a promise that He had made in giving this law. If His inviolable promise makes it possible for her to obtain her wish by a subterfuge, He may as well give her a child straightaway.

Among further examples of Hannah's "insolence," the following is given.

> "Now Hannah, she spoke in her heart" [1 Sam. 1:13]. Rabbi Eleazar said in the name of Rabbi Jose ben Zimra: "She spoke concerning her heart. She said before Him: 'Sovereign of the Universe, among all the things that Thou hast created in a woman, Thou hast not created one without a purpose, eyes to see, ears to hear, a nose to smell, a mouth to speak, hands to do work, legs to walk with, breasts to give suck. These breasts that Thou hast put over my heart, are they not to give suck? Give me a son, so that I may suckle with them.' " (Ibid.)

This time Hannah addresses God not as the giver of the Torah, but as her Creator. She demands that God respond to a fundamental need that He Himself has created in women. He should not create organs for a definite purpose and yet deny them the opportunity to realize that purpose. Like Rabbi Eleazar's previous example, this is not the prayer of a weak human being who feels a need to be self-apologetic, to offer fulsome praise to God before submitting requests. Hannah feels that she is requesting not undeserved grace, but her legitimate due, and she prays accordingly.

Besides Hannah, Rabbi Eleazar asserts that Elijah and Moses also "spoke insolently toward heaven." When Elijah said, "For Thou didst turn their heart backward" (1 Kings 18:37), he implied that God Himself bore the responsibility for Israel's lapse into idolatry. Moses was insolent when God threatened to destroy Israel for worshiping the golden calf.

> "Now therefore let Me alone, that my wrath may grow hot against them and that I may consume them, but of you [Moses] I will make a great nation" [Exod. 32:10]. Rabbi Abbahu said: "Were it not explicitly written, it would be impossible to say such a thing. This teaches that Moses took hold of the Holy One, blessed be He, like a man who seizes his fellow by his garment, and said before him: 'Sovereign of the Universe, I will not let Thee go until Thou forgivest and pardonest them.' " (Ibid. 32a)

These rabbinic homilies reflect an element that exists in the biblical text itself.[3] There is an authoritative tone, for instance, in the prayer with which Moses besought God not to destroy Israel. Instead of humbly begging pardon for the community, Moses pointed out that God's intention would discredit God in the eyes of the world, as well as violate past promises.

> And Moses besought the Lord his God and said: "O Lord, why does Thy anger burn against Thy people whom Thou hast brought out from the land of Egypt with great power and with a mighty hand? Why should the Egyptians speak, saying: 'With evil intent He brought them out to kill them in the mountains and to destroy them from the face of the earth'? Turn from Thy burning anger and change Thy mind about doing harm to Thy people. Remember Abraham, Isaac, and Israel, Thy servants to whom Thou didst say: 'I will multiply your descendants as the stars of the heavens, and all this land of which I have spoken I will give to your descendants, and they shall inherit it forever.' " So the Lord changed His mind about the harm which He said He would do to His people. (Exod. 32:11–14)

For a moment, Moses is the leading partner in the covenant. For a moment, he knows better than God what is in God's best interest, since he foresees that the Egyptians will mock God if Israel is destroyed. He also points out that God's intention is invalid anyway, since it contradicts His covenantal promises. It is this profound aspect of covenantal mutuality that is captured by the comments of Rabbi Eleazar and the other talmudic sages.

In discussing the prayers of Hannah, Elijah, and Moses, the Talmud recognized that prayer is not only an experience of humility and awe, even if this is acknowledged to be the dominant aspect of prayer. It is also legitimate in prayer to confront God and argue with Him, not merely to plead for mercy and beg for grace. In prayer, Jews are not restricted to yearning for God's love; they can make demands upon their Beloved. Covenantal mutuality implies that God is committed to taking seriously the requests and recommendations of His covenantal partners. God even invites comments on His intentions, as in the case of Abraham before the destruction of Sodom and Gomorrah. Moses sensed a similar invitation to respond when God proposed to destroy Israel over the golden calf. The "insolence" ascribed by the Talmud to Moses and the others is therefore not an expression of rebellion against God, but an expression of sensitive listening to God. The religious consciousness to which it gives expression is a covenantal relational consciousness and not a rebellious autonomous consciousness.

Joy and Terror in Judgment

The themes of awe before God and covenantal self-confidence are also found blended together in the rabbinic understanding of the period of divine judgment between Rosh ha-Shanah and Yom Kippur. The character of this period in the Jewish year naturally evokes in the worshipers an emphasis upon trepidation and human insignificance before God.

> O Lord, before I was formed, I had no worth; and now that I have been formed, I am as though I had not been formed. Dust am I in my life; yea, even more so in my death. Behold I am before Thee like a vessel filled with shame and confusion. May it be Thy will, O Lord my God and the God of my fathers, that I sin no more, and as for the sins that I have committed before Thee, purge them away in Thine abundant mercy, but not by means of affliction and suffering.

The liturgy also states that the angels themselves quake at this time, for "even they are not guiltless in Thy sight." The Hallel prayer is omitted on these High Holy Days because, as the Babylonian Talmud explains, its joyous praise is out of place.

> . . . on Rosh ha-Shanah Hallel is not said. What is the reason? Rabbi Abbahu replied: "The ministering angels said in the presence of the Holy One, blessed be He: 'Sovereign of the Universe, why should Israel not chant hymns of praise before Thee on Rosh ha-Shanah and Yom Kippur?' He replied to them: 'Is it possible that the King should be sitting on the throne of justice with the books of life and death open before Him, and Israel should chant hymns of praise?' " (Rosh ha-Shanah 32b)

Yet all is not gloom and despondency. The Jerusalem Talmud notes (Rosh ha-Shanah 1:3) that on the day that judgment begins, Jews eat and drink and dress with a general attitude of confidence. The prospect of divine judgment upon all the misdeeds and lapses of the previous year generates a serious mood, but not exclusively terror before a severe authoritarian God. Although Jews realize that the humblest expressions of repentance are required of them, they can nonetheless stand erect when the time of judgment begins, knowing that they are "significant others" in God's eyes.

The Jerusalem Talmud brings out the dialectical relationship between the humbling experience of judgment and the self-assurance of the judged by noting that it is we, and not God, who are empowered to decide when the period of judgment shall begin.

Hurnah said: "What nation is like this nation? It is the custom among men that if the ruler says 'The trial is today' and the accused say 'The trial shall be tomorrow'—to whom do you listen? Surely to the ruler. With regard to God, however, this is not the case. If the [human] court declares, 'Today is Rosh ha-Shanah,' God says to the ministering angels: 'Set up the [heavenly] court, let the defense attorneys arise, let the prosecuting attorneys arise, because My children have declared that today is Rosh ha-Shanah.' If the [human] court deliberates and decides to postpone it to the next day, God says to the ministering angels: 'Remove the [heavenly] court, let the prosecuting attorneys leave, because My children decided to postpone it to tomorrow. . . . ' " (*Rosh ha-Shanah* 1:3)

By giving humorous expression to the incongruity of the situation, this rabbinic parable reminds us that God turns to His covenantal partner even at the moment when the latter has most to fear Him. In acknowledging the awesome right of God to judge, we need not become paralyzed by feelings of human depravity or crushed by an infantile sense of dependency.

Hukkim *and* Mishpatim

In these examples, prayer and Rosh ha-Shanah, the theme of awe before God is not allowed to annul the theme of covenantal mutuality. Here, rather, the two themes complement each other, whereas in the examples given earlier in this chapter they were antithetical. But whether they occur as antithetical or as complementary, we can see how the Judaic tradition frequently sought to bring them together in the same experience. I believe that it would be correct to see the distinction between *mishpatim* (ordinances) and *hukkim* (statutes) also as an attempt by the tradition to integrate those two themes into the legal framework of the *halakhah* itself. The distinction arises in connection with the attempt to find *ta'amei ha-mitzvot*, the reasons for the divine commandments. With many *mitzvot*, one can cite universal grounds of ethics or human well-being that make their observance worthwhile for human beings in general. But other *mitzvot* resist attempts at rational explanation; there are so many of them that the presence of such inexplicable commandments in the Torah seems also to be part of the divine purpose. The Judaic tradition gave expression to this situation by employing the terms *mishpatim* and *hukkim* for these two kinds of *mitzvot*. In the Babylonian Talmud, the distinction is derived from the verse "My ordinances shall you

do and my statutes shall you keep, to live in accord with them; I am
the Lord your God" (Lev. 18:4).

> Our rabbis taught: "My ordinances shall you do"—that is, such com-
> mandments which, if they were not written [in scripture], they should
> by right have been written, and these are they: [the laws concerning]
> idolatry, immorality and bloodshed, robbery, and blasphemy. "And My
> statutes shall you keep"—that is, such commandments to which Satan
> objects: they are those relating to the wearing of sha'atnez [a fabric of
> wool and linen], the halitzah [a ceremony whereby a widow releases her
> brother-in-law from the obligation of levirate marriage] performed by a
> sister-in-law, the purification of the leper, and the he-goat-to-be-sent-away.
> And perhaps you might think these are vain things, therefore scripture
> says: "I am the Lord," that is, I the Lord have made it a statute and you
> have no right to criticize it. (Yoma 67b)

In seeing ethical and humanitarian reasons for the mishpatim, we are
encouraged to believe that the well-being of the community is central
to God's purpose in revelation. They enable us to see God as the compassionate teacher, who shows us how to realize our own human powers
within the framework of life provided by the Torah. Hukkim, on the
other hand, seem to have no purpose other than to demonstrate Israel's
readiness to give unconditional allegiance to God.

The hukkim themselves can be divided into two kinds. On the one
hand, there are those which admittedly seem to bring no benefit, yet
they also do no harm. The examples mentioned in the above quotation
from Yoma fall into this category. The world may regard the Jews as silly
and superstitious for their meticulous preoccupation with foodstuffs and
the composition of dress materials, but there is nothing morally offen-
sive in such practices. Other hukkim, however, do violate the human
sense of justice, as the rabbis themselves were ready to admit on occasion. Midrash Rabbah on Leviticus 24:10 cites an interpretation of Ecclesiastes 4:1: "So I returned, and considered all the oppressions that
are done under the sun: and behold the tears of such as were oppressed,
and they had no comforter; and on the side of their oppressors there
was power; but they had no comforter."

> Daniel the Tailor interpreted the verses as applying to bastards. "And
> behold the tears of such as were oppressed." If the parents of these bas-
> tards committed transgression, what concern is it of these poor sufferers?
> So also if this man's father cohabited with a forbidden woman, what sin
> has he himself committed and what concern is it of his? "And they had
> no comforter," but "on the side of their oppressors there was power."
> This means, on the side of Israel's Great Sanhedrin, which comes to

them with the power derived from the Torah and removes them from the fold in virtue of the commandment: "A bastard shall not enter into the assembly of the Lord" [Deut. 23:3]. "But they had no comforter." Says the Holy One, blessed be He: "It shall be My task to comfort them."

It was bold of the rabbis to protest against a law that they saw as fundamentally unjust. Nevertheless, they accepted it with the proviso that in the world to come God will correct the injustice. Laws like this call in question the covenantal principle that encourages the human moral sense to play a creative role in the covenantal relationship, whereas laws of foodstuffs and ritual purity simply have nothing to do with that principle, but without actually contradicting it.

Mishpatim enable us to see divine revelation as anthropocentric in the spirit of covenantal mutuality. *Hukkim* to the rabbis represent the spirit of unconditional submission, whose extreme form is symbolized by the Akedah of Isaac. The creation and employment of this terminological distinction in the Talmud amounts to incorporating in the very heart of the *halakhah* the two contrasting themes that I have been examining in this chapter.

3

"Halakhic Man": Soloveitchik's Synthesis

AS WE HAVE JUST SEEN, the biblical and rabbinic traditions contain two contrasting themes: one that emphasizes the dignity of human responsibility, intellectual adequacy, self-confidence, and covenantal mutuality with God, and another that demands utter silence and resignation before the inscrutable transcendent will of God. The rabbinic tradition does not attempt any higher unity or integration of these opposing religious moods. It posits both and does not explain whether they complement each other. The respective weight that a Jew gives to either of them is not prescribed in advance. Which of the two elements will play a dominant role in one's spiritual appreciation of Judaism is not dictated by the texts themselves. Selection and emphasis remain the responsibility of the reader.

Modern Jewish thinkers have responded to these apparently diametrically opposed faith experiences in different ways. Erich Fromm, for example, strove to uncover the humanistic nonauthoritarian frameworks in the Judaic tradition.[1] He constantly emphasized stories in the Talmud that assert the intellectual dignity of human beings, their right to argue with God. He appreciated the covenantal notion according to which God obligates Himself to act in harmony with human beings. These humanistic notions enabled Fromm to claim that in this tradition

God is not an authoritarian force outside of humanity, but rather reflects its higher powers.

I believe that Fromm's identification of God with the human being's ultimate powers is a mistaken appreciation of biblical and rabbinic senses of human autonomy. Be that as it may, Fromm claims to discern an evolutionary pattern and believes that, although there are regressive tendencies, nevertheless the higher form of the religious life in Judaism is not those stories in which God is portrayed as an arbitrary figure, but those in which human beings are encouraged to unfold their own powers. To the degree to which we can assert our own dignity, creativity, and spontaneity, God is not a force and a power outside of us who acts independently of our higher nature. When we are encouraged to unfold our own powers of love, when human creativity is considered a virtue, and when God is not frightened of human assertiveness—at that moment there occurs the true unfolding of the religious impulse that understands human beings to exist in the image of God. The true spirit of the Judaic tradition emerges when we come to understand that God is a symbol of the deepest spiritual powers present in the human condition.

Walter Kaufmann was correctly critical of Fromm's polarization between authoritarian and humanistic religion and showed that both dimensions are present within the Judaic framework.[2] Abraham both argues against God and unconditionally submits. One must take note of both dimensions simultaneously, and Fromm's attempt to perceive an evolution does not do justice to the presence of this paradoxical feature throughout the tradition.

Yeshayahu Leibowitz has moved in the opposite direction to Fromm. He does not see the humanistic, assertive ethical features of Judaism as a higher expression of Judaism. What typifies Judaism for him is Abraham's readiness to sacrifice Isaac. The act of worship reaches full purity only when the human being's total sense of personal dignity is negated, when a person willingly places worship of God outside of any categories that are intelligible to one's ethical sense. Worship out of love demands total submissiveness. Leibowitz admits that there are humanistic features in the Judaic tradition, such as the attempts to make the commandments intelligible to human reason and to link their observance with social and economic benefits. But this, according to Leibowitz, represents only the first stage in the religious development of a Jew. In order to motivate human beings to worship, one appeals to their self-interest. Leibowitz calls this worship *she-lo li-shemah*, worship of God not for its own sake, where human needs and human rationality lie at the center of the religious life. Religious maturity comes only when a Jew is able to achieve worship of God *li-shemah*, for its own sake. It expresses itself in a love of God that is totally dominated by theocentric passion. Leibowitz recognizes no covenantal category that would in some important way involve mutuality between God and the Jewish community. For Leibowitz, one chooses either a human-centered religion or a God-centered religion.

Paradigmatic for Leibowitz's understanding of Judaism is the Akedah, the readiness of Abraham to sacrifice his only son, Isaac, and thereby to sacrifice all human concerns and values in unconditional obedience to God's will. There is therefore no category of ethics in Judaism; humanism is an atheistic, secular category that is in no way tied to Jewish worship. To Leibowitz, in opposition to Fromm, true worship is where Jews totally negate themselves as significant beings and accept that their whole worth stems from their standing before God in worship. Leibowitz would understand the statement of God to Moses, "Be silent, for such is my decree," not in the sense that God has a plan for history that is unintelligible to human beings, since Leibowitz denies any theology of history, but rather that Jews are called upon to worship God even in an unintelligible reality that defies all human expectations of God. The act of worship in Judaism is sui generis and unrelated to whatever events occur in history; it should in no way be integrated into the universe of discourse where human rational and ethical categories are operative. Worship of God is beyond the ethical, beyond the rational, beyond the possibility of translation into cultural categories that can be shared with all human beings irrespective of religious commitment. There is a unique dimension to worship that cannot be reduced to any other human category.

Both Fromm and Leibowitz, therefore, try to eliminate one of the two conflicting themes by regarding it as merely a starting point for an evolution into the other and superior theme. Whereas Fromm sees Judaism as evolving historically from a submissive to a humanistic conception of God, Leibowitz sees the individual Jew as rising from an anthropocentric to a theocentric attitude to worship. There is, however, a modern Jewish thinker who seeks not to eliminate one of the two themes by treating it as an inferior form of religious passion, but rather to integrate them together in the religious life of the Jew. He is Rabbi Joseph Soloveitchik, considered by many to be the leading Orthodox Jewish theologian of the present century, whom it was also my good fortune to have as a teacher.

In Soloveitchik, both dimensions of the Judaic tradition—the assertive and the submissive—are given full expression. Moreover, whereas in rabbinic literature there is no attempt to explain how the two fit together, Soloveitchik seeks to bring them into a higher ideological unity. Submission to the inscrutable divine will, the denial of human rationality, the inability to appropriate the divine reality through humanistic ethical categories, the surrender of all that is dear to a human being—these features of the faith experience are raised by Soloveitchik to an ultimate heroic dimension of Jewish spirituality.

Soloveitchik's appropriation of those two dimensions of the Judaic tradition has enabled him to participate in modernity, to enter into the larger framework of contemporary culture, and yet at the same time to retain Orthodox Jewish submission to the authority of the past as expressed in the unchangeability of the *halakhah* and the permanent status of Judaic dogma. Fromm wishes that we remain at the moment of Abraham's intercession with God for Sodom. Leibowitz demands that we march on to the moment of the Akedah. Soloveitchik shows how an interplay of both themes may continue at the most mature stage of Jewish religious life.

The Intellectual Dignity of "Halakhic Man"*

It will be necessary to look at several of Soloveitchik's writings, because although both themes are always latently present, sometimes one and sometimes the other is given greater emphasis. Thus, it was the theme of human autonomous creative power that dominated his first major essay, *"Ish ha-halakhah,"* published in 1944, which I shall quote from its recent English translation as *Halakhic Man*. In it we may see how deeply Soloveitchik's thinking and philosophical outlook have been influenced by the emphasis on learning that he inherited from his own family. The *lamdan*, the student who masters completely the intricacies of the *halakhah* (the Judaic legal tradition in its entirety), the one who can define clearly and distinctly the conceptual issues involved in a complex talmudic text, is the spiritual hero type from whom Soloveitchik draws his religious inspiration in *Halakhic Man*. Not prayerful piety or moral introspection, not mystic retreat or elaborate philosophical and theological sophistication, but the hard, disciplined daily work of the talmudic

---

*"Man" in such expressions as "halakhic man" and "covenantal man" appearing in this book refers to all human beings, men and women. The word "man" has been retained in quoted passages.

student who draws joy from uncovering the inner logical coherence of the vast corpus of halakhic literature—this is what nourished Soloveitchik's initial and most significant philosophic work. In writing it, Soloveitchik had before him the image of his father, his grandfather, and the whole Lithuanian halakhic tradition that emerged from the Gaon of Vilna, powerful legal minds that manifested great spiritual energy in the disciplined act of learning. Soloveitchik's philosophic work was an attempt to show how a whole philosophy of life could be constructed upon the felt experience of the individual who is devoted to the process of learning. The freedom, boldness, intellectual integrity, and uncompromising rigor that are present in the act of study were the model for Soloveitchik's description of "halakhic man."

Whether the learning model can adequately serve as a sufficient grounding for a total religious worldview is too vast a question for exhaustive discussion within the framework of this book. What is important in the present context is how the experience of learning, the primacy of scholarship, found in the Lithuanian tradition served Soloveitchik as symbolic of a total spiritual outlook, as an Archimedian point from which he could move to a total vision of Judaic creativity and halakhic autonomy. This is the matrix within which Soloveitchik brought halakhic man into discussion with Socrates, who had claimed that virtue is knowledge, and with Kant, who had argued that the dignity of a human being lies in his or her sense of moral autonomy. Soloveitchik thus introduced halakhic Judaism into the world of Western philosophic thought not in the manner of Buber and Scholem, who found a point of contact in the pietistic existential experience of the mystic, but by demanding respect and recognition for the intellectual acumen of the talmudic scholar in the tradition of Brisk, the hometown of Soloveitchik's immediate ancestors. Such a scholar, with his day-and-night engagement with the details of Judaic law, was for Soloveitchik a human type whose stature could rival that of the modern mathematician, scientist, and philosopher.

Soloveitchik's methodology is to offer sharp, contrasting human typologies in order to bring home the point he is trying to establish. His first major philosophic essay employs a contrast between two mutually opposed human types whom he terms "cognitive man" and *homo religiosus*. The former is typified by the modern natural scientist advancing confidently from triumph to triumph. *Homo religiosus*, on the other hand, is the mystic, the transcendentalist seeking mystic union with God, the pietist fearful of this world, who is grace-oriented and ridden with a sense of guilt, who believes that this world is an affront to God and that the ultimate significance of the religious life is to transcend the imperfect body together with the imperfect social and political reality. Soloveitchik then brings onto the stage a third figure, "halakhic man," who shares some of the features of the other two and thereby rises above both.

Halakhic man is the spiritual individual who emerges in the Judaic tradition, who is no less deeply committed to God than *homo religiosus*, but whose ideal halakhic system is no less brilliant than an abstruse mathematical universe and whose creative ingenuity need fear no comparisons with the spirit of modern technical advance. The essay concentrates, however, on contrasting the deficiencies of *homo religiosus* with the virtues of halakhic man. Although Soloveitchik occasionally says that halakhic man is himself a *homo religiosus*, mostly the latter term denotes a kind of spirituality over which halakhic man excels through being a superlative version of "cognitive man."

In terms of the themes that I have developed in the preceding chapters, the personality of Soloveitchik's halakhic man corresponds in some important ways to my emphasis on the dignity that emerges from covenantal consciousness. In Soloveitchik's conceptual scheme, however, the impulse to abhor passivity and become a partner with God does not emerge exclusively or even primarily from the covenantal moment of Sinai, but comes from the mandate assigned to man and woman on the sixth day of creation. Soloveitchik accepts the fundamental rabbinic viewpoint that the whole of the Torah, including the narrative passages, is to be studied for its normative content. The elaborate story of the six days of creation has no descriptive significance for Soloveitchik. It is not meant to offer us a cosmological theory; rather, its fundamental implication is that it invites us to see in the story of creation an activity of God that must be imitated by human beings.

Here, indeed, Soloveitchik goes beyond rabbinic precedent, since he does not merely draw normative conclusions from God's manner of creation, but infers that human beings must participate in the act of creation itself: God has made them partners in the creative process. The principle "and you shall walk in His ways" (Deut. 28:9) and the whole idea of *imitatio Dei* were never taken in the rabbinic tradition to imply that as God is a creator, so must the human being be a creator. They were related by the rabbis to notions of mercy, justice, kindness, visiting the sick, clothing the naked, that is, attributes of God that are imitated in the ethical and social realms of human life.[3] That God's creation of a cosmos should *itself* be viewed as an act to be imitated is Soloveitchik's bold exegetical move, whereby he makes the notion of human creativity

and the notion of dignity of action play central roles in his whole understanding of halakhic consciousness.

Soloveitchik is so bold as to claim that God deliberately created an
imperfect universe so as to leave scope for humankind to act creatively.
The notion of *creatio ex nihilo*, he argues, implies that God is also the
source of the initial chaos described in the opening verses of Genesis.
Inasmuch as that chaos was not totally reduced to order by God in the
sequel, God is the source of the nonformed and the incomplete in our
world, not only the source of frameworks of structure and law. The
creation of an imperfect universe was an act of love, since it enabled
the human species to undertake the task of perfecting that which God
brought into being in an imperfect and incomplete form. Correcting
the evil in the world is a task for human beings. Soloveitchik emphasizes
his point with a *midrash* according to which the Jewish festival of the
new moon atones for the imperfection of creation; it is an atonement,
as it were, for God's sin in creating an imperfect world.

> The Jewish people bring a sacrifice to atone, as it were, for the Holy
> One, blessed be He, for not having completed the work of creation. The
> Creator of the world diminished the image and stature of creation in
> order to leave something for man, the work of his hands, to do, in order
> to adorn man with the crown of creator and maker. (p. 107)

For Soloveitchik, therefore, creation is not only an ethical and social
category. It expresses itself in the total creative gesture of man, be it
mathematical theorizing, be it technological innovation, be it an expression of art and beauty. All realms which express the creative impulse
constitute an *imitatio Dei*. The impulse to creativity is the highest human act and gives expression to holiness. Human curiosity, which leads
to the creation of thought systems, is seen by Soloveitchik as a profound
religious impulse. The instinct to bring something new into being is the
hallmark of human dignity.

> If a man wishes to attain the rank of holiness, he must become a creator
> of worlds. If a man never creates, never brings into being anything new,
> anything original, then he cannot be holy unto his God. That passive
> type who is derelict in fulfilling his task of creation cannot become holy.
> (p. 108)

Within the Judaic way of life, however, human creativity does not
burst out spontaneously in every arbitrary direction, but is channeled
and delimited by the *mitzvot* revealed to Moses. Soloveitchik must therefore face the question that is implicit in the Kantian critique of revelation as heteronomous morality. How can a revelatory system of

morality be compatible with the Kantian sense of dignity that grows from man as the autonomous legislator of his own morality?

In *Halakhic Man*, furthermore, Soloveitchik was writing not about the Zionist pioneer, the new Jew who was engaged in building a total Jewish society. Soloveitchik was describing eastern European Jewish spirituality as exemplified by the Lithuanian learning tradition of Brisk. He was defending that tradition against all those, including the socialist Zionists, who saw it as the antithesis of dignity, responsibility, and creativity. The bold Promethean spirit that Soloveitchik described as the authentic impulse of Judaism was mirrored for him and mediated to him by an elitist intellectual tradition that to many seems overwhelmed by legal details and totally antipathetic to initiative and spontaneity. How does a religious Jew of eastern European influence, who lives by a disciplined *halakhah*, who feels enormously the weight and authority of the past, who believes that change in the law is prohibited and that the whole framework of the tradition should claim Jews totally—how does such a spiritual type manifest for Soloveitchik the bold spirit of Kantian autonomy?

The answer is partly that, as was already noted, Soloveitchik's essay is largely devoted to contrasting halakhic man with *homo religiosus*. It is in comparison with the latter that halakhic man is portrayed as a model of creativity and dignity. *Homo religiosus* lacks those characteristics because, not being endowed with the *mitzvot* and the *halakhah*, he is the victim of his alternating moods of religious exaltation and depression.

> On the one hand, he senses his own lowliness and insignificance, his own frailty and weakness . . . the one biological creature who has misused his own talents for destructive ends, who has failed in the task assigned to him. On the other hand, he is aware of his own greatness and loftiness, how his spirit breaks through all barriers and ascends to the very heights, bores through all obstacles and descends to the very depths. Is he not the crown of creation to whom God granted dominion over all the work of His hands? . . . From a religious perspective, man, in his relationship to the world, oscillates between the two poles of self-negation and absolute pride. . . . *Home religiosus* can never be free of this oscillation. (pp. 67–68)

Homo religiosus—Soloveitchik's depiction of the universal natural religious type—is a torn personality. He oscillates between self-affirmation and self-negation. For Soloveitchik, this is the permanent feature of the human situation in general and is crystallized out of the ambiguity within the religious consciousness. Man is a mere speck of dust and yet also but a little lower than the angels. Elation and depression are the natural accompaniments of his religious consciousness. But halakhic man, although he is himself a kind of *homo religiosus*, is protected against the manic-depressive condition. His possession of a permanent, ordered system of life in which he lives constantly with the command of God, which does not oscillate in terms of his subjective experience, but is a normative objective order, lifts him above the existential antinomy and gives him a permanent sense of legitimacy and worth.

> And let the Halakhah itself be proof! God commanded man, and the very command itself carries with it the endorsement of man's existence. If man, when confronted by God, would revert to nothingness and naught, then the command, which is the very foundation of the Halakhah, would be incomprehensible. For certainly God would not make a mockery of His Torah! The fact that God linked Himself with man and prescribed for him laws, statutes, and judgements bears witness that He, may He be blessed, does not nullify and obliterate man's being. (p. 71)

Yet if one agrees with Soloveitchik that halakhic man has the advantage over *homo religiosus* because he knows that he is always accepted by God and because the performance of the *mitzvot* confirms a deep sense of legitimacy and covenantal responsibility, is this a sufficient answer to the charge that an all-encompassing external coercive dimension is present in a disciplined normative life governed by the Orthodox *halakhah*? There is no facet of human existence that is not touched by the laws given in the Torah. Spinoza in his *Tractatus* regarded the elaborate system of laws in the biblical tradition as a way of encouraging slave morality. The all-encompassing law, he claimed, enabled a slave people to avoid the challenge of living according to a moral sense and personal responsibility, because the *halakhah* is the antithesis of personal responsibility and Judaism does not encourage a moral sense. There are no situations in which Jews have to call on their own conscience and face life through their own energies and strengths. This type of critique of the *halakhah* continued from Spinoza onward. Soloveitchik, who is thoroughly committed to the Orthodox *halakhah*, rejects the critique of Spinoza and Kant by claiming that halakhic man is able to view this intricate system of life as his own autonomously created norm.

> However, while *homo religiosus* accepts the norm against his will, "as though a demon compelled him" [cf. *Nedarim* 20b], halakhic man does not experience any consciousness of compulsion accompanying the norm. Rather, it seems to him as though he discovered the norm in his innermost self, as though it was not just a commandment that had been imposed upon him but an existential law of his very being. (pp. 64–65)

Here Soloveitchik insists that it appears to halakhic man that he is acting by a law of his own innermost self. It is the existential law of his very being. The total normative system that for Spinoza enslaved the traditional Jew becomes for Soloveitchik the highest expression of the human being's personal sense of autonomy and freedom. The felt experience of living by Judaism is for Soloveitchik conformity not to an extraneous authority called God, but to the halakhic community's own personal creation. The *halakhah* expresses humanity rather than compels humanity. Judaism begins with revelation, but it is lived as if it were the expression of the individual. It is a testimony that a totally disciplined, normative existence can nevertheless be an expression of human autonomy and freedom.

I recall the enormous sense of intellectual courage and daring that Soloveitchik would manifest in a talmudic lecture. No figure of authority would intimidate him, no quoting of Jewish sources would in any way inhibit his own piercing creative mind. Maimonides and Akiva, all the revered teachers of the past, were his colleagues as he studied the Talmud. He argued with them, he struggled with them. They were living people who engaged him in a discussion. His own uncompromising commitment to intellectual honesty, his refusal to say that he understood as long as anything remained unclear, his ability to assert his own intellectual independence in the face of the whole tradition— this was Soloveitchik's own manifest experience of talmudic learning in the Brisk tradition. Since learning itself is regarded as a religious act by Orthodox Jews, one cannot experience such independence and yet not have this spill over into the normative life which that learning seeks to elucidate. Because Judaism is filtered through the cognitive dimension of learning, through the all-enveloping passion of day-and-night engagement with learning in an autonomous spirit, Soloveitchik claims that the biblical law is not experienced by Orthodox Jews as something extraneous and coerced, but is felt to be the personal existential law of their own being. Spinoza did not understand how learning in the talmudic tradition makes the biblical law into an expression of personal dignity and autonomy.

It is the learning experience that enables Soloveitchik to bring Judaism into the modern world. When Soloveitchik wrote his essay in the early 1940s, he was aware of the attractions exercised by modern intellectual achievements upon bright young people in the Jewish community. In order to win back the creative spirits in his own tradition who seemed to be totally enamored of the boldness of the secular intellectual endeavor, Soloveitchik compared halakhic man favorably also with cog-

nitive man. The a priori constructions of the mathematical genius, the
Platonic indifference to the real world and love for the pure form, these
were compared by Soloveitchik with the talmudist's indifference to practical reality. The rabbinic dictum "Great is learning if it leads to practice" is understood by Soloveitchik to refer not only to the importance
of bringing the norm into the world, but to the intellectual freedom of
halakhic man in constructing the norm itself.[4] This interesting distortion of the initial talmudic text is also a reflection of how far the intellectual passion has gone within the Jewish religious tradition.[5] The
concern with practice, with how the norm is going to be lived within
the daily life of the community, does not trouble the mind of the talmudic theoretician. He studies long-inoperative laws, or even ones that
have never been put into practice, out of a spirit of intellectual curiosity,
and is happy to engage in *hiddush* (innovation), the creation of pure a
priori constructs. Soloveitchik thus presents the impulse to halakhic
learning, the rigor involved in the Brisk method of talmudic study, the
resultant bringing of order to the data on the basis of coherent conceptual constructions, as a counterbalance to the allure of the Western
intellectual tradition. He advises modern Jewish intellectuals to return
to their own garden, where they will discover in the intensity of learning
the same joy, the same rigor, the same dignity as exists in the modern
university, only in an even higher degree.

> Halakhic man is a spontaneous, creative type. He is not particularly sub-
> missive and retiring and is not meek when it is a matter of maintaining
> his own views. Neither modesty nor humility characterizes the image of
> halakhic man. On the contrary, his most characteristic feature is strength
> of mind. He does battle for every jot and tittle of the Halakhah, not only
> motivated by a deep piety but also by a passionate love of the truth. He
> recognizes no authority other than the authority of the intellect (obvi-
> ously, in accordance with the principles of tradition). He hates intellec-
> tual compromises. . . .
> This autonomy of the intellect at times reaches heights unimaginable
> in any other religion. (p. 79)
>
> No other scholarly discipline has woven crowns for its heroes to the
> extent that the Halakhah has done. In no other field of knowledge has
> man been adorned with the crown of absolute royalty as in the realm
> of Torah. The glorification of man reaches here the peak of splendor. (p.
> 81)

The scholar who can compete with and surpass "cognitive man" is
aware that he is a mighty ruler in the kingdom of the intellect. Everything is under his sway and heeds his command. Such a bold description

of an Orthodox Jew who lives by the Torah of God sounds paradoxical. Unless one claims that Soloveitchik is consciously exaggerating and distorting what is fact takes place in reality—which I believe not to be true—one has to see in Soloveitchik the integrity of the *talmid hakham* who is mirroring the world that he has seen and lived with throughout his talmudic life. Nothing intimidates the accomplished halakhic scholar. He bows before none. He is not frightened of any human being. He disregards the pressures of social conformity. His integrity and learning free him from all submission to earthly kingdoms. He is a master in what Kant called the kingdom of ends.

Halakhic Man and the Concrete

There is, however, a deep antinomy within halakhic man. On the one hand, his learning frees him from concern with the real world. The attachment to learning for its own sake and not for the sake of transforming the world makes halakhic man like the mathematician who does not ask to what degree the geometrical triangle or circle conforms to the real world. The *halakhah*, according to Soloveitchik, describes primarily an ideal world created by the mind of the talmudist; only after that ideal has been constructed do we concern ourselves with how far it can be realized in the world of our present historical reality. Yet the content with which halakhic man deals does not consist of mathematical forms. It consists of legal norms that govern practice. He is engaged in an intellectual adventure of elaborating new details of *mitzvot*, divine commandments that are meant to be realized in the real world. His method of study is a process of pure a priori creation whose paradigm is the activity of the mathematician, but the content is a norm that leads halakhic man to seek to anchor himself in this world and banish the mystic yearning of *homo religiosus* to escape from the world. Here the paradigm for halakhic man is the activist impulse of the modern world, an activism that also characterized the modern religious sensibility in the United States at the time that Soloveitchik was struggling to present halakhic man as an attractive model for Orthodox Judaism in the modern era. In this respect, Soloveitchik's distinction between *homo religiousus* and halakhic man leads not to an intellectualization of religious life, but rather to an activist existential posture of halakhic man as distinct from *homo religiosus* with his posture of withdrawal from worldly matters. The basic difference between these two postures, as Solovietchik formulates it, is that *homo religiosus* wants to rise from his earthly life to heaven, whereas halakhic man brings heaven down to earth.

> ... The only difference between *homo religiosus* and halakhic man is a change of courses—they travel in opposite directions. *Homo religiosus* starts out in this world and ends up in supernal realms; halakhic man starts out in supernal realms and ends up in this world. *Homo religiosus*, dissatisfied, disappointed, and unhappy, craves to rise up from the vale of tears, from concrete reality, and aspires to climb to the mountain of the Lord. He attempts to extricate himself from the narrow straits of empirical existence and emerge into the wide spaces of a pure and pristine transcendental existence. Halakhic man, on the contrary, longs to bring down transcendence into this valley of the shadow of death—i.e., into our world—and transform it into a land of the living. (p. 40)

Halakhic man, this passage implies, seeks to build a sanctuary in the midst of this world. He seeks to make God's presence visible in the material structures of reality. His body is not a source of embarrassment. He is not ridden by a sense of guilt and sin. He is not a naive simpleton or a philistine moralist impressed by his own righteousness, but a person who believes that God has totally accepted the human situation and invited humans to be partners in the creation of the world. God did not ask the Israelite community to leave the earth, but instead descended to them on the mountain of Sinai. God came to meet them in their situation instead of asking them to find a point of spirituality that mirrors eternity and not temporality.

When Soloveitchik portrays the activism of halakhic man, his source of inspiration is not merely the covenantal *mitzvah* in the abstract, but also—once again—the felt experience of the talmudic tradition of Brisk.

> Halakhic man is a man who longs to create, to bring into being something new, something original. The study of Torah, by definition, means gleaning new, creative insights from the Torah *(hiddushei Torah)*. "The Holy One, blessed be he, rejoices in the dialectics of Torah" [a popular folk saying]. Read not here "dialectics" *(pilpul)* but "creative interpretation" *(hiddush)*. This notion of *hiddush*, of creative interpretation, is not limited solely to the theoretical domain but extends as well into the practical domain. The most fervent desire of halakhic man is to behold the replenishment of the deficiency in creation, when the real world will conform to the ideal world and the most exalted and glorious of creations, the ideal Halakhah, will be actualized in its midst. The dream of creation is the central idea in the halakhic consciousness—the idea of the importance of man as a partner of the Almighty in the act of creation, man as creator of worlds. (p. 99)

Here, too, the boldness of Soloveitchik's claim for halakhic man is startling. Not only is the Judaic norm said to express the existential laws of halakhic man's own being, not only is halakhic learning said to appropriate an extraneous moral system and transform it into an expression of the autonomous self, but learning creates an activist, a revolutionary, a creator of worlds, a person who fervently strives to realize the ideal *halakhah* in the concrete world. Halakhic man's intellectual involvement in the details of the law is only a manifestation of a much larger commitment to take the details of human suffering with extreme seriousness. Moral sloppiness, indifference to social and political exploitation, silence before human suffering, all these will be alien to halakhic man as Soloveitchik describes him.

Yet, one is forced to ask, does Soloveitchik's transformation of the devoted scholar into a creator of worlds correspond to the empirical reality of Jewish life in Lithuania? The examples that Soloveitchik offers to give concrete expression to his enormous claim are some incidents in which his grandfather was concerned. For instance, his grandfather ensured that the burial society buried a poor man before a rich man in accordance with the rule that the one who dies first must be buried first, although the burial society wanted to bury the rich man first because it had received a handsome payment on his behalf. Do such examples suffice to justify the seemingly exaggerated claim that halakhic man is a mighty activist, transforming the world, anchored to the concrete, fighting the causes of social injustice? Was it not rather those who cast away the whole intellectualist world of talmudic study who became the pioneers of the activist impulse in recent Jewish history? What worlds did halakhic man create? Was he in the forefront of social endeavors to transform the economic injustices of the world? Although the examples of the personal morality of Soloveitchik's grandfather show the latter to have been a courageous defender of halakhic propriety, examples on a far greater scale would be needed to confirm Soloveitchik's claim for the activism of halakhic man. When Soloveitchik pits halakhic man against cognitive man, the modern Western intellectual, there is some prospect that Soloveitchik's hero will hold his own, but it is difficult to see how halakhic man can win out against the modern social activist.

Soloveitchik has located one experience of halakhic man, the learning adventure, and attempted to construct a total personality type out of that single experience. The autonomous creativity of the talmudic student is a positive and praiseworthy feature of the Brisk tradition which somehow has to do battle alone on behalf of Orthodox Judaism against all the attractions of modern secular society. Just as all attempts to build a total unified perception of reality out of one insight must be impoverished because they will lack the complexity and dynamics of the multiple concrete, so, too, must the attempt to characterize a total religious culture on the basis of the experience of learning be incomplete and fail to give a plausible description of the reality of that culture.

How the person of learning becomes a person of action is a serious question. Aristotle knew that the contemplative life and the activist life do not easily go together.[6] Maimonides at the end of his *Guide of the Perplexed* faced the intense struggle in the soul of a philosopher between the yearning for the perfection that grows from a contemplative life and the felt duty to be active in the community. It has always been a serious question how to integrate theory with practice and prevent the fullness of intellectual passion from overcoming all of one's activist instincts. The question cannot be answered with the simple assertion that one who learns Torah loves to create in his or her intellectual adventures and therefore expands his or her creative impulse into the practical as well as the theoretical realms of life.

The weight of Soloveitchik's claim thus cannot be borne by learning alone. Rather, one needs to invoke the fact that *mitzvah* plays a central role in the whole normative life of Judaism. The fact that all the commandments deal with the real world could have suggested to Soloveitchik that halakhic man is committed to deal with this world seriously. But then he would need to face the fact that learning can be a form of spiritual alienation, that intellectual discussion of *mitzvot* about this world can be a substitute for taking the world seriously. It is possible for learning to become not an expression of one's yearning to act, but a mental construction that enables one to escape the complexities of the real world. The world of thought can be an island to which one escapes from the often tragic failures that may result from attempts to do something in the concrete world. Thought always confers a feeling of completeness and purity that material involvement in the social and economic evils of the world cannot promise. That intellectual involvement in Torah study might be a source of alienation from the real world is not given serious consideration in Soloveitchik's essay.

Self-Creation

In the second half of the essay, Soloveitchik describes the creative impulse of halakhic man not so much in terms of his transforming social and political structures as in terms of his own *self*-creation. He may not be noted for great achievements in the public marketplaces, but he has them in his own personal life.

> Judaism declares that man stands at the crossroads and wonders about the path he shall take. Before him there is an awesome alternative—the image of God or the beast of prey, the crown of creation or the bogey of existence, the noblest of creatures or a degenerate creature, the image of the man of God or the profile of Nietzsche's "superman"—and it is up to man to decide and choose. . . . Herein is embodied the entire task of creation and the obligation to participate in the renewal of the cosmos. The most fundamental principle of all is that man must create himself. It is this idea that Judaism introduced into the world. (p. 109)

We see here how Soloveitchik shifts the emphasis from halakhic man as a creator of worlds to self-creation. If the primary task of human beings is seen to be to bring order into their personal lives, and if every human life is a world in itself, then there is a restricted and metaphorical sense in which Soloveitchik's claim that halakhic man is creator of worlds may be granted. Halakhic man is creative in allowing himself to grow into a unique personality, in ensuring that his own life is not doomed to become an endless repetition of his past failures, in treating the future as a wide-open option for his spiritual potential, in recognizing that personal renewal is a permanent possibility. This leads Soloveitchik to a favorite theme: repentance (*teshuvah*), the opportunity to liberate oneself from the failures of the past and demonstrate that the laws of psychological determinism need not control human destiny.

Although it is in repentance that Soloveitchik finds the broadest aspect of the self-creative activity of halakhic man, two other aspects are also discussed in this part of the essay. These are prophecy and the attitude to divine providence. The Judaic notion of providence, according to Soloveitchik, is not only a view of God's relationship to the world; it is above all a challenge to each human being not to remain at the level of behaving simply as a member of a species, in the manner of other animals, but to develop into a unique individual whose behavior is not species-determined. Individuality is not endowed at birth, but must be achieved in one's growth and development. One must transform a biological species existence into a personal, individual, humanly willed existence. The significance of the doctrine of divine providence is that it implies that the possibility of such a transformation and development is available to human beings. Judaism thereby invites the individual to develop an authentic existence by seeing oneself as unique and different from the species.

Man is obliged to broaden the scope and strengthen the intensity of the
individual providence that watches over him. Everything is dependent
on him; it is all in his hands. When a person creates himself, ceases to
be a mere species man, and becomes a man of God, then he has fulfilled
that commandment which was implicit in the principle of providence.
(p. 128)

The highest aspect of human self-creation in Soloveitchik's thought
is manifested in the emergence and mission of the prophet. Although
there is no prophecy without divine grace, no one can become a
prophet without thorough self-preparation for the role.

> To be sure, the outpouring of the spirit, the divine overflow, is dependent
> upon heavenly grace; nevertheless, the preparation for prophecy and the
> task of self-creation has been entrusted to man. . . .
>   The prophet creates his own personality, fashions within himself a new
> "I" awareness and a different mode of spiritual existence, snaps the chains
> of self-identity that had linked him to the "I" of old—to man who was
> just a random example of the species. (p. 130)

In prophecy, the primary focus is not on divine grace, but on human
initiative, on self-growth through knowledge, on lifting up one's self into
a unique personality. Divine providence does not depend on God's be-
stowing His gracious love upon the individual, or on a man's or a woman's longing for undeserved merit on the part of God, but rather presents
him or her with the challenge of leaving mere species existence and
becoming a unique individualistic being. Although repentance features
prominently in *Halakhic Man*, it has no grace dimension either. Soloveitchik distinguishes carefully between the act of verbal confession (*vi-
dui*), which seeks atonement (*kapparah*), and the act of repentance
(*teshuvah*). The latter is an experience of self-renewal and self-creation
that grows from reflection and a powerful resolution of the human will.
The emergence of a reborn personality does not depend at all on atonement, which is grace-given. This view of repentance reflects the total
sense of adequacy and assertiveness that accompanies halakhic man
throughout Soloveitchik's essay.

There is no moment in this essay at which halakhic man senses resignation and defeat. The self-adequacy and activist spirit of the student
in the talmudic hall of learning permeates all aspects of human consciousness. This stance may not be conspicuous in its concern for a
social and political order that mirrors political justice, but it manifests
itself in the uniqueness, authenticity, and inner integrity of the individual. It would appear from Soloveitchik's focus on self-creation that the

inactivity of halakhic man in the public realm may be overlooked if his spirit of activism focuses upon his personal life.

Existentialist philosophy with its commitment to authenticity and individuality is able to welcome the talmudic scholars of Brisk into the modern world. They do not cower before influential notables. They are not intimidated by people of wealth. They are concerned with caring for the oppressed in their neighborhood, with the life of compassion, with the courage not to be conformist. All these characteristics were truly embodied in the personal lives of Soloveitchik's grandfather and father. Soloveitchik derives halakhic man's sense of adequacy from the personal examples of these individuals and expands their learning experience into a vision of a total culture. There remains, however, a fundamental question that cannot be ignored from the perspective of the present book. If there is so little empirical evidence that Soloveitchik's halakhic man manifested his creativity in the renewal of society, to what extent can the spirit of the Lithuanian talmudic hall of learning serve as an inspiration in the circumstances of Israel, where the task is to create a total Jewish society on the basis of political independence? Indeed, the same question can be asked with regard to any society that invites Jews to participate in shaping the quality of life of the total society.

"The Lonely Man of Faith"

Soloveitchik's first major work does not contain the dialectic present in "The Lonely Man of Faith" and other later writings that give expression to both the assertive and the self-negating features of halakhic consciousness. Only the assertive dimension of Jewish spirituality is emphasized. The feelings of inadequacy, crisis, defeat, nothingness, and longing for redemption, which play a crucial role in Jewish spirituality according to Soloveitchik's other writings, are here ascribed explicitly only to *homo religiosus*. The only hint that they may also be felt by halakhic man is when the latter is said to be a kind of *homo religiosus* as well. The essay concentrates exclusively on what distinguishes halakhic man from the universal type of *homo religiosus*. Creative involvement in the world is ascribed to the former, whereas the latter either withdraws from the world or makes a total separation between his religiosity and his worldly life.

It is in his writings of the last two decades that Soloveitchik gives ample space also to the self-abnegating features in the Judaic tradition.

Crucial in this respect was "The Lonely Man of Faith," published in 1965. As in *Halakhic Man*, Soloveitchik builds his essay upon two initial contrasting human types, derived this time from the two creation stories in Genesis. "Adam the first" is the human being of the first chapter of Genesis, who was created in the image of God and ordered to fill the earth and subdue it by a God Who is called only Elohim in the Hebrew text. The second chapter of Genesis introduces "Adam the second," who was fashioned from the dust of the ground by a God Who is called both Elohim and Adonai (the Tetragrammaton). The differences between Adam the first and Adam the second, as Soloveitchik depicts them in this essay, are rather similar to the differences between cognitive man and *homo religiosus* of *Halakhic Man*. Since Soloveitchik derives the possibility of the covenant from Adam the second, his characterization of the Orthodox Jew, whom he now calls "covenantal man" rather than "halakhic man," gives greater emphasis to the self-abnegating features of Judaism, although the Jew as a human being also participates in the assertive attitudes of Adam the first. The thrust of the essay is therefore very different from that of *Halakhic Man*: instead of the self-confident adequacy of halakhic man, the Jew is portrayed as oscillating between two extremes. The man of faith in the Judaic tradition sometimes advances confidently in the spirit of Adam the first, but then is obliged as Adam the second to sacrifice every achievement and withdraw in defeat.

Soloveitchik ingeniously divides familiar human characteristics between the two Adams. The first creation story tells us basically only two things in the biblical text. Man and woman are created together, so there is no place for the loneliness of Adam without Eve; and both are told to go out into the world and master it. Adam the first is therefore typified for Soloveitchik by all the outward-oriented activities of human beings, culminating in their modern scientific and technological domination over nature. To Adam the second, by contrast, Soloveitchik ascribes everything that belongs to the inner needs of human beings as opposed to their external activity in the world. "It is not good for the man to be alone" (Gen. 2:18) is for Soloveitchik not a description of a utilitarian functional need, but reflects the fact that the human's existence as a significant being cannot be realized in isolation and separateness. Only in the framework of relationship, only in the framework of love and intimacy, can the human person find a deeper sense of personal fulfillment. The drama in the second creation story is psychological and existential. The problem is not how to subdue and harness nature, but how to become a whole human being. Soloveitchik finds this distinction also in the different names by which God is denoted in the two stories. The God of the man and woman who confront a hostile nature is Elohim, the impersonal God of the cosmos. The man or woman who is aware of a personal existential psychological drama of loneliness is met by a God whose name is the Tetragrammaton; this is the personal God of revelation, the God Who meets the human being in an intimate personal encounter. Elohim is God revealed in being and in the mysterious powers of nature. Adonai is the God of *mitzvah*, the God of the covenant, the God Who establishes a direct relationship with the human community and the human being.

To Soloveitchik, therefore, there are two fundamental mandates and drives within biblical spirituality and Judaic spirituality. One is focused toward mastery and power and technological boldness, the other toward the in-depth human need for love and intimacy, toward what Soloveitchik sees as the need to ground one's existence in that which is of ultimate significance. The latter drive is the quest to be part of a normative history that transcends the problems of personal death and temporality. It is the need for a God who meets me in the framework of intimacy, who addresses me as His "thou" and lives with me in covenantal mutuality.

When Soloveitchik speaks of God as Elohim Who inspires the human being to become a creator, he continues the assertive thrust developed in *Halakhic Man*, the insistence upon the dignity that comes with power. "The Lonely Man of Faith," then, gives a halakhic validation of the technological quest for power. The halakhic concern for human responsibility becomes in this essay a justification for the whole modern technological spirit, which has often been viewed as a threat to the religious quest. Religious humility does not demand technological impotence.

Where the two essays differ is that in *Halakhic Man* the assertive autonomous dignity of halakhic man was not in any way negated; there was no indication that halakhic man might experience deep existential crises that create in him a yearning for redemption. In "The Lonely Man of Faith," by contrast, redemption is a major concern, not as a category related necessarily to sin, but as an existential psychological category related to the human sense of loneliness and lack of permanent worth. There is a human need for relationship, a need for in-depth communication, a need to feel that one's life is confirmed by God's love. This need, Soloveitchik claims, can be realized only if one is prepared to respond to God's command not only when God encourages the human being to express his or her assertive dignity, but also when God demands unconditional commitment, sacrifice, defeat, and retreat. The "man of faith" accepts this demand, although it violates the categories of the intellect.

> The intellect does not chart the course of the man of faith; its role is an a postiori one. It attempts, ex post facto, to retrace the footsteps of the man of faith, and even in this modest attempt the intellect is not completely successful. . . . The very instant . . . the man of faith transcends the frontiers of the reasonable and enters into the realm of the unreasonable, the intellect is left behind and must terminate its search for understanding. The man of faith animated by his great experience is able to reach the point at which not only his logic of the mind but even his logic of the heart and of the will, everything—even his own "I" awareness—has to give in to an "absurd" commitment. The man of faith is "insanely" committed to and "madly" in love with God. (pp. 60–61)

The man of faith is lonely because he cannot translate this ultimate experience of defeat, the nonrational element that is essential in his faith gesture, into the functional, rational categories of those who live only with the experience of God Who commands humans to become adequate before the forces of nature, those who form what Soloveitchik calls the "natural work community" or the "majestic natural community" whose values are those of Adam the first alone. The covenantal faith community created by Adam the second longs not for adequacy but for redemption from finitude, but its members can experience redemption only to the degree to which they retreat and are prepared to sacrifice all that they gained when they acted in the spirit of Adam the first. Yet God wants men and women to engage in the pursuit of dignity as well as redemptiveness. The man of faith is required to be both the creative free agent, majestic and assertive, and the obedient servant of God who yields all that he has achieved as a sacrificial act to his God. He is required to participate in the majestic natural community as well as in the covenantal faith community. As a result, "The dialectical awareness, the steady oscillating between the majestic natural community and the covenantal faith community renders the act of complete redemption unrealizable" ("Lonely Man of Faith," p. 49). The man of faith who "finds redemption in the covenantal faith community by dovetailing his accidental existence with the necessary infinite existence of the Great True Real Self" (ibid.) has his longing rejected because he is commanded by God also to carry the burden of the majestic community, in which the striving for adequacy and living with the impersonal is a permanent feature of reality. Hence the loneliness of the man of faith.

The ultimate resolution of this desperate and painful yet exhilarating experience of loneliness will be achieved only in the eschatological moment of redemption, since in the present condition the man of faith is obliged to oscillate constantly between two competing demands (p. 55). He is required by God to participate in the modern technological world, to join in the adventure of controlling nature so as to bring dignity to human beings. At the same time, however, he must stand alone before the world as one whose way of life is unintelligible, because he is the carrier of a faith dimension that cannot be translated into categories based upon human reason. Here Soloveitchik departs from the attempt of his earlier essay to portray the *halakhah* as a quasi-Kantian system of morality. No longer do we have halakhic man who transforms an externally given norm into an autonomous product of his own creative intellect. Instead, covenantal man is prepared to sacrifice his own autonomy and rationality for the sake of an unconditional commitment to God. This move is inconceivable for any Kantian or quasi-Kantian approach to morality; it belongs rather to Abraham's "suspension of the ethical" as described by Kierkegaard in *Fear and Trembling*.

Victory and Defeat

In "The Lonely Man of Faith," Soloveitchik speaks only in general terms of the need for the man of faith to experience and accept failure and defeat. We encounter passages that use terms such as "recoil," "retreat," "confronted and defeated," "overpowered," and "crisis and failure" (e.g., pp. 24–25), but nowhere does Soloveitchik give a specific content to these terms. For his precise meaning, we must turn to other essays, notably "Majesty and Humility" and "Catharsis."

In "Majesty and Humility," as the title indicates, Soloveitchik writes of two kinds of moment in human life that constitute two kinds of experience of God. There are moments when we feel that we can soar above the heavens, that there are no limits to our desire for experience. These are moments of joy and love when we feel a sense of adequacy and power. They correspond to the experience of God in the abundance of being, in the overflow and majesty of reality. But there are also moments of tragedy and defeat and suffering, when we experience God as Someone very intimate and close, constricted within the narrow confines of human existential despair. We then encounter "not *magestas Dei* but *humilitas Dei*" (p. 35).

These two experiences also create two ethical-normative frameworks of orientation to life. There is the ethic of victory, which calls upon human beings to subject nature to human needs, to build a true and just society and an equitable economic order, to become partners with God in the creation of an ordered and just world. There is, however, in Judaism also an ethic of defeat, which the "victory-minded and success-oriented" Western philosophical tradition cannot comprehend. The "ethic of retreat or withdrawal" is seen by Soloveitchik as rooted in the kabbalistic mystery of *tzimtzum* (self-contraction), "without which, not only the building of the sanctuary, but even the creation of the world, would have been impossible" (p. 35). Not only God's creative activity, therefore, but also His self-contraction and withdrawal become an ethical example for the Jew to follow.

> If God withdrew, and creation is a result of his withdrawal, then, guided by the principle of *imitatio Dei*, we are called upon to do the same. Jewish ethics, then, requires man, in certain situations, to withdraw.
>
> Man must not always be a victor. From time to time triumph should turn into defeat. Man, in Judaism, was created for both victory and for defeat—he is both king and saint. He must know how to fight for victory and also how to suffer defeat. (pp. 35–36)

It may be noted that Soloveitchik had used the concept of *tzimtzum* in a very different way in *Halakhic Man*. There it served as an invitation to human beings to join God in the task of creation, whereas here it serves as an exhortation to accept defeat. There is no need to seek to harmonize the discrepancy between the two uses of *tzimtzum*. In both essays, rather, the concept possesses the emotive quality of making the religious person believe that in some way God's conduct provides an example for human conduct.

In "Majesty and Humility," unlike "The Lonely Man of Faith," Soloveitchik gives a detailed description of the acceptance of defeat with a number of specific examples from the Bible and the *halakhah*.

> What was the most precious possession of Abraham; with what was he concerned the most? Isaac. Because the son meant so much to him, God instructed him to retreat, to give the son away. . . . What of the ordinary person? Is there, for example, and more sensitive area in the lives of two young people—man and woman—than their love relationship? Therefore, the principle of self-defeating action must govern the relationship in this area. Sex, if unredeemed, may turn into a brutal, ugly performance which man shares with the beast. Sex, therefore, is in need of redemption. It must be purged of its coarseness and animality. What action did Judaism recommend to man in order to achieve this purpose? The movement of withdrawal and self-defeat. Only in light of this prin-

ciple can we begin to understand many of the strict halakhic rules of separation.

What does man cherish more than the intellect, around which his sense of dignity is centered? Precisely because of the supremacy of the intellect in human life, the Torah requires, at times, the suspension of the authority logos. Man defeats himself by accepting norms that the intellect cannot assimilate into its normative system. . . . In a word, withdrawal is required in all areas of human experience and endeavor; whatever is most significant, whatever attracts man the most, must be given up. (pp. 36–37)

The examples given by Soloveitchik in the above passage make clear what was meant by the general remarks about defeat and retreat in "The Lonely Man of Faith": asking a father to sacrifice his son, the paradigm model of the Akedah; asking young lovers to live in sexual withdrawal in the most intimate moments of passion and love on the night of their marriage, because the wife suddenly discovers that she has begun to menstruate. It is in such moments that heroism is given even to ordinary daily life. It is being able to say no to one's quest for intellectual integrity and to the supremacy of reason. Those who can commit themselves to all laws in the Bible, even those which are unintelligible to human reason, have been purged of the arrogance of modern humanity's insatiable intellectual hungers.

Defeat, however, does not imply that one necessarily remains permanently in a posture of self-negation.

What happens after man makes this movement of recoil and retreats? God may instruct him to resume his march to victory and move on in conquest and triumph. The movement of recoil redeems the forward-movement, and the readiness to accept defeat purges the uncontrollable lust for victory. Once man has listened and retreated, he may later be instructed to march straight to victory. (p. 37)

Here Soloveitchik adds a further dialectical thrust: once the intellect has been redeemed, it is invited to participate again in the cognitive majestic drama. Abraham is defeated, but Abraham finds victory in defeat because Isaac is spared. Yet success is not guaranteed even by submission and acceptance of defeat, as is exemplified by the case of Moses.

Moses was less fortunate. He withdrew; he gazed upon the land from afar; but his prayers were not fulfilled. He never entered the Promised Land which was only half a mile away. He listened, though his total obedience did not result in victory. God's will is inscrutable. (p. 37, n. 21)

In retreat, we are not unconditionally promised further renewal and further victory. It is at this point that Soloveitchik falls back on the ultimate principle of authoritarian religion: God's will is inscrutable. Yet Soloveitchik does not speak the language of authoritarianism. He does not argue from legal categories for the maintenance of the authority of *halakhah.* He does not assert that Jews must submit to the unchallengeable authority of the sages of the tradition. Nor does he argue that modern humanity is impoverished through lacking the spiritual grandeur and dignity of the generations of the past and that therefore the modern Jew must give in to the wisdom of tradition, because the further one gets away from Sinai, the less one's spiritual powers are capable of asserting themselves. On the contrary, Soloveitchik encourages modern humanity to assert its dignity, to build, to engage in a cosmic drama with a feeling of adequacy. He does not create the sense that to be born later is to be spiritually inferior, as for many Orthodox Jews original sin is being born later. He allows a Jew to submit totally to the Orthodox *halakhah* without negating the modern experience. Through giving an existentialist significance to unconditional submission to the *halakhah,* Soloveitchik has offered modern Jewish orthodoxy a basis for maintaining its strict adherence to the law and yet at the same time participating in the building of a modern anthropology.

Halakhic "Catharsis"

Similar ideas are found in Soloveitchik's essay "Catharsis," whose title alludes to Aristotle's theory of Greek tragic drama, according to which the sufferings of the dramatic hero produce a catharsis, or purging of the emotions of the audience. The essay seeks to show that Judaism contains a conception of the heroic that is superior to the Greek conception. Here the ambivalence of Soloveitchik's attitude to Western culture manifests itself. On the one hand, he seeks to protect Judaism from being undermined by modern secular society, through arguing that Judaism is the finest, noblest, and truest expression of humanity's ultimate needs. On the other hand, he has a genuine esteem for the Western intellectual tradition. He does not want to confine the halakhic Jew to the ghetto. His work from his earliest period onward was an attempt to bring the eastern European talmudic student into dialogue with the best of Western philosophical and scientific experience.

Soloveitchik's later writings constantly reflect this ambivalence. He upholds the value of modern culture, but at the same time he senses that if there were a total translation of the halakhic experience into Western rational categories, commitment to *halakhah* would be weakened. In his work, there is always both commendation and an effort to negate all that he admires in Western culture. "Catharsis" is a good example. In that essay, the Greek conception of heroism is said to be merely "aesthetic" (p. 41), rather as in "Majesty and Humility" Greek ethics is said to be "victory-minded and success-oriented" (p. 35). Greek culture does not penetrate into the in-depth notion of humanity. Modernity is vulgar. Terms of this nature have the evocative quality of reassuring the Orthodox student that even though he is called upon to admire Western culture, he must know that true depth and authenticity, including genuine heroism, are found only within his own tradition. He will achieve the fullness of existential authenticity only to the degree that he can live a dialectical experience in which he also fully embraces Torah learning and observance. Only if he can make that total commitment will he discover how modern secular culture can enrich his faith experience.

In "Catharsis," too, Soloveitchik teaches that at every level of our total existential experience—the hedonic, the emotional, the intellectual, and the moral—we must engage in the dialectical movement by alternatively advancing and retreating. Jewish heroism is a case in point. Jacob wrestled all night with a mysterious stranger and then allowed him to go free at the moment at which he had conquered him (Gen. 32:24–32). This episode enables Soloveitchik to exalt Jewish above classical Greek "aesthetic" heroism.

> The classical man was an aesthete, endowed with a demonic quality; he longed for vastness. His creative fantasy was boundless and reached for the impossible. . . . In short, the hero of classical man was the grand figure with whom, in order to satisfy his endless vanity, classical man identified himself: hero worship is basically self-worship. The classical idea of heroism, which is aesthetic in its very essence, lacks the element of absurdity and is intrinsically dramatic and theatrical. . . .
>
> Biblical heroism is not ecstatic but rather contemplative; not loud but hushed; not dramatic or spectacular but mute. The individual, instead of undertaking heroic actions sporadically, lives constantly as a hero. Jacob did not just act heroically upon the spur of the moment. His action was indicative of a resolute way of life; he was not out to impress anybody. (pp. 41–42)

Whereas classical heroism is demonstrated only by stage heroes, the *halakhah* enables heroism to be a genuine experience for Orthodox Jews in their ordinary, everyday life. Soloveitchik's example is the woman who discovers on her wedding night that she has begun to menstruate, with the result that bride and bridegroom are obliged by the *halakhah* heroically to postpone the sexual consummation of their marriage. Just as in *Halakhic Man* the talmudic learning experience allows every Jew to become a creator of worlds, so in "Catharsis" the *halakhah* turns every Jew into an unsung hero.

> The heroic act did not take place in the presence of jubilating crowds; no bards will sing of these two modest, humble young people. It happened in the sheltered privacy of their home, in the stillness of the night. The young man, like Jacob of old, makes an about-face; he retreats at the moment when fulfillment seems assured. (p. 46)

This story of bride and bridegroom shows how human beings purge their hedonic desires at the bidding of the *halakhah*. But Soloveitchik goes further: the *halakhah* also tells Jews what they are allowed to feel. They must discipline not only their pleasures, but also their emotions. Soloveitchik's example of emotional catharsis is the story I mentioned in the previous chapter regarding the sudden tragic death of Aaron's two children. Central to Soloveitchik's understanding of the story is the fact that the law enjoined Aaron not to mourn for the death of his children.

> The commitment or consecration of a priest to God is ultimate, all-demanding, and all-inclusive. . . . Aaron belonged to no one, not even to himself, but to God. Therefore he was not even free to give himself over to the grief precipitated by the loss of his two sons; he had no private world of his own. Even the heart of Aaron was divine property.
> What does all this mean in psychological terms? God wanted Aaron to disown the strongest emotion in man—the love for a child. (p. 48)

Soloveitchik considers that not only was the public manifestation of grief prohibited to Aaron, but even the internal experience of grief. The *halakhah* similarly asks mourners who have buried a dear relative just before a holiday to cast off their garments of mourning and participate in the festive spirit of the community (pp. 48–49). It is not only external social behavior that is demanded, but an internal experience of joy.[7]

A third area of life where Judaic catharsis manifests itself is the human intellect.

> If the scholar, simultaneously with the ecstasy of knowing, experiences also the agony of confusion, and together with the sweetness of triumph over Being, feels the pain and despair of defeat by Being, then his cognitive gesture is purged and redeemed. Then, and only then, does this gesture become heroic. (p. 51)

The human mind is purged of its arrogance, continues Soloveitchik, when it recognizes, first, that it cannot penetrate the mystery of being, and second, that human-made rules of behavior cannot replace the moral law given at Sinai. In other words, the "man of faith" must reject the whole Kantian notion of moral autonomy and admit his inability to develop serious moral philosophy.

It is not surprising, then, that for Soloveitchik the fourth area in which "man must be ready to accept defeat" is "in the moral-religious world, in his relationship to God" (p. 52). The excesses of religious fanaticism show that "if one has not redeemed his religious life he may become self-righteous, insensitive, or even destructive" (ibid.). Judaism is able to purge us also of this misdirected religious passion.

> Catharsis of religious life consists exactly in the awareness of the long interludes during which man finds himself at an infinite distance from God. . . . The breaking of the covenantal tablets is an experience every committed individual must endure. Only after Moses had lost everything he was questing for, did he ascend Mount Sinai to receive, not only two new tablets of stone but also the radiant countenance and the great mission of transmitting and teaching Torah to the covenantal community. (p. 53)

From all these examples, we see how Soloveitchik seeks to reconcile the two conflicting themes discussed in our previous chapters and combine them into a higher unity. It is by postulating that "man moves toward the fulfillment of his destiny along a zig-zag line; progress frequently superseded by retrogression; closeness to God, by the dark night of separation" (p. 53). The problem with this solution is that it is implausible when compared with our experience. Does Soloveitchik's redemptive cathartic experience teach us always to withdraw from an enemy who still harbors in his heart thoughts of destruction? As he admits, nothing guarantees that in the act of recoil and in self-defeat one will also move forward to new victories. In reality, the act of self-defeat may be an invitation to further destructive action on the part of one's enemy.

All of Soloveitchik's examples of the cathartic-dialectic experience are problematic. What happens to the emotional life of a person who, like Aaron, is commanded to extinguish all natural sentiments of love for his or her children? Can Isaac truly live anymore with Abraham after seeing his father place a blade next to his throat? Can he continue to feel confidence in his father's love? Can Abraham allow himself freely to love his son, knowing that the command of God can at any time again instruct him to kill him? Can there be natural joy and spontaneous love in the relationship of husband and wife if in the moment of deepest passion they must deny their natural instincts? Can the intellect be encouraged to feel its own strength, but also to deny its own ability to create a moral conception of life?

Although the concept of Judaic catharsis is ingenious and has genuine applications, it is insufficient to provide the systematic answer that Soloveitchik seeks. Ultimately, as in "Majesty and Humility," his approach has to fall back upon accepting the inscrutable will of God. Ultimately, Soloveitchik requires Jews to recognize that in all realms of existence the authority of God is total and that their existence is willed by God to the degree that they can control their existence through the discipline of the normative *halakhah*. Whether Soloveitchik speaks of catharsis, heroism, redemptiveness, or in-depth existential living, the bottom line is that Jews have a right to think, to feel, and to love only to the degree that they are prepared to submit totally to whatever God will demand of them. Soloveitchik was a brilliant innovator in his attempts to portray Orthodox Judaism as a plausible way of life in the modern world and to allow the characterology of the modern existentialist temperament to find its roots in the *halakhah*. Yet even he, in his attempt to reconcile the conflicting tendencies found in Judaic spirituality, could maintain plausibility only up to a certain point, beyond which one is required to accept unquestioningly the inexplicable demands of God and the authority of the tradition.

Lying behind Soloveitchik's demand that Jews oscillate between two communities, that they interrupt advance with retreat, is concern lest the Jewish community be carried away by hubris. The enormous elation that halakhic man feels in exercising his creative powers in the majestic gesture of subduing nature must be counteracted by the move of sacrificial surrender based on the Akedah. I would argue, however, that this drastic cure is unnecessary because the disease need not arise in the first place. Judaism contains its own internal corrective mechanisms, which can protect against any inclination to hubris. Halakhic Jews are aware, in the first place, that they are creatures as well as creators. Second, they know that they were given the *mitzvot* in order to fulfill a purpose of God's choosing, such that their consciousness of covenantal autonomy is always subject to and restricted by a sense of normative direction. If one's religious life is permeated by creatureliness and the demands of the *mitzvot*, then one's sense of adequacy and belief in one's ability to cope with reality can be contained within a healthy religious perspective that includes the virtues of humility as well as feelings of personal dignity.

4

Ethics and Halakhah

W HEN ASKED to explain their total allegiance to *mitzvot* that appear to conflict with generally accepted notions of morality, halakhic Jews influenced by Soloveitchik have often cited to me the importance of an Akedah-like resignation for the spiritual life of Judaism. Solo-veitchik's existential appreciation of Judaism, consequently, is not merely a character description of "covenantal man," but serves to legitimize a total way of life. The poetry of his Midrashic portrait of halakhic life has serious behavioral moral consequences. The *halakhah* in its totality can be made plausible for the modern Jew if it is understood as a heroic manifestation of insane love for God and of unconditional surrender to God's will as mediated in the *halakhah*. Admittedly, Soloveitchik por-trays the negation of our intellect and ethical sense not as a passive submission to authority but as an active heroic gesture. Nevertheless, his religious anthropology gives support to the claim that Judaism must create obedient personalities who give total allegiance to authority with-out allowing any independent moral or rational considerations to enter into their evaluation of their obligation to the norms and theological claims of the *halakhah*.

This chapter will argue that the surrender of human rationality and the sacrifice of one's human ethical sense are not required by Judaic faith. In demonstrating this, I shall build upon certain aspects of Maimonides' religious anthropology that provide a different religious emphasis from that of Soloveitchik. Subsequently, I shall claim that passionate commitment to God and Torah gives expression to Jewish particularity and not to Jewish isolation. The loneliness of the "man of faith" is not constitutive of the Sinai covenant.

Mitzvot *Without the Surrender of Reason*

Maimonidean religious anthropology is in no way similar to Soloveitchik's existentialist portrayal of "covenantal man." Covenantal Jews, as Maimonides depicts them, move in the direction of the fullness of religious vitality when they connect the purpose of the law with truth and rationality. The harmony between reality and the religious norm, the understanding that there is a unified spirit of intelligibility permeating both natural causality and divinely revealed law, is what Maimonides believes will bring Jews closer to a dedicated intimacy with the God of the covenant. Contrary to Soloveitchik, he does not ask us to live as a covenantal community of faith oscillating between the "majestic" role offered by the God Who created nature and an unconditional surrender and self-negation demanded by the God of revelation. There is no dichotomy between "majesty" and covenantal faith.

In contrast to Maimonides, for Soloveitchik it is the human will and not the intellect that makes possible the highest achievement in the religious life. For Maimonides, love of God grows from understanding; for Soloveitchik from total surrender.[1]

Maimonides held that it is possible to discern a rational divine purpose in all the mitzvot given to Moses. Traditionally, the mitzvot were divided into mishpatim (ordinances), those for which a rational explanation could be given in terms of human personal and social needs, and hukkim (statutes), those for which no such explanation could be given and which had to be obeyed simply because they were the revealed will of God. One of Maimonides' theological innovations was to transform this distinction into one between those mitzvot whose rational purpose was self-evident and those whose rational purpose could be discerned only after careful reflection. All the mitzvot, then, were rational and could in principle be justified in terms acceptable to medieval philosophers, Jewish or non-Jewish.

Soloveitchik, however, maintains the traditional form of the distinction between mishpatim and hukkim. Indeed, in *Reflections of the Rav*, he uses it to argue against Maimonides for the centrality of the human will and not the intellect in Judaism.

> The Bible teaches that in all of creation man is unique; only he was created in God's image. What is this singular, distinguishing character- istic which differentiates man from the animals, plants, and the rest of creation? What endowment reflects the Divine image which is the source of man's status and dignity? Maimonides and other medieval philoso- phers regarded man's *logos*, his thinking capacity, his ability to acquire knowledge, as man's most singular characteristic. . . .
>
> If man's thinking capacity constitutes his singularity, how could God ask man to commit himself to precepts, the rationality of which eludes him and of which some actually conflict with his reason? If man's dignity and humanity are rooted in his intellect, would God command a *hukkah*, a *mitzvah* which is beyond human understanding? . . .
>
> We are, therefore, inclined to follow the masters of the Kabbalah, who taught that not man's rationality but his *ratzon elyon* (higher will) con- stitutes the singular endowment which distinguishes him from the rest of creation. This will makes decisions without consulting the intellect. It is in the center of the spiritual personality and constitutes man's real identity. Man's pragmatic intellect, which weighs pros and cons, is of subordinate stature in man's personality and is called *ratzon tahton*, the lower, practical will. (pp. 91–92)

For Maimonides, no less than for Soloveitchik, the Jewish commit- ment to the *mitzvot* should issue from a passionate love for God. Yet Maimonides does not suggest for a moment that the covenantal faith commitment therefore cannot be viewed in rational categories. On the contrary, his whole spiritual enterprise presupposes that human beings can approach God in love and total commitment not by abandoning their sense of the reasonable, but through perceiving the supreme ra- tionality of God's gift of the *mitzvot*.

Maimonides believed that there was something lacking in a Jewish soul that finds love of God incompatible with rational understanding of the laws given by God to the Israelite community.

> There is a group of human beings who consider it a grievous thing that causes should be given for any law; what would please them most is that the intellect would not find a meaning for the commandments and pro- hibitions. What compels them to feel thus is a sickness that they find in their souls, a sickness to which they are unable to give utterance and of which they cannot furnish a satisfactory account. For they think that if those laws were useful in this existence and had been given to us for this or that reason, it would be as if they derived from the reflection and the understanding of some intelligent being. If, however, there is a thing for

which the intellect could not find any meaning at all and that does not lead to something useful, it indubitably derives from God; for the reflection of man would not lead to such a thing. (*Guide* 3:31)

The closing chapters of the *Guide of the Perplexed*, where the above quotation occurs, are devoted largely to a long and detailed demonstration that each of the laws of the Torah was intended by God to fulfill a rational purpose. It is here that Maimonides rejected the traditional understanding of the division of the *mitzvot* into *mishpatim* and *hukkim*. It was the supposed unintelligibility of the *hukkim* that so fascinated those whom Maimonides criticizes, although the Torah itself implied that we should be able to perceive that the *hukkim* expressed amazing wisdom.

> It is as if, according to these people of weak intellects, man were more perfect than his Maker; for man speaks and acts in a manner that leads to some intended end, whereas the deity does not act thus, but commands us to do things that are not useful to us and forbids us to do things that are not harmful to us. But He is far exalted above this; the contrary is the case—the whole purpose consisting in what is useful for us. . . . And it says: "[For that is your wisdom and your understanding in the sight of the peoples] which shall hear all these *hukkim* and say: 'Surely this great community is a wise and understanding people' " [Deut. 4:6]. Thus it states explicitly that even all the *hukkim* will show to all the nations that they have been given with "wisdom and understanding." (Ibid.)

The Battle Against Idolatry

In the closing chapters of the *Guide*, Maimonides argues that the real difference between the two kinds of *mitzvot* is that the *mishpatim* concern the social and ethical requirements of human beings in every situation, whereas the *hukkim* were formulated by God to deal with the specific historical situation of the Israelite community at the time of its escape from slavery in Egypt. The greatest weakness of the community was that during its long stay in Egypt it had become deeply addicted to the idolatrous worship practiced by the Egyptians and indeed by all other peoples of that time. God devised the *hukkim* as a means of weaning the community away from idolatry. It was important, however, that the mass of the community should not be aware of the true purpose of the *hukkim*, since they would have refused to believe that any god could issue commands that contradicted all established religious practice. God in His wisdom therefore made the *hukkim* sufficiently similar to current practice in order to be acceptable to the Israelites, yet so subtly different as to lead them gradually away from idolatry. By the time of Maimonides, on the other hand, the practice of offering sacrifices to idols had long since ceased, both among the Jews and among their Christian and Muslim neighbors. In the absence of the actual practice of idolatry, it was difficult even to imagine how deep a hold it had once had upon the Israelites. Thus neither in ancient times nor in the time of Maimonides had the rational divine purpose behind the *hukkim* been easily discernible. "People of weak intellects" therefore supposed that they were irrational demands of God. In fact, however, *hukkim* as well as *mishpatim* had a rational purpose, but whereas the rationality of the latter was easily perceived by all, it took profound philosophical reflection to discern the rationality of the former.

It would be beyond the scope of this book to discuss all the detailed proofs given by Maimonides for the rationality of the *hukkim*. All the same, an examination of how Maimonides related certain *hukkim* to the battle against idolatry will be instructive, since it will shed light on the basic religious anthropology assumed by Maimonides both in his *Guide of the Perplexed* and in his *Mishneh Torah*. Maimonides, unlike Judah Halevi,[2] does not attribute any special ontological dimension to the Jewish people. He believes that the same basic psychology, describable in Aristotolian categories, is operative both in Jews and in other human beings. When, therefore, he speaks of the susceptibility of the Israelites to idolatry, he is describing how he sees the primitive religious impulses of humankind in general.

Maimonides realized that human beings in an unredeemed world feel themselves to be at the mercy of illness, poverty, war, natural disasters, and other forces beyond their control. These basic features of the human condition make them vulnerable to anybody who seeks to exploit them by offering an interpretation of reality that promises some degree of security, success, and material well-being. Although magic, astrology, and demon worship have no empirical scientific basis, according to Maimonides, their practitioners are able to attract the masses, who seize any opportunity to escape from their misery. The gullibility of human beings, combined with the desperation of their situation, is what explains their readiness to become enslaved to idolatry.

To take a Maimonidean example (*Guide* 3:37), consider a father who witnesses the deaths of young children around him. How vulnerable is he to anyone who offers any possible hope for his sick child. How easy it is for him to adopt idolatrous practices that promise security and life and well-being for his child. Similarly, farmers live constantly with the terror of drought and pests, knowing that they may lose all their crops and become impoverished. How easy it is to manipulate their anxiety. How quick they are to accept explanations that offer ways of dealing with unknowable and unpredictable natural forces and that promise some degree of control over the tragic dimension in the human situation. The utter helpless dependency of human beings upon forces beyond their control makes them permanently vulnerable to the influence of pagan priests who offer all forms of solutions to the problems of the human condition.

Although the promises of the idolatrous priests were false, people believed them wholeheartedly because they clutched at any straw that might protect their children and their property. Consequently, it would have been pointless for Moses to try to convince the Israelites with scientific arguments that they would lose nothing by abandoning idolatrous practices. Nobody would have listened to him. The only way for Moses to influence their behavior was for him to enter into their mentality. If pagan priests had exploited their fears in order to induce them to worship idols, Moses had to use those same fears in order to make them turn away from idolatry and worship God. The very practices that paganism claims will bring a blessing become in the Torah actions that will bring a curse.

For instance, whereas the priests had promised that the children of idolators would live long lives, Moses announced that those who worshiped pagan deities would actually suffer the loss of their children. Whereas they had been told that specific practices would ensure the growth of their crops, Moses proclaimed that it was because of such idolatrous practices that the whole economy would be undermined and the community would be prone to the very calamities and fears that it had sought to overcome through idolatry. The law pronounced a curse on those who took fruit from trees during the first three years from the planting. The people therefore refrained from plucking the fruit and offering it to idols—and discovered that the trees grew just as well without recourse to idolatry.

Moses was speaking within an emotionally charged religious universe, deeply influenced by idolatrous perceptions of reality. For Moses to succeed in the battle against pagan priests' manipulation of human affairs, he had to master the logic of the pagan world. He could not combat paganism if he ignored the rules and the sensibilities of the pagan imagination. This was a key for Maimonides' understanding of how the biblical *hukkim* function. You must announce the very opposite promised by the pagan world, bring all your persuasive influence and authority to bear, and make God sufficiently vivid and important in the imagination of the community in order to compete adequately and effectively with the promises offered by idolatrous priests. If you confine yourself to speaking a language of love of God, you cannot win over the masses from a pagan priestly order that maintains its hold over them by showing how its worldview responds to human fears. The God you offer to the community must compete successfully with the pagan conception of reality if monotheism is to become an effective force in history.[3]

The atmosphere of the temple, the laws of the sacrifices, and the details of ritual purity, which many have regarded as the carrier of a numinous dimension in Judaic spirituality, are not seen by Maimonides as nonrational features of the religious life that elevate the Jew above the rational. Instead, they belong to the Judaic battle against mythology and for the triumph of the rational over the nonrational. It is not the mysterious, awesome holiness of God that Maimonides finds in the laws of Leviticus, but a God Who appreciates the vulnerability and susceptibility of limited human beings to mythic magical imagination. Moses could not battle against the overwhelming attraction of pagan ritual life unless sacrifices to God were held in great esteem and there was a deep fear of violating the sanctuary (*Guide* 3:45). Moses did not legislate an extensive law with massive details and restrictions for the reason suggested by Judah Halevi, who claimed that all the details were necessary in order to endow Israel with a unique mysterious spiritual power.[4] Rather, Moses knew that if the community did not acquire a serious appreciation of every detail of ritual, it would remain permanently vulnerable to the pagan image of the world. Detail communicates importance. The enormous detail of the laws of ritual purity and sacrifice was elaborated not because Judaism is ultimately grounded in the nonrational, but because in battling with the nonrational it was necessary to ensure that the institution created to educate people away from idolatry would be able to capture the public imagination to an even greater extent than the elaborate detail of idolatrous ritual.

Like most of the later Judaic tradition, Soloveitchik rejects Maimonides' rational explanation of the *hukkim*. He follows that trend in the tradition that regards the *hukkim* as expressing the absolute authority of God in the religious life. In "The Community," for instance, he writes (p. 23): "We also try to tell the child the story of statutes whose meaning we do not fully grasp. We tell him the story of *hukkim*, laws whose rationale is beyond our grasp, of man's surrender to his Maker, the story of the suspension of human judgment in deference to a higher will." It is my claim, by contrast, that one can sustain the covenantal anthropological spirit of Maimonides without necessarily feeling bound to accept his historical explanations of the particular *mitzvot*. What I share with Maimonides is the conviction that the *hukkim* do not imply that one must sacrifice the quest for intelligibility and that passionate love for God does not require the surrender of the intellect.

Beyond the Ethical

The social and ethical laws called *mishpatim* reflect the moral and ethical concerns that the Judaic community shares with all of humanity. Parallels to the ethical *mitzvot* in Judaism can be found in many other civilized religious or nonreligious communities. The question of what makes for a viable social and moral order is not a problem confined to the particular context of a Jewish state. All nations that seek the well-being of their citizens require an appreciation of what constitutes a just and ethical order. But the importance of Judaism's moral concerns is in no way diminished by the fact that those concerns are shared by other communities. In order to appreciate the seriousness with which Judaism takes the ethical *mitzvot*, it is not necessary to claim some special Jewish ethical sensibility or to adduce the moral genius of the Hebrew prophets.

Though the Jewish people and Judaism share and reflect universal needs, covenantal religious authenticity is not defined exclusively by the ethical category of universalizability. The *mishpatim*, that is, are not exhaustive of Judaic spirituality. There are also features in Judaic spirituality that symbolically reflect the particular history and existence of the Jewish people. The norms of the festivals, for example, mirror the way the community understands the intimate personal relationship between itself and God. Many of these *hukkim*, as *mitzvot* that structure Judaic particularity and provide a vivid framework for expressing the community's particular passion for its God, resemble intimate family customs. Through them the community builds familial solidarity grounded in a common memory and destiny. Such *hukkim* allow Jews to appreciate their own particular religious identity, but without having to justify their particularity in terms of a framework of universal significance for all humanity. They complement and absorb the ethical. They express and enhance the richness of Judaic religious consciousness by widening one's appreciation of the complexity of the nonrational dimensions in Judaism. Their observance, however, does not require Jews to be unquestioning, obedient personalities who sacrifice their own ethical and rational understanding before the unconditional authority of the *halakhah.*

Judaism reduced to ethical activism and moral seriousness, without the religious intimacy and mystical dimensions expressed through many of the symbolic ritual *mitzvot,* would be deprived of much of the richness of the spiritual life. A family seriously committed to the ethical life does not only engage in social and political action. The family enjoys music, art, strolling in the country, intimate family meals and discussions, and the joy of just being together in familial solidarity. It would be a strange family indeed, a rather cold and lifeless family, if the only thing defining its members' familial identity, the only thing they did together, was ethical and political action directed toward making the world a better place to live in.

Ethical seriousness is not the only value in the covenantal appreciation of the religious life; the community and social action do not exhaust the yearning of the religious soul for God. Prayer, religious awe, and the nonrational retain their place in the religious life even as one makes the ethical a controlling category for the development of the *halakhah.* At the same time, however, the divine power and mystery must never be used as a justification to undermine the category of the ethical.

A single-minded vision, emphasizing only one aspect of the religious soul's yearning for God, undermines the richness that Judaism allows one to appreciate in its integration of the passion of covenantal particularity with concern for the social and political well-being of humankind. The prophetic teachings regarding the ethical must not lead one to identify Judaism with the ethical or with the role of the Jewish people in the universal redemption of humanity. Nor, on the other hand, should the covenantal intimacy with God expressed through the *hukkim* lead one to build a covenantal identity that focuses on Jewish separateness and distinctiveness from the world. One also misunderstands Judaism as a total way of life if one seeks to define it exclusively in terms of what makes it unique. Judaism as a way of life can never be defined only by what sets it apart from the rest of the world.

The full unfolding of our rational and ethical capacities is implicit in the notion of the covenantal relationship with God. If covenantal mutuality is to be taken seriously, one's ethical and rational capacities must never be crushed, as Soloveitchik demands when he makes the Akedah the supreme paradigm of religious authenticity. In asking the Judaic community to interpret and expand the norms of Judaism to cover all aspects of life, the God of the covenant invites that community to trust its own ability to make rational and moral judgments.

Ethics Without Revelation

Maimonides states that when philosophical opinion clashes with the literal meaning of the Bible, we must ask whether the philosophical assertion has been truly demonstrated. If not, then we should accept what the Bible says literally, but if it has been demonstrated, we are obliged to reinterpret the Bible figuratively (*Guide* 2:25). That is, he allowed that the Torah might challenge some common philosophical views, but he could not imagine that the Torah required us to sacrifice our human powers of reason. Similarly, I allow that the Torah may challenge some accepted current patterns of behavior, but I cannot imagine that it requires us to sacrifice our ability to judge what is just and fair.[5] The covenant invites a community to act and to become responsible for the condition of its human world. This invitation to full responsibility in history would be ludicrous if the community's rational or moral powers were negated in the very act of covenantal commitment. How can a community be called to become responsible to implement Torah and simultaneously be told not to trust those powers? The "ought" of *mitzvah* implies respect for how human beings are to appropriate and apply the Torah in human life. That means that the development of the *halakhah* must be subjected to the scrutiny of moral categories that are independent of the notion of halakhic authority. Just as Maimonides utilized the human capacity to know truth independently of revelation and rabbinic authority to determine the meaning of religious language, so too must our human ethical sense shape our understanding of what is demanded of us in the *mitzvot*.[6] Maimonides, the master halakhist of Jewish history, was not embarrassed to read the Bible and the Talmud with the help of Aristotelian philosophy. In that same spirit, contemporary halakhic Jews need not apologize for using the best of ethical thought to learn how to apply the *mitzvot* that touch upon ethical and moral considerations in everyday life.

My claim that ethics is central to the covenantal revelation should not be confused with the assertion that without revelation ethical norms have no rational obligatory grounding. Human history has shown that individuals are capable of developing viable ethical systems not rooted in divine authority. God's revelation of the ethical is not meant to compensate for a presumed inability of human reason to formulate an ethical system. Maimonides, too, saw no difficulty in accepting the legitimacy of an Aristotelian ethical worldview based upon an understanding of human nature. Indeed, he identified much of the ethical teachings of Aristotle with the halakhic principle of *imitatio Dei* (MT *Hilkhot Deot* 1:5–6). In incorporating the Aristotelian framework of ethics within his understanding of Judaism, Maimonides demonstrated that covenantal halakhic spirituality is in no way threatened or undermined by admitting the validity of ethical norms whose source is independent of the notion of revelation.[7]

In his introduction to his commentary on *Pirkei Avot*, Maimonides shows how the *halakhah* educates toward the notion of moderation and the avoidance of extremes and is therefore ultimately a material realization of Aristotle's understanding of what constitutes a healthy moral character. The *halakhah* in this view does not give authority to what constitutes moral character, but rather is a way of life that effectively fosters those principles of healthy moral character dispositions that are known through reflection on the nature of the human individual. Those principles do not require extraneous halakhic authority to make a substantive moral claim upon us. Similarly, in suggesting a way in which halakhic Jews may appropriate ethical criteria within their religious life, I am not making any claim regarding the possibility or nonpossibility of ethical frameworks independent of revelation and certainly do not seek to delegitimize such frameworks. A critique of ethical humanism is not essential for explaining why Judaism can be a living option for a modern Jew. Indeed, the ethical sense that must be used to define the direction of the *halakhah* will draw upon the moral discussion of individuals who do not necessarily share the presuppositions of a commitment to an authoritative halakhic system.

In seeing the ethical as constitutive of the covenant, we may be able to correct what I believe to be a serious misunderstanding in the way some contemporary philosophers deal with the relationship between God and the ethical. MacIntyre, in his *Short History of Ethics*,[8] focuses the problem sharply when he tries to show that God has no essential place in the foundation of morals. He uses an argument that goes back to Plato's *Euthyphro*.

> Why should I do what God commands? . . . "Because He is good." Since the answer has to function as a reason for obedience to God, it follows that *good* must be defined in terms other than those of obedience to God, if we are to avoid a vacuous circularity. It follows that I must have access to criteria of goodness which are independent of my awareness of divinity. But if I possess such criteria, I am surely in a position to judge of

good and evil on my own account, without consulting the divine commandments. (pp. 112–113)

To MacIntyre, if one is able to build independent criteria for the
evaluation of what is to count as good, God is redundant with respect
to the ethical. From a covenantal perspective, however, the dichotomy
presented by MacIntyre does not exist. If we live in a framework of
relationship to God, then we need to know what presuppositions play
a role in defining the rules of that relationship. Consider how we react
when different *mitzvot* appear to contradict each other. If we believe that
the ethical is a presupposition for our understanding of God's revelation, then it provides a standard for weighing *mitzvot* in situations of
value conflict. The sacredness of human life, for example, is the decisive
criterion when a conflict arises between the observance of the Sabbath
and the saving of a human life.

For religious individuals shaped by the tradition of the covenant,
ethics are not acted out in a spirit of human isolation. Such people are
always acting in response to and within a relationship with their God.
The point of departure for their perception of reality is always covenantal, and they always view themselves in the context of being in the
presence of God. They do not live in Kant's ethical universe because
they do not perceive human beings as totally self-legislating individuals.
They can never understand an "ought" in isolation from the presence
of God. The heteronomous quality of revelation arises not from a need
to compensate for the failure of human reason to provide justifiable
reasons that would substantiate ethical obligations, but rather from the
way covenantal ethical thinking reflects the building of a common life
between the community and God.

Since *mitzvah* mediates this relationship with God, the manner in
which one understands the content of *mitzvah* colors one's whole perception of the God with Whom that relationship is being built. It affects
our notions of worship, of *imitatio Dei* and walking in God's ways, of
what pleases our beloved God over and above what is strictly required
by *mitzvah*. The question of the relation between revelation and the
ethical is much broader than the simple either/or of MacIntyre. It is
therefore a mistake to claim that God is redundant in revealing the
ethical simply because ethical norms may have other sources of authority than revelation.

In absorbing and recognizing the serious role of the ethical within
the framework of *mitzvah*, one need not, as Soloveitchik did, deny human reason's ability to formulate a viable ethical system, but only rec-

ognize that fundamentally ethics in Judaism functions within categories that mirror relationship rather than autonomous self-sufficient moral reason. One can be an ethical human being without faith in the covenantal God, but one cannot commit oneself to the fullness of the covenantal *mitzvah* without appreciating the way the ethical impulse is intrinsic to Judaism as a way of life.[9] That is to say, one can be ethical without being religious, but one cannot be covenantally religious without an ethical passion.

The Torah provides for a way of life, and everything that is part of individual and communal existence is absorbed into the framework of *halakhah*. Covenantal spirituality contains both the devotional passion of prayer and the command of a God Who seeks to be sanctified in the midst of a community. Accordingly, the ethical and moral concerns found in the Torah are not an imperfect preliminary stage to be overcome in the act of unconditional surrender in the life of worship. Nor may our appreciation of what is considered just and fair ever be undermined through appeals to the absolute authority of *halakhuh.*

Loneliness and Criticism

For Soloveitchik, however, when a Jew abandons his autonomous sense of ethical competency, when he knows that his reason is inadequate to understand the Torah and the universe, when he bows unconditionally before the authority of the halakhic tradition, he becomes the profound and authentic "lonely man of faith" destined to oscillate between the community of majesty and the community of faith—to live with the unbridgeable gap between the God of nature·and revelation. The world must be a lonely place for Soloveitchik's covenantal man, since persons who do not share the faith commitment of *halakhah* cannot understand the religious passion that derives from Sinai and from the total halakhic way of life that is mediated by the talmudic tradition.

The belief that loneliness is an essential feature of the halakhic life was used by Soloveitchik in "Confrontation" to justify his decision prohibiting the Orthodox community to enter into a religious dialogue with other faith communities.

> The word, in which the multifarious religious experience is expressed, does not lend itself to standardization or universalization. The word of faith reflects the intimate, the private, the paradoxically inexpressible cravings of the individual for and his linking up with his Maker. It re-

flects the numinous character and the strangeness of the act of faith of
a particular community which is totally incomprehensible to the man of
a different faith community. Hence, it is important that the religious or
theological *logos* should not be employed as the medium of communication between two faith communities whose modes of expression are as
unique as their apocalyptic experiences. The confrontation should occur
not at a theological, but at a mundane human level. There, all of us
speak the universal language of modern man. (pp. 23–24)

The covenantal Jewish community can live with other faiths only on
the plane of "majesty." Jews can participate with Christians to improve
the social condition of humanity, to alleviate suffering and poverty, but
in no way is it possible for them thereby to speak out of the framework
of their own revelatory faith experience. The inner religious life of the
Jew is hermetically sealed off from the rest of humankind. The Jewish
community is the carrier of a unique spiritual system that cannot be
made available to the understanding of people who do not share its
practices and faith. Loneliness is therefore essential to the very life of
halakhic faith: it is not to be explained as arising from misunderstandings about Judaism in non-Jewish society, since the latter can have no
real understanding.

Loneliness is bearable, isolation from broader cultures can be a welcome and exhilarating experience, if one identifies loneliness with
uniqueness.[10] "Jewish identity can only be understood under the aspect
of singularity and otherness" ("Confrontation," p. 18). "Lonely man is
profound: he creates, he is original" ("The Community," p. 13). The
fact that one is not understood then does not indicate any limitation
in oneself and in one's practice, but is the necessary result of what it
means to live in the world as a unique faith community. One can even
revel in the unintelligible as an external confirmation and sign of one's
own uniqueness. Such an attitude can have dangerous implications.
When the faith experience is insulated from outside criticism, there is
a risk of moral sloppiness and religious arrogance. People can feel self-
righteous and morally secure in their private faith language, if they
believe that their community is the repository of absolute truth. Soloveitchik tries to guard against this danger by including religious self-
righteousness among those features of the "man of faith" that require
catharsis. But the danger is innate in any theology that exalts the Torah,
as the revealed word of God, above the limitations that are part of
normal human rationality. If the practical meaning of the biblical revelation is not self-evident, but requires as well as living tradition mediated by commentary, then the revelatory system of Judaism is not

immune from the limitations and imperfections of the human mind. The safeguard against falling victim to those limitations is to subject one's own thought to the criticism of others. In this way, the errors of judgment that finite human beings make have a possibility of correction. Being sensitive and appreciative of the criticism of others allows human beings to approximate the highest degree of the reasonable available to them.[11] A religious worldview that grows only from a discussion among its own in-group members, and that does not participate in nor is exposed to broader frameworks of discussion, runs the danger of perpetuating its own weaknesses, mistakes, and prejudices. A religious culture has greater opportunities for inner purification and depth when it widens its range of perception through exposure to modes of thought and experiences that stem from other cultural frameworks.

When the faith commitment has been insulated from and is unresponsive to rational criticism, there is nothing that cannot be justified in the name of tradition. History has shown the dangers that result when religious traditions claim to transcend the limits of human finitude and to embody absolute universal truth. People who believe that authentic faith requires that they follow the model of the Akedah may sacrifice thousands of innocent human beings in the name of their "insane" love for God.

Soloveitchik seeks to justify the faith posture of "loneliness" by making severe *ad hominem* attacks on "majestic" Western culture. "The Lonely Man of Faith" concludes with such an attack (p. 60ff.), besides those in "Majesty and Humility" and "Catharsis" mentioned in the previous chapter. Western spiritual persons of the majestic faith temperament, claims Soloveitchik, expect reciprocity from God in their faith gesture. They demand that faith adopt itself to the mood and temper of modern times. They subordinate faith to transient interests in their demonic quest for dominion. They are completely claimed by utilitarian interests. Their faith commitment does not understand the meaning of sacrifice or unconditional commitment, but is concerned with convenience. They prefer an "aesthetic" rather than a covenantal experience. They are of the "compromising" type that cannot grasp the strength and total commitment of the covenantal man of faith. They do not understand what it means to be "madly in love" with God and "insanely committed" to Him. At the center of their cultural edifice lies the quest for success and the gratification of human needs.

All these *ad hominem* accusations make it easier for the halakhic community not to respond to what may be serious moral criticism. If one can cast aspersions on the integrity and sincerity of all outsiders, it is not a serious problem if one is not understood. One feels pain in one's loneliness only if one is rejected by groups or individuals whom one respects. Soloveitchik's accusatory style, therefore, can be used by observant Jews to ignore criticism through priding themselves on the fact that they alone live in the realm of the unchangeable, in the eternal quest for redemption. They need not value the utilitarian, aesthetic, success-driven communities that live only in the present.

I call these accusations *ad hominem* because Soloveitchik has not presented any solid argument to show that the denounced failings are instrinsic to Western culture, to show that the community outside of the covenantal faith framework must necessarily be dominated by self-interest and demonic in its quest for success. These features of human life can certainly be seen in many members of the nonhalakhic community, but it would be hypocritical to ignore the fact that they also characterize both individuals and groups found inside the halakhic community itself. Soloveitchik admits that all human beings are susceptible to such failings; he has not shown that Western culture is innately less capable of coping with them than is the covenantal faith community. His denunciations of Western spiritual people could easily be construed as encouraging the very form of religious self-righteousness of which he wished to purge covenantal man in his article "Catharsis."

If a person claims to be overcoming the finite limitations of his or her mind by giving absolute allegiance to a divine revelation, then that person is engaging in self-deception. Those very limitations can lead him or her to misunderstand the purport of the revelation, however clear its formulation may seem to be. Since our finite minds are vulnerable to misunderstanding God's plainest words, we can never have infallible assurance that we are acting exactly according to divine command. All the more so when it comes to the manifold implications that the halakhic tradition has inferred from the original *mitzvot* over the generations.

The rabbis sought to cope with their human limitations in the only possible way when they subjected one another's views to critical examination. Typical of the Talmud is its preservation of intricate arguments between rabbis and its recording of minority views as well as the general consensus. It was always open to a later generation to revive the argument and come to a fresh conclusion.[12] Soloveitchik, as we have seen, is an excellent example himself, being ready to take issue with traditional commentaries when he believed that they had misunderstood a talmudic text.

There is no justification, moreover, for confining the debate exclusively to insiders of the halakhic tradition and disregarding totally the views and intellectual presuppositions of people outside the covenantal faith community. Both insiders and outsiders have the same finite human limitations, and each community has the opportunity of understanding its own internal matters better through intelligent contact with the other. Here, too, Soloveitchik is an example, since he employs the terminology and implicitly appeals to the values of existentialist thought in his claims for covenantal man. Similarly, his earlier *Halakhic Man* sought to appropriate values of Western "cognitive man" for Judaism. Blanket denunciations of Western culture and spirituality are therefore out of place; the latter should indeed be examined critically by Jews, but also recognized as a stimulus to internal Judaic reappraisal and renewal.

Like Soloveitchik, I believe that Jews have no reason to be ashamed of having a particularistic way of life that distinguishes them from the general style of Western culture. But I also believe that particularism is the healthier for developing in the context of larger frameworks of rational discourse, so as to help itself to discover possibilities for moral renewal and for overcoming intellectual sloppiness and arrogance.

This is how I understand why Maimonides chose to begin the *Mishneh Torah*, his recodification of the Judaic body of law, with four chapters on universal themes of philosophy. Later in the same work, he defined the moral characteristics of the prudent Jew (the *hakham*) and the saintly Jew (the *hasid*) with the aid of concepts drawn largely from the ethics of Aristotle. Much of the introduction to his commentary on *Pirkei Avot*, as I mentioned, is devoted to discussing the human soul in largely Aristotelian terms and showing that halakhic practice leads to health of the soul as thus conceived. As these examples show, Maimonides constantly sought to locate the halakhic frame of reference within a larger rational discourse. The halakhic law of Judaism and the universal truths of philosophy must, he was convinced, be significantly interrelated. The election of Israel and the resultant particularistic Jewish culture did not remove Jewish spirituality from the universal framework of human rationality and wisdom.

Maimonides requires no particularized spiritual sensibility and disposition in order to make sense of halakhic spirituality. There is no ontological uniqueness to the Jewish people that explains their election. Israel's uniqueness is not ontological but normative: it reflects the sanctifying power of the Mosaic legislation to rescue human beings from idolatry and allow them to show what it means to be created in the image of God.

Central to Maimonides' whole approach to Israel as a faith community is his belief that their destiny must be anchored within a framework of universal intelligibility. He opposes any approach to the normative and theological structure of the Torah that will be unintelligible to those who do not participate in the Judaic religious framework. If Jews build a normative system grounded in a private language that is in no way convincing to intelligent human beings, if they allow aggadic theological pictures to contradict what is known by scientists throughout the world, they desecrate their spiritual destiny and mission. In *Helek*, his introduction to the tenth chapter of the Mishnaic tractate *Sanhedrin*, Maimonides speaks about such Jews in pity as well as anger.

> One can only regret their folly. Their very effort to honor and exalt the sages in accordance with their own meager understanding actually humiliates them. As God lives, this group destroys the glory of the Torah and extinguishes its light, for they make the Torah of God say the opposite of what it intended. For He said in His perfect Torah: "The nations who hear of these *hukkim* shall say: 'Surely this great community is a wise and understanding people' " [Deut. 4:6]. But this group expounds the laws and the teachings of our sages in such a way that when the other peoples hear them they say that this little people is foolish and ignoble.

Accordingly, Maimonides demands not merely that the *mitzvot* must be seen as having a rational basis, but also that Midrashic statements about the nature of reality must be understood in a way that is intelligible to human beings in general. Both parts of the rabbinic tradition, the *aggadah* as well as the *halakhah*, must excite the world's admiration for their wisdom.[13] If the rabbinic sages made an aggadic statement about the nature of reality that any sane person knows to be false, says Maimonides (ibid.), then we must assume that they did not intend that statement to be taken literally, but were deliberately talking in riddles.

Maimonides makes no distinction in this respect between the factual claims of the *aggadah* about nature and the normative demands of divine revelation. He does not create a rupture between the God Who speaks to all humankind through nature and the God Who speaks to Israel through the revelation of the Torah. He does not split humanity, as Soloveitchik does, into a "majestic" community that lives according to a scientific understanding of nature and a covenantal faith community that is governed by partly unintelligible *mitzvot*. On the contrary, he constantly brings the religious quest to know God through the study of the Torah together with the religious quest to know God as

He is manifested in nature. There are not two incompatible cognitive gestures. There are not two separate roads to God that are totally unrelated and that speak a different logic.[14] This for Maimonides would be a violation of the unity of God.[15]

From my own anthropological perspective, I would say that Soloveitchik's division into two Adams and two communities is a violation of Judaism's concern with bringing all of life into the service of God. It forces the Jewish community into an impossible situation where, on the one hand, it shares with all humans a desire to build an ordered social and political world, yet, on the other hand, in its own internal faith structure it must posit a unique logos that is totally unavailable to all humans outside its ranks. The openness to all of humanity in the "majestic" gesture must not be abandoned when one begins to appropriate the faith experience. Otherwise one becomes schizophrenic. The unity of the human personality as well as the unity of Torah as a way of life is violated.

At the end of the *Guide*, Maimonides teaches that the philosophic passion that leads one to the highest peaks of devotional solitude and contemplative love of God leads as well to total commitment to social and political action. The God we love with the depth of faith is found not only in moments of retreat, but above all in full involvement with the world.

In the modern world, the covenantal Jew need not split the public from the private realm. The attempt to find a way in the modern world to share and discuss our respective faith commitments with persons of other faiths should not be identified with medieval polemical discussions as to who has the true faith. The readiness of religious individuals to listen to others, found often in the modern world,[16] is a healthy sign that we have also been freed from the mistaken notion of the Enlightenment that only if Jews appear in a neutral universalist garb can they find a place in the public arena of human civilization. The elevation of loneliness into an existential ideal for the Jewish community, by appealing to the ontological uniqueness of every individual and faith community, is not the way for a dignified people to meet the new spiritual possibilities for mutual understanding that modernity makes possible.

If our faith is to express our total human personality, it is absurd to expect that when we act for the well-being of society we put on a neutral humanist cap that is unrelated to our total faith posture. Moral concern is not an appendage to the life of faith. It flows from the total covenantal relational identity of one committed to the life of *mitzvah*. When moral action is expressive of character and personal identity, one cannot leap out of one's self-understanding as a covenantal faith personality upon meeting persons of other faiths or upon meeting human beings generally who are concerned with the ethical well-being of society. The self-exposure of the halakhic Jew in the public arena of life need not be filled with trepidation and fear of being swallowed up by the majority culture.[17] The dignity of particularism and the joy of living by the *mitzvot* can give the halakhic community the ease and security to be present within the world as a covenantal faith community.

5

Human Beings
in the Presence of God

SOLOVEITCHIK AND Leibowitz have much in common in their way
of viewing the problem of a modern religious anthropology of Judaism.
Both see halakhic practice as the defining characteristic of Judaism, both
seek to liberate the enormous achievements of the Judaic halakhic tradition from the mistaken identification with legalism, both discern the
antinomy between the assertive and the submissive themes in the tradition, both take the Akedah to be a paradigm, and both find a major
inspiration in Maimonides. But their approach to resolving the antinomy between the assertive and the submissive, between *mitzvah* as expressive of the divine concern with human well-being and as the
unconditional human surrender to God that transcends human understanding, is completely different. Whereas Soloveitchik seeks to combine these two themes in a precarious dialectical union, Leibowitz sees
them as representing two successive stages in the Judaic religious life.

In his critique of my book *Joy and Responsibility*, Leibowitz charges
that I am not aware of "the danger of viewing religion as a means to
satisfy human material, spiritual or psychic needs or for the realization
of human values."[1] For Leibowitz, the attempt to place human purposes
at the center of halakhic practice is antithetical to the core meaning of
Judaism, and possibly borders on idolatry.

The crucial issue between Leibowitz and myself is whether worship of God and human self-realization are mutually exclusive. Leibowitz's theocentric Akedah model of worship drives a wedge between consciousness of God and consciousness of self. There is no place for a covenantal religious consciousness in his system. The *mitzvot* are completely one-directional, representing solely the will of the individual to worship. It is because the covenant is abandoned in Leibowitz's perception of Judaism that he can force one to choose between humankind and God, between the ethical and the *mitzvot*. But when, as in my view, the *mitzvot* are seen as embodying the full covenantal interaction of human beings with God, then our humanity remains an essential component of our relationship with God.

Mitzvah *as Worship*

Leibowitz confronts the modern Jew with the following either/or decision in his article "Mitzvot ma'asiyot": either the human being or God must be considered the center of absolute value. An ethical vision of life places human dignity, human autonomy, and the intrinsic significance of human life at the center of its universe. A Judaic religious perspective, however, for Leibowitz must claim that Jews are dignified and have significance only because they are called upon to act in the presence of God. Outside of the life of worship, the human being has no value. For Leibowitz, this is given vivid expression at the conclusion of the Day of Atonement service.

> What are we? What is our life? What is our goodness? What is our virtue? What our help? What our strength? What our might? What can we say to Thee, Lord our God and God of our fathers? Indeed, all the heros are as nothing in thy sight, the men of renown as if they never existed, the wise as though they were without knowledge, the intelligent as though they lacked insight. Most of their actions are worthless in Thy sight. Their entire life is a fleeting breath. Man is not far above the beast, for all is vanity. Yet from the first Thou didst single out mortal man and consider him worthy to stand in Thy presence. Who can say to Thee what art Thou doing? Even though man be righteous, what can he give Thee?

As Leibowitz understands it, this prayer expresses the essence of Judaism. On the one hand, it declares the absolute insignificance of the human being. The human being is as nothing before God. His or her intelligence, wisdom, and power, all human achievements and culture, pale into nothingness before God. Yet in spite of this insignificance, the human being is invited to stand before God. Judaism gives human beings a unique status, separating them from the world of beasts and other objects of nature by calling upon them to live the life of *mitzvot*. Outside of a life constituted by *mitzvot*, human dignity and uniqueness are absolutely denied.

> In Judaism, man is not a value in himself, but he is an image of God who gets his meaning and value from this fact. The duty of loving one's neighbor does not derive from the status of a person as a person but from his status before God. (*Yahadut*, p. 27)

Human actions reflecting an ethical and moral spirit have significance in Judaism only if they can be done as *mitzvot*. The Bible does not teach ethical imperatives as such. The Torah does not say merely, "Love your neighbor as yourself"; rather it states: "Love your neighbor as yourself: I am the Lord" (Lev. 19:18). Only within a context of *mitzvot* and worship, only from a commitment to God, does "Love your neighbor" have significance, according to Leibowitz. In Leviticus, this statement appears in the context of *mitzvot* whose purpose is to bring about a holy community. Holiness is a religious category, which must not and cannot be reduced to humanistic ethical concerns.

Although ethical concerns shape his appreciation of *mitzvah*, Leibowitz refuses to recognize ethics as an autonomous category. That is to say, though the sense of the ethical is found in Judaism, the Judaic emphasis upon worship of God cannot allow the intrinsic dignity of the human being to count as a sufficient justification for ethical action. The life of worship through *mitzvot* and the quest for human self-realization are fundamentally incompatible categories.

> Every reason given for the *mitzvot* which bases itself on human needs from any consideration of the concept need, whether intellectual, ethical, social, national—voids the *mitzvot* from every religious meaning. If they are meant to benefit society or if they maintain the Jewish people, then he who performs them does not serve God but himself or society or his people. In any case, he does not serve God but uses the Torah of God for his benefit and as a means to satisfy his needs. The reason for the *mitzvot* is the worship of God. (p. 26)

For Leibowitz, Judaism is exclusively an institutional communal framework of worship within which the individual's particular human situation never surfaces. Similarly, individual spiritual action outside the normative framework of *halakhah* has no significance. Halakhic Judaism has no interest in developing personal inwardness or in talk about religious experiences. *Halakhah* does not express the inner psychic sensibility of the individual. It only calls upon the individual to act in conformity with the halakhic demand. *Halakhah*'s total indifference to the inner spiritual life of the individual and to his or her particular religious situation explains how it can obligate a community to act in total uniformity. What is more, nothing happens to one's character through the observance of the *mitzvot*. When it comes to Judaic practice, one always remains a beginner.

> The fulfillment of the *mitzvot* is the way leading a person toward his God. A person has to know that the way is eternal. He goes on it and he is always at the same point. This is the religious faith realized in the fixity, continuity, permanence of the *mitzvot*. . . . Therefore the content and meaning of doing the *mitzvah* is the effort that a person puts forth to reach the religious goal. (p. 24)

Leibowitz insists, however, that living by the *mitzvot* should not be considered an abandonment of human autonomy and freedom. Commitment to *mitzvot* should not be equated with subjugation to external authority. On the contrary, for Leibowitz it is only by living a life dedicated to *mitzvot*, which are in no way connected to human needs and are in radical opposition to nature, that worshipers can express their own human autonomy.

> . . . there is no freedom from the chains of nature except through accepting the yoke of Torah and *mitzvot*. . . . "The only free person is he who is concerned with Torah." . . . He is free from enslavement to nature since he lives a life contrary to nature as revealed in the world and in the nature of man. (p. 30)

Under nature, Leibowitz includes all human biological, psychological, spiritual, intellectual, ethical, and aesthetic needs. The halakhic sense of duty obligates one to perform acts whose explanation refers not to those needs but only to the acceptance of the *mitzvah* to worship God. *Halakhah* as worship of God frees one from attachment to nature. In other words, it is precisely because *halakhah* does not provide a framework for human self-realization that it is able to express human freedom. The educational philosophy that guides Leibowitz in his approach to *mitzvot* is the belief that only a Torah which is in opposition to nature, and thus to humanism, can offer a modern person a compelling religious option.

A person will not undertake this way of life unless he sees divine service as a goal in itself and not as a means to achieve any other purpose. (p. 24)

Leibowitz's philosophic approach to *mitzvot* is influenced by Maimonides' teaching on the radical transcendence of God. For Maimonides, all descriptions of God are either false or inadequate and come close to idolatry, because of the radical otherness and uniqueness of God. The conceptual categories used to describe human life cannot be applied to God. Biblical, anthropomorphic descriptions of God are concessions to our limited human understanding. Maimonides' rejection of all positive descriptions of God is based fundamentally on logical considerations deriving from the concept of the unity of God, since ascribing positive attributes to God would violate God's unity. In the case of Leibowitz, the reason for insisting upon radical divine transcendence is not only logical but, above all, religious. For Leibowitz, moral descriptions of God are not only false, they are also religiously inappropriate. To pray to God for the sake of your need is to make God an instrument in the service of human purposes. That, he believes, violates the spirit of worship implicit in the prayer recited at the end of the Day of Atonement, "The Lord, He is God." For Leibowitz, any explanation beyond that statement—the Lord is God—reduces worship to a conditional value.

Worship and History

Maimonides' insistence upon the radical transcendence of God enables Leibowitz to make the important claim that religious language is totally prescriptive. For Leibowitz, one cannot talk about God but can only act in His presence. All of Judaism can be translated into a way-of-life language that does not require any theological metaphysical claims about the nature of God and the way He acts in history. Whereas empirical descriptions have to be confirmed or falsified by the canons of scientific and logical thought, God talk cannot be made intelligible outside of the normative language of the *mitzvot*. Halakhic Jews, therefore, should not look to nature or history in their religious quest. That quest is fully exhausted in their participation in the framework of the *halakhah*. Jews worship God through the life of *mitzvot*, and the life of *mitzvot* is constitutive of what they mean when they speak of the reality of God.[2] Leibowitz believes in God because there is a *mitzvah*, and he observes the *mitzvah* because it is God's command. This is the inherent and fascinating circularity in Leibowitz's religious philosophy.

Leibowitz is very much within the Orthodox tradition in the sense that the Talmud defines for him how he responds to the biblical text. But he goes further than the tradition by making the bold claim that *only* the normative authority of the Talmud and not historical revelation endows the books of the Bible with sanctity. Judaism and the Jewish people are unique, in Leibowitz's view, not by virtue of the divine election of Israel in history, but because of the decision of the community to utilize the Torah as a guide for worship. He argues that the Bible itself teaches us that God's miraculous involvement in history failed to mold the religious quality of the community. Even after the great spectacle of the revelation at Sinai, the community reverted to worship of the golden calf. The liberation from Egypt was followed by constant rebellion. The biblical descriptions of the failures of God's actions in history to transform the community into a committed religious spiritual nation are meant to show that events in history have no influence in building a holy community.

Leibowitz, therefore, has nothing in common with modern theologians such as Emil Fackenheim who talk of the commanding voice of God speaking in the modern world through Auschwitz or through the significant military victories of the Israeli army.[3] In his view, neither reborn Israel nor the tragic suffering of Jews in the twentieth century has any particular religious significance. Events in nature and history are in themselves religiously indifferent.

Leibowitz's understanding of Judaism has made him a lone voice within Israeli society. His radical polarization between human needs and worship does not often find a responsive echo in a society in which Judaic symbols have been integrated into the daily life of the nation. Israeli society, struggling to find its roots within the Jewish historical past, has appropriated many features of the tradition that enhance and give direction to the national identity. But Leibowitz refuses to allow Judaism to become an instrument for securing group survival. He is fiercely critical of applying religious models such as the Akedah and *kiddush ha-shem*, the sanctification of God's name, to the heroism of Israeli soldiers in battle. For Leibowitz, to do so is idolatrous, since it substitutes loyalty to the nation for loyalty to God. Patriotism must never be confused with the life of worship. The needs of the nation must not become the ultimate value giving significance to Judaism. The intimate connection between Jewish nationhood and Judaism must never lead to the approach of Mordecai Kaplan, who understood Ju-

daism as a civilization that promotes and secures the survival of the
Jewish people. All attempts to explain Judaism as providing for the
meaningful continuity of a people in history are considered by Leibowitz
to be modern forms of idolatry. *Mitzvah* is not an instrument for Jewish
continuity. From the perspective of *halakhah*, Jewish nationhood has
significance only because *mitzvot* and the worship of God have eternal
meaning.

Leibowitz, whose religious passion is drawn from Judaism's struggle
against idolatry, refuses to apply the category of *kedushah* (holiness) to
any human institution or any human purpose. *Kedushah* introduces one
to the notion of absolute value and must therefore never be identified
with the political concerns or survival of the nation. Only God warrants
absolute allegiance. All human institutions, including the Jewish state,
have only conditional or instrumental value.

The centrality of *mitzvah* in Judaism implies for Leibowitz that God
is the source of demand, not a guarantor of redemption. In Leibowitz's
system, God promises nothing regarding the direction of human life and
history. The given world, without hope for redemption, is sufficient to
contain the living drama of worship through *mitzvot*. That, for Leibowitz, is the essential difference between Judaism and Christianity. Christianity promises to serve the deepest human spiritual needs. Its religious
impulse is nurtured by the promise of redemption and the promise of
liberation from finitude and sinfulness. In Judaism, however, human
beings are called upon to live within the given world in accordance with
the eternal demand of *mitzvah*, which in no way offers hope or promise
of redemption. Judaism is characterized by the Akedah model, which
recognizes our insignificance before the unconditional demand of *mitzvah*, in contrast to the crucifixion symbol of Christianity, which points
to the need for redemption.

> Christianity's highest symbol is the crucifixion, and sacrifice which God
> brings for man, whereas the highest symbol of faith in Judaism is the
> Akedah where all man's values are cancelled and cast aside for reverence
> and love for God. (p. 23)

There are therefore three basic religious conceptions within Judaism
that enable Leibowitz to construct his religious anthropology and deal
philosophically with the challenges of Kant and linguistic philosophy.
First is the absolute primacy of the Talmud over the biblical tradition.
Torah in its biblical sense is for Leibowitz a formal category announcing
the notion of *mitzvah*. *Mitzvah* is given material content only through
the rabbinic oral tradition. The Kantian spirit of autonomy can find its

place within Judaism, since it is not revelation but the Talmud and the
religious community, through its sages, which define what is binding in
the *halakhah*.

Second, it is common practice, and not theology, that identifies and
unites the Jewish religious community across history. The central role
given to practice above theology in Judaism enables Leibowitz to propose that religious language has only a prescriptive meaning.

Third, the categories of *she-lo li-shemah* and *li-shemah*, which for him
characterize the development of Judaic religious consciousness from anthropocentrism to theocentrism, enable him to defend Judaism against
all modern reductionist critiques and historicist perceptions of Judaism.
Using those categories, he can embrace the Akedah model and provide
a way of making sense of Judaism in a world that has experienced the
devastating effect of Auschwitz.

Leibowitz's rejection of any concern with discovering the human
implications of the *mitzvot* thus relies heavily upon the categories of
li-shemah and *she-lo li-shemah*. Those categories, however, are not sufficiently exhaustive and precise to serve as the unique criterion for clas-
sifying and evaluating religious behavior. In the Talmud, *she-lo li-shemah*
denotes a normative act motivated by considerations extraneous to the
proper purpose of the act itself.[4] However, what will be considered an
extraneous reason for performing a *mitzvah* depends on how the significance of the *mitzvah* in question is understood. If one gives charity
so that one's sick child will become healthy, or if one studies Torah to
gain honor, or if one fulfills the *mitzvot* so that God will reward one
with economic wealth or military victory, then the reason for performing the act is clearly extraneous to the *mitzvah* itself. Such acts of *she-
lo li-shemah* differ markedly from religious acts done for reasons connected with the religious significance of particular commandments. Take,
for example, observance of the laws of the Sabbath. In observing the
Sabbath, I become fully conscious that God alone is the Creator of the
universe. The Sabbath, awakening my sense of creatureliness, directs
me to understand that I must not relate to nature and to other persons
as an absolute master. And so, in observing the Sabbath, I am educated
to realize that all those who work for me must never be reduced to
instruments serving my needs. To cite this educational function of the
Sabbath as a justification for observing it is not to give a reason that is
extraneous to the religious significance of the Sabbath. As this example
shows, willing submission to God is not the sole religious reason that
can be given for performing a *mitzvah*. What one takes to be the significance of the *mitzvah* will determine how one decides whether par-

ticular reasons for doing a *mitzvah* are intrinsic or extraneous to that *mitzvah*. The reasons for the observance of the Sabbath described above are intrinsic to the *mitzvah* of Sabbath observance. To classify these reasons for observing the Sabbath, as Leibowitz does, together with doing it so that my team will win a soccer game as two instances of *she-lo li-shemah* is to reduce the category of *she-lo li-shemah* to absurdity. *She-lo li-shemah* ceases being a religiously useful concept when it fails to discriminate between the religious value of such clearly different motivations.

Leibowitz and Maimonides

The basic differences between Leibowitz's halakhic anthropology and my own are related to our respective understandings of Maimonides.[5] For Leibowitz, Maimonides is the paradigm of the "man of faith" who exemplifies how the human is transcended totally in the life of worship. Although I appreciate Leibowitz's theocentric passion, I reject his claim that Maimonides ascribes an anthropocentric focus to the *mitzvot* only in a preliminary stage in the life of worship of God. As I understand it, Maimonides' appreciation of the reasons for the *mitzvot* makes human well-being a permanent feature of the religious life.

There are especially two sections of the *Guide of the Perplexed* that are crucial for deciding between our interpretations of Maimonides. One comes from the closing chapters in which Maimonides describes the highest form of worship; the other concerns the Book of Job.

In his various writings, Leibowitz repeatedly cites the following passage from the end of the *Guide* to support his own religious anthropology.

> Know that all the practices of the worship, such as reading of the Torah, prayer and the performance of the other commandments, have only the end of training you to occupy yourself with His commandments, may He be exalted, rather than with matters pertaining to this world; you should act as if you were occupied with Him, may He be exalted, and not with that which is other than He. (*Guide* 3:51)

For Leibowitz, the distinction Maimonides makes here between occupying oneself with the commandments and occupying oneself with matters pertaining to this world reflects Leibowitz's own distinction between the world of the commandments and nature. Accordingly, when Maimonides tells his reader that one must occupy oneself with the commandments and not with matters pertaining to this world, this for Leibowitz means that the worshiper must turn aside from all the human purposes discussed in the preceding chapters of the *Guide*. That is to say, the reasons for the *mitzvot* elaborated by Maimonides in *Guide* 3:25–50 must no longer play any part in the moment of worship. At the same time, Leibowitz takes Maimonides' statement to imply that in Judaism the *only* way one can be occupied with God is through performing *mitzvot*. In this manner, Leibowitz seeks to ascribe to Maimonides his own view that knowledge of God, love of God, and faith in God have no religious meaning apart from the fact that they can be channeled into a normative performance that exemplifies God's commanding will. A God Who cannot be seen and cannot be identified with any aspect of reality cannot be experienced in any way familiar to the human relational world. The only content one can give to the notion of love of God is acting by the *mitzvot*.[6]

This passage is central to Leibowitz's way of understanding the radical transformation that Maimonides offers as the ultimate stage of the religious life. Whereas previously it had been legitimate to bring the needs of this world into the performance of *mitzvah*, now there is a clear radical bifurcation between human ethical concerns and the commitment to the *mitzvot*. The *mitzvot* have now become an end in themselves. They are the only framework through which one can intelligently make sense of disinterested worship of God.

I believe that Leibowitz's interpretation of this passage is mistaken and that it cannot bear the weight he asks it to carry. This is seen when we consider the meaning of this text in its larger context, as the immediately following words show.

> If, however, you pray merely by moving your lips while facing a wall, and at the same time think about your buying and selling; or if you read the Torah with your tongue while your heart is set upon the building of your habitation and does not consider what you read; and similarly in all cases in which you perform a commandment merely with your limbs— as if you were digging a hole in the ground or hewing wood in the forest— without reflecting either upon the meaning of that action or upon Him from Whom the commandment proceeds or upon the end of the action, you should not think that you have achieved the end. Rather you will then be similar to those to whom it is said: "Thou art near in their mouth and far from their inward parts" [Jer. 12:2]. (Ibid.)

Maimonides clearly indicates what he means by not being occupied by the things of this world while performing *mitzvot*. He is referring to the distraction that comes from the economic needs of daily survival, the problems of family life, of children in school, and the like. It is from thoughts about these problems that Maimonides tells his reader to free himself when performing the *mitzvot*. Whoever performs a *mitzvah* should instead reflect "upon Him from Whom the commandment proceeds," but *also* "upon the meaning of that action" and "upon the end of the action." Far from abandoning the reasons for the *mitzvot* elaborated in the previous chapter, Maimonides is expressly telling his reader to reflect upon them. For Maimonides to confirm the viewpoint of Leibowitz, he should have said "reflect upon Him from Whom the commandment proceeds and *not* upon the meaning or the end of the commandment," since for Leibowitz these are two antithetical forms of reflection. Thinking about Him from Whom the commandment proceeds belongs to authentic *avodah li-shemah*, worship for its own sake. Thinking about the end of the action is concern with its purpose in human terms, which for Leibowitz is *avodah she-lo li-shemah*, worship not for its own sake. Maimonides, however, does not see the human purposes of the *mitzvot* as antithetical to service of God for its own sake, and so he joins the two together.

Furthermore, his words "you should act as if you were occupied with Him" do not mean in this context that the *mitzvot* are the *only* content of worship. On the contrary, Maimonides is telling his reader that this manner of performing *mitzvot* can lead to a form of worship that transcends the performance of *mitzvot*. In this chapter, Maimonides invites his philosophic halakhic reader to utilize the time during the performance of many *mitzvot* for developing the disciplined habit of meditation about God, a habit leading to contemplative love of God. The philosophic halakhist, he points out, can find ample time for dealing with the needs of everyday life, namely, "while you eat or drink or bathe or talk with your wife . . . " (ibid.). Having given those needs their due, the worshiper can easily dismiss them from thought at the times of the reading of the Torah and of the recitation of the Shema, so as to use those times for the development of the ability to meditate upon God. Similarly, all the *mitzvot* structure fixed and legitimate times for developing the powers of contemplative love of God, which is the highest form of worship. They are then instrumental in training the person for this intellectual contemplative worship, which focuses upon discerning how the structure and course of nature manifest God's governance in the world He created. This worship can be expressed in those rarer moments when one is totally free from the demands of everyday life, including the concrete demands of the *halakhah*.

. . . while performing the actions imposed by the law, you should occupy your thoughts only with what you are doing, just as we have explained. When, however, you are alone with yourself and no one else is there and when you lie awake upon your bed, you should take great care during these precious times not to set your thought to work on anything other than that intellectual worship consisting in nearness to God and being in His presence. . . . (Ibid.)

The contemplative mode of worship here described by Maimonides is not expressed through halakhic action. It would be a serious mistake to identify Maimonides' view of the contemplative worship of the philosopher with a halakhic framework. In contrast to Leibowitz's halakhic understanding of worship, the mode of contemplative worship introduced at the end of the *Guide* is individualistic and not patterned according to the daily obligatory framework of institutional worship. Maimonides also says that one should not attempt this form of worship until one has had careful training in philosophy and acquired the unique psychological powers of the philosopher.

Philosophy and Halakhah

Leibowitz fails to give sufficient weight to the role of philosophy in Maimonides' conception of worship. He is mistaken in his claim that philosophy for Maimonides has only the function of helping one overcome the dangers of idolatry.[7] Love of God in Maimonides is related not to the will to worship, as Leibowitz would have it, but is a natural unfolding of the passion of the mind in its quest to understand God. For Maimonides, knowledge and performance of the *mitzvot* based on traditional authority lead one around, but not into, "the palace of the king," as he puts it in *Guide* 3:51. You are still outside if the *mitzvot* are your only framework. It is philosophy that leads to Maimonidean intimacy with God. The end of the *Guide* does not offer a new understanding of how *mitzvot* lead from an anthropocentric to a theocentric focus. It shows, rather, how the philosopher can utilize the structure of *halakhah* to prepare for what is in fact a meta-halakhic experience.[8] That is to say, *mitzvot* for Maimonides do not exhaust or exclusively structure the life of worship. To replace worship based on philosophic knowledge with worship based on the will to worship is to distort Maimonides' appreciation of the significance of philosophy in creating love for God. One cannot translate Maimonides' intellectualism into a heroic existential attempt to free oneself from all that is natural within the human world. I agree with Leibowitz that there is an enormous theocentric passion in Maimonides, a lovesick individual's yearning for his Beloved. But this passionate love for God cannot be separated from the method and direction through which Maimonides gave it substance. Leibowitz, coming after Kant and the modern critique of metaphysics, understands that contemplation of God's creation can in no way establish necessary knowledge regarding divinity. From a modern perspective, knowledge of the world of nature is religiously indifferent. This modern epistemological framework, however, cannot be used to understand Maimonides. It is not his world. For him, the view of the world seen from the vantage point of Aristotelian physics and astronomy has ultimate religious significance. For Leibowitz, it cannot have this role. Leibowitz, therefore, is reduced to making *halakhah* the exclusive vessel of the life of faith and worship. (*Halakhah* must become an essential constituent of the notion of worship.) Since all truth claims regarding God lack any cognitive value, the only thing left over from Maimonides for Leibowitz is the yearning to worship. Leibowitz compresses the Maimonidean passion into the will to worship, but in doing so he cuts off that passion from the intellectual roots that nourished it.

Maimonides speaks of extra-halakhic worship not only in the *Guide*. In the *Mishneh Torah*, too, he mentions a significant religious life not channeled through the framework of the *halakhah*.

> Why did the tribe of Levi not acquire a share in the land of Israel and in its spoils together with their brothers? Because this tribe was set apart to serve God and to minister to Him, to teach His straight ways and righteous ordinances to the multitude, as it is written: "They shall teach Jacob Thy ordinances, and Israel Thy law" [Deut. 33:10]. Therefore they were set apart from the ways of the world. They do not wage war like the rest of Israel, nor do they inherit land or acquire anything for themselves by their physical prowess. They are rather the army of God, as it is written: "Bless, Lord, his substance!" [Deut. 33:11]. He, blessed be He, acquires goods for them as it is written: "I am your portion and your inheritance" [Num. 18:20]. (MT *Hilkhot Shemitah ve-Yovel* 13:12)

After writing about the status of the tribe of Levi, who were set apart to be God's particular servants and who represent the highest rung of holiness within the community, he goes on to write what I believe to be one of his boldest philosophic statements in the *Mishneh Torah*.

> Not only the tribe of Levi, but every single individual from among the world's inhabitants whose spirit moved him and whose intelligence gave him the understanding to withdraw from the world in order to stand

before God to serve and to minister to Him, to know God, and he walked upright in the manner in which God made him, shaking off from his neck the yoke of the manifold contrivances which men seek, behold this person has been totally consecrated and God will be his portion and inheritance for ever and ever. God will acquire for him sufficient goods in this world, just as He did for the priests and Levites. Behold, David, may he rest in peace, said: "The Lord is the portion of my inheritance and of my cup; Thou maintainest my lot" [Ps. 16:5]. (Ibid., 13:13)

The holiness of the Levites and priests results from their being consecrated to a life of service to God. Such holiness, however, is not exclusive to Israel. It can be attained by individuals throughout the world whose intelligence and intellectual efforts lead them to dedicate their lives to standing before God, to serving and ministering to Him. Philosophic reflection on being opens up the spiritual way to all individuals drawn by a passionate yearning to understand how all of being is anchored to divinity.

Judah Halevi argued that the way to God was available only through the revelation of mitzvot and the elaborate detail of the halakhah.[9] Maimonides, though an incomparably greater halakhist than Halevi, did not believe that for halakhah to be considered a serious spiritual road, it must become an essential constituent of the notion of worship. On the contrary, he believed that only if Jews could appreciate a spiritual life beyond the particular framework of the Judaic tradition and recognize how all of reality mirrors divinity would they truly understand the meaning of love of God. For Maimonides, if one is to understand the fullness of the life of worship, one must go beyond the mediative framework of mitzvah.

Mitzvah is seen by Maimonides as a covenantal political category brought to Judaism through Moses.[10] In giving the category of covenantal mitzvah to the nation, Moses sought to organize a political community that would mirror in the human world the way God manifests Himself within the patterns of nature.[11] Mitzvah anchors the spiritual life in history and the community, keeping individuals from the mistaken notion that they can build a full spiritual life in isolation from a community. Thus the philosopher understands that the mitzvot are not meant only for training in spiritual meditation, since they also organize and serve the well-being of the nation. The philosopher appreciates that they are above all a communal framework and that through them God commands one to remain permanently active in the community. The anthropocentric focus that Maimonides elaborates in his approach to the mitzvot is therefore not a stage to be overcome. Withdrawal, solitude

and contemplative love of God are always balanced by the seriousness
with which one takes a spiritual life mediated by the framework of *mitzvah* found in the Torah.

Maimonides' halakhic Jew is guided to appropriate two frameworks
for the spiritual life. In one, *mitzvah* mediates God's personal covenantal
address to the individual and the community. In that framework, God,
appreciating the limited capacities of the human situation, speaks in the
language of human beings. The second framework for the spiritual life,
the framework of contemplative love of God, mediates the divine power
in its plenitude. When the framework is covenantal, the spiritual life is
earthbound, history-oriented. The *mitzvot* point to God's acceptance of
human beings and encourage them to accept full responsibility in building a covenantal society. Human well-being is not extraneous to them.
On the contrary, it is by way of it that God guides human beings to
His worship. In the fourth chapter of his introduction to *Pirkei Avot*,
for example, Maimonides felt no embarrassment in pointing out how
the disciplined framework of *halakhah* contributes to psychic health.
When one moves beyond covenantal consciousness to the second spiritual framework, however, one recognizes that there is nothing in Judaism that demands belief that all that exists in the world was meant
for human beings, and one begins to appreciate the true place of the
human individual and the community within the hierarchy of being.[12]

This double passion, a spiritual way that grows from *mitzvah* and a
spiritual way born from reflection on God's creation, finds its clearest
expression at the end of the *Guide*, when Maimonides distinguishes between four levels of human perfection. The first is the perfection of
possessions, the second of bodily constitution, shape, and health. The
third is the perfection of moral excellence, the fourth the acquisition of
rational excellence. In reference to the final perfection, Maimonides
writes: "This is in true reality the ultimate end; this is what gives the
individual true perfection, a perfection belonging to him alone, and it
gives him permanent perdurance; through it, man is man" (*Guide* 3:54).
Yet Maimonides does not end the *Guide* on this rung of perfection.
After introducing his reader to the solitary passion of the perfected intellect, he returns to the sphere of the community and history.[13] Having
contemplated God's "grace, justice and righteousness in the earth" (Jer.
9:23), one must imitate God by manifesting those three characteristics
in one's life among one's fellow human beings, "for in these things I
delight" (ibid.). There is a movement to and fro between the two frameworks, which may remind us of the dialectical movements so characteristic of Soloveitchik as we encountered them earlier in this book. The

difference is that Maimonides sees no contradiction between the two frameworks; they complement each other and must be in ultimate harmony with each other.

Even so, it is not easy to integrate the way of worship mediated by covenantal *mitzvah* and the way of philosophic eros, or to find the right balance between them. Only Moses and the patriarchs were capable of total integration (*Guide* 3:51). Maimonides adds that he himself was unable to integrate them harmoniously, but that he appreciated those rare moments when he was able to give expression to his theocentric philosophic passion. Though Maimonides does not show how one balances both dimensions to become a harmonious integrative personality, it would appear that he did not believe that a single-minded personality whose life mirrors just one of the passions is the ideal religious type. His philosophic system is an attempt to allow both passions their full vitality.

Job and Philosophy

Leibowitz is prima facie on stronger ground with respect to the second passage mentioned above, namely, Maimonides' discussion of Job. The climax of the Book of Job is the "speech from the whirlwind," where God tells Job that since he possesses infinitesimally smaller powers than his Creator, he has no right to question God's will. Maimonides, himself, moreover, undoubtedly appreciated that theme in the Judaic tradition which dwells on the insignificance of human beings in comparison with God. Near the beginning of the *Mishneh Torah*, for example, he asserts that human beings have a far more insignificant place in the hierarchy of being than angels and the planets, let alone God.

> When a man reflects on these things, studies all these created beings from the angels and [heavenly] spheres down to human beings and so on, and realizes the divine wisdom manifested in them all, his love for God will increase, his soul will burst, his very flesh will yearn to love God. He will be filled with fear and trembling as he becomes conscious of his lowly condition, poverty and insignificance and compares himself with any of the great and holy bodies; still more when he compares himself with any one of the pure forms that are incorporeal and have never had associations with corporeal substances. He will then realize that he is a vessel full of shame, dishonor and reproach, empty and deficient. (MT *Hilkhot Yesodei ha-Torah* 4:12)

The feeling of awe and shame noted in the *Mishneh Torah* is given fuller philosophical expression in the sections on divine providence in the *Guide*. There Maimonides argues that much confusion regarding God's supposed indifference to human beings is the result of a mistaken appreciation of the place of them and their history within the hierarchy of being. To Maimonides, it is an arrogant and grave mistake to perceive God's creation as revolving around us and our needs. Above us, he agrees with Aristotle, there exist heavenly bodies whose very matter is superior to that in our bodies, while above them there are angels who exist as separate intellects without any material bodies at all.

> Be not misled in your soul to think that the [heavenly] spheres and the angels have been brought into existence for our sake. For it has explained to us what we are worth: "Behold the nations are as a drop of a bucket" [Is. 40:15]. Consider accordingly your substance and that of the spheres, the stars and the separate intellects; then the truth will become manifest to you and you will know that man and nothing else is the most perfect and the most noble thing that has been generated from this [inferior] matter, but that if his being is compared to that of the spheres and all the more to that of the separate beings, it is very, very contemptible. (*Guide* 3:13)

Awe, trepidation, and a sense of insignificance in comparison to God and other vastly superior beings expressed for Maimonides, both in his philosophic and in his halakhic works, the mature feeling of one who has arrived at a philosophical understanding of the nature of reality and of God. This feeling, Leibowitz might fairly object, does not seem to enhance, enrich, or support the feelings of adequacy and dignity that I have claimed represent Maimonides' anthropology. Nor does Maimonides treat this feeling as merely a transient moment of religious growth. At the end of the *Guide*, he asserts unequivocally that the same feeling exists in an enhanced form in the individual who has achieved understanding of reality through training in logic and mathematics, physics and astronomy, and who has pushed the possibilities of metaphysical knowledge to their uttermost limits. The philosophical halakhist with a highly developed intellect adopts a humble stance and is always filled with trepidation, since there is no place in the world in which this individual does not sense the awe-inspiring presence of God. God is present in the intimate precincts of home as well as in the public marketplace. There is no hiding, no privacy, no area of reality that does not reveal the awesome gap separating this person from God.

Know that when perfect men understand this, they achieve such humility, such awe and fear of God, such reverence and such shame before Him, may He be exalted—and this in ways that pertain to true reality not to imagination—that their secret conduct with their wives and in latrines is like their public conduct with other people. . . .

This purpose to which I have drawn your attention is the purpose of all the actions prescribed by the law. For it is by all the particulars of the actions and through their repetition that some excellent men obtain such training that they achieve human perfection, so that they fear, and are in awe and dread of, God, may He be exalted, and know who it is that is with them and as a result act subsequently as they ought to. (Guide 3:52)

Leibowitz rightly discerns that for Maimonides the sense of human insignificance before God is a theme of fundamental importance and that it enters essentially even into what Maimonides regards as the highest form of worship. Nonetheless, the existence of this theme in Maimonides does not contradict what I have said about the sense of human adequacy and dignity in Maimonides' anthropology, since Maimonides never allows this theme to place a question mark over God's adherence to the Sinai covenant. As we have seen, that highest worship is a meta-halakhic experience, even though the Jew can utilize the life of halakhah in preparing for it. Within the framework of the covenant of mitzvah and its halakhic elaboration, on the other hand, human adequacy is never undermined. When Maimonides brings the theme of God's awesomeness into the Mishneh Torah, his halakhic code, it is to prevent his readers from ever imagining that their relationship to God is mediated exclusively by the covenant with its concern for human well-being. God is also their Creator and as such the Creator of beings far superior to themselves. They should realize and never forget that God ultimately wants them to worship Him with a passion that reflects His full reality and not merely the partial aspect of His reality that is expressed in the covenant.[14]

These basic conceptions of Maimonides also underlie his discussion of the Book of Job (Guide 3:22–23). Maimonides asserts that the book's prologue, in which Satan is given permission to tempt Job, is a parable in which Satan is synonymous with the yetzer ha-ra, the base instinct that exists in every human being. The sufferings of Job, on the other hand, may be a parable or they may really have occurred. Job, in his initial reactions to those sufferings, exemplifies for Maimonides any Jew whose approach to God is mediated by only one of the two frameworks that we have just mentioned. He lacks the knowledge that makes possible disinterested contemplative love of God.

> The most marvellous and extraordinary thing about this story is the fact that knowledge is not attributed in it to Job. He is not said to be a wise or a comprehending or an intelligent man. Only moral virtue and righteousness in action are ascribed to him. For if he had been wise, his situation would not have been obscure for him, as will become clear. (*Guide* 3:22)

Here Maimonides makes use of the distinction between the "moral virtues" (moral excellence) and the "intellectual virtues" (intellectual excellence) that is drawn in the first book of Aristotle's *Nicomachean Ethics*. In the subsequent books, Aristotle explains how his celebrated doctrine of the mean provides a general understanding of the moral virtues, namely, of those character dispositions that a human being needs in order to play a proper role in society. The climax of the *Nicomachean Ethics*, however, comes when Aristotle shows how the intellectual virtues—wisdom and scientific knowledge and the like—enable one to come as close to a godlike existence as is possible for human beings. Maimonides makes use of this distinction in the manner in which he distinguishes between the halakhic framework of the covenant and the meta-halakhic framework of disinterested love of God. In *Hilkhot Deot* of the *Mishneh Torah*, for example, he defines the character dispositions appropriate to halakhic life with the aid of many concepts borrowed from Aristotle's discussion of the doctrine of the mean. In the *Guide*, he shows how scientific knowledge and metaphysics make possible the highest form of worship of God. Thus, when he says of Job that he possessed moral virtue but not knowledge, wisdom, and intelligence, the implication is that Job's worship of God was characterized by practice rather than philosophical knowledge. This was why Job spent so much time bemoaning his incomprehension of why great suffering had befallen him.

From Anthropocentrism to Theocentrism

Since Job is certain that he has committed no major sin, the notion of reward and punishment fails to help him to understand his own suffering. He concludes, therefore, that the righteous and the evildoers are regarded by God as equal and that the undeserved suffering of the righteous reflects divine contempt for the human species. As long as human history is viewed as the exclusive mediator of the spiritual life, Job has no alternative but to reject God, for he refuses to allow his moral integrity to be crushed. The turning point in his distress comes when he realizes that the greatest happiness consists in knowing God. In comparison, all the things that he had previously supposed constituted happiness—such as possession of wealth and many children—are unimportant, and so he does not need to impute enormous iniquities to himself in order to account for their loss. He is brought to this turning point through the impact of contemplating the manifestation of God's activity in the magnificent structure of the world of nature (the activity described in the "speech from the whirlwind"), in which human beings are just one small component. Once Job moves beyond the framework of the tradition with its focus on the affairs of the human community, once he grasps how the divine reality is also manifested in a larger framework where divine and not human purposes lie at the center of the religious worldview, then no suffering can weaken his acceptance of and love for God.

> This is the object of the Book of Job as a whole. I refer to the establishing of this foundation for the belief and the drawing attention to the inference to be drawn from natural matters so that you should not fall into error and seek to affirm in your imagination that His knowledge is like our knowledge, or that His purpose and His providence and His governance are like our purpose and our providence and our governance. If a man knows this, every misfortune will be borne lightly by him. And misfortunes will not add to his doubts regarding the deity and whether He does or does not know, and whether He exercises providence or manifests neglect, but will on the contrary add to his love. . . . (*Guide* 3:23)

Job discovers a new joy, a new meaning to existence, when he perceives the world from this theocentric focus. His new perception of reality does not explain his suffering, but it enables him to see it in a different proportion and thus to bear it. This larger spiritual vision enables him to return to human life, to build a family afresh, and to begin a life of worship that cannot be destroyed by the vagaries of human fortunes. Job is now fortified by his commitment to a religious vision of the universe that is immune to skepticism about God's reality even in the face of so much suffering in human history. His philosophic perception of God acts as a sustaining framework when the covenantal justice model becomes inadequate on its own. Job can reforge his commitment to the life of *mitzvah* because history does not exhaust the totality of the meaning he gives to the living God.

Leibowitz understood fully well that Maimonides describes the religious passion of Job from a perspective in which human ethical concerns have lost their urgency. He is mistaken, however, in taking this as ultimately the only model in Maimonides for religious authenticity and in maintaining that the political anthropocentric framework of the *mitzvot* must be overcome by one who has moved in the way of Job. The tension that Maimonides presents between the theocentric and anthropocentric foci should not be explained away as forcing a decision between the centrality either of man or of God. Maimonides' religious anthropology rather builds upon the ability of an individual to *alternate* between theocentricity and anthropocentricity, between solitude and social commitment, between silent reflection and moral activism. Thus the appreciation of human self-realization within the life of *mitzvah* is not a *she-lo li-shemah* perception of worship. Man is not chosen *above* God. What the framework of the covenant mediates is man and woman *in the presence* of God.

Maimonides never abandons the Judaic concern with history. History and messianism remain central to philosopher-halakhists who understand the path of the *Guide of the Perplexed*. They can take history seriously precisely because they have a spiritual anchorage that does not point exclusively in the direction of historical realization in a messianic society. This is the inner dialectic of Maimonides. Only those who go beyond the *halakhah* can appropriate the true telos of the *halakhah*. Only those who can transcend history can take history seriously. Only those who can appreciate the insignificance of the human being can return to a spiritual vision whose primary focus is human action and the building of a total human spiritual community. The philosophers can be in history, accept the covenant with full seriousness, and sustain their struggle to realize it, because they have found a way of building conviction that does not depend on the material realization of the messianic idea within history. Their theocentric love for God can sustain them in the darkest moments of historical tragedy. They have discovered a moment in the religious life whose self-sufficiency is capable of enabling them to bear the burden of an unredeemed historical world.[15]

This manner of transcending history does not imply its negation. On the contrary, philosopher-halakhists understand that the spiritual life was not meant to be lived in solitude, but is to be materialized within the concrete frameworks of a social-political order. They appreciate that the ultimate goal of the halakhic community's spiritual vision is to create social and political conditions that liberate human beings to love God from a theocentric focus.

Leibowitz's approach to the Akedah and the experience of Job can help one to remain spiritually intact despite the cruel vicissitudes of history, but it destroys the possibility of understanding the *mitzvot* in a way that permits the full presence of the human being in the religious life. In his way of transcending history, Leibowitz has also departed from treating the covenant—in which the community is a full partner—as the guiding principle for understanding Judaism. And in establishing the passion of Job as the exclusive model for understanding the *mitzvot*, he has sacrificed the rich complexity of the Maimonidean religious anthropology.

Torah as an eternal way for the Jewish people must not lead to a Judaism that is indifferent to history, but to one that demands that Jews in every particular historical context discover how the human significance of the *mitzvot* can be applied within their own historical situation. I accept, like Leibowitz and halakhic Jews in general, the primacy of the oral law above the written law; but I take this primacy to imply that the eternal significance of the Torah is that it constitutes a God-given challenge that must be met in every generation by a covenantal community that trusts its own autonomous rational and moral judgments in applying the Torah to life.

6

The Spirit of Judaic Prayer

U P TO NOW, this book has drawn its direction for a modern covenantal anthropology chiefly from the activist spirit implied by the notion of *mitzvah* and from the intellectual freedom with which rabbinic
teachers interpreted the biblical text. But if our anthropology is to express the richness and complexity of the religious life, it cannot ignore
another major dimension of the life of faith, namely, the dimension of
prayer.

The classic prayer in the Judaic tradition is the Amidah, the standing, silent devotional prayer consisting of three benedictions of praise,
thirteen of petition, and three of thanksgiving. The Talmud (*Berakhot*
34a) sees this structure as mirroring the way a humble servant would
supplicate a master. It is not appropriate, according to the rabbis, to
begin immediately with one's needs. A servant first gives words of praise
to the master and only then petitions for the servant's needs. After
stating these petitions, the servant offers thanksgiving. However, the
fundamental driving force in approaching the master remains need and
dependency. The praise and thanksgiving are just ways of giving one's
petition a respectful aesthetic form.

Human beings are needy, and the Jewish people, until the messianic
kingdom, are a needy community. The *siddur*, their daily prayer book,

reflects their sense of exile, wandering, and longing for a renewed political kingdom and a redeemed Jerusalem. That, together with supplication for the forgiveness of sins and to be spared poverty, hunger, and
disease, forms the core of their prayerful petition. Whereas *mitzvah*
and Torah learning encourage adequacy, assertion, personal initiative,
and dignity, prayer could seem to encourage surrender, resignation, and
feelings of total helplessness and dependency upon God. But must petitional prayer diminish the sense of responsibility implied by covenantal *mitzvot* and undermine the confidence of the rabbinic scholars
who insisted that the Torah "is not in heaven"? Must the presence of
this dimension of the Judaic faith experience contradict my claim that
a covenantal religious anthropology can minimize appeals to divine grace
and encourage the development of human initiative? Or, to adapt Soloveitchik's language, can the covenantal prayer community become a
covenantal "majestic" community prepared to face courageously the
burdens of living in an unredeemed world? Or must the prayer community wait on the margins of history for the Messiah to bring miraculous redemption? Is the door to traditional halakhic prayer closed to
a modern Jew who is not prepared to wait for the Messiah before Jews
assume full responsibility for their social, political, and economic existence? Are Torah learning and *mitzvah*—but not prayer—the only significant mediators of the covenant for one who is grateful for the
newfound human powers made possible by modern technology?

In this and the following chapter, I shall consider these questions
from the contrasting viewpoints of Soloveitchik's dialectical anthropology with its aspects of defeat, resignation, and surrender, Leibowitz's
theocentric focus with its emphasis on *mitzvah* as pure duty, and my
own covenantal perspective, which completely rejects the Akedah model
for covenantal *halakhah*. The analysis will show how our anthropologies
influence, and are influenced by, our different approaches to prayer.

Soloveitchik, Leibowitz, and I disagree, first of all, as to how the
essential pathos of the prayer experience is to be understood. For Soloveitchik, the inner spirit of the experience of reciting the Amidah is
a sacrificial offering of one's whole being to God. For Leibowitz, by contrast, Judaic prayer is totally indifferent to the inner life of the worshiper. Its vitality is derived exclusively from the formal notion of *mitzvah*
found in Judaism. In fact, for Leibowitz, prayer is the paradigm for understanding how living by the *mitzvot* is totally unrelated to the particular life situation of the individual and the community. As for myself,
I shall argue against Leibowitz in the next chapter that prayer cannot
be understood in the same way as other *mitzvot*. Here I agree with So-

loveitchik that there is a particular experiential dimension in prayer, the *kavvanah* (the devotional attitude and intention), not found in other *mitzvot*. But I shall first show, in contrast to Soloveitchik, that the Judaic prayer experience does not epitomize self-surrender but reflects the mood of covenantal acceptance and intimacy before God. Spontaneity and individual responsibility will be shown to have a definite place in the tradition that emphasizes supplicatory prayer. Nor need those vital features of my covenantal anthropology be crushed by the *halakhah's* standardization of the language of prayer and its establishment of a fixed daily routine of worship.

As we have seen, the emphases in Soloveitchik's different descriptions of the halakhic experience are not always consistent. At times his focus is on human initiative and autonomy, bold new adventures of the spirit, openness to new possibilities, faith in one's capacity to cope with the challenges of human existence. At other times his portrait is much more subdued, reflective, and self-conscious. The optimistic mood gives way to a melancholy spirit marked by doubt and resignation, helpless surrender in terror before the mysterious power of God, and a desperate longing to break out of one's isolation. There are moments where Soloveitchik invites you to celebrate with him the excitement of an existence in which his halakhic man looks upon the world as inviting his creative potential. And yet at other times the universe does not appear as an inviting place and you find yourself being dragged down into feelings of self-reproach and unworthiness. The oscillations in the way covenantal man lives by the *mitzvot* are also powerfully evident in Soloveitchik's treatment of prayer.

Prayer and Love

The depiction of the prayer experience in Soloveitchik's "Lonely Man of Faith" is essentially optimistic. Here, in contrast to other writings of his, worshipers do not doubt their own legitimacy or ability to enter into the prayer experience. In prayer, the Jew addresses God as Thou and relives the covenantal revelatory experience in which God redeems the human being and the community from torturous isolation. God's revelation in history, as distinct from His manifestation in nature, makes possible the emergence of a new individual and a new community. On the natural level, as Soloveitchik portrays it, existence is impersonal. The challenge nature poses the community and the individual is how to overcome its cruel indifference in order to survive. The urgency to survive creates a cooperative human effort to build a society capable of mastering the arts of existence. On the cosmic natural level, there is thus cooperation, but love and personal intimacy are absent. To use Buber's language, God as He is perceived in nature creates the relational ontology of "I–It" and not "I–Thou." Only when God directly encounters human beings and is present in personal speech as a Thou does the human being find the resources to go beyond surface communication and to develop those human feelings and experiences that enable him or her to become what Soloveitchik calls an in-depth personality. Only through God's revelation to the human being as a personal reality do love and sacrificial action in human relationships become possible. The covenant at Sinai corresponds to an existential human need to discover love, intimacy, and total commitment in relationships. From Soloveitchik's religious perspective, the emergence of these powers requires God's revelatory presence. They do not come about within human beings in their own isolation and autonomy, but are made possible as God makes Himself present in a new way in the human world. It is revelation in history that creates new human potentials for love. That revelation is not a terrifying experience that overwhelms its recipients and reduces them to feelings of insignificance; it is a redeeming experience. Because of revelation, Adam is no longer shut up within himself, cut off from feelings of love necessary for his fulfillment as a total human personality. God as Thou transforms the whole framework of interpersonal relational possibilities.

> If God had not joined the community of Adam and Eve, they would have never been able and would have never cared to make the paradoxical leap over the gap, indeed abyss, separating two individuals whose personal experiential messages are written in a private code undecipherable by anyone else. Without the covenantal experience of the prophetic or prayerful colloquy, Adam *absconditus* would have persisted in his he-role and Eve *abscondita* in her she-role, unknown to and distant from each other. Only when God emerged from the transcendent darkness of He-anonymity into the illumined spaces of community-knowability and charged man with an ethico-moral mission, did Adam *absconditus* and Eve *abscondita*, while revealing themselves to God in prayer and in unqualified commitment,—also reveal themselves to each other in sympathy and love on the one hand and common action on the other. Thus, the final objective of human quest for redemption was attained; the individual felt relieved from loneliness and isolation. ("Lonely Man of Faith," p. 45)

From this perspective, the human being's powers of love are energized as a result of encountering God in prayer. Prayer makes it possible for one to become a revealing being. Adam and Eve, symbolic of all interpersonal human relationships, become transformed human beings, in-depth personalities, when they are addressed by God. God's presence to them as Thou energizes their whole being and enables them to move from a utilitarian to a covenantal plane of existence. The later generations of biblical history continue this movement. Personal and intimate speech flows from their being as they participate in the prophetic community of ancient Israel and in the prayer community that becomes institutionalized after the return from Babylonian exile. There is a parallelism between the encounter with God in prayer and the interpersonal encounter on the human plane, and indeed, Soloveitchik's understanding of covenantal prayer and the covenantal faith community is intimately connected to his description of the human condition and of human relationships.

Prayer and Prophecy

Soloveitchik depicts the institution of fixed communal prayer as a conscious response by the Jewish community to the waning and disappearance of prophecy. The Great Assembly organized by Nehemiah and Ezra decided that if God had stopped talking to them in revelation, then they must initiate a continuation of the dialogue through prayer.

> While within the prophetic community God takes the initiative—He speaks and man listens—in the prayer community the initiative belongs to man: he does the speaking and God, the listening. The word of prophecy is God's and is accepted by man. The word of prayer is man's and God accepts it. The two Halakhic traditions tracing the origin of prayer to Abraham and the other Patriarchs and attributing the authorship of statutory prayer to the men of the Great Assembly reveal the Judaic view of the sameness of the prophecy and prayer communities. Covenantal prophecy and prayer blossomed forth the very instant Abraham met God and became involved in a strange colloquy. At a later date, when the mysterious men of this wondrous assembly witnessed the bright summer day of the prophetic community full of color and sound turning to a bleak autumnal night of dreadful silence unillumined by the vision of God or made homely by His voice, they refused to acquiesce in this cruel historical reality and would not let the ancient dialogue between God and men come to an end. For the men of the Great Assembly knew that with the withdrawal of the colloquy from the field of consciousness of the Judaic community, the latter would lose the intimate companionship of God and consequently its covenantal status. In prayer they found the salvation of the colloquy, which, they insisted, must go on forever. If

God had stopped calling man, they urged, let man call God. ("Lonely Man of Faith," pp. 36–37)

The men of the Great Assembly's refusal to allow the absence of God's revelatory word to be a permanent feature of history, their refusal to acquiesce in God's silence in history, speaks volumes for their felt sense of dignity and their awareness that they were playing an essential role in maintaining the ongoing intimacy and dialogue between God and Israel. They knew that God must be present and involved with the community. They refused to admit the possibility that with the end of prophecy the passionate intimate dialogue between God and Israel had come to an end. If God stops speaking to Israel through prophets, it is time for human beings to take the lead in the dialogue between God and Israel. The absence of revelation and of overt miraculous divine involvement in history did not drive them into feelings of self-doubt, terror, inadequacy, and rejection. It is interesting to note Soloveitchik's use of the expression "they refused to acquiesce" in explaining their response of initiating statutory prayer, as if God were not free to choose whether or not to be present among them. It is their response which defines for the community God's continuous involvement in its life. This understanding of how prayer developed reflects the spirit of talmudic teachers who define for the community how God responds to violation of the law by Jews. Israel as a convenantal learning community defines how the divine word is appropriated and understood in history. Just as they are competent to define the consequences and scope of revelation, they are equally competent to decide what are the human needs to which God may be expected to be responsive. Prayer reflects the activist spirit of the covenantal community which insists on maintaining a continuous intimate dialogue with God.

The continuity claimed by Soloveitchik between the prophetic community and the prayer community is one of the most significant expressions by a contemporary halakhic thinker of the sense of adequacy and dignity of rabbinic covenantal religious consciousness, since it implicitly disregards the miraculous features of God's revelatory encounter with the community. We may see this in the three-fold covenantal connection that, according to Soloveitchik, the prayer and prophetic communities share. To begin with, the paradigm for prayer in "The Lonely Man of Faith" is the face-to-face encounter of God with Moses. It is the speech of a friend. It is the speech of a prophet who feels adequate and dignified in the encounter with God. There is no dread and awe of the numinous.[1]

Only within the covenantal community which is formed by God descending upon the mountain and man, upon the call of the Lord, ascending the mount is a direct and personal relationship expressing itself in the prophetic "face to face" colloquy established. "And the Lord spoke unto Moses face to face as man speaketh unto his friend." (p. 34)

It is this biblical description (Exod. 33:11) of the face-to-face encounter between God and Moses that Soloveitchik wants his readers to focus upon as he relates prayer to the prophetic experience. The universe in which the prophetic and prayer communities live invites the personal encounter between the human being and God. The essence of prayer is the existential awareness that one lives in the presence of God in a personal and intimate way and that this divine presence can be addressed through direct and warm speech. This is the covenantal God Whose name is the Tetragrammaton. Reflection on the impersonal God of nature, designated by the term "Elohim," does not lead to prayer because the essence of prayer for Soloveitchik is covenantal relational intimacy.

The cosmic drama, notwithstanding its grandeur and splendor, no matter how distinctly it reflects the image of the Creator and no matter how beautifully it tells His glory, cannot provoke man to prayer. (p. 35)

Only the framework of prophetic revelation makes prayer as personal encounter possible.

Prayer as the continuation of the prophetic experience must not, therefore, be confused with the technical prayer recital required by the *halakhah*. The *halakhah* tries to give concrete form to the awareness of standing in the presence of God, but the language in which prayer is cast and the elaborate rituals the *halakhah* requires one to perform are only formal means for expressing the encounter with God as a personal Thou. The halakhic tradition's decision to fix the content of prayer is ascribed no significant weight in Soloveitchik's attempt to define prayer as an intense reliving of the covenantal prophetic encounter in the individual's daily life.

A second feature that prophecy and prayer share is commitment to the community. Prophecy from a Jewish perspective is not a private ecstatic experience. The prophet brings an urgent normative message from a God Who seeks to be embodied in the life of the community. The prophetic experience does not isolate the prophet from the community, but places him in a matrix of social and political action.[2] Prayer reflects this same pattern, as is shown by the plural form present in all the petitional prayers. In Judaic prayer one never prays for oneself alone, but always begins with a prayer on behalf of the community whose style is "Heal *us*, redeem *us*, restore Thy *people* to Jerusalem." As one stands before God, the drama of Jewish history and the urgent need of the total community is engraved in one's consciousness.

As the prayer consciousness fills the heart of the worshiper, preoccupation with self falls away and is replaced by solidarity with the needs of others and an awareness that one's being is inextricably linked to the destiny of one's community. This commitment to the community leads to a third feature shared by the prayer and prophetic communities. Both the prophet and the praying individual recognize the centrality of normative action in their covenantal experience with God.

> When confronted with God, the prophet receives an ethico-moral message to be handed down to and realized by the members of the covenantal community which is mainly a community in action. . . . Prayer likewise consists not only of an awareness of the presence of God, but of an act of committing oneself to God and accepting His ethico-moral authority. . . . Prayer is always the harbinger of moral reformation. (pp. 39–42)

Prayer is here defined as a prologue to practice. Its essence, which is drawn from the covenantal encounter, is to awaken the worshiper to the centrality of acting with justice in the world. As the continuation of the prophetic encounter, prayer casts the individual into social action. It is not resignation, helplessness, or withdrawal. It is not quietism or a relinquishment of personal responsibility. Prayer as encounter, as discovery of God as Thou, is consummated only in moral action. In prayer the powers of love and solidarity become so intense that the prayerful individual must become an active being within the social and political reality. From this perspective, petitional prayer extends the covenantal dignity of *mitzvah* and is in no way its antithesis.

Prayer and Self-Discovery

The role of prayer in promoting human dignity is also prominent in Soloveitchik's essay "Redemption, Prayer, Talmud Torah," which depicts the relationship of petitional prayer to the growth and development of the human person. Petitional prayer is here interpreted as a process of self-discovery. In learning how to utter petitional prayer, people are transformed from mute beings, unable to articulate their pains and needs, into dignified beings who can express them in meaningful linguistic structures. Judaic prayer began when "the children of Israel sighed by reason of their bondage and their cry came up to God" (Exod. 2:23), but it reaches maturity only when the outpouring of human needs is subjected to the discipline of the mind in the Amidah.

> In the final stage, the word appears; the outcry is transformed into speech. Man, at this level, not only feels his needs but understands them as well; there is a logic of prayer which opens up to man when he is in possession of the word. . . . The hierarchy of needs, clearly defined and evaluated, is to be found in the text of the Amidah, where not only the emotional need-awareness, but also the logos of need and with it the human being himself are redeemed. The outpouring of the heart merges with the insights of the mind. To pray means to discriminate, to evaluate, to understand, in other words, to ask intelligently. I pray for the gratification of some needs since I consider them worthy of being gratified. I refrain from petitioning God for the satisfaction of other wants because it will not enhance my dignity. (pp. 66–67)

To use Soloveitchik's terms (ibid., p. 70), this experience of petitional prayer leads toward the pole of self-acquisition, self-discovery, self-objectification, self-redemption. The focus is not on how God will respond to the words uttered in prayer but on how those words change the human being.[3] Soloveitchik regards human beings as discovering their essence when they are able to comprehend and articulate the fundamental needs that define the proper aspirations of humankind. Halakhic prayer emphasizes petition, which articulates the human being's proper needs, because it is crucial not to be confused as to what is an essential human need. To misunderstand those needs is to misunderstand the essence of being human. From this posture, the mood of prayer is philosophic and analytic and close to the reflective learning experience found in *Halakhic Man*. It is therefore not surprising when Soloveitchik relates *tefillah* (prayer) to the Torah learning process.

> It was for a good reason that Moses and Ezra integrated *kriat torah* [reading from the Torah] into the framework of *tefillah*. Without *talmud torah* [the study of the Torah], it would be difficult for *tefillah* to assure man of total redemption. (p. 68)

Soloveitchik ends his essay, however, with a sudden dialectical leap toward the opposite pole: having led us to self-acquisition, prayer requires from us total self-sacrifice.

> When *tefillah* and *talmud torah* unite in one redemptive experience, prayer becomes *avodah she-be-lev*. What does this term denote? Not service by the heart, but the *offering* of the heart; Judaic dialectic plays "mischie-

vously" with two opposites, two irreconcilable aspects of prayer. It announces prayer as self-acquisition, self-discovery, self-objectification and self-redemption . . . Yet there is another aspect to prayer: prayer is an act of giving away. Prayer means sacrifice. (p. 70)

Here Soloveitchik offers no explanation for this unexpected complete shift of direction, apart from the different connotations of the word *avodah*: "sacrifice" as well as "worship" and "service." To understand his intention, we must turn to other writings and especially to his article in Hebrew "Ra'ayonot al ha-tefillah" (where prayer and specifically the Amidah are characterized without any emphasis on human dignity).

Petitional Prayer and Self-Sacrifice

Petitional prayer, rather than being a vehicle leading to self-discovery or expressing human solidarity and commitment to the well-being of others, is understood now as self-sacrifice. Worship of the heart, which finds its fullest expression in the middle petitional benedictions, does not lead to the humanizing encounter with God as the eternal Thou, but is now total surrender to the awesome terror of divinity. It is an act of sacrifice, an act of casting oneself down before the Lord and acknowledging His unlimited rule and the complete feebleness of man ("Ra'ayonot al ha-tefillah," p. 102). In petitional prayer, we urgently seek out God's grace and help because we are overwhelmed by feelings of insignificance and worthlessness.

In *Reflections of the Rav*, Soloveitchik prefers the Hebrew word *tehinnah* over *bakkashah* as the appropriate term for petitional prayer because *bakkashah*, the customary term, suggests a claim upon God, whereas *tehinnah* etymologically "suggests an unearned grace, something not due to us." "Christians and mystics considered *tehinnah* an unworthy form of prayer," he observes, "a sacrifice for a recompense, a self-directed prayer" (p. 84). Nonetheless, he explains, *tehinnah* is emphasized in Judaism because the emotion of dependence and helplessness is singled out above all others as the central existential posture of worship. The feeling of wretchedness is paramount for authentic prayer.

When the covenantal identity is grounded in *mitzvah*, we know we have dignity because we are called upon to be active and responsible in history. When covenantal identity grows from prayer, as the latter is portrayed in "Ra'ayonot al ha-tefillah," one discovers dignity only after having gone through a process of total self-negation.

The worshipper negates himself in order to regain himself. Out of prayer one emerges exalted and refreshed, finding one's redemption through the loss of oneself. (p. 104)

For Soloveitchik, the sacrificial gesture of prayer is not only reflected in the thirteen petitional benedictions. He discovers (ibid.) the most exalted petition in the opening benediction of the third section of the Amidah, which states:

> Be pleased, Lord our God, with Thy people Israel and with their prayer. Restore the worship through Thy most holy sanctuary. Accept Israel's offering and prayer with gracious love, and may the worship of Thy people Israel be ever pleasing to Thee.

Soloveitchik understands the words "Accept Israel's offering and prayer with gracious love" as an offering of the self to God. The whole Amidah, in fact, is seen as a declaration of the human being's utter insignificance and helplessness before God, thereby signifying the total sacrifice to God of one's own being.

The worshiper's consciousness of total dependency is not derived only from social, political, and economic needs. For Soloveitchik it is ontological. Prayer as self-sacrifice touches upon the very legitimacy of human existence and the very essence of what it means to be a finite creature before God. Its paradigm is the Akedah of Isaac.

> Build an altar. Arrange the pieces of wood. Kindle the fire. Take the knife to slaughter your existence for My sake—thus commands the awesome God Who suddenly appears from absolute seclusion. This approach is the basis of prayer. Man surrenders himself to God. He approaches the awesome God and the approach expresses itself in the sacrifice and Akedah of oneself. (p. 95)

Prayer and Dread

Soloveitchik, as we have seen, believes that prayer is related to the prophetic experience. Rabbinic prayer continues the prophetic biblical dimension. However, in "Ra'ayonot al ha-tefillah" the portrait of the prophetic experience is radically different from that found in "The Lonely Man of Faith." Gone is the emphasis on Moses' friendly face-to-face encounter with God, with the ease and acceptance that characterized it. The prophetic experience is now in no way analogous to the interpersonal relationship of friendship and love. Instead, Soloveitchik calls upon biblical texts that emphasize the terror and awe felt in the prophetic encounter with God.

In "Ra'ayonot al ha-tefillah," the covenantal community's experience at Sinai is an awesome terrifying experience in which human finitude is overwhelmed in the encounter with divinity. When it meets the infinite, the finite human being, says Soloveitchik, must lose all sense of ontological legitimacy and dignity (pp. 94–95). It is therefore no wonder that the people are terrified and awestruck at the revelatory moment of Sinai and cry out to Moses to act as their mediator. Revelation, rather than confirming dignity, creates the terror of death: "All the people witnessed the thunder and lightning, the blare and the mountain smoking. And when the people saw it they fell back and stood at a distance. 'You speak to us,' they said to Moses, 'and we will obey. But let not God speak to us lest we die' " (Exod. 20:18–19). This dread is what every individual should feel who dares approach God in prayer.

Soloveitchik's paradigm is now (p. 88) not Moses' face-to-face encounter with God, but a Moses who hides his face because he is afraid to look at God in the burning bush, a Moses who is told: "You cannot see My face because no man can see My face and live" (Exod. 23:20). Soloveitchik deliberately selects those biblical descriptions which bring home to his reader the enormous terror that should fill the heart of a human being who encounters the presence of God. Prayer as continuing the prophetic experience takes on a radically new meaning when it is the prophet's terror before God that is portrayed.

When prayer ceases to have the friendly personal dimension nurtured by the covenantal "we" consciousness, and when one forgets how dignified the men of the Great Assembly felt when they insisted that the covenantal dialogue with God continue, one may wonder how prayer itself is possible. Those who think about the awesome terror of God may doubt their own worthiness to approach Him, address Him as Thou, and bring to Him their needs, concerns, and hopes.

> The Halakhah never let its attention be distracted from an aspect [of prayer] which constituted for it an almost insoluble problem and an amazing paradox. In the eyes of the sages of the tradition, having recourse to God in speech and entreaty seemed a bold and adventurous action. How can mortal man, who is here today and in the grave tomorrow, approach the King of the kings of kings, the Holy One, blessed be He? Can we say that permission is given to a common person to talk to a high and exalted King and to request his needs from Him?
>
> Evidently, the experience of fear and trembling, which is an integral part of the religious life, complicates the problem of prayer and turns it

into a marvelous riddle. On the one hand, it is impossible for man to approach God. To the extent that man approaches God, his finite human existence is contradicted. Finitude is swallowed up in infinity and expires in its recesses. . . . The personality and self-confidence of man are as nothing in comparison with the majesty of God and the splendor of His glory. The question bursts out: how is it possible for prayer to exist? (pp. 87–88)

According to Soloveitchik, the agonizing dialectic between the desperate necessity of prayer and the total unworthiness of human beings to pray accompanies the worshiper throughout the whole Amidah experience. Already in the rabbinic period, the Amidah was prefixed by the verse "O Lord, open Thou my lips and my mouth shall declare Thy praise" (Ps. 51:15). When Soloveitchik's ideal worshiper is pronouncing this introductory sentence, he or she is filled with anxiety over the virtual impossibility of prayer and is begging God to help him or her to utter any words at all.

One who comes to begin entreating and petitioning [God] is full of fear: his initial immediate reaction expresses itself in paralyzing terror and alarmed trembling. He asks himself: how is it possible to conduct a conversation between man and his Creator? As his lips move, he expresses with quivering and trembling his weakness and insignificance. He begins saying: "O Lord, open Thou my lips and my mouth shall declare Thy praise." That is to say: "I do not know how to move my lips and find suitable words in order to express my thoughts. God, do that for me. I entreat Thee not only about the fulfillment of my petitions and the supply of my needs, but about the matter of the prayer itself. Foolish I am and I know nothing." This is the general introduction. A confession of dejection about his baseness, his distress, and his despair. See, he is entreating the Holy One, blessed be He: "Teach me how to pray." (pp. 90–91)

There is an internal conflict in the soul of this worshiper. On the one hand, prayer is urgent and necessary. The worshiper's religious life would be sapped of all its vitality if one could not pour out one's deepest needs and feelings before God. Yet, on the other hand, the mere human being is terrified, frightened and overwhelmed by the reality of God. How dare we presume that God can be approached? It is this haunting sense of unworthiness that underlies the introductory quest for God to help one to pray.

Since this inner contradiction weighs so heavily on the worshiper, the first benediction of the Amidah tries to reassure us that we are welcome before God.

> Blessed art Thou, O Lord, our God and God of our fathers, the God
> of Abraham, the God of Isaac, and the God of Jacob, the great, the
> mighty, and the awesome God, the most high God, who bestows abun-
> dant grace, and creates all things, and remembers the gracious deeds of
> [Himself to] the fathers, and will bring a Redeemer to their children's
> children for His name's sake out of love. O King, Supporter, Savior, and
> Shield: blessed art Thou, O Lord, the Shield of Abraham.

From terror the worshiper moves to feelings of acceptance, sensing God's
abundant grace as mirrored in the creation of nature. The first benediction, which recalls God's relationship to the patriarchs, mediates for
the worshiper the way Abraham discovered God, His wisdom and His
love, in the structure of being (p. 90). The worshiper who utters the
words "the God of Abraham, the God of Isaac, and the God of Jacob"
is inspired with feelings of legitimacy and worth. It is for this reason (p.
91) that the words *melekh ha-olam*—"King of the Universe"—do not appear in the first benediction of the Amidah. The intimacy of God's love
in this benediction precludes focusing on God's majestic glory.[4] The
patriarchs who found God in nature bring God's overflowing grace to
the consciousness of the worshiper.

What a shift in the view of the manifestation of God in nature between "The Lonely Man of Faith" and "Ra'ayonot al ha-tefillah"! In the
former, reflection on nature does not lead to prayer. Nature mirrors an
impersonal God. Only in revelation of God as a personal Thou at the
covenantal moment of Sinai does prayer become possible. Here, there
is the opposite move. The God of revelation inspires terror and silence.
It is the God of nature who liberates the human being and creates prayer
as a vital living possibility. Creation is now the carrier of love, revelation
the carrier of terror. But creation does not give legitimacy to the worshiper in his or her own right. Only the worshiper who participates in
prayer as a member of a historical covenantal community can stand
before God: "On his own he who prays is worth nothing; together with
the generations he reflects the image of the father of the generations:
Abraham!" (p. 91). Although nature mirrors God's overflowing love to
every single individual, for Soloveitchik prayer is possible only through
participation in the covenantal experience of Abraham.[5]

Soloveitchik, however, expects a great change of mood in the worshiper who passes from recalling God's love and acceptance to the second benediction, which describes the power of God and the utter
helplessness and insignificance of the human being. "Pride sinks down
and humility springs up" (p. 92). The mood of self-negation and terror
acquires even greater intensity as the worshiper pronounces the third

and last of the benedictions of praise: "Thou art holy and Thy name is holy, and holy ones praise Thee every day. Blessed art Thou, O Lord, the holy God." When worshipers are conscious of God as holy, trepidation fills their hearts. They doubt their own legitimacy and are prepared to sacrifice everything to God.

For Soloveitchik, the animal sacrifices were not only a substitute for the human sacrifices of the Israelites' neighbors; rather, God only excused the Israelites from sacrificing their *bodies* on the altar, but expected them to understand that in bringing an animal sacrifice they were vicariously bringing their total personality as a sacrifice before God.

> With regard to the sacrifice as an experience the Holy One, blessed be He, demands a human sacrifice. Sacrificing an animal is only a symbolic act. The chief correlative of the external act is a spiritual act of offering a soul in sacrifice. . . . The Akedah of Isaac, which occupies such an important place in the liturgy and world view of Israel, signifies: the Akedah and sacrifice of a man. The law of sacrifices demands a human sacrifice clothed in the form of an animal. (pp. 94–95)

After the destruction of the second temple, animal sacrifices were no longer possible. Prayer then became the vehicle through which the spirit of human self-sacrifice continued as a live religious experience. Today Jewish prayer contains a sacrificial dimension when the worshipers acknowledge total dependency and helplessness before God, that only He is mighty and not they, that He is holy and they are but dust and ashes (p. 96).

Prayer and Precedent

According to Soloveitchik, it is because human beings are so insignificant and helpless before God that they are dependent upon precedent in order to dare to pray at all. For that reason, Soloveitchik considers it impossible to make the slightest change today in the forms of prayer. This not only excludes the innovations introduced in Reform Jewish worship, but even *tefillat nedavah*—spontaneous voluntary prayer. The three fixed daily prayers, in the morning, the afternoon, and the evening, are all that are permitted to a Jew.

Since it is only the distant past that legitimates prayer today, there must be absolute commitment and conformity to the prayer forms of the tradition. In utilizing the fixed forms of the tradition, I admit my own unworthiness to pray. The words of the prayer book are a gift of the tradition—I pray because my ancestors prayed. My thoughts and feelings are sacrificed on the altar through my voluntary renunciation of the possibility of introducing new prayers. By submitting to the prayer forms that the tradition has given me, I both acknowledge the absolute urgency to stand in prayer before God and confess my sense of personal unworthiness to do so.

Soloveitchik does not portray the absolute authority of *halakhah* as enslavement to tradition or as crushing human poetic passion and creativity. The willing renunciation of innovative or spontaneous prayer expresses the heroic self-sacrificial feature of Soloveitchik's dialectical anthropology. Jews submit to the halakhic form of prayer because of the existential terror that finite man feels before the infinite God, not because Judaism enslaves one to the past.

The existential characterology of self-negation is also used, in *Reflections of the Rav*, to justify opposition to the custom in Reform synagogues of allowing men and women to sit together, as opposed to the Orthodox practice of having them in separate parts of the synagogue.

> Out of this sense of discomfiture prayer emerges. Offered in comfort and security, prayer is a paradox, modern methods of suburban worship and plush synagogues notwithstanding. The desire for proximity of wife and children at services comes from a need for security and comfort. Real prayer is derived from loneliness, helplessness, and a sense of dependence. (p. 81)

Similarly, in "Ra'ayonot al ha-tefillah," there is no place for *tefillat nedavah* in Soloveitchik's approach to prayer. *Nedavah*, the free, spontaneous gift, would presuppose that God is easily approachable. Only one who feels welcome to stand before God could look upon *tefillah nedavah* as a legitimate form of prayer. For Soloveitchik, however, there is no one alive today who is qualified to act in that spirit. As individuals with their own particular religious longings, Jews have not been able to pray for centuries. They can pray only collectively as the children's children of the patriarchs, whose unique ability to initiate prayer was consolidated by the scribes and sages of the tradition. Only within the ordered framework of ritual prayer is one given the legitimacy to express petitional needs. Any outpouring of the soul that is not grounded in total subordination to the liturgical form of the Amidah must be viewed as egocentric expressions by an arrogant individual who has forgotten that prayer is a gift from the tradition and not a normal expression of covenantal consciousness.

If it is not within the worshiper's ability to present before God the whole arrangement of the prayer in its original formulation, to arrange the praise of the Lord and to request permission for his daring approach, to recall the merit of the patriarchs and also the gracious deeds of the Holy One, blessed be He, Who is responsive to the needs of all creatures—the worshiper does not have permission to ask for his own needs. An egoistic supplication which falls outside the form of prayer that was instituted by the men of the Great Assembly is forbidden. (p. 103)

Soloveitchik's covenantal man sees himself as able to stand before God exclusively because he is a remote descendant of those who received the Torah at Sinai. In his view, the covenantal community, which extends across the generations, redeems the individual Jew from an existence that is fundamentally worthless and empty of significance. It keeps us from being overwhelmed and crushed by a devine reality that seems to repulse human beings and negate their right to approach Him in prayer. We must use the absolutely immutable forms of Judaic prayer, according to Soloveitchik, because we can pray only as tiny components of a vast historical drama, not as contemporary individuals with our own sentiments and concerns. If we dare step outside the fixed structure and language of prayer handed down by the tradition, we lose the right to speak.

Prayer and the Covenant

In all of his recent writings, Soloveitchik treats all human achievements as ephemeral and insecure, liable to be snatched away at any moment by a God Who demands sacrifices. The bold, assertive actions of the patriarchs, the prophets, and the men of the Great Assembly are unique exceptions, unique both in the history of Israel and even in the lives of the persons concerned. Hence the manner in which Soloveitchik employs them as precedents: later generations are not endowed with the ability to act in the *spirit* of Abraham, Moses, or Ezra in those founding moments of covenantal history, but are merely granted the favor of being permitted to reproduce their specific actions on those occasions.

I cannot accept this position, for the simple reason that it does not do justice to the eternity of the covenant. God said to Abraham: "I will establish My covenant between Me and you and your generations for an everlasting covenant" (Gen. 17:7). And again, as Moses said to the people: "I make this covenant, with its sanctions, not with you alone, but both with those who are standing here with us this day before the Lord our God and with those who are not with us here this day" (Deut. 29:13–14). Creativity, adequacy, and boldness of spirit were not permitted by God only to those who participated in the founding covenantal moments; rather, they define the ongoing vitality of the eternal covenant between God and His human partners in every generation. They are essential features of a life lived in the spirit of a constantly reaffirmed covenant.

The men of the Great Assembly were not burdened by Soloveitchik's antinomies when they decided to introduce statutory prayer as a natural expression of covenantal intimacy. The patriarchs were not crushed by self-doubt when they approached God in prayer. Their covenantal consciousness, imbued with a sense of God's irrevocable love and acceptance, must remain a permanent feature of covenantal anthropology. One cannot separate God's covenantal commandments from His acceptance of those commanded. One cannot separate legal obligation to the covenant from its implied anthropology.

Soloveitchik tries to minimize this problem by making sacrifice into a heroic voluntary act, but it is a heroism of resignation and surrender rather than a heroism of freedom and adequacy. He supports the motif of self-sacrifice in prayer by focusing on the prophet's terror before God and viewing that as paradigmatic for the way that we should feel when we stand up to pray. I believe that this identification of prayer with the rare moments of prophetic experience is mistaken. The astonishment of Moses at the burning bush and the terror of the community at Mount Sinai have not been constant normative features of the religious life of Israel. They were unique intense moments in which an individual or a community was enveloped by a very singular overwhelming manifestation of God. Such experiences do not represent the norm of what it means to live in covenantal relationship with God.

Prayer, rather, is part of a total way of life organized by *mitzvah*. It is part of living with the knowledge that one has particular obligations and that God is concerned about and responsive to the human situation and to the way human beings live. *Mitzvah* mediates God's commanding will and His presence in everyday life. In insisting that the community observe the *mitzvot*, Judaism taught both that human beings can fulfill the divine commandments and that they have no need to feel overwhelmed, terrified, and awestruck by the divine presence when it is mediated by the commanding will present in *mitzvot*. For a covenantal Jew committed to *mitzvot*, this is a normal perception of everyday reality. Just as one regularly fulfills the *mitzvot* without terror, so also one prays regularly without terror, since prayer is part of the *mitzvah* life.[6] This is not to deny that there are possibly moments of enormous religious intensity within the prayer experience. However, they are not paradigmatic for the way one stands before God in prayer, any more than for the way one fulfills God's will in performing the different *mitzvot*.

Prayer is related to the normative experience of Judaism in which we live before God *without* being overwhelmed and terrified. It mirrors the normal religious consciousness of the believer in a personal God. The exalted rank of the prophet or the ecstasy of the mystic is not a precondition for feeling invited to participate in the prayer experience. The covenant was given to the whole community and was also meant for the most ordinary member of the community in the most elementary situations of life. Judaism as a total way of life for a whole community sets the grounds for the prayer encounter. When the community turns from its daily activities to its daily prayer, it is not demanded to make a leap from the prosaic to the ecstatic, but to express and clarify in words what its covenantal relationship with God signifies in its way of life. The relational intimacy of prayer grows out of the normative life of Judaism; it is not its antithesis.

The centrality of petitional prayer in the tradition confirms that being a needy creature and being a responsible person are not antithetical religious postures. The *mitzvah* was not given exclusively to heroes who are free from the pains and sufferings of the human condition. The covenant of *mitzvah* does not require the indifference of the stoic sage. God, in entering the covenant, accepts fully the limited and fragile features of a human life. Finitude can stand before Infinity if the ground of the relationship is covenantal. Judaic prayer, therefore, does not have to be the antithesis of the sense of dignity that grows from both the normative and the learning dimensions in Judaism.

APPENDIX

Halakhic Critique of Soloveitchik's Approach to Prayer

Soloveitchik's claim to be describing the true nature of Judaic prayer in "Ra'ayonot al ha-Tefillah" is not persuasive. The traditional texts that he cites as precedents for his interpretation are not convincing. In many cases, they suggest a posture to worship that differs from the one that he himself proposed.

Let us begin with the relationship of prayer to self-sacrifice. Soloveitchik cites Nachmanides for the idea that the burning animal represents the sacrificer. It is possible to find such statements in Nachmanides, but their theological purport is quite different. Soloveitchik cites a passage in Nachmanides' commentary on Leviticus 1:9, a passage that I shall quote more fully. The words cited by Soloveitchik are italicized.

It is more fitting to accept the reason for the offerings which scholars say, namely, that since man's deeds are accomplished through thought, speech, and action, therefore the Lord commanded that when man sins and brings an offering, he should lay his hands upon it in contrast to the evil deed committed. He should confess his sin verbally in contrast to his evil speech, and he should burn the inwards and the kidneys of the offering in fire because they are the instruments of thought and desire in the human being. He should burn the legs of the offering since they correspond to the hands and feet of a person, which do all his work. *He should sprinkle the blood upon the altar, which is analogous to his blood. All these acts are performed in order that when they are done, a person should realize that he has sinned against his God with his body and his soul, and that his blood should really be spilled and his body burned were it not for the grace of the Creator, Who took from him a substitute* and a ransom, namely, this offering, so that its blood should be in place of his blood, its life in place of his life, and that the chief limbs of the offering should be in place of the chief parts of his body.

When the whole passage is read, it becomes evident that the central idea of Nachmanides is the *sinfulness* of the human being, whereas Soloveitchik's argument centers upon his *insignificance* and *helplessness* in the face of God. As far as Soloveitchik's account goes, even were the human being completely free from sin, his mighty Creator would still be demanding animal sacrifices as an outward sign of human self-sacrifice. Soloveitchik's argument really has nothing to do with the sacrifices in the temple, but rather is concerned with the Akedah of Isaac.

Although the Babylonian Talmud establishes a connection between the *times* of the sacrifices and of prayer, it does not make the sacrifices determine the exclusive *content* and *spirit* of the daily Amidah. The Talmud (*Berakhot* 26b) traces the three daily prayers back to three prayerful moments in the lives of the patriarchs and uses the times of the daily sacrifices to define the exact hours at which the daily prayers should be said. In the Amidah of these prayers, however, it is only the seventeenth benediction that is concerned with the sacrifices, where God is asked to restore the temple and its forms of worship. It is only the additional prayers for the Sabbaths, new moons, and festivals that concentrate upon the sacrifices. In this case, the thirteen middle benedictions are replaced by one long benediction that quotes the biblical laws of sacrifice, but again its theme is a plea for God to restore the temple.

Immediately before this discussion in the Babylonian Talmud, the rabbis indeed make it clear that the sacrificial motif is not the most important factor in determining the *halakhah* of daily prayer: the theme of prayer as supplication for mercy (*rahamim*) overrides the theme of prayer as a replacement for sacrifice.

The question was raised: if a man erred and did not say the afternoon prayer, should he say it twice in the evening? Should you argue from the fact that if he erred in the evening he prays twice in the morning? [I may reply that] this is because it is all one day, as it is written: "And there was evening and there was morning, one day" [Gen. 1:5]. But in this case, prayer being in the place of sacrifice, since the day has passed, the sacrifice lapses. Or should we rather say that since prayer is supplication for mercy, a man may go on praying as long as he likes? Come and hear: for Rabbi Hunah ben Judah said in the name of Rabbi Isaac reporting Rabbi Johanan: "If a man erred and did not say the afternoon prayer, he says it twice in the evening and we do not apply here the principle that if the day has passed, the offering lapses." (Berakhot 26a)

The rabbis decided that here one does not apply the principle that "if the day has passed, the offering lapses," because daily prayer is a supplication for mercy.[7] Since God is attentive and responsive to human needs, a human being must be allowed to express those needs in worship even if from the perspective of the sacrificial motif for prayer they should be prohibited. The medieval commentary *Tosafot* remarks on this passage that the additional prayers for the Sabbaths, new moons, and festivals are *not* mentioned here; since they are so closely tied to the sacrifices, they lapse if the corresponding time has passed, "but all the other prayers count as 'supplications for mercy,' and 'would that a man would go on praying the whole day,' and there is no 'its time has passed' here on account of [the time having come for] another prayer."

That the rabbis regarded supplication for mercy as the dominant theme of the Amidah is shown by their decision to make reciting the Amidah obligatory no less for women than for men. Ordinarily, the *halakhah* excuses women from all *mitzvot* whose performance is determined by a fixed time schedule. This might be expected to apply equally to the Shema and the Amidah, since both are recited at fixed times of day. But the Mishnah rules: "Women, slaves, and minors are exempted from the Shema and from *tefillin*, but are obligated to the prayer [i.e., the Amidah], to the *mezuzah*, and to grace after meals" (Berakhot 3:3). The Jerusalem Talmud comments here: "Is it not evident that in prayer each person asks for mercy upon himself?" How can we say that men shall request divine mercy but not women? Is it not a basic need of all human beings to feel invited to stand before God in prayer? The urgent human need to supplicate for mercy overrides the technical ruling that would excuse women from *mitzvot* performed at set times.

The halakhic precedent of the sacrificial service in the temple and the formal halakhic status of women in *mitzvah* break down before the natural religious yearning of human beings for God's mercy. Soloveitchik's understanding of prayer as self-sacrifice and requiring justification from traditional precedents does not seem to fit this rabbinic approach to prayer. Prayer as yearning for mercy is the antithesis of the Akedah experience in its implications for religious behavior. It does not inhibit the worshiper, as Soloveitchik claims it must do, from freely expressing petty needs before God.[8]

> Accordingly, the Halakhah was insistent about the official character and orderliness or prayer, about the form and wording of prayer, and forbade license and arbitrariness in the approach of man to God. Were it not for the biblical passages that speak of prayer, it would be impossible to utter it. Accordingly, let us not add to it. . . . No Jew has the authority to add to the three prayers that were instituted by the scribes and sages of Israel. We do not have the authority to compose new prayers. And this is how a permanent halakhic ruling is formulated in the Talmud: "Rabbi Judah also said in the same of Samuel: 'If one was standing and saying a prayer and remembered that he had said it, he stops even in the middle' " [*Berakhot* 21a]. It is forbidden to say an obligatory prayer twice. Once is enough. One who adds is as if he had twice offered the regular sacrifice. "Rabbi ben Abba said: 'If one prays long and looks for fulfillment of his prayer, in the end he will have vexation of heart' " [*Berakhot* 32b]. We are not qualified to compose *tefillat nedavah*. Therefore, we do not now pray it. ("Ra'ayonot al ha-Tefillah," p. 89)

Neither of the passages that Soloveitchik quotes from the Babylonian Talmud implies that the terror of standing before God obliges us to rely totally upon precedent in the forms of our prayers. The first passage (*Berakhot* 21a) asserts that if someone begins reciting, say, the afternoon prayer and then suddenly remembers having already recited it earlier in the day, then that person must stop immediately—even in the middle of a blessing. This halakhic ruling simply reflects a basic halakhic principle that one does not repeat the performance of such a *mitzvah*. Once one has said the afternoon prayer fully and properly, the duty to say it has been totally exhausted, and one's obligation is now to say the evening prayer when it becomes due. A repetition of the afternoon prayer can fulfill no *mitzvah*, unlike a repetition of an act of charity. It is true that some of the medieval commentators on the passage raise the question "Could he decide to continue to recite his prayer as *tefillat nedavah?*" (spontaneous voluntary prayer) and answer it negatively. Yet this ruling, too, does not result from the awe, terror, and insignificance of man before God. It simply reflects the principle that when one begins a prayer, one must be aware of the appropriate intention. One cannot begin with the thought of offering obligatory prayer and then suddenly switch in the middle to making a voluntary offering.[9]

The same applies to his second quotation.

> Rabbi Hanin said in the name of Rabbi Hanina: "If one prays long, his
> prayer does not pass unheeded. Whence do we know this? From Moses
> our master, for it says: 'And I prayed to the Lord' [Deut. 9:26; but prob-
> ably "And I fell down before the Lord forty days and forty nights" in
> Deut. 9:18 is meant]. And it is written afterward: 'And the Lord heard
> me that time also' [Deut. 9:19]." But is that so? Has not Rabbi Hiyya ben
> Abba said in the name of Rabbi Johanan: "If one prays long and looks
> for the fulfillment of his prayer, in the end he will have vexation of heart,
> as it says: 'Hope deferred makes the heart sick' [Prov. 13:12]"? What is
> his remedy? "Let him study the Torah, as it says: 'But desire fulfilled is
> a tree of life' [ibid.]. And the tree of life is nothing but the Torah, as it
> says: 'She is a tree of life to them that lay hold on her' [Prov. 3:18]."
> There is no contradiction: one statement [Rabbi Johanan] speaks of a
> man who prays long and looks for the fulfillment of his prayer, the other
> of one who prays long without looking for the fulfillment of his prayer.
> (Berakhot 32b)

The Talmud here emphasizes two valid points that complement each
other. On the one hand, it is not wrong—but even commendable—to
pray long and earnestly about a matter that is close to one's heart. On
the other hand, it is a fundamental error to believe that everything can
be obtained from God if one prays sufficiently long and earnestly. People
who have that belief may destroy themselves with frustration and dis-
appointment if their deep wish is constantly refused. The passage does
not in any way suggest the importance of fixed forms of prayer.

Later in the article, Soloveitchik quotes another passage from the
Babylonian Talmud as proof that Jews are not allowed to formulate their
own private prayers.

> Our rabbis taught: "One who passes through a place infested with beasts
> or robbers says a short prayer." And what is a short prayer? Rabbi Eliezer
> says: "Do Thy will in heaven above and grant relief to them that fear
> Thee below and do that which is good in Thine eyes. Blessed art Thou,
> O Lord, Who hears prayer." Rabbi Joshua says: "Hear the supplication
> of Thy people Israel and speedily fulfill their request. Blessed art Thou,
> O Lord, Who hears prayer." . . . Others say: "The needs of Thy people
> Israel are many and their understanding is small. May it be Thy will, O
> Lord our God, to give to each one his sustenance and to each body what
> it lacks. Blessed art Thou, O Lord, Who hears prayer." (Berakhot 29b)

Soloveitchik points out (p. 103) that although a variety of formulas is
offered, none of them mentions the specific concerns of the endangered

traveler. The longest of the formulas offered, he claims, begins to be like the Amidah in that it confesses the inability of the worshiper to pray, yet even this only permits him to ask for the fulfillment of the needs of the individual members of the community, not specifically for help in his own dangerous situation. Personal supplications are impossible even in the situation where their need is most felt.

In this argument, there is a supposition that begs the question. It is assumed that the short prayers suggested by the rabbis are the *only* prayers that they allow the endangered traveler to offer, although this is nowhere said in the text. But this is the very point at issue: when the rabbis devised fixed forms of prayer, was their intention to supplant spontaneous prayer, or to supplement spontaneous prayer with obligatory forms that ensure that the enthusiastic, spontaneous worshiper forgets nothing essential, or to provide guidelines for satisfactory spontaneous prayer, or what? Nothing in the text enables us to answer this general question.

Still, if we want to discover what the Talmud really thinks about praying with a sense of freedom and ease, there is little to be gained from looking at passages that makes no explicit allusion to it. Rather we must consider texts that clearly discuss the possibility.

> Rabbi Eleazar says: "If one is in doubt whether he has recited the Shema or not, he says the Shema again. If he is in doubt whether he has said the prayer [i.e., the Amidah] or not, he does not say it again." Rabbi Johanan, however, said: "Would that a man would go on praying the whole day!" (*Berakhot* 21a)

Rabbi Johanan wanted individuals to feel free to pray as often as they desired to stand before God. He was happy to encourage them even if they simply wanted to repeat the fixed Amidah many times. His attitude to *tefillat nedavah* was the very contrary of the spirit of inadequacy, unworthiness, and trembling that Soloveitchik requires in one who dares to address God. Maimonides gave the same ruling in his *Mishneh Torah*.

> If a person wishes to pray the whole day, he may do so. And the prayers he adds are accounted to him as if he brought free-will offerings. He must accordingly add in each of the middle benedictions a thought appropriate to the particular benediction. If this is done in one of the benedictions only, that is sufficient, the object being to make it manifest that the prayer is voluntary and not obligatory. In the first three and last three benedictions, there must be no addition, diminution, or change. (MT *Hilkhot Tefillah* 1:11)

This ruling occurs in the context of an outline of the history of Judaic prayer. From the time of Moses onward, says Maimonides, there was a duty to say prayers daily. Until the Babylonian exile, there were no fixed rules governing the exact hours and wording of prayer, except that prayer should have the structure of praise, petition, and thanksgiving. One prayed according to one's personality, situation, and religious yearnings in an almost completely individualistic and spontaneous manner.

> One who was fluent would offer up many prayers and supplications. If one was slow of speech, he would pray as he could and whenever he pleased. Thus also the number of times of prayer depended on an individual's ability. One would pray once daily, others several times in the day. (MT *Hilkhot Tefillah* 1:3)

This situation changed, continues Maimonides, only when the Israelites were exiled to a foreign land and foreign powers ruled their own land. Their children grew up speaking an incoherent mixture of Hebrew and other languages.

> Consequently, when anyone of them prayed in Hebrew, he was unable adequately to express his needs or recount the praises of God without mixing Hebrew with other languages. When Ezra and his court of law saw this situation, they ordained the Eighteen Benedictions in their present order. . . .
> The object aimed at was that these prayers should be in an orderly form in everyone's mouth, that all should learn them, and thus the prayer of those who were not expert in speech would be as perfect as that of those who had command of a chaste style. (Ibid., 1:5–6)

It is this introduction to *Hilkhot Tefillah*, together with the shorter discussion in Maimonides' *Book of Commandments*, for which Soloveitchik terms Maimonides the "redeemer" of the notion of prayer in "Ra'ayonot al ha-tefillah," because Maimonides thereby demonstrated daily prayer to be a *mitzvah* from the Torah (p. 85). But Maimonides did not see himself as having legitimized a virtually impossible activity. Before the exile, every Israelite—not merely unique individuals such as Moses and the patriarchs—was capable of praying freely at least once a day. The loss of this capacity was due not to an innate human unworthiness to stand before God, but to the harmful effects of changed political circumstances upon children's learning of language. Prayer was given a specific form not in an Akedah spirit of self-negation, but simply to enable all members of the community once again to feel ease and fluency of speech in the moment of prayer. Institutionalized prayer implied no restriction upon those whose language had remained unimpaired; they could continue to pray spontaneously as well as saying the fixed prayers. For those who had little command of language, institutionalized prayer also made *voluntary* prayer much easier, since if they were at least capable of making a small change in one of the middle benedictions, they might "pray the whole day" if they wished to.

If one looks to Maimonides as the great halakhist who confirmed the central importance of prayer in Judaism, it is unwarranted to build a religious anthropology that is antithetical to Maimonides' understanding of how prayer is possible from a halakhic perspective. For him, the freedom and spontaneity of prayer in the earlier biblical periods was not lost, but rather regained, after prayer was given a structured form in rabbinic Judaism. The possibility for the individual to go beyond the fixed communal forms of worship remains a permanent feature of the life of Judaic faith.

The passages quoted above from the Talmud and Maimonides encourage the worshiper to add to the fixed formulas of the Amidah, albeit with explicit qualifications. In the same Judaic sources, however, there is also a classic discussion that insists on the immutability of certain expressions in the Amidah. Since Soloveitchik alludes to that discussion in "Ra'ayonot al ha-tefillah," let us see whether it could lend any support to his ban upon *tefillat nedavah*.

The starting point of the discussion is in the Mishnah, which asserts that a reader in the synagogue who says, "We give thanks," twice at the beginning of the eighteenth benediction must be silenced.

> If [a reader] says, "May Thy mercies extend to a bird's nest," "Be Thy name mentioned for well-doing," or "We give thanks, we give thanks," he is silenced. (*Berakhot* 5:3)

In its commentary on the passage, the Babylonian Talmud explains that the latter two utterances are forbidden because they detract from the unity of God.

> We understand why he is silenced if he says, "We give thanks, we give thanks," because he seems to be acknowledging two powers. Also if he says, "Be Thy name mentioned for well-doing," because this implies for the good only and not for the bad, and we have learned: "A man must bless God for the evil as he blesses Him for the good." (*Berakhot* 33b)

The rabbis did not want the community to be influenced by the Persian religion or the gnostic heresy. The former saw history as a battle between a god who is the source of all the good in the world and an-

other who is the source of all the evil; the latter distinguished between
the totally good supreme god and an inferior god who created the world
and spoke through the prophets. It was therefore vitally important not
to use a formula of thanksgiving that could hint at the existence of two
divinities. One also had to obey the dictum about blessing God for evil
as for good (an allusion to *Berakhot* 9:5). Especially during the sufferings
and wanderings of the Jewish people after the destruction of the second
temple, the community was vulnerable to the view that God has no
power over the evil that occurs in history or that the God of Israel is
not supremely good.

Daily prayer is not worship alone; it is also a powerful educational
influence upon the community. People who hear and recite certain descriptions of God every day are bound to internalize those descriptions.
The rabbis therefore had to take the greatest care in formulating them.
This is how the Talmud explains the restrictions on the formula of
thanksgiving in the eighteenth benediction of the Amidah. It is also
why the Talmud goes on to mention a restriction on the formula of
praise in the first benediction: we are not allowed to multiply praise of
God beyond saying "the great, the mighty, and the awesome God."

> A certain [reader] went down [before the ark of the Torah] in the pres-
> ence of Rabbi Hanina and said: "O God, the great, the mighty, the awe-
> some, the majestic, the powerful, the terrible, the strong, the fearless,
> the sure, and the honored." [Rabbi Hanina] waited till he had finished;
> and when he had finished, he said to him: "Have you concluded all the
> praise of your Master? Why do we want all this? Even with these three
> [attributes of praise] that we do say, had not Moses our master men-
> tioned them in the law [Deut. 10:17] and had not the men of the Great
> Assembly come and inserted them in the prayer [cf. Neh. 9:32], we should
> not have been able to mention them, and you say all these and still go
> on! It is as if an earthly king had a million denarii of gold, and someone
> praised him as possessing silver ones. Would it not be an insult to him?"
> (*Berakhot* 33b)

Fulsome praise of God is an insult, according to Rabbi Hanina, because it presupposes that human beings have the ability to utter adequate praise of God, whereas anything that they say falls incomparably
short of the plenitude of the divine reality. Even if the reader had hon-
orable intentions, he revealed how little he appreciated that God Whom
he sought to describe so admiringly.

The dictum of Rabbi Hanina forms an important testimony for Maimonides in those chapters of his *Guide of the Perplexed* in which he is
developing his "negative theology." Maimonides finds that there is no
way in which we can express God's true nature in human language. We

cannot use adjectives that describe the physical world, since God has no body. When it comes to evaluative as opposed to descriptive language, we cannot use any adjectives of praise because they are all inadequate to describe the excellence of the divine reality. Given that true praise of God is impossible, Maimonides suggests, we might well be guided by verses like "Silence is praise to Thee" (Ps. 65:2) and "Commune with your own heart upon your bed and be still" (Ps. 4:5). It is "the dictum of this perfect one," Rabbi Hanina, that explains why we can nevertheless say "the great, the mighty, and the awesome God"— but no more—in the first benediction of the Amidah. The prayer is not even allowed to include further expressions of praise of God that occur in the Bible.

> . , , it will become clear to you from this statement [of Rabbi Hanina] that we are not permitted in our prayers to use and cite all the attributes ascribed to God in the books of the prophets. For he not only says "had not Moses our master mentioned them, we should not have been able to mention them," but poses a second condition: "and had not the men of the Great Assembly come and inserted them in the prayer"—whereupon we are permitted to use them in our prayers. (*Guide* 1:59)

Here is a statement of a halakhic master that makes the language of prayer totally dependent upon ancient precedent and forbids all innovations. *This* is the kind of statement that Soloveitchik needs from classic Jewish sources on which to base his claim that petitional prayer is a virtually impossible activity that only precedent sanctions and his claim that *tefillat nedavah* is impossible today. Indeed, Soloveitchik cites the dictum of Rabbi Hanina in "Ra'ayonot al ha-tefillah" (p. 91), at the point where he starts arguing that the three attributes "the great, the mighty, and the awesome" should lead the worshiper from an initial feeling of confidence before God to a feeling of utter insignificance, helplessness, and dependence. But the discussion of Maimonides in the *Guide* makes only *praise* of God utterly dependent upon precedent. Nor has the prohibition upon exaggerated praise anything to do with an alleged impossibility of approaching God. Like the prohibition upon saying, "We give thanks, we give thanks," it is concerned not with the petitions that the worshiper may wish to address to God, but with protecting the worshiper against false notions about the nature of the God Who is being addressed. The other previous quotations from the Talmud and Maimonides also expressly place restrictions only upon the benedictions of praise and thanksgiving in the Amidah, but not upon the thirteen middle petitional benedictions. On the contrary, both sources expressly permit the worshiper to vary the wording of the middle benedictions so as to be able to "go on praying the whole day."

7

Individual and Community
in Prayer

D URING MY STUDENT DAYS at *yeshivah*, I was disturbed by the halakhic ruling that required one to pray even when one was unable to
concentrate and bring the proper devotional attitude to the prayer service. In seeking an explanation for this ruling, I was told by my teachers
that the *halakhah* is above all concerned with practice, and not necessarily with the *kavvanah*, the attitude and intention of the worshiper.
It would be praiseworthy if one could pray with *kavvanah*, but that is
not a necessary condition for prayer to be considered a *mitzvah*. The
important thing is to pray (*davin*), and hopefully *kavvanah* will come. If
it does not, at least you prayed (*davin*ed) in accordance with the demands of the *halakhah*.

I was never satisfied either with this halakhic ruling or with the explanations that were offered. From the perspective of this ruling on
prayer, it would seem that Judaism is more concerned with uniform
practice in the community than with developing religious inwardness.
Is conformism and the loss of one's own religious sensibility the price a
loyal halakhic Jew must pay for commitment to the halakhic structure
of prayer? The strong emphasis on the fixed liturgical forms and the
necessity to offer thrice daily the same Amidah prayer would seem to
suggest just that. Halakhic routine would seem to numb and alienate

one from one's own personal psychic religious vitality.[1] I do not deny that there are exceptional individuals who are able to retain their own individualistic approach to God in prayer, irrespective of the deadening weight of a prayer routine. However, if one looks at the general mode of halakhic behavior in the community, it may appear that the prayer discipline nurtures a conformist personality conditioned to think about duty and not about one's personal relationship with God. If that were the only way of understanding prayer in Judaism, it would seem to be a factor undermining the critical independent spirit I believe is necessary for the full flowering of a mature covenantal relationship with God.

Prayer and Human Needs

What is a serious problem from my perspective on Judaism is for Leibowitz a welcome indication of the true nature of halakhic worship. He sees in the absence of personal identification with the content of the prayers, and in the routine of going through the mechanical motions of worship three times a day, a perfect example for his understanding of Judaism. Halakhic prayer, he argues in "Al ha-tefillah," reflects Judaism's total indifference to the individual. Judaic prayer simply is the discharging of a duty that stems from the commitment to serve God through the performance of the *mitzvot*.

> Fixed obligatory prayer includes two elements. It is not a prayer that a person wishes to pray, but one that he is required to pray. Not a prayer that he originates, but a prayer that one demands of him. Two, it is a fixed prayer. It does not change in conformity with the conditions, circumstances, and situations, objective or subjective, in which the person who prays finds himself. (*Yahadut*, p. 385)

As a communal duty, prayer obligates different individuals regardless of their particular psychological or human situation. Leibowitz is quick to observe that the bridegroom, whose universe is filled with hope, joy, and new possibilities for intimacy and warmth, is required to say the same benedictions of the Amidah, the same Shema, the same joyful prayer celebrating the gift of life as people mourning the death of their children.

> There is only the same Amidah prayer for the bridegroom entering the *hupah* and for a widower returning from the funeral of his beloved wife. Only the very same sequence of psalms and songs for the happy person and the melancholy one, the very same sequence of supplications for whoever feels the need and whoever feels no such need. (p. 386)

Leibowitz's indifference to the covenantal framework for explaining *mitzvah* spills over to his understanding of prayer. The relational interpersonal features of the covenant have no place in the significance of prayer any more than in providing reasons for the *mitzvot*. It matters little to Leibowitz if the worshiper is bored by the prayers or fails to identify with their content. On the contrary, indifference to what is being said may in fact be requisite for authentic worship. Left to their own normal religious impulses, individuals would not dream of saying or doing what halakhic prayer has them say or do. As Leibowitz claims about *mitzvah* in general, so too about prayer: in its very estrangement from the individual's particular sensibility resides its strength.

The particular benedictions and the structure in which the Amidah is cast—praise, petition, and thanksgiving—have the same significance for Leibowitz as that which Maimonides ascribes to the choice and number of animals offered in sacrifice. Just as Maimonides argued that it would be nonsense to inquire why seven lambs and not eight were prescribed in the Torah for some particular sacrifice (*Guide* 3:26), similarly, claims Leibowitz, it would be a mistake to try to explain the particular linguistic form of the worship service. To function as a communal *mitzvah*, prayers like the sacrifices have to receive some particular form. Leibowitz's worshipers, therefore, utter the nineteen benedictions of the Amidah because they are commanded by the *halakhah* to use precisely those benedictions in prayer. If the *halakhah* had demanded that prayer consist entirely of thanksgiving or praise or whistling or silent body movements, the worshipers would comply from a sense of duty in the same way.

In denying the significance of the language of prayer, Leibowitz believes that he has resolved the thorny problem of God's response to prayer. The notion of unanswered prayer would be a contradiction in terms since one prays only because it is a *mitzvah*.

> There is no prayer which is not answered, since true prayer is only the expression of the purpose of the worshiper to serve God. The very prayer itself is the attainment of the purpose. In other words, answered prayer is a tautology, and a prayer which has not been answered is an absurd concept like a triangle that doesn't have three sides. (p. 389)

Leibowitz's approach to prayer relies not only on authoritative Judaic texts or prior legal precedents, but above all on the way the community acts out its daily religious life. Judaism as practiced by the community takes precedence for him over the authoritative texts of the tradition. Although talmudic teachers warned against making prayer a fixed routine, Leibowitz claims that the practice of daily worship as found in the *siddur*, the traditional prayer book, was victorious in Jewish history over the earlier rabbinic concern with spontaneity and individual expression in prayer. He argues that the act of reciting the same prayer three times day by day is conceptually more coherent if we ignore the individual's personal feelings and focus upon halakhic prayer as reflecting the commitment to serve God through the *mitzvot*.

For Leibowitz, consequently, the halakhic demand that one recite the Amidah prayer with *kavvanah* should not be understood as requiring the individual to reflect upon or identify with the words uttered, or to bring any specific prayerful feelings to worship. Indeed, he claims, a Jew is not required to adopt any particular devotional attitude when engaging in the *mitzvah* of prayer. *Kavvanah* in prayer is similar to the *kavvanah* that one must have when performing all *mitzvot*. It is, to use the halakhic term, *kavvanah latzet*, the intention of discharging one's obligation to God, not *kavvanat ha-lev*, a heartfelt devotional attitude.

I take issue with Leibowitz's approach to prayer on three points. The first is the *kavvanah*, the attitude and intention to be adopted in prayer. Prayer and the Shema must be recited not only from a sense of obligation to God's law, but above all as expressing the inner yearning for intimacy with God. Like Soloveitchik and many medieval commentators, I believe that *kavvanah* with regard to the Shema and Amidah is unique and should not be identified with the formal sense of duty that one brings to the performance of *mitzvot* such as *matzot* on Passover and *lulav* on Sukkot.[2] Although, for the individual Jew, the covenantal community mediates the hearing of all the *mitzvot*, nevertheless prayer and the Shema must be appropriated in a way that expresses the individual's particular sensibility and human situation. Second, I believe that the Talmud and the Judaic tradition are better understood not as sacrificing spontaneity to structure, but as seeking to maintain a balance between them.

The third and basic point is our respective appreciation of prayer as illustrative of the halakhic life. For Leibowitz, it is an example of how the *halakhah* in its entirely is constituted by collectivization of the religious consciousness. I, by contrast, view prayer and the Shema as reflecting that tendency in the *halakhah* which encourages personal initiative and responsibility within the communal system of the *halakhah*.

Leibowitz sets up an opposition between an individual who prays to bring information to God or to attain the benefits of God's power and an individual who prays because it is a *mitzvah* to worship God for no other reason than that He is God. There is, however, a third possibility, in which the worshiper neither just seeks to gain benefits nor acts exclusively out of a sense of duty. Worshipers of this third type offer prayer because they seek to express their faith in God's covenantal concern and acceptance.

It is impossible for Leibowitz to subsume any of the worshiper's personal needs under the rubric of prayer because for him need and pure worship are opposing categories. But he has failed to distinguish between two different kinds of need. There is the need of a helpless dependent person who cries out for help in economic distress or asks the doctor to heal his sick child. Different from this, at least potentially, is the need of lovers to share with each other the situations of vulnerability that either may experience. When you discuss your needs in a love relationship, you do not necessarily expect your beloved to solve your problems. Reassurance and comfort may be gained simply through knowing that your beloved listens to you in your anguish and that you are not alone in your plight. I understand petitional prayer as expressing the need of covenantal lovers of God to share their total human situation with God.

The Dependency of Covenantal Love

Some halakhic teachers have argued that the memory of the Exodus story creates the proper theological frame of reference for petitional prayer.[3] The memory of a God who miraculously intervenes in history inspires one with hope and confidence that one's personal and communal petitional needs will be answered by God. I believe, however, that halakhic prayer, with its central emphasis on petition, can be understood in the framework of the covenantal moment at Sinai.

It is interesting to observe that in early rabbinic traditions the community recited the Ten Commandments together with the Shema. This would seem to suggest that the recital of the Shema was meant to be a reliving of the covenantal moment at Sinai. Even though the recital of the Ten Commandments was discontinued, because the rabbis feared that the community would give undue importance to them at the expense of the entire Torah, the significance of the Shema as a reassertion of the Sinai covenant was never lost.[4]

In reciting the Shema, we hear God addressing the community. The emphasis, so to speak, is "Hear, O Israel, study, reflect, and be attentive to the revelatory message of Torah." It is the moment of commitment of the community to God and His Torah. In the Shema and its bene-dictions, one captures the felt immediacy of the revelatory moment of Sinai. God invites the community to enter into the covenant. The re-living of the revelatory moment of Sinai does not create a sense of hu-man helplessness, but rather it is followed by the Amidah prayer with its many petitions, in which the community gives expression to its se-curity and confidence in God's accepting love. The covenant of Sinai encourages one to come before God in direct worship.[5] Petitional prayer reflects how the worshiper feels unembarrassed to bare his or her total human situation and needs before the reality of a personal God Who demonstrated His acceptance of our humanity in the giving of the *mitz-vot* to the community at Sinai. No human need is petty or trivial before the covenantal God, Who commands a total way of life.

I believe Leibowitz is mistaken in considering the recitation of the Shema as if it were merely one among the many other *mitzvot* of the Torah. Rather, by liturgically reenacting the founding of the covenantal relationship between Israel and God, it sets the theological orientation for the worshipers' observance of the *mitzvot*.

Duty and Relational Intimacy

The Shema and the Amidah are expressive of how the covenantal Jew performs *mitzvot* from an enlivened sense of God's presence and not only from a sense of commitment to God's authoritative will as me-diated by the *halakhah*. There is a profound difference between one's sense of God during the performance of many *mitzvot* in which *kavvanah* as an expression of duty is sufficient, and one's sense of God during the Shema and prayer. It is the difference between responsibility and inti-macy. It can be compared to the difference between a man's sense of his family when he is out in the larger world trying to fulfill his manifold obligations to provide for them and when he is at home experiencing their direct presence at a family meal or discussion. With many *mitzvot*, likewise, one's manifest activity demonstrates awareness of God's com-manding authority in one's life, but the situation is markedly different when one is performing *mitzvot* through which God is experienced in His immediacy as a vivid personal reality.

We should therefore distinguish between *mitzvot* performed from a sense of duty, which require merely *kavvanah latzet*, and *mitzvot* as ex-pressive of a personal relationship, which have *kavvanat ha-lev*. Leibo-witz, in recognizing only *kavvanah latzet* and subsuming all *mitzvot* under the rubric of the Kantian notion of duty, ignores the important distinction between relational intimacy and normative responsibility. The *mitzvot* that express relational intimacy demand of the individual a distinct *kavvanah* and invite the bringing of all his or her individual spiritual yearnings into the practice of the *halakhah*. It is not the will alone that is invited to be active in such *mitzvot*, but the human being as a total personality. Even though the individual Jew hears all *mitzvot* within the context of the community, nevertheless *mitzvot* such as prayer and the Shema, which structure the relational dimension of covenantal immediacy, must be appropriated in a personal individual way. Behavioral conformity, acting from a sense of duty and commitment to halakhic rules, suffices only when the relational dimension is not the dominant spirit of the *mitzvah*.

The unique status of the *mitzvot* of prayer and the Shema can be observed in the way the Talmud deals with the ruling that the individual must decide whether he or she is capable of reciting them with the proper *kavvanah*. On the one hand, we notice in the Talmud the tendency to emphasize the importance of a fixed liturgical form, to insist that everyone is required to pray the same prayers three times daily, to pray in a quorum, and that even when praying alone at home one should try to pray at the same time as the community. Everywhere one should pray in the direction of Jerusalem. Although these disciplined elements, which create a sense of solidarity with the community, are present in prayer, the significance of the individual was not denied. Prayer and the Shema retain an important individualistic stamp through the important halakhic teachings in the Talmud that Jews must decide individually whether they are capable of bringing the proper devotional attitude to them. Not only did the Talmud require that individuals decide beforehand whether they can pray with *kavvanah* and that they repeat the Amidah if it was recited without the proper *kavvanah*, it even tells of rabbis who did not pray for three days on that account.

> Rabbi Hiyya ben Ashi citing Rav, ruled: "A person whose mind is not at ease must not pray. . . . " Rabbi Hanina did not pray on a day when he was agitated. . . . Rabbi Eliezer ruled: "A man who returns from a journey must not pray for three days. . . . " On returning from a journey, Samuel's father refrained from prayer for three days. . . . (*Eruvin* 65a)

The attitude to prayer reflected in this passage has its counterpart in rabbinic attitudes to reciting the Shema. The Mishnah discusses whether a bridegroom is capable of reciting it in the proper frame of mind on his wedding night. Do we obligate a man to engage in that *mitzvah* when we imagine that he cannot avoid being dominated by other concerns?

> The bridegroom is exempt from reciting the Shema on the first night until the outgoing of the Sabbath if he did not perform the act [of sexual consummation]. It happened that Rabban Gamaliel recited it on the first night when he married. His disciples said to him: "Our master, you have taught us that a bridegroom is exempt from reciting the Shema [on the first night]." He said to them: "I will not absolve myself from [acknowledging] the kingdom of heaven even for a moment." (*Berakhot* 2:5)

Although the Mishnah excuses the bridegroom from reciting the Shema, it taught that the option can be given to the bridegroom to decide whether he is capable of bringing the proper devotional concentration to it. In the continuation of this passage, Rabban Simeon ben Gamaliel suggests that this option is not available to ordinary human beings and must be reserved exclusively for people of exceptional devotional piety (ibid., 2:8). What is important for our purposes is that from these rabbinic discussions regarding prayer and the Shema we learn that individuals are not obligated to those *mitzvot* if their personal situation prevents them from adopting the proper devotional attitude. What conditions will prevent one from being able to concentrate on those *mitzvot* cannot be predetermined and are an individual matter. Furthermore, individuals are trusted to decide for themselves whether they are capable of *kavvanah*. Thus the *halakhah*, despite its concern with communal worship and common practice, insisted that individuals must take into account their own personal psychic and emotional situation before participating in those two *mitzvot*.

Allowing the individual to decide whether he or she is capable of bringing the proper *kavvanah* to prayer and the Shema would seem to support the claim that there is a unique *kavvanah* required in these two cases. Practices such as the eating of *matzot* on Passover or the taking of the *lulav* on Sukkot, on the other hand, are obligatory irrespective of the personal psychological mood of the person who performs them. *Kavvanah* in these *mitzvot* is *kavvanah latzet*, expressing the sense of duty and commitment to the shared practices of the community. It does not touch upon the inner personal relational feelings of the practitioner. Regarding these practices, we can indeed find rabbinic teachers who claim that one has fulfilled one's obligation to the *halakhah* even if they are performed without *kavvanah latzet*: it is sufficient to have acted in conformity with the whole community for the action to be considered a *mitzvah*. But regarding the Shema and prayer, there is agreement among commentators on the Talmud that these *mitzvot* must be performed "with *kavvanah*," meaning *kavvanat ha-lev*, since they are not related exclusively to the formal notion of duty but to the act of consciously standing before God.[6]

What the passages quoted above show is that rabbinic teachers were not afraid to allow individuals to act in a way that is different from the entire community. They were not disturbed by the fact that individuals might not pray for an extended period of time. They refused to make prayer and the Shema into habitual mechanical acts to be performed irrespective of one's personal human situation.

Structure and Spontaneity

The rabbinic approach to prayer, rather than pointing to the collectivization of Jewish religious consciousness, encourages individuals within the community to discover the personal dimension of Judaic spirituality within the communal life of the *halakhah*. In prayer and the Shema, the rabbis sought to allow the personal to be present in the framework of halakhic practice by joining individual initiative to structure, discipline, and order. They insisted that habit not triumph in the life of prayer, and they constantly admonished the community that prayer must not be a gesture that one repeats unthinkingly. They insist that one must not pray today just because one prayed yesterday. Personal supplication must be brought within the fixed framework of the petitional benedictions of the Amidah. One must even strive to bring novel elements into daily petitional prayer. This is not to deny that discipline and fixed structure can inhibit the free and natural outpouring of personal prayer. The Talmud was awake to this possibility, and it relates stories of individuals who were afraid to insert new prayers because they felt that they would lose the proper order of the service (*Berakhot* 29b). The heavy emphasis on form and reciting the fixed ritual may create a religious personality overconcerned with praying in the right way and not necessarily concerned with expressing one's own personal feelings before God. The fixed communal forms of the *halakhah* and the inner personal religious *kavvanah* are apt to struggle with each other in the life of worship. Nevertheless, talmudic teachers wanted the community to face the challenge of uniting prayer in its standard halakhic obligatory framework with prayer as a personal expression of relational intimacy with God.

Confirmation that this rabbinic attitude to prayer is still reflected in the practice of the Jewish community today is given to me by childhood memories of how my mother prayed during the synagogue service. It was very moving to listen to the way she spoke with such feelings of loving intimacy with God. In the midst of the service, I could hear her asking God to ensure that her adult sons would find good brides and that her husband would be able to support his family with dignity. Her prayers gave expression to her personal yearnings as a wife and mother. Her language was in no way inhibited or stunted. As I listened to her prayers, I did not sense that she felt unworthy to approach God with "petty" personal needs. She would have been astonished if someone had told her that the significance of prayer is to manifest an Akedah consciousness and asked how she dared feel so relaxed and easy before God. My mother, a deeply traditional Jew, prayed in the manner of generations of Jewish mothers. She continued a tradition that she received from her own family.

From my mother's prayers, I learned that commitment to structure and form does not necessarily inhibit personal expression. The personal and intimate can live within the structured formal framework of halakhic liturgy. Both together have always been part of the Judaic experience of prayer. The communal dimension is made possible through having a fixed language and appointed times for the service. The tradition endowed this aspect of prayer with seriousness, not because it believed that prayer becomes possible only through sacrificing one's own personal identity, but because halakhic Jews do not stand before God only as single individuals. They include the community in the life of worship. The community as a whole enters into the covenant of *mitzvah*, and in the prayer experience the individual Jew gives expression to his or her covenantal communal consciousness. Centrality of the community, however, was never meant to negate or crush the individual's natural impulse to pray.

The two distinct legitimizations of prayer in the Babylonian Talmud (*Berakhot* 26b)—"Prayers were instituted by the patriarchs" and "Prayers were instituted to replace the daily sacrifices"—exemplify the combination of the individual and communal dimensions in Judaic prayer. By relating the prayer service to the sacrifices of the temple, the rabbis provided a framework for the ongoing drama of communal worship even after the destruction of the temple. The morning and afternoon sacrifices had been communal in nature. They had provided a symbolic form in which the total community could recognize that it stood as a unit before God. The motif that prayer replaces sacrifice is an attempt to keep the former communal consciousness alive in the prayer experience, since the liturgy, too, provides a structure for the total community to stand as one before God. The motif that prayer was initiated by the patriarchs, on the other hand, demonstrates the essential naturalness an individual Jew feels before God. The patriarchal experience reflects the role of the individual in prayer, whereas the memory of the sacrifices expresses the role of the community. The Talmud thereby unites both the individual and the communal dimensions of prayer. The two can live together. Neither need negate or repress the other.

The fixed petitional prayers express the fundamental needs of Israel as a total community. Through those prayers, the primacy of the community is established in each individual's consciousness. Simultaneously, however, the Talmud encourages individuals to bring their own individual requests before God during their recitation of those very same petitional prayers for the community.[7] They express their personal needs before God within a structured liturgical framework that demonstrates their concern for the well-being of a total society. The communal dimension has the role of widening the range of individual consciousness, not the role of redeeming it from an exaggerated sense of nothingness and lack of worth. It is built, however, upon the dignity that individual Jews feel as worshipers who are encouraged by talmudic teachers to offer their own spontaneous prayers before God.

Both Soloveitchik and Leibowitz understand *tefillat hovah*, obligatory prayer, as expressing the highest form of religious worship. From what I have tried to show up till now, I believe, on the contrary, that the obligatory, fixed formulas of Judaic prayer determine how one *begins* the life of worship as a member of the covenantal community. To that fixed formula one can and should ultimately bring personal prayer. The test of the vitality of obligatory prayer is whether it succeeds in liberating and encouraging each individual to express what is personal in his or her dialogue with God. In contrast to both Leibowitz and Soloveitchik, I maintain that an absence of voluntary spontaneous prayer, *tefillat nedavah*, is a sign that obligatory prayer has crushed something essential to the prayer experience. The relational intimacy of the covenant has been undermined when the individual disavows any personal natural piety and feeling before God. In being thus inhibited, the worshiper demonstrates that the covenant is not a source of acceptance and dignity but of intimidation and self-negation. Judaism, through prayer and the Shema, encourages individual expressions of love of God within the communal framework of the *halakhah*. The prayer of the bridegroom and the mourner cannot be identical in a covenantal religious culture that makes prayer expressive of a personal relationship with God.

The Collectivization of Religious Consciousness

The delicate and sensitive rabbinic balance between the importance of shared practice and personal initiative and individual expressiveness in prayer was not easily digested by later halakhic teachers. Eventually, some of them rejected completely the earlier talmudic emphasis on *kavvanah* as expressive of one's personal and particular human situation. Within the medieval period, leading halakhists insisted that one is required to pray whether or not one is able to bring a proper devotional *kavvanah* to prayers. This new tradition found its most radical expression and culmination in the ruling of *Hayyei Adam*, the early-nineteenth-century halakhic code, which wholly denies the legitimacy of *tefillant nedavah*, spontaneous prayer.[8] Both Soloveitchik's and Leibowitz's respective approaches to prayer would seem to have their roots in this later halakhic tradition. Let us examine it carefully, as its implications for the role of the individual in Judaism are far-reaching.

Taking up the question of whether a bridegroom can recite the Shema, the commentary *Tosafot* writes (on *Berakhot* 17b):

> In our day nobody ever recites the Shema with proper *kavvanah*. So the bridegroom's lack of proper concentration should not be a bar to his reciting it. And if he does recite it, he cannot be charged with arrogance because there is no pretence to reciting it with *kavvanah*, since nobody ever does. Indeed, if he does not read it, he will surely be guilty of arrogance, for it would amount to him saying: "Today I do not recite the Shema because I cannot do it with *kavvanah*," as if to imply that at other times he recites it with *kavvanah*.

An interesting distinction is introduced here between the time of the Talmud and the time of *Tosafot* (later Middle Ages), in terms of the capability of praying with (proper) *kavvanah*. One cannot help asking: on what grounds is it claimed that nobody in that time recited the Shema with *kavvanah*? Had the Jewish people fallen prey to spiritual degeneration or been infected by some deep inner corruption? We know, however, that the Jews of medieval Europe demonstrated tremendous heroism in their loyalty to the Torah and the *halakhah* despite profound suffering and oppression, as evidenced by the martyrdom of simple Jewish families in France and Germany. *Tosafot* is clearly not referring to Jews whose devotion to *halakhah* is weak or shallow. How strange, therefore, for *Tosafot* to assume that *kavvanah* was available only for those who lived in the time of the Talmud, as if there is some notion of sin in the tradition by which Jews born later must necessarily be considered spiritually inferior to prior generations.

Both the *Tur* and the *Shulhan Arukh*, two major medieval halakhic codes, in many respects take a similar line. Wherever the Talmud encouraged individuals to decide whether they are able to have *kavvanah*, it is asserted that this was only for talmudic times, because then people were able to pray with *kavvanah*. "In our times," however, this is no longer so. Accordingly, the law that those who pray without *kavvanah* must repeat the Amidah is suspended.[9]

It is strange that when the *halakhah* had triumphed and won the full devotion of the community, it was nevertheless claimed that the community was unable to pray with *kavvanah*. This claim could be understood as a mode of response to the difficulty of balancing concern with objective, meticulously delineated ritual demands, which must be shared by all members of the community, against concern with personal initiative and responsibility for the *mitzvot*. Halakhic jurists did not want to burden individuals with difficult decisions regarding their own *kavvanah*. They were concerned lest the worshiper be overtaken by paralyzed self-doubt: "Am I able to pray with *kavvanah*? Did I really pray with *kavvanah*? Did I bring my full heart into the proper devotional attitude in my intimate dialogue with God? Perhaps I should pray again?" It may well be that to free individual Jews from torturous self-doubts regarding their relationship with God, the halakhists ruled: "We need not today repeat the Amidah or the Shema if we said it without *kavvanah*, or concern ourselves with our personal, psychological human situation. It is sufficient if we recite the prayers, and we can be assured that we have fulfilled our duty."

I prefer, however, to believe that this important halakhic claim was not descriptive of the contemporaneous religious condition of the community, but was rather a legal construction meant to prevent the formal halakhic structure from being invaded by the anarchistic possibilities that may result when individuals are given the responsibility to decide whether they are able to pray with the proper *kavvanah*. I believe that this is so for several reasons. First, as was noted, the medieval Jewish community took the *halakhah* very seriously, as the enormous bulk of *responsa* literature in this period also testifies. There is no reason to believe, therefore, that the religious devotion of this self-enclosed halakhic community was in any way inferior to that of the talmudic period. Second, if it was believed that the community was spiritually inferior and therefore unable to bring the proper devotional attitude to the recitation of the Amidah and the Shema, why was true *kavvanah* depicted in such lofty terms? The *kavvanah* one should have in prayer is described in far more rigorous and demanding terms in the *Tur*, the *Shulhan Arukh*, and the later code *Hayyei Adam* than in the Talmud.[10] It would have been odd to bring such expectations to a community believed to be in some very important way spiritually inferior. To expose the community to such exalted demands concerning *kavvanah* and yet claim categorically that "in our time we cannot have *kavvanah*" is like inviting great spiritual excellence from a friend and then defining him as fundamentally sinful and corrupt. You do not excite the imagination of weak, limited, and inferior human beings to strive for spiritual excellence unless you are in some way infected with a spirit of sadism, which these rabbis were not.

Furthermore, if the claim "We do not have *kavvanah*" is descriptive of the prayer condition of the community and not just a legal construct used to prevent the individualization of the spiritual life within the *halakhah*, why was *tefillat nedavah* (voluntary prayer) permitted? These halakhists knew of the tradition of Asher ben Yehiel (c. 1250–1327), who claimed that *tefillat nedavah* should not be engaged in unless one is certain of being able to pray with *kavvanah*. Consequently, if the claim "We in our time do not have *kavvanah*" was descriptive of the actual condition obtaining in the community, these halakhists should also have ruled out *tefillat nedavah*, as indeed *Hayyei Adam* later did. The fact that they allowed *tefillat nedavah*, although they proclaimed that all the strict demands of the Talmud regarding *kavvanah* were no longer applicable to *tefillat hovah* (obligatory prayer), would seem to suggest, therefore, that they were not describing the realities of the community in claiming, "We do not have *kavvanah*," but trying to prevent the structure of halakhic obligation from being infused with the spirit of individualism. They could allow *tefillat nedavah*, however, because individual discretion did not threaten anarchy when it did not touch on the obligatory framework of the *mitzvot*.

The concern for shared practice and an ordered religious community seems to have won out in the structure of halakhic obligation at the expense of retaining personal initiative and responsibility. As long as *halakhah* is objective, communal, and ordered, the system is in no way threatened by the anarchic possibilities of individualism. That triumph may ensure that the community will act in a uniform way. A heavy price, however, is paid for the security of such halakhic standardization. It builds into religious life a sense of spiritual inferiority in relation to prior generations, which undermines the dignity that comes with belief and trust in one's own creative religious powers and intuitions. A model of worship of God that denies that praying with devotion is equally available to all generations destroys something vital in the religious life.

Prayer in Maimonides

The master halakhic codifier who did not move in this direction, who did not create a qualitative distance between the religious capabilities of individuals in his generation and those of the Talmud, was Maimonides. He did not assume that the ability to pray with *kavvanah* was available to those who lived in the talmudic era and not to Jews living in his own time. In the *Mishneh Torah*, he makes the same demand for *kavvanah* as the Talmud had made, giving individuals the same freedom to decide whether they are able to recite their prayers with *kavvanah*. Similarly, he applies the Talmud's prohibition against prayer by a person who is emotionally agitated or exhausted to Jews living in his own time. In Maimonides, there is no radical distinction between the halakhic Jews of his time and those of the Mishnaic and talmudic discussions.[11]

By not accepting that there is a necessary spiritual degeneration in history (that is, that the further a generation is from Sinai, the more inferior its spiritual capacities), Maimonides enabled loyalty to tradition not to turn into slavish obedience nurtured by a sense of guilt and inadequacy.[12] The laws of the Shema and the Amidah appear in *Sefer Ahavah* in the *Mishneh Torah*. This book, which invites the individual to consider how specific *mitzvot* point to the ideal of love of God, contains a halakhic framework that encourages individual decision making, initiative, and personal responsibility. Where there is an emphasis on love in the *halakhah*, there must be a readiness to allow individuals to break from routine and give expression to their total personality. This is possible if individuals can be trusted to decide whether they are capable of *kavvanah*. Love and joy become possible in the halakhic community when rigidity and anxious concern for uniform practice do not totally dominate its worship.[13]

Both Soloveitchik and Leibowitz believe that their respective approaches to Judaism and prayer reflect the teachings and spirit of Maimonides' philosophy of Judaism. For Soloveitchik in "Ra'ayonot al hatefillah," the Maimonidean emphasis on prayer as *avodah she-be-lev*, service of the heart, should be understood to mean that prayer is an act of total self-sacrifice and surrender before God. In Leibowitz's view, the dimension of service of the heart should not be understood as allowing for individual experiential feelings in the life of worship. Central to his concern is the emphasis that Maimonides places on prayer as *mitzvah*.

I believe, however, that Maimonides' understanding of prayer as *avodah she-be-lev* is an invitation to individuals to discover their own personal and individual mode of worship within a system in which common practice and community are so heavily emphasized. In contrast to Leibowitz, it reminds the halakhic Jew that common religious practice is no bar to individualized religious love. In contrast to Soloveitchik, it does not require the sacrifice of the personal dignity of the individual before the weight of the authoritative framework of the halakhic tradition. The community, for Maimonides, is not the exclusive ground of legitimization for prayer.

Stages in the Life of Worship

As we saw in chapter 4, Maimonides devoted much of the last book of his *Guide of the Perplexed* to showing that a rational justification could be given for the *hukkim*, which had traditionally been regarded as *mitzvot* that Jews observe because of God's unconditional authority. In clarifying the way the biblical historical context influenced the revelation of the different *mitzvot*, Maimonides makes a statement that encapsulates his understanding of the whole purpose of the giving of the Torah at Sinai as well as defines the successive stages of worship through which God intended to lead the Israelite community.

> At that time, however, the way of life generally accepted and customary in the whole world, and the universal service upon which we were brought up, consisted in offering various species of living beings in the temples in which images were set up, in worshipping the latter, and in burning incense before them, since the pious ones and the ascetics were at that time . . . the people who were devoted to the service of the temples consecrated to the stars. Therefore His wisdom, may He be exalted, and His gracious ruse, which is manifest in regard to all His creatures, did not require that He give us a law prescribing the rejection, abandonment, and abolition of all these kinds of worship. For one could not then conceive the acceptance of [such a law], considering the nature of man, which always likes that to which it is accustomed. (*Guide* 3:32)

At Sinai it was impossible to explain to the community the higher forms of worship that God truly desired, because the Israelites, as a result of their extended stay in Egypt, knew only of animal sacrifice as the way one approaches a god. The Torah had to provide the community with a slow educational process that would start with its current conception of what constituted proper worship and gradually introduce it to higher forms of worship. The starting point of Maimonides' understanding of worship is the claim that in evaluating what is appropriate to a given community, we must take into account the particular intellectual and emotional sensibilities of its members. Forms of worship that are a close approximation to the highest relationship that human beings should have with God cannot be utilized if they are unrelated to the particular psychological sensibility of the worshiper. To ask in biblical times that worshipers give up the visual drama of the sacrifice, that their relationship to God be expressed merely through refined forms of language, would have been to ask them to adopt forms of worship that were alien to their temperament and contradicted their perception of how one expresses a living relationship with God.

Maimonides offers a striking analogy to bring home to the reader the reason for the biblical legitimization of biblical sacrifices.

> At that time this would have been similar to the appearance of a prophet in these times who, calling upon the people to worship God, would say: "God has given you a law forbidding you to pray to Him, to fast, to call upon Him for help in misfortune; your worship should consist solely in meditation without any works at all." (Ibid.)

From the above passage, it would appear that Maimonides recognized three different stages in the life of Judaic worship. In the first stage, the community is instructed to offer sacrifices. The main concern during this stage of worship is to wean the community away from idolatry. The second stage is when the community's worship centers upon petitional prayer. This stage is described in the closing sentence: "to pray to Him, to fast, to call upon Him for help in misfortune." It was this second stage that defined the form of worship both in talmudic times and in the medieval period of Maimonides. The closing sentence of this quotation suggests the existence of a third and yet higher stage of worship. The words "this would have been similar to the appearance of a prophet in these times" hint unambiguously that the highest form of worship should consist solely in meditation, namely, the contemplative worship mentioned in chapter 5.

Although the biblical stage of animal sacrifice had been left behind, the mass of the community was still not ready for contemplative worship. Daily worship centered upon petitional prayer. In times of crisis, they would fast and cry out to God. The majority of the community believed that the essential significance of prayer was to seek out God's intervention and help. If the community had been instructed that worship should consist in contemplation, then God would quickly have ceased to be a living reality for them. Maimonides understood that only rare individuals are able to worship God in a spirit of disinterested love.

He did not expect that the mass of the community in the historical conditions then prevailing could be drawn toward worship of that kind. An oppressed and frightened community burdened with political and economic hardships could hardly be expected to transcend its needy situation in the moment of worship. It is difficult to educate a community in the direction of contemplative love when one is faced with the suffering of hungry children and the current threat of religious persecution. The significance of the messianic era for Maimonides was precisely that the political and economic situation of the community would have so improved that its relationship to God would open up greater possibilities of love of God.[14]

Maimonides understands the *halakhah* not only as prescribing forms for the community, but also as providing opportunity for individuals to advance in their spiritual growth *ahead* of the general level of the community. When he asserts in the *Mishneh Torah* that daily prayer is a commandment from the Torah, he also notes that prayer in the biblical period was an individualistic form of worship.

> The number of prayers is not prescribed in the Torah. Nor does the Torah prescribe a fixed time for prayer. . . . One who was fluent would offer up many prayers and supplications. If one was slow of speech, he would pray as he could and whenever he pleased. Thus, also, the number of separate services depended on an individual's ability. One would pray once daily; others several times in the day. (MT *Hilkhot Tefillah* 1:2–3)

Thus the Torah on the one hand prescribed detailed forms of sacrificial worship binding upon the community as a whole, but on the other hand, with its commandment of daily prayer, it encouraged different members of the community to rise to whatever level of worship each was capable of achieving. Some would pray in simple and slow speech, others with eloquence; some would pray just once a day, others frequently.

The above understanding of prayer, quoted from the *Mishneh Torah*, is taken a stage further at the end of the *Guide*. As Moses through bringing down the Torah from Sinai enabled singular individuals to find their way in a context of sacrificial worship, so Maimonides in the *Guide* sought to provide the opportunity for individuals to aspire toward contemplative love of God in a halakhic context of worship based on petitional prayer.

In contemplative love, now equated with "service of the heart" at the end of the *Guide*, God is worshiped simply because He is God. The anthropocentric stimulus to worship has given way to the theocentric one. The consciousness of divinity felt in this moment of philosophical reflection makes it possible to embrace God fully within the world as it is given. When this moment of worship is achieved, the worshiper has transcended the petitional need structure of halakhic prayer. He or she has moved from worship based upon fear of God to worship grounded in love.[15]

Philosophy paves the way for the highest stage of worship of God. In reflecting on the universe and in enjoying the orderly causal patterns of nature, one is not simply studying physics. This reflective experience is filled with the passion and joy of a God-intoxicated lover who seeks to be claimed exclusively by the manifestation of the divine reality in the causal order of the world. It is apprehension of God through knowledge of His governance of the universe, Maimonides tells his reader, that lets you "afterwards engage in totally devoting yourself to Him, endeavor to come close to Him and strengthen the bond between you and Him" (Guide 3:51). It is what leads to that contemplative love of God that constitutes the fullest expression of "service of the heart."

When the objective reality of God takes hold of the mind, one is freed from relating to God out of any sense of deprivation. In joyfully appreciating and accepting the orderly patterns that reflect God and nature, one transcends modes of worship that center on expecting God to transform the given condition of human nature and society. One makes contact with God out of the given and not out of a framework of anticipation.[16]

The very same Judaic sources that Maimonides uses in the Mishneh Torah to show that prayer is a commandment from the Torah are used in the Guide to identify the highest form of worship as contemplative love of God based upon the valid apprehension of Him and His acts. This confirms my contention that for Maimonides "service of the heart" signifies the worship that individuals offer over and above their duty to participate in institutional communal worship: prayer in the biblical period, contemplative love in the time of Maimonides. Service of the heart began as a mitzvah of daily prayer in the biblical period, when it enabled and encouraged the individual to rise above the level of sacrificial worship. In the Mishneh Torah, Maimonides shows how the halakhic elaboration of that mitzvah established a central place for prayer in the communal life of Judaism, with a dominant emphasis on petitional prayer. The Guide, however, makes it clear that the ultimate goal of service of the heart is not the disciplined pattern of communal halakhic prayer. Service of the heart finds its ultimate realization in the way a philosopher transcends the halakhic focus of communal petitional prayer.

In my appreciation of prayer, I have striven to continue what I believe to be the spirit of Maimonides' understanding of *mitzvah* and *halakhah*. For Maimonides, *halakhah* can be an expansive and accommodating system. It can withstand the critical passion of the philosopher. It can absorb ways of spirituality that are expressive of the unique capacities of individuals rather than be merely the standard legal practices of a community.

Spinoza misunderstood the role of the individual in Judaism because he rejected Maimonides' integration of philosophy into the four cubits of the *halakhah*. Spinoza sees only law and obedience as constituting the essence of Judaism. Maimonides charts a path for the individual by showing how Judaism enables one to move from sacrifices through petitional prayer to the passionate lovesickness of one who is dazzled by the beauty and reality of God's creation. To pray in the spirit of Maimonides is to open up the halakhic system to the dignity of the individual. In contrast to both Leibowitz's and Soloveitchik's models of prayer, patterned either after the Kantian notion of duty or the Akedah of self-sacrifice, I understand prayer as capturing the relational intimacy of the covenant. Rather than self-negation and self-effacement, prayer reflects the worshiper's confident mood of being fully accepted by God as a total person.

PART TWO

The Covenant
and the Living God
of History

8

Rabbinic Responses to Suffering

I N THIS WORK, I am not arguing for either the superiority or the necessity of a covenantal orientation to life for the realization of human responsibility and dignity. In thinking about Judaism, I cannot ignore the fact that atheists act with moral dignity and compassion in the world. I believe, in contrast to many contemporary religious thinkers,[1] that secular humanism is a viable and morally coherent position. What I am claiming is only that neither the critique of halakhic Judaism found in the Christian tradition nor the moral critique found in Spinoza is convincing. There are many different approaches to human life that encourage initiative, intellectual freedom, responsibility, and the sense of personal adequacy and dignity. I am not arguing that faith is necessary in order to have these values, but only that faith in the covenantal God of Judaism does not have to contradict or undermine them.

I have sought to show, accordingly, that the posture of the human partners to the covenant need not be one of submission and helpless dependency. Dignity has been conferred upon them by the divine call to undertake the broad range of responsibility implicit in the covenantal *mitzvot*. Nor need their failures to live up to that responsibility create in them a fear of rejection by God, since the doors of repentance, as the rabbis say, are always open.[2] The acceptance of that responsibility therefore need not entail the paralyzing sense of guilt alleged in Paul's criticism of the law. Nor does *mitzvah* demand unconditional obedience without rational discernment, since the *halakhah* expects from Jews not just a dedicated will to serve God but also a reflective, sensitive, and critical moral disposition.

To establish my claim, however, it is not enough to indicate, as in the previous chapters, that such values manifest themselves in the different domains of the halakhic way of life. This would be to focus exclusively upon the human partners to the covenantal relationship while ignoring the role attributed to God in that relationship. Such an approach might well be accused of reducing the Torah to a humanistic ethical system by omitting what the Torah has to say about God. The God of Sinai does not merely hand over responsibility for the *mitzvot* to Israel and then take His leave. He also commits Himself to permanent involvement in the history of the community, promising magnificent rewards for observance of the *mitzvot* and threatening terrible punishment for transgressions against them. Long and dramatic lists of those promises and threats are given in Leviticus and Deuteronomy. Since rabbinic times, Jews have daily recited part of such a passage as the second chapter of the Shema.

> And it shall come about, if you listen obediently to my commandments which I am commanding you today, to love the Lord your God and to serve Him with all your heart and all your soul, that He will give the rain for your land in its season, the early and the late rain, that you may gather in your grain and your new wine and your oil. And He will give grass in your fields for your cattle, and you shall eat and be satisfied. Beware, lest your hearts be deceived and you turn away and serve other gods and worship them. Or the anger of God will be kindled against you, and He will shut up the heavens so that there will be no rain and the ground will not yield its fruit; and you will perish quickly from the good land that the Lord is giving you. (Deut. 11:13–17)

The rabbinic as well as the biblical perspective upon the covenant is one in which Jews cannot judge their own actions independently of what they believe to be God's response to those actions, namely, subsequent events in nature and in history. This perspective constitutes a serious challenge to my claim that the covenant encourages human dignity and adequacy. Let me explain. The Bible and the rabbinic literature attest that Jews *failed* to find direct, stable, and predictable connections between their behavior, whether as individuals or as a community, and subsequent events. When meticulous attempts to live up to covenantal responsibilities were followed by unexpected disasters, was it because of some undetectable flaw in apparently exemplary behavior, or was it because of the sins of earlier years or even of previous generations?[3] When the wicked prospered, on the other hand, how long would one have to wait for divine punishment? One cannot ascribe a sense of dignity to people who are burdened by such questions and are unable to handle their understanding of how God responds to their lives.

The rabbis were deeply concerned with this problem. This chapter examines how they offered possibilities for coping with it in the life of the individual, while the next chapter will indicate how they dealt with it on the level of the community as a whole. In the final chapters of the book, I shall offer a conception of a personal God mediated exclusively through Torah and *mitzvot*.

Events and the Living God

Let us now examine, accordingly, how the rabbis dealt with the problem of the impact of natural and historical events upon the religious consciousness of the individual Jew. It would be a mistake to think that this was not a serious problem for the rabbinic tradition because the relational immediacy of the living God of revelation had been neutralized by the talmudic emphasis upon study of Torah and questions of legal authority and practice. The enormous concern with exegesis and fine legal distinctions should not be thought to have diminished the vitality of the covenantal passion for God. Rabbinic teachers brought the religious intensity of the living God present at the revelatory moment of Sinai into their daily experience of the study of Torah. That study, they claimed, should indeed be felt as an experience akin to revelation. It should take place "in dread and fear and trembling and quaking" just like the Sinai experience (*Berakhot* 22a). If even only two people sit together and occupy themselves with the Torah, the divine presence rests between them (*Pirkei Avot* 3:6).

In talmudic as in biblical times, Jews perceived every aspect of reality in their world as expressive of the personal will of God. Schematically speaking, we may say that the covenantal community experienced God as an active personal will in three basic ways: in its consciousness of (1) its physical existence, (2) its sociopolitical existence, and (3) its normative daily life. First, the creation of the physical world and the human species was not perceived as merely a single act of the divine will in the distant past. Rather, as the first benediction of the Shema puts it, Jews saw God as Him Who "in His goodness renews every day by day the work of creation." At every present moment, the will of God decided whether their physical existence should continue or cease. Second, their sense of history and social consciousness took its beginning from and never forgot the story of Exodus, in which a stupefied mass of slaves had been transformed into a living social reality through God's decision to lead them out of the social chaos of Egypt. Just as nature was not to be explained without the God of Creation, so the community owed its social and historical existence to the Lord of History through Whose intervention it had been born. Neither the physical nor the communal existence of Jews was intelligible without reference to a transcendent personal will. Third, there was the Torah, which functioned as a permanent mediator of God's personal relationship to the community. The *mitzvot* are not abstract demands implied by a Platonic form or a Kantian categorical imperative; they are demands made by a personal will and presuppose a personal relationship to God.

Given, therefore, that the rabbis lived in a universe in which everything was related to a personal God with a spontaneous will, how did the rabbinic tradition educate Jews to sustain commitment to that personal God in spite of the serious gap that developed between their expectations based on the biblical promises and their actual experience? Unpredictable relationships, in which one never knows how one will be treated, do not leave an individual unscarred. They are not conducive to the development of spontaneity and feelings of self-worth, especially if one's total sense of personal worth is measured by the perceived responses of the divine covenantal partner to one's actions.

A covenantal religious consciousness is always vulnerable to self-doubt and to feelings of rejection and guilt. When suffering and tragedy have struck without any explanation once, twice, and repeatedly, individuals in the community no longer know what kind of world they are living in. Like Job, they may ask: "Why do You hide Your face and treat me like an enemy?" (Job 13:24).

When drought occurs and hunger becomes a real threat, rabbinic Jews are taught to fast, pray, and sit as mourners. The lack of rain not only brings economic hardship but also awakens feelings of rejection and alienation. One confronts the unpredictable events of nature as a rejected mournful son of the covenant. "If all these fast days are past and they have not been answered, they place limits on business transactions, building, and planting, on betrothals and marriages, and on mutual greetings, as benefits persons under divine displeasure" (*Ta'anit* 1:7).

Similar in spirit to this statement from the Mishnah was my father's reaction one year on the first night of Sukkot when a sudden rainstorm forced our family to leave the *sukkah*. Our family had built a beautiful *sukkah* in joyful expectation of celebrating the festival, which reenacts God's providential protection of the community in its desert wanderings. The Sukkot holiday educates the community to trust in God's love. I cannot forget my father's explanation to his children as we left the *sukkah*. "God must be displeased tonight with the community of Israel. He does not welcome us into His 'canopy of peace.' " The rain was seen as a sign of divine anger and rejection.[4] A perception of God that understands a simple rainstorm as a manifestation of divine displeasure can have destructive psychological consequences. If such a perception typifies covenantal consciousness, it calls into serious question my claim that the covenant encourages human dignity and initiative.

In examining how the rabbis sought to handle this problem, we may say that their approach belongs more to what we would now call religious anthropology than to philosophical theology. This distinction is of basic importance. To the philosopher or theologian concerned with the problem of theodicy, the existence of morally indifferent causes of suffering appears to be incompatible with the existence of an all-powerful and benevolent God. Such an individual is faced with the problem of reconciling what seems to be an incompatibility of facts and beliefs. How is it logically possible to claim that God is the just Lord of History in the light of the senseless evil manifest in the world?[5] The problem of suffering appears in a different light, however, when the focus is more on its anthropological than its theological implications. The question then becomes: How do we respond to events that can call into question our whole identity as God's relational partners? Can we allow ourselves to embrace a personal God, knowing that chaos can at any moment invade our reality and arbitrarily nullify all our efforts and expectations? Do we have the strength to open ourselves to a personal God in a world filled with unpredictable suffering? When her child dies, the question a mother faces is less how to explain the logic of God's omnipotence than whether she has the strength and emotional energy to love again.

From the anthropological perspective on the problem of evil, therefore, the prime concern is not so much to defend the notions of divine justice and power. It is rather, as in other personal relationships, to determine what measure of continuity, stability, and predictability can enable the relationship with God to survive all shocks. It is to identify the cluster of beliefs that supports a person's will to persist in the face of tragedy and suffering. If the world I live in requires that I become overly vigilant because of the threat of danger striking at any moment, then how can I sustain commitment to a way of life predicated on God's covenantal love and justice?

God's Promises of Reward and Punishment

How the rabbis confronted the problem[6] will be shown by examining some texts, of which the first contains a discussion of two conflicting descriptions of divine providence.

> He who performs one *mitzvah*, good is done to him, his days are prolonged, and he inherits the land. But he who does not perform one *mitzvah*, good is not done to him, his days are not prolonged, and he does not inherit the land. (*Kiddushin* 1:10)

Although some authorities take "and he inherits the land" to mean "and he has a part in the world to come," the emphasis in this statement is decidedly this-worldly. Indeed, this statement from the Mishnah is hardly different in spirit from the Bible. The biblical perspective is earthbound. It typically invites one to expect prosperity in this world if one is loyal to God's *mitzvot*, to anticipate rain in due season, abundant crops, many children, security from adversity, a long and good life.

The Talmud finds this statement problematic but not so much because it does not accord with observed fact. After all, the Bible itself already contains dissentient voices (Job, Ecclesiastes) that point out that virtue is not always automatically rewarded. By the time of the Mishnah, Jews had had much more than enough experience to controvert biblical optimism. What arouses the talmudic sages is not that the statement appears to be false as an assertion of fact, but that it is contradicted by a *baraita*—another authoritative statement from the age of the Mishnah.

> But the following [*baraita*] contradicts [the statement of the Mishnah]. He whose good deeds outnumber his iniquities, evil is done to him, and he is [punished by God in this world] as if he had burnt the whole Torah, not leaving even a single letter [so as to be free of punishment in the world to come]; while he whose iniquities outnumber his good deeds, good is done to him, and he is [unpunished by God in this world] as if he had fulfilled the whole Torah, not omitting even a single letter [because he will receive punishment in the world to come]. (*Kiddushin* 39b)

This *baraita* claims that when people strive to be righteous in this world, God's response is to inflict upon them suffering that will expiate their sins, so that they can enjoy complete bliss in the world to come. But people who prefer iniquity to righteousness are allowed to prosper in this world, because they have already ensured themselves punishment in the world to come. The succeeding discussion shows the talmudic sages to be concerned to know, in the first place, whether the Mishnah and the *baraita* actually do contradict each other. Abbaye points out that if we reinterpret "good is done to him" in the Mishnaic statement to mean "he suffers as much as is necessary to purge him of his sins," then it is identical in meaning with the *baraita*. Rava points out that this *baraita* accords with Rabbi Jacob's interpretation. Rabbi Jacob had said that there was no reward for *mitzvot* in this world and that wherever the Torah promises a reward for a *mitzvah*, the reward is to be expected only in the next world. To illustrate his assertion, Rabbi Jacob told a story of a child who died immediately after fulfilling two *mitzvot*: the child obeyed his father, who had told him to take birds from the loft, and he obeyed the biblical requirement of letting the mother bird go free before taking the young ones. Yet, although the Bible promises long life to those who fulfill either of these *mitzvot*, on descending from the loft the boy fell and was killed.

> There is not a single *mitzvah* in the Torah whose reward is [mentioned] alongside it which is not dependent on the resurrection of the dead [for receiving the reward]. In connection with honoring parents, it is written: "that your days may be prolonged and that it may go well with you" [Deut. 5:16]. In reference to the dismissal [of the mother bird] from the nest it is written: "that it may be well with you and that you may prolong your days" [Deut. 22:7]. Now, if one's father said to him, "Ascend to the loft and bring me young birds," and he ascends to the loft, dismisses the mother, and takes the young, but on his return falls and is killed— where is this person's happiness and where is this person's prolonging of days? But "that it may be well with you" means on the day that is wholly good; and "that your days may be long"—on the day that is wholly long. (Ibid.)

"Wholly good" and "wholly long" allude to the time of the world to come. Rabbi Jacob's example awakened the interest of the talmudic sages. Was it a hypothetical example, or had he witnessed such an event himself?

> Yet perhaps there was no such happening? Rabbi Jacob saw an actual occurrence. Then perhaps [the boy] was meditating upon a transgression [at the moment when he fell]? The Holy One, blessed be He, does not treat an evil thought as a [corresponding] act. Yet perhaps he was med-

itating idolatry, and [in this case just the thought is enough, as] it is written: "[Any man of the house of Israel who sets up his idols in his heart . . . I the Lord will be brought to give him an answer in the matter . . .] in order to lay hold of the hearts of the house of Israel [who are estranged from Me through all their idols]" [Ezek. 14:4–5]? That too was precisely [Rabbi Jacob's] point: should you think that mitzvot are rewarded in this world, why did the mitzvot [that he had just fulfilled] not shield him [as a reward] from being led to [such] meditation? (Ibid.)

Rabbi Jacob's judgment that there is no reward for mitzvot in this world resulted from a personal experience. Let us for a moment try to reconstruct dramatically the course of events as he may have experienced them. He saw the eagerness on the child's face when the child went to perform the father's wishes. He felt the joy of the father, who was giving his child the opportunity of a long and prosperous life, as the Torah promises to whoever fulfills the relevant mitzvot. Moments later, however, he witnessed the sharp and ironic contrast between the father's confident solicitude and the unanticipated tragedy of the child's sudden death.

One who sees such an incident cannot remain unaffected. Life appears ludicrous, bizarre. Reality appears to mock all human anticipations and dreams. The abyss separating the father and son's joyful expectancy and what in fact took place forced Rabbi Jacob thenceforth to live the covenantal life exclusively in anticipation of the eschatological moment of resurrection. Only in a redeemed world, he concluded, can we witness the full realization of the covenantal promise. The world of the present is open to much suffering. Our task is to be loyal to the mitzvot no matter what ensues, to understand that in an unredeemed world our will must be anchored to the performance of the mitzvot of God. This is all we can have in this world. Joy, ease, and prosperity belong to the world to come. The unredeemed world of the present is too fragile a vessel for the biblical promises.

This radical reinterpretation of the biblical promises is not allowed to pass without serious questioning. "Perhaps there was no such happening?" One wonders, however, what difference it made whether Rabbi Jacob did or did not see the incident. The discussants knew that there was evil and suffering in the world. The child was not the only innocent or righteous individual to suffer or die prematurely despite, or even because of, loyalty to the mitzvot. Yet it is interesting to note that the focus here is on one particular incident.

When the Talmud begins to question the right of Rabbi Jacob to make his judgment on the basis of what he saw, it is not the larger drama of history that is invoked, but whether Rabbi Jacob could truly claim to have seen an innocent child going to perform two *mitzvot*. Possibly what he really saw was a child with sinful thoughts, a child meditating on idolatry. Since there is a hidden world of human thoughts not available to the observer, empirical evidence cannot provide an infallible basis for claiming to understand what has in fact occurred. That being the case, how could Rabbi Jacob use personal experience to set aside the patent meaning of biblical verses? Can human beings with their limitations ever know reality sufficiently to make such far-reaching judgments on God's relation to the covenantal community?

The answer given by the Talmud, whose gist is "If there is any reward in this world, then God should have protected the child from thinking such evil thoughts," can be read as implying that we have no other alternative but to judge on the basis of what we see. It would strain the plausibility and credibility of the covenantal outlook if we were allowed to suspect that behind the manifest performance of *mitzvot* by Jews there might lie a pagan idolatrous mentality. The justification of the death of a child on the basis of unprovable sins of idolatry is incompatible with an understanding of *halakhah* that encourages individuals to render judicial decisions on the basis of what they see. The Talmud prefers to believe that there is no reward in this world rather than let unsupported suspicion destroy our confidence in our ability to distinguish between obedience and disobedience to the *mitzvot*. It therefore grudgingly accepts the testimony of Rabbi Jacob and allows him to reinterpret the divine promises in the Bible on the basis of his own experience.

Even so, the Talmud is still not satisfied. How could the incident have happened, since there is a tradition from Rabbi Eleazar that suggests that the child should have enjoyed divine protection?

> Yet Rabbi Eleazar said: "Those who are sent on a *mitzvah* are never harmed"? There, when they are on their way, it is different. But Rabbi Eleazar said: "Those who are sent on a *mitzvah* are never harmed, either on their way or on their return"? It was a rickety ladder, so that injury was likely, and where injury is likely one must not rely on a miracle. (Ibid.)

The tradition of Rabbi Eleazar embodies a crucial principle of the covenantal outlook. God may not reward *mitzvot* with long life and prosperity and security, but He surely does not deny Jews the opportunity to fulfill the very demands that He Himself requires of them. This is a talmudic version of the philosophical notion that "ought" implies "can." There cannot be *mitzvot* if God does not ensure the conditions enabling one to fulfill His will. That is, even if you maintain that there is no reward for *mitzvot*, it is reasonable to expect that God will protect you from unforeseeable danger when you go to perform them.

Behind this talmudic discussion, there is an attempt to uphold as much of covenantal vitality as possible. The feeling of trust in an ordered universe, the belief that God will protect one from the intrusion of irrational and unanticipated tragedy, is not totally abolished. Although the full biblical promise is postponed, an attempt is made to retain something of the promised unity between *mitzvot* and the material conditions of reality. The talmudic teacher carves out moments of order within a universe filled with chaos and unpredictability by circumscribing the biblical promise to the moment that one goes to perform *mitzvot*. The sense of God's love during the performance of a *mitzvah* permits the Jew a feeling of security and well-being, a feeling that may linger on—Rabbi Eleazar is suggesting—even for a brief time after completion of the *mitzvah*. All the same, the Talmud adds, that feeling of security must not lead to reckless behavior. God's protection does not include the performance of miracles to save us from dangers we can reasonably foresee, such as a rickety ladder.

As a metaphysical explanation of God's actions in the world, this talmudic text makes little sense. For if God is benevolent, if He could split the sea, rescue an enslaved people, and bring manna to the hungry community in the desert, why would He not protect a child from a rickety ladder? The discussion becomes intelligible, however, when seen as dealing not with the problem of evil in the world but with the question: what expectations can Jews permit themselves when they look for coherence between the world of *mitzvah* and the world of everyday life? What expectations will allow Jews to live the life of *mitzvah* without oscillating between boundless hope and utter despair?

The upshot of the guidance offered by the Talmud is that Jews should be sober and careful when performing a *mitzvah*. God will give you the protection needed to perform His *mitzvot*, but belief in God's protection should not make you oblivious to real dangers. You must combine your trust in God's protective love with a healthy respect for reality. The talmudic sages warn against exaggerated expectations, because they know that if Jews anticipate too much now, the result will be disillusionment and profound frustration. Bring the living biblical God into as much of reality as appears currently possible, they advise. Even if only for a circumscribed moment, life can at least embody a foretaste of the abundant love and joy awaiting the Jewish community in a redeemed future world.

Risk and Postponed Gratification

The Mishnah and the *baraita* embody different kinds of expectations that individuals may permit themselves in their living relationship with God, different risks that they are prepared to take in the light of that felt relationship. Since the aim of the talmudic discussion is to find a viable way of life, not a metaphysical truth, the Talmud does not give exclusive preference to any of the ways offered. Some Jews may find one outlook more consonant with their sensibilities and personal experience, others may feel more at ease with another. The teachings of the Mishnah and of the *baraita* are both authentic, because both seek to preserve commitment to the *mitzvot*. Both those who formulated the mishnaic statement and Rabbi Jacob knew that theirs was a world filled with undeserved suffering. Their differences do not concern the basic facts of the world but the response to that world. Whereas the former chose to respond with a nearly biblical optimism about this world, Rabbi Jacob found himself forced to postpone all his hopes to the world to come. Witnessing the undeserved death of one child was too much for him.

Rabbi Jacob refused to expose people to the risk of expecting that their obedience to the *mitzvot* will ensure them material prosperity and a long life. For when people hold such expectations, the sudden death of a child who has just performed *mitzvot* that promised long life may create a total value disorientation. That may happen because for the covenantal Jew the *mitzvot* are not abstract categorical imperatives, but express the commanding will of a personal God. If things happen that suggest that the promises of this God cannot be relied upon, trust in Him and readiness to perform His *mitzvot* may collapse. When the expectations based on a relationship are in disorder, the entire relational framework, which includes norms and values, may break down. The solution chosen by Rabbi Jacob was simple and drastic. Eliminate every expectation of reward in this world for the performance of *mitzvot*. Remember that the covenantal relationship with a personal God does not end with death. Look forward to the promised resurrection of the dead. Never forget that God loves you and that this is why He gave you the Torah and the *mitzvot*, which will guarantee you reward in the world to come.

The authors of the statement in the Mishnah, on the other hand, preferred to educate Jews to believe that everyday reality can also contain joy. Although, as the *baraita* shows, views like those of Rabbi Jacob were already known in their time, these authors were unwilling to accept those views and take the risk of teaching Jews not to have any expectations of this world. To give up anticipation of reward in this world for mitzvot could destroy the vitality of the sense of personal relationship with God that animates covenantal religious life. The distant promise of the resurrection of the dead is too weak a peg to bear the entire weight of human expectations on its own. The living God of the Bible must be seen to be active also in present reality if Jews are not to grow weary of God's covenant and despair of His love. If we are taught to expect rewards for mitzvot also in this world, then sometimes we may be disappointed, but we will also attach greater significance to the joyful moments in our lives by seeing them as signs of divine approval. When the impetus to live that joyful moments provide is thus reinforced, we will also be able to take the disappointments in our stride.

The rabbis of the Mishnah and Rabbi Jacob did not disagree regarding belief in a personal God. Both also share the same objective reality: a world of painful tragedy and undeserved suffering, of people snatched away in the midst of performing noble deeds. Nonetheless, they are able to have different expectations of a personal God and different styles of living the covenantal life. The choice between the different views is left to the sensibilities of the individual reader. All that the Talmud demands of its readers is that they find some approach that will enable them to maintain their commitment to the mitzvot in the world as they experience it. There is even nothing to prevent the same person from alternating between the different approaches at different moments in his or her life.

The Response of a Lover

That the very same person could in different circumstances interpret the workings of providence in completely different ways is exemplified in rabbinic literature by Rabbi Akiva. We find rabbinic traditions reporting that Akiva sometimes interpreted joy and suffering with a this-worldly reference, but also rabbinic statements that he sometimes saw them as pointing to the next world.[7] Neither view is more evidently the authentic Akiva than the other. It would appear that Akiva adhered to no single dogmatic line on the workings of divine providence, but had recourse to different views on different occasions in accordance with his evaluation of the circumstances. Whenever he saw suffering, he sought to bring comfort, while wherever he saw joy, he sought to make it a means of reinforcing loyalty to the mitzvot.

When Rabbi Akiva was tried and executed for teaching the Torah in defiance of an edict of the Roman authorities, the lesson he drew had nothing to do with reward and punishment.

> Once when Rabbi Akiva was being tried before the wicked Tineius Rufus, the time arrived for reading the Shema and he began to recite it joyfully. Said [Rufus]: "Old man, old man, either you are a magician or you bear pain with contumacy." Rabbi Akiva answered him: "Woe to that man! I am neither a magician nor do I bear pain with contumacy; but all my life I have read this verse: 'And you shall love the Lord your God with all your heart and with all your soul and with all your might' [Deut. 6:5—the second verse of the Shema]. I loved Him with all my heart and I loved Him with all my wealth [i.e., might], but I was never called upon to face the ordeal of 'with all my soul' [i.e., at the cost of my life]. Now that I experience 'with all my soul,' and the time for reading the Shema has arrived, and I have not thrust it aside, therefore I am reciting the Shema with joy." (JT Sotah 5:5)

Rather than focus on repentance and on suffering in this world in order to receive reward in the next, Akiva interpreted his own suffering as an occasion to realize his great religious dream to love God unconditionally, with a passion that transcended the normal human instinct of self-preservation. It was Akiva who had taught that the Song of Songs is the holy of holies as far as scripture is concerned, because the erotic passion found in it is a symbolic expression of the relationship between God and Israel. This lover of God did not focus on reward and punishment at the moment of his death, not because he rejected this view of providence, but because, as a lover of God, it would have been beside the point for him to seek to draw comfort from the fact that his suffering was a down payment for future reward.[8] By his refusal to be intimidated by the edict of the Romans and by reciting the Shema while under torture or even at the time of his execution, Akiva heroically demonstrated that no external force could break his loyalty to God and the Torah. His statement is less a testimony to God's metaphysical justice than to the power of the Torah to inspire love for God. Akiva's response to his impending death was a heroic demonstration that acceptance of God's Torah does not depend on threats and rewards and does not require victorious manifestations of divine power in current history. It exmplifies the achievement of rabbinic Judaism in internalizing the Torah within the soul of the people.

In general, the rabbis sought to transform suffering, even their own, into a means of deepening their understanding of the Torah and the *mitzvot*.[9] When tragedy occurred, their characteristic question was

"What can we learn from this?" and typically they taught that repentance (*teshuvah*) was always a proper response to suffering.

> If a man sees that painful sufferings visit him, let him examine his conduct. For it is said: "Let us search and probe our ways, and return to the Lord" [Lam. 3:40]. If he examines and finds nothing, let him attribute it to the neglect of the study of the Torah. For it is said: "Happy is the man whom Thou chastenest, O Lord, and teachest out of Thy Torah" [Ps. 94:12]. If he did attribute it [to that], and still did not find [anything amiss], let him be sure that these are chastenings of love. For it is said: "For whom the Lord loves, he corrects" [Prov. 3:12]. (*Berakhot* 5a)

By utilizing tragedy and suffering as a catalyst for active moral renewal, the Judaic tradition prevents political powerlessness from creating feelings of personal impotence and loss of self-esteem. If events in the larger world are unpredictable, if the nation is subject to the violence and whims of foreign rulers, the rabbinic mind does not fall victim to despair, disillusionment, and escapism, but rather focuses on the personal and the communal as the framework to contain its activist dignity. The call to repentance—"If a man sees that painful sufferings visit him, let him examine his conduct"—should not, therefore, be seen as a metaphysical justification of evil. Rather, it is advice that encourages the Jew to sustain and give meaning to the covenantal relationship despite the mystery of suffering.[10]

The covenantal spirit of Sinai is crushed when a person feels paralyzed to act. It is broadened and deepened, however, when it is discovered that suffering can energize us to strive actively for moral renewal. The shift of focus from the might of the Roman legions to the moral quality of the community's behavior as the cause of exile does not reflect a naive, self-centered moralism that explains everything in terms of one's own feelings, thoughts, and actions. Rather, it gives expression to a covenantal activism that strives to salvage some degree of human dignity and responsibility in an unpredictable, chaotic world. From the viewpoint of religious anthropology, the emphasis on repentance as a response to suffering helps sustain the significance of *mitzvah* action by its focus on what I can do, what I am called upon to achieve. It deflects attention from absorption with irrational forces to areas of human adequacy. It encourages questions such as: In what sense is my own world capable of receiving some normative order? To what degree can I build into that normative order sufficient dignity to countervail the forces dominant in the larger arenas of history, which are beyond my control?

The "Chastenings of Love"

Although the dominant model for understanding suffering is the need for repentance, there is as well a suggestion in the above-mentioned talmudic text that sufferings are an expression of "chastenings of love" and not punishment for sins. It will be illuminating to consider how different rabbinic teachers responded to the notion that suffering may express God's love.

> Rabbi Jacob ben Idi and Rabbi Aha ben Hanina differ with regard to the following. The one says: "Chastenings of love are such as do not involve the intermission of study of the Torah. For it is said: 'Happy is the man whom Thou chastenest, O Lord, and teachest out of Thy law' [Ps. 94:12]." And the other one says: "Chastenings of love are such as do not involve the intermission of prayer. For it is said: 'Blessed be God, Who has not turned away my prayer, nor His mercy from me' [Ps. 66:20]." (Ibid.)

The Talmud goes on to add the view of an earlier sage, Rabbi Johanan: "Both of them are chastenings of love. For it is said: 'For whom the Lord loves, he corrects' [Prov. 3:12]."

These three rabbinic teachers each have a different understanding of how to apply the notion of "chastenings of love." One believes that the highest religious goal is coming to love God and to understand God's will through studying the Torah. He cannot then believe that he is experiencing God's love in his suffering, if he is prevented from engaging in that very activity which brings him to an intimate love relationship with God. To the second teacher, prayer rather than study is the experience that creates this intimacy. He infers that if God truly loves him, God will not bring about conditions that prevent him from engaging in the intimate dialogue of prayer with his Beloved. To Rabbi Johanan, suffering enables one to achieve greater spiritual heights than either prayer or Torah learning. He believes, consequently, that suffering is an expression of divine love even when it prevents him from engaging in prayer or study of the Torah.

The Talmud records these three views, but it does not decide which is the correct understanding of suffering. On the contrary, it teaches that people are not obliged to accept suffering as a loving gift of God if they personally do not want such a gift. It points out that even Rabbi Johanan did not demand that others must willingly accept suffering, although he believed that it was a gift offered by God.

> Rabbi Hiyya ben Abba fell ill and Rabbi Johanan went in to visit him. He said to him: "Are your sufferings welcome to you?" He replied: "Neither they nor their reward." He said to him: "Give me your hand." He gave him his hand and he raised [i.e., cured] him. (Ibid., 5b)

A similar dialogue and cure took place when Rabbi Johanan went to visit the sick Rabbi Eleazar. Moreover, the Talmud emphasizes, Rabbi Johanan himself found suffering to be too onerous a divine gift on an occasion when he was the one who fell ill.

> Rabbi Johanan once fell ill and Rabbi Hanina went in to visit him. He said to him: "Are your sufferings welcome to you?" He replied: "Neither they nor their reward." He said to him: "Give me your hand." He gave him his hand and he raised him. Why could not Rabbi Johanan raise himself? They replied: "The prisoner cannot free himself from jail." (Ibid.)

These illustrations of how different teachers were prepared to experience suffering indicate that the Talmud is not making a propositional judgment on the way God acts with love in the world. Sufferers are not lectured to the effect that they must interpret pain as an expression of divine love. Rather, they are asked whether such a conception can enhance their religious appreciation of God. Without denying the theoretical possibility of "chastenings of love," sufferers who reply, "Neither they nor their reward," declare that for them the unbearable pain cancels out any potential deepening of the love relationship with God. Such persons, the Talmud implies, need not a metaphysical explanation but rather a "helping hand." How and if one uses the notion of "chastenings of love" depends on the ability of the chastened to interpret their experience in that light without jeopardizing their sense of personal worth before God.

Living with a Personal God

When the Talmud presents the change in Rabbi Johanan and mentions other teachers who refuse to live with suffering, it gives us an appreciation of the moods, strengths, and sensibilities of different individuals who strove in their own ways to make sense of tragedy and painful situations in order to live with the God of the covenant. Rabbinic teachers did not offer one single model of how to respond to suffering and how to anticipate the divine response to observance of the *mitzvot*. The context, the situation, all that has occurred in a person's life, will influence the type of perception that that person will bring to God in a particular situation. The consciousness of a living personal God that grows out of the biblical story of God the Creator and Sustainer of life, God the Redeemer of Israel from slavery, and God the Source of the commandments at Sinai does not permit a consistent single-dimensional theology. Rabbinic Judaism forswore systematic theology, not because the rabbis could not think in a coherent philosophical way, but because systematic theology could not do justice to the vitality and complexity of experience.

Within human relationships, there are moments of happiness, love, tenderness, and intimacy; there are feelings of mutual appreciation, respect, dignity, and creativity. There are also, however, moments of pain, fear, rejection, loneliness, estrangement, terror, anger, and intimidation. Mature human relationships have ways of incorporating the whole range of these feelings and attitudes. Similarly, one cannot expect that worship within a theistic framework could be understood and contained within one model or posture, especially if one seeks to make all of life an occasion for worship. The alternate rhythms of reality, the pains and joys, sufferings, loneliness, ecstasy, terror—all these complex feelings will have to find some way of being absorbed in one's personal relationship with God.

One must seek ways of dealing with moments when it appears that God is distant, strange, and alien, but also ways of dealing with moments when He appears to speak as a loving Father, a concerned Teacher, or a commanding Judge. There are moments of intimacy and moments of distance, moments of God's unconditional authority and moments when God invites one to understand and to participate in a spirit of mutuality.

The relationship between an Aristotelian philosopher and the God of Aristotle may function effectively within the single model of contemplative love. But a personal God Whose actions in history cannot be predicted, Who is not tied to the universe through patterns of causal necessity, Who is considered to be the source of all that occurs in reality, will always be perceived in multiple relational models by those who seek to relate to Him, just as all dynamic human relationships that contain aspects of unpredictability and uncertainty have to be organized from more than one perspective.[11]

The rabbis did theology by telling stories of how individual people built their relationship with the God of the covenant. In not laying down as authoritative a line on theology as they did with regard to practice, they refrained from constricting the multiple possibilities that one may develop in making sense of the covenantal relationship with

God. One can claim, I believe, in the spirit of the rabbinic tradition that so long as the centrality of *mitzvah* and the eternity of the covenant are not undermined, there is enormous room for building multiple images of God and of His relationship to the community, nature, and history, a multiplicity that enables the covenant to remain a living option. Maimonides followed in the spirit of the rabbinic tradition and suggested multiple theological models for understanding divine providence. He did not, however, embrace all that the rabbinic teaching tradition permitted, as he personally rejected the view of chastenings of love.

> As for us, we believe that all the human circumstances are according to the desserts, that He is exalted above injustice, and that among us only those deserving punishment are punished. . . . However, in the discourse of the sages, there occurs something additional over and above what is to be found in the text of the Torah, namely, the dictum of some of them regarding the chastenings of love. For according to this opinion, sometimes misfortunes befall an individual not because of his having sinned before, but in order that his reward should be greater. (*Guide* 3:17)

Although, as I have shown, Judaism strove to unify common practice within the community, it never eliminated the role of the individual in the spiritual life. Judaism was not concerned only with obedience to the authority of the *halakhah*. It above all strove to make the *halakhah* expressive of the covenantal relationship with God. As long as the relationship with God is held before Jews as the telos of halakhic practice, they will continue in the spirit of the rabbinic tradition and tell different stories of how they organize their relationship with the God of the covenant.

The problems I have been discussing concern primarily the psychological and existential vitality of the covenantal relationship with God. A constant gap between our perception of our relationship to a personal God and the reality of the world that we believe He created and rules is liable to give rise to repeated frustration. The question then is: How long can *any* attempt to cope with the frustration succeed in containing it? How long is it before we decide that the relationship no longer exists or that it is not worth having?

To this question there is no single universal answer applicable equally to all human beings. The situation is like that of one's relationship to other persons. When we have a deep commitment to a relationship, but our partner begins to behave in ways that we find problematic, then our normal reaction is to seek ways of interpreting that behavior which will enable us to feel that the partner's love and commitment to the relationship continue to exist. We do not readily believe that a beloved parent, spouse, or friend has rejected us. If the problems continue, however, we may reach a breaking point, at which attempts to cope no longer have any attraction for us. *Whether, when,* and *how* a breaking point is reached depend very much on the individual concerned. One couple may have had problems for years but only started heading toward a divorce after one partner ignored the other's birthday. Others may tolerate repeated frustrations in their relationship and may remain together for a whole lifetime on the strength of a memory of the passionate love felt at the beginning of their marriage. Although those earlier moments are only a memory, the two of them nevertheless live together in the hope of somehow renewing the tenderness they once felt in their relationship.

It is in such terms that one must seek to understand the Jewish people's long romance with God. The Jewish people were living through a painful age when the Talmud was compiled. But they had marvelous memories from their youth and the years of their maturity: the Exodus from Egypt, the kingdom of David and Solomon, the miraculous rescue from Haman, the Maccabean restoration. The Jews had tasted deep love and hoped to taste it again. They continued to feel manifestations of that love in their daily life of *mitzvah* and on their great festive occasions, even though that love failed to shield them from historical realities.

On the level of the Jewish community, the rabbis succeeded in preserving a remnant throughout the centuries. On the level of the individual Jew, the approaches of the rabbis inevitably sometimes succeeded and sometimes failed. It is hardly possible to predict how long a given individual can continue to interpret suffering as an expression of God's love or as a call to repentance and spiritual growth. As in relationships between human beings, it depends upon whether the particular experiences and memories of that specific individual have the power to carry him or her through difficult moments that cast doubt upon the quality of love in the relationship. Human relationships and relationships with God are so individual, they are so closely tied to the unique sensibility of a particular person, that it is hard to be sure why some people are sustained for years by memories of joy, whereas others have a low threshold for tolerating pain. Some abandon the covenant after the death of a single loved one, but others retain belief in God's love for and commitment to themselves despite having lost their whole family in the Holocaust. One human being leaves Auschwitz as an atheist and another as a person whose belief has grown stronger.

Some find the unpredictable dimensions of reality to be so overwhelming that they cannot bear the strain of not knowing whether God loves them or has turned away from them. Theism gives them the feeling that to live religiously is to be doomed to remain psychologically a manic-depressive. For them, suffering is bearable if it results from the limitations of finite human beings, but it becomes terrifying and demonic if it is seen as part of the scheme of their all-powerful Creator. Others would find life unbearably chaotic if they could not believe that suffering, tragedy, and death were part of God's plan for the world. Feeling that there is meaning and order in the world and that God in His wisdom decided to terminate the life of their loved one makes their tragedy bearable.

Both of these religious sensibilities exist within the Jewish community and within other theistic communities. It is therefore a mistake to ask what would have to occur, or have to have occurred, in order to confirm or falsify theism.[12] There is no definitive set of factual conditions, applicable equally to all human beings, that makes them incapable of maintaining their belief in a personal God. Similarly, there is no set of factual conditions that will equally induce all human beings to accept theism. The Bible already implies this when it emphasizes that the Israelite community wanted to return to Egypt only a few days after its miraculous liberation from Pharaoh, or that the community built the golden calf while Moses was receiving the Sinai revelation. Yet the Talmud reflects the community's persistence in maintaining faith in that same revelation despite tragic historical conditions.

The Jews' tenacious refusal to abandon the God of the covenant despite the often dismal facts of Jewish history should therefore not be understood as reflecting the power and hold of irrational beliefs on human beings. The power of Judaism for people who normally would be considered intelligent and who in their daily life display a healthy respect for facts should alert us to the possibility that before us is a very complex phenomenon.

I do not claim that religious statements are merely expressions of normative judgments or are no more than imaginative stories meant to sustain a moral vision of life. Besides serving as carriers of meaning and normative commitment, religious statements also suggest existence claims. God is not only a term used to describe one's religious commitment. "God talk" is not exhausted by the subjective way of life of the individual. For people who have religious faith, their prayers of praise, thanksgiving, and petition refer to a definite objective reality.[13] Accordingly, I do not accept attempted translations from apparent factual statements in Judaism to "ways-of-life" statements having no objective reference. I do claim, however, that a theistic religious vision that guides human action is more complex than ordinary descriptions of objective phenomena.

As history has shown, the human being is not only a fact-seeking animal, but equally, and possibly more so, a value-hungry individual seeking direction and significance in life. We hunger for a frame of reference that orders and orients everyday existence into some meaningful pattern. In spite of the extreme importance of facts, their range does not exhaust the sources from which one constructs a vision of life that gives meaning and direction to existence.

The values people live by are usually absorbed from other human beings, from admired and loved persons, and from treasured communal traditions. This does not mean that objective conditions of reality are irrelevant to the plausibility and reasonableness of a value system. Ultimately, however, the commitment to live in a theistic or an atheistic framework has its source in the individual concerned and in the influence of other human beings, individually and collectively, on the value system of that individual. That is why Judaism, with its emphasis on the covenant, will remain a living possibility for Jews for as long as there is a Jewish community that organizes itself on the basis of *mitzvah*. The certainty of the eventual ingathering of exiles, like the vividness of the memory of redemption from bondage, was nourished among Jews by a story and a way of life that were passed on from parents to children. Out of this living tradition was born a substantial religious community that is a source of living values and significance. If Jewish theism was not destroyed by two thousand years of exile, it should not be imagined that even the Holocaust could destroy it. Those theologians who pronounced God dead or dethroned since Auschwitz misunderstood the source and staying power of covenantal theism.

In trying to understand the power and hold that the Judaic tradition has had over individuals for thousands of years, one must recall that the end of wisdom includes knowing the limits of what one can fully judge. "Hands off" is what William James would advise us when encountering the mysterious phenomenon of covenantal faith.[14] Philosophy done in the spirit of James teaches us to be sensitive listeners rather than passers of judgment on visions of life that are possibly far more complex than some of our theories of truth and meaning can handle.

9

The Rabbinic Renewal
of the Covenant

IN THE BIBLE, the covenant and the *mitzvot* are explicitly linked with divine promises both for the individual Jew in his or her everyday life and for the Jewish community in its course through history. In both respects, therefore, Jews have always had to ask themselves what expectations those promises imply and how they should respond when their expectations are fulfilled or disappointed. Rabbinic literature, too, reflects awareness of the problem both on the level of the individual and on that of the community as a whole. As the previous chapter showed, the rabbis deliberately provided a variety of ways of handling the expectations of the individual Jew, since no single way could suit all individuals or even all the situations encountered by one particular individual. In this chapter, I shall show how the rabbis used a similar approach when handling the historical expectations of the Jewish people.

Self-Perception and Historical Experience

From the rabbinic period onward, there was an enormous gap between the internal world of the Jewish community and the public world, between Israel's self-understanding as God's elect and the attitudes and actions of the nations of the world, which treated Israel with hostility or derision. The gulf between the claim to represent God's design for history and the experience of abuse or indifference from the dominant political power structures was a permanent source of pain and shame for the Jewish people.

The struggle not to allow the external world to undermine the coherence of Jewish self-perception presented rabbinic Judaism with a profound psychological challenge. Schizophrenic tendencies may result from an unbridgeable gap between one's self-perception and external reality. Ghettoization in its various forms was a way for Jews to build a healthy sense of personal worth, as well as a policy imposed upon Jewish communities by their host countries. Voluntary ghettos were created in the freedom of the United States by Jews who had escaped from the compulsory ghettos of European despotisms. It is understandable why Jews living in exile felt the need to live within self-enclosed Jewish communities and to disassociate themselves from people who did not confirm their self-perception.

It is in this context, too, that one has to see the rejection of non-Jewish culture by Jews. Jewish hostility to non-Jewish science and philosophy, let alone literature and the arts, was not simply or even primarily the rejection of an epistemological challenge to the truth of revelation. Rather, it was a refusal to recognize any value in the cultures of peoples whose attitudes and behavior contradicted Jewish self-understanding. Jews were seen by others at most as having had a place in the early beginnings of history as forerunners of what was to come to fruition in Christianity or Islam. The contemporary Jewish religious experience, encompassing the ever-expanding rabbinic tradition, was generally ignored in the broader intellectual environment, or it was misrepresented and despised to the extent that it was known. The antipathy shown by Jewish religious communities toward "alien knowledge" was due in large measure to the demeaning experience of not encountering their own culture in any way within the conceptual frameworks of the surrounding civilizations. It is extremely painful to respect an intellectual environment that treats oneself as a cultural nonentity.

I do not claim that the psychological need for personal dignity and sanity is the exclusive category within which to comprehend rabbinic evaluations of alien cultures. But I do believe that if one forgets the need of human beings to encounter what confirms the validity of their own reality and to disregard what denies them significance, then one will fail to discern the whole complex social and psychological frame-work relevant to a coherent perception of rabbinic theology.

The problem of bridging the gap between self-perception and exter-nal reality is not exclusive to Judaism. It is liable to occur with any comprehensive religious or philosophical outlook. In Judaism, however, the problem is made particularly acute by the fact that if one is loyal to the biblical description of reality, then one cannot confine one's re-ligious view of life within the realm of private, individualistic experience. Because the Sinai covenant was made between God and a community, it is as a member of that community that the individual Jew addresses God. A Jew's worship of God cannot be exhausted by what takes place in his or her individual religious life. Despite the theological flexibility of the rabbis in other respects, Judaism could never embrace the belief that the redemption of the individual soul, the freeing of the inner life from attachment to reality, is the ultimate goal of the religious quest.[1] On the contrary, Judaism requires the individual to encounter reality with communal expectations. The Bible, the rabbinic literature, and the liturgy alike constantly remind Jews that they are members of a cov-enantal nation. God is not revealed to Jews in the lonely night of the soul, in the deep struggle of the individual mortal who seeks eternity, but in the creation of a community at Sinai. Jewish messianism is not an otherworldly category, not an offer of salvation to the individual, but a historical hope for a renewed community.

In the biblical perspective, God's involvement in the drama of hu-man history is channeled through the life of the Israelite community. Just as the sanctuary is the location at which God's presence is concen-trated in the world, so the people of Israel is the vehicle whereby God manifests His Lordship in history.

It is relatively easy to fit the earlier part of Israelite history into this scheme. The Creator chooses to involve Himself with a particular com-munity of descendants of one man, Abraham. His love for that com-munity and promise to be its God are vindicated in its miraculous deliverance from the clutches of Pharaoh, its preservation throughout the harsh conditions of the wilderness, and its progressive conquest of the Promised Land, culminating in the kingdom of David and Solomon. Thereafter, however, it becomes increasingly difficult to find confir-mation in world history for the biblical perception of God's relationship to Israel. The stage is dominated by the great empires of Assyria, Bab-ylon, Persia, Greece, and Rome, which barely allow the Israelite com-munity to survive and prove able to desecrate the sanctuary of God's presence.

Responses to Paganism

The rabbis were consequently faced with a great gap between the Jewish people's self-definition as God's elect in history and the apparent historical triumph of idolatrous nations that defied God's power and negated God's promises to Israel. In the ancient world, it must be remembered, the triumph or defeat of a people was seen as a triumph or defeat for its deities.[2] The rabbis therefore offered a variety of explanations for why God tolerated the existence and apparent victory of idolatry in the world.[3] In part, this variety parallels the variety of explanations that they gave for the workings of providence in the life of an individual Jew, as was discussed in the previous chapter. One approach used in both spheres was to postpone the reckoning to a distant future. Just as the individual might be urged to expect reward or punishment only in the next world, so the visitation of divine wrath upon the idolaters might be postponed to a future day of judgment. An example of how this was done is found at the beginning of the tractate in the Babylonian Talmud that deals with idolatry. Of the long aggadic exposition, it will suffice to give some extracts that indicate its gist.

In times to come, the Holy One, blessed be He, will take a scroll of the Torah in His embrace and proclaim: "Let him who has occupied himself herewith, come forward and take his reward." Thereupon all the nations will crowd together in confusion, as it is said: "All the nations are gathered together [. . . let them bring their witnesses that they may be justified . . .]" [Isa. 43:9]. . . . Thereupon the Kingdom of Edom [i.e., Rome] will enter first before Him. . . . The Holy One, blessed be He, will then say to them: "Wherewith have you occupied yourselves?" They will reply: "O Lord of the Universe, we have established many marketplaces, we have erected many baths, . . . and all this we did only for the sake of Israel, that they might [have leisure to] occupy themselves with the study of the Torah." The Holy One, blessed be He, will say in reply: "You foolish ones among peoples, all that which you have done, you have only done to satisfy your own desires. You have established marketplaces to place courtesans therein; baths, to revel in them. . . . "
. . . They will then depart crushed in spirit. On the departure of the Kingdom of Rome, Persia will step forth. . . . The Holy One, blessed be He, will ask of them: "Wherewith have you occupied yourselves?" And they will reply: "Sovereign of the Universe, we have built many bridges, we have captured many cities, . . . and all this for the sake of Israel, that they might engage in the study of the Torah." Then the Holy One, blessed be He, will say to them: "You foolish ones among peoples, you

have built bridges in order to extract toll, you have subdued cities so as to impose forced labor. . . . " . . . They, too, will then depart crushed in spirit. . . . And so will every nation fare in turn. . . . (*Avodah Zarah* 2a–b)

This text belongs to a time when the Jewish people were politically powerless. It depicts a future when God will pass final judgment on history and when Israel, which was then a minority group threatened by the surrounding pagan societies, will become the triumphant center of history, while Rome and Persia, then the major powers of the world, will find justification only in proportion to their services to God's elect people. The text reflects the mood of a people that longs to retaliate for its humiliation.

It would be a mistake, however, to read the text without noticing its context. It is the introductory aggadic discussion in the talmudic tractate on idolatry, that is to say, in a commentary on the corresponding Mishnaic tractate. The latter is a compendium of laws concerning how a Jew should relate to idols, to pagans, and to the whole framework of social intercourse that Jews are exposed to in the pagan world. Those laws provide guidelines for Jewish behavior in a larger pagan society and restrict Jews from giving support to or being influenced by the alien values of that society. The Torah, therefore, is not merely the bar before which the idolatrous nations of the world will be called to justify themselves in the distant future. On the contrary, both the talmudic and the Mishnaic tractate are chiefly about how Jews use the Torah to combat idolatry *in the present*. The aggadic discussion gives assurance that the small partial victories against idolatry that are achieved now will turn into a universal victory at a time of God's choosing.

As the previous chapter argued, a complex range of attitudes and feelings is always present in a personal relationship to God, because such a relationship cannot be defined in terms of a unique coherent theological model that makes God's actions predictable in the way that the Aristotelian God, for example, exerts a predictable and uniform influence upon the world. This applies to God's interventions in history no less than to His interventions in the life of an individual Jew. The biblical model says: because Israel indulged in idolatry, it was conquered and exiled by the idolatrous world empires. In the time of the rabbis, the Jewish people had largely put idolatry behind them, yet they were still subject to idolatrous Rome in the land of Israel and to idolatrous Persia in Babylon. The rabbis therefore adopted alternative models to account for God's interventions and noninterventions in history. A later passage in the same talmudic tractate accordingly gives various explanations for why God tolerates idolatry in the world. The passage begins with the relevant quotation from the Mishnah.

> The [Jewish] elders in Rome were asked: "If [your God] has no desire for idolatry, why does He not abolish it?" They replied: "If it were something unnecessary to the world that was worshiped, He would abolish it. But people worship the sun, moon, stars, and planets. Should He destroy His world on account of fools?" [The questioners] said: "If so, He should destroy what is unnecessary for the world and leave what is necessary for the world." They replied: "We should [then] merely be strengthening the hands of the worshipers of the latter, because they would say: 'Be sure that these are deities, for behold they have not been abolished.' " (*Avodah Zarah* 4:7)

This is not just a clever argument with which the Jewish elders outwitted heathen philosophers in Rome. The point that the Mishnah is making is that the existence of idolatry must *not* be interpreted as a sign that God is *indifferent* about the world that He created or about our relationship to Him. On the contrary, it is out of concern for the world and for humankind, including His chosen people, that He does not adopt the only course that could assuredly make idolatry impossible. When this view is adopted, the existence of idolatry need not put an end to biblical personalism or undermine the theistic passion.

Another approach to the existence of idolatry is given by the Talmud in its commentary on the above Mishnaic passage, through a rewording of the reply of the Jewish elders.

> They replied: "If it were something of which the world had no need that was worshiped, He would abolish it. But people worship the sun, moon, stars, and planets. Should He destroy the world on account of fools? *The world pursues its normal course*; and as for the fools who act wrongly, they will have to render an account. Another illustration: suppose a man stole a measure of wheat and went and sowed it in the ground. *It is right* that it should not grow. But *the world pursues its normal course*; and as for the fools who act wrongly, they will have to render an account. Another illustration: suppose a man has intercourse with his neighbor's wife. *It is right* that she should not conceive. But *the world pursues its normal course*; and as for the fools who act wrongly, they will have to render an account." This is similar to what Rabbi Simeon ben Lakish said: "The Holy One, blessed be He, declared: 'Not enough that the wicked put My coinage to vulgar use, but they trouble Me and compel Me to set My seal thereon!' " (*Avodah Zarah* 54b, emphasis added)

Superficially, this is similar to the first talmudic passage discussed above: everything will be put right on a future day of divine judgment.

There is a difference, however, when we ask: what attitudes to the existence of idolatry do the two talmudic passages seek to inculcate? The passage quoted at the beginning of this chapter seeks to reinforce the courage of Jews by enabling them to rejoice privately over the ultimate discomfiture and downfall of the idolaters. The present passage focuses on the deliberate contrast between our personalist moral expectations of God and the natural world created by God, between "it is right" (din hu) and "the world pursues its normal course" (olam ke-minhago noheg). It makes this emphasis in a way that enables the reader to assent to both of these contrasting perceptions of the world. The pious Jew is correct in feeling that the stolen wheat ought not to grow, that the adulterous wife should not conceive. For indeed, the thieves and the adulterers will eventually have to render account for their deeds. At the same time, however, the Jew must accept the existence of a natural order and can do so without disavowing all personalist expectations of God. The immutability of the natural order is not amoral; its moral significance is that the guilt of the fools will be so much the greater in their hour of judgment, since they have frustrated God's purposes by exploiting the natural order that He created, thereby compelling Him to set His seal on their wicked acts. Unlike the earlier passage about the future judgment, the present one faces the fact that the natural order created by God plays a role in idolatry and in the successes of idolaters—and it enables the Jew to handle and accept this fact.

In the continuation of the passage last quoted, three distinct and even contradictory answers are given by the Babylonian Talmud to the question: are idols endowed with any real power?

> A philosopher asked Rabbi Gamaliel: "Is it written in your Torah: 'For the Lord your God is a devouring fire, a jealous God' [Deut. 4:24]. Why, however, is He so jealous of its worshipers, rather than of the idol itself?" He replied: "I will give you a parable. To what is the matter like? To a human king who had a son, and this son reared a dog to which he attached his father's name, so that whenever he took an oath he exclaimed: 'By the life of this dog, my father!' When the king hears of it, with whom is he angry—his son or the dog? Surely he is angry with his son." He said to him: "You call the idol a dog, but there is some reality in it." [Rabbi Gamaliel asked:] "What is your proof?" He replied: "Once a fire broke out in our city, and the whole town was burnt with the exception of a certain idolatrous shrine." He said to him: "I will give you a parable. To what is the matter like? To a human king against whom one of his provinces rebelled. If he goes to war against it, does he fight with the living or the dead? Surely he wages war with the living." (Ibid.)

According to Rabbi Gamaliel, idols are dead objects. Since they have no reality, God does not bother to destroy them, but toward the idolaters God is the "devouring fire" of biblical idiom, burning down their entire city except for the shrine of the lifeless idol. Gamaliel's answer upholds the biblical view of God as a "jealous God" intervening in history to punish idolaters; he shows how even the supposedly miraculous preservation of the shrine actually confirms and does not contradict that view.

Immediately following, however, the Talmud gives a second and distinct way whereby Jews can handle the miracles ascribed to idolatrous shrines.

> Zunin said to Rabbi Akiva: "We both know in our heart that there is no reality in an idol. Nevertheless, we see men enter [the shrine] crippled and come out cured. What is the reason?" (Ibid., 55a)

Akiva's answer is that the people concerned just chanced to go to the shrine when the disease would have left them anyway. Although he speaks in terms of an oath that is imposed upon afflictions when they are sent upon someone, his answer is similar to the modern answer which would say that disease is an organic process that follows its own natural course.[4]

> At the time they are sent upon a man, the oath is imposed upon them: "You shall not come upon him except on such an such a day, nor depart from him except on such and such a day, and at such an hour, and through the medium of so and so, and through such and such a remedy." When the time arrives for them to depart, the man chances to go to an idolatrous shrine. The afflictions plead: "It is right that we should not leave him and depart, but because this fool acts in an unworthy way shall we break our oath?" (Ibid.)

This answer agrees with that of Gamaliel to the extent that all reality is denied to idols, but it differs in making no attempt to uphold the biblical picture. Rather, it is an answer in terms of *olam ke-minhago noheg*, according to which it appears that God is "compelled to set His seal" upon the folly of the idolaters, and yet the reader is simultaneously told that one is right to feel that the man should not have been healed.

The third answer, with which this section of the Talmud ends, differs from both the first and the second in admitting that idols do have a reality in a certain sense. Like these answers, it is given in response to a miracle ascribed to an idolatrous shrine.

> Rava, son of Rabbi Isaac, said to Rav Judah: "There is an idolatrous shrine in our place, and whenever the world is in need of rain [the idol] appears to [its priests] in a dream, saying: 'Slay a human being to me and I will send rain.' They slay a human being to it, and rain does come." (Ibid.)

Rav Judah cites an answer of Rav, the purport of which is that it is God Himself Who sends the rain, thereby enabling the idol to deceive the idolaters in order "to banish them from the world." Whether this refers to the idolaters slaughtered as human sacrifices or to a future day of judgment, the implication is that human beings can indeed obtain their desires through idolatrous practices, but only so that the very success of idolatry can lead to its ultimate elimination. This is a partial but not total departure from the biblical view: God does not intervene immediately to punish idolaters, but He does hasten them on their path to oblivion. As the Talmud notes:

> This is similar to what Rabbi Simeon ben Lakish said: "What means that which is written: 'Surely He scorns the scorners, but He gives grace to the lowly' [Prov. 3:34]? If one comes to defile himself, he is granted facilities for so doing, and if one comes to purify himself, support is given to him." (Ibid.)

These are three distinct approaches: one seeks to uphold the biblical world view against appearances, the second distances itself from that view, the third partially reinstates it. What is common to all three—and here they all differ from the biblical outlook—is that they imply that there is no simple criterion of success or failure that will decide whether God is active in history. The same events may be claimed as successes both by the idolaters and by the Jews, depending on how those events are interpreted. The ongoing validity of Judaism thus hangs not upon individual events, but upon the perception of history as a whole. If there is a perception of God's involvement in history that allows Jews to adjust to disappointed expectations of God, then their attachment to Judaism as what gives meaning to their whole life is not threatened. On the contrary, when instant successes against idolatry are no longer a criterion for perceiving the active presence of God, then that presence can be felt all the more strongly in the day-to-day observances and practices of Judaism. The positive significance of observing the mitzvot for Jews can thus more than outweigh experienced misfortunes, provided that they have some perception of history that enables them not to see those misfortunes as calling the very validity of Judaism in question.

Renewing the Covenant

A similar abandonment of the theology of instant success is found in another part of the Talmud, which discusses the differences between the return from exile as anticipated by the biblical prophets and as realized by Nehemiah and Ezra. Jeremiah and Ezekiel were correct in prophesying that the exiles would eventually return and create a new commonwealth in the land of Israel. But they had anticipated a return of the nation in triumph, not the selective return engineered by Jewish courtiers who had the ear of the Greek King of Persia. They expected a Jerusalem rebuilt in its old grandeur, not the furtive patching of the walls organized by Nehemiah under constant threat from his fellow officials of the Persian empire. The new temple of Zerubbabel was not the magnificent structure envisaged by Ezekiel, but started as a modest building that evoked mixed feelings in those who remembered the temple of Solomon (Hag. 2:3, Ezra 3:12).

Indeed, it had been prophesied that the return would outshine the original entry into the land, since it would be sealed by a new covenant with a new kind of human being.

> "Behold, days are coming," says the Lord, "when I will make a new covenant with the house of Israel and with the house of Judah, not like the covenant that I made with their fathers in the day I took them by the hand to bring them out of the land of Egypt, My covenant which they broke, although I was a husband to them," says the Lord. "But this is the covenant that I shall make with the house of Israel after those days," says the Lord, "I will put my Torah within them and on their heart I will write it; and I will be their God and they will be My people." (Jer. 31:30–32)

> "Then I will sprinkle clean water upon you and you will be clean; I will cleanse you from all your filthiness and from all your idols. Moreover, I will give you a new heart and put a new spirit within you; and I will remove the heart of stone from your flesh and give you a heart of flesh. And I will put My spirit within you and cause you to walk in My statutes; and you will be careful to observe My ordinances." (Ezek. 36:25–27)

In these passages, Jeremiah and Ezekiel offer a solution to the problem that covenantal mutuality imposes on any theory of history. If human freedom to choose is an essential condition of a covenantal perception of history, then the possibility of sin and failure is built into communal political structures. Since social and political institutions are vulnerable to the mistaken judgments that result from free human choices, how can any people feel secure in what it is building in history? How can the Israelite community dare to build a second commonwealth if it has no assurance that the factors that led to the destruction of the first commonwealth have been removed? Will it not just be inviting fresh suffering upon itself? The answer of Jeremiah and Ezekiel is that God will create a new kind of human being from whose heart the inclination to sin, which destroyed the first commonwealth, will be erased.[5]

The creation of the second commonwealth did not bear out this prophetic aspiration. Just as Nehemiah and Ezra did not emulate Joshua by entering the land at the head of a victorious army, they were not the mediators of a new and greater covenant than that given through Moses at Sinai. Instead, as the closing chapters of Nehemiah relate, they organized the Great Assembly of the people to renew the *existing* covenant.

> Behold, we are slaves today. And as to the land which Thou didst give to our fathers to eat of its fruit and its bounty, behold we are slaves on it, and its abundant produce is for the kings whom Thou hast set over us because of our sins. They also rule over our bodies and over our cattle as they please; and we are in great distress. Yet despite all this, we are making an agreement in writing, sealed by our leaders, our Levites, and our priests. (Neh. 9:36–10:1)

Ezra and Nehemiah and the men of the Great Assembly do not turn away from God because of the gap between promise and reality. On the contrary, *despite* their distress (*u-ve-khol zot*) they are prepared to reaffirm the covenant. Despite the gap between the prophetic promise and their own historical reality, they are prepared to act and take steps to create a new commonwealth. That is their great spiritual bequest to the ongoing covenantal drama of Jewish history.

Commenting on the renewal of the Sinai covenant in those chapters of Nehemiah, the Babylonian Talmud first makes it clear that the inclination to sin was *not* totally eradicated. To eradicate the *yetzer ha-ra*, the base instinct that inclines people to idolatry and immorality, would be to undermine the foundations of life and of the world itself. This the Talmud shows with a *midrash* that depicts the *yetzer ha-ra* in human form as the source of all of Israel's sufferings.

> "And they cried with a loud voice to the Lord their God" [Neh. 9:4]. What did they cry? "Woe, woe, it is he who has destroyed the sanctuary, burnt the temple, killed all the righteous, driven all Israel into exile, and is still dancing around among us. Thou hast surely given him to us so that we may receive reward through [resisting] him. We want neither

him nor reward through him!" . . . They ordered a fast of three days and three nights [cf. Neh. 9:1], whereupon he was surrendered to them. He came forth from the holy of holies like a young fiery lion. . . . The prophet said to them: "Cast him into a leaden pot, closing its opening with lead, because lead absorbs the voice," as it is said: "And he said: 'This is wickedness. And he threw her down into the midst of the measuring pot and he threw the weight of lead upon its opening' " [Zech. 5:8]. They said: "Since this is a time of grace, let us pray for mercy for the tempter to evil." They prayed for mercy and he was handed over to them. He said to them: "Realize that if you kill him, the world goes down." They imprisoned him for three days, then looked in the whole land of Israel for a fresh egg and could not find it. Thereupon they said: "What shall we do now? Shall we kill him? The world would then go down. Shall we beg for half mercy? They do not grant halves in heaven." They put out his eyes and let him go. It helped inasmuch as he no more entices men to commit incest. (*Yoma* 69b)

This *midrash* reflects the fact that in the second commonwealth, Jews succeeded in overcoming the infatuation with idolatry, which had been the prime reason why God had allowed the first commonwealth to be destroyed. It suggests that this was done by expunging idolatry from human hearts, recalling Jeremiah and Ezekiel's vision of a new covenant inscribed in the hearts of Jews. Nonetheless, the aspiration for total victory over the inclination to sin is shown to be an illusion. Encouraged by its suppression of idolatry, the community wants to go on to suppress all the passional human instincts that are sources of sin. But it discovers that behind those instincts lies the force that is also responsible for the creation of life. There can be no "granting of halves," no way of retaining the constructive potential of the force while eliminating all possibility of risk associated with it.[6] Yet even here a partial victory is achieved: the force can be curbed so that it no longer finds an outlet in incest.

Rethinking Divine Power

The *midrash* depicts the second commonwealth as a tribute to the ability to create within the partial, to achieve spiritual growth without the full realization of the biblical promise. Choice is not limited to either total exile and subjugation or to a new world in which the good and love are totally triumphant. There is an intermediate possibility: to promote Judaic dignity in a world dominated by a foreign empire, creativity without total independence, progress without redemption.

Having thus vindicated the decision of Nehemiah and Ezra to build a new commonwealth without the certainty of success, the Talmud goes on to use their example in developing a new understanding of the notion of divine power in history. It gives an exegesis of "Ezra blessed the Lord the *great* God" (Neh. 8:6) that explains why "the *Great* Assembly" was the name given to the assembly of the people called by Nehemiah and Ezra to renew the covenant.

> Rabbi Mattena said: "[Ezra blessed the *great* God when] he said: 'the great, the mighty, and the awesome God' [Neh. 9:32]." The interpretation of Rabbi Mattena seems to agree with what Rabbi Joshua ben Levi said. For Rabbi Joshua ben Levi said: "Why were they called men of the Great Assembly? Because they restored the crown of the divine attributes to its ancient completeness. Moses had come and said: 'the great, the mighty, and the awesome God' [Deut. 10:17]. Then Jeremiah came and said: 'Aliens are frolicking in His temple; where then are His awesome deeds?' Hence he omitted the 'awesome' [in Jer. 32:18]. Daniel came and said: 'Aliens are enslaving His sons; where are His mighty deeds?' Hence he omitted the word 'mighty' [in Dan. 9:4]. But [the men of the Great Assembly] came and said: 'On the contrary, therein lie His mighty deeds that He suppresses His wrath, that He extends long-suffering to the wicked. Therein lie His awesome powers, for but for fear of Him, how could [our] one nation persist among the nations?' " But how could rabbis [i.e., Jeremiah and Daniel] abolish something established by Moses? Rabbi Eleazar said: "Since they knew that the Holy One, blessed be He, insists on truth, they would not ascribe false things to Him." (Ibid.)

Moses, who is the authority for the correct notion of divine power as well as for the normative behavior of the community, had described God in prayer as "great, mighty, and awesome" (Deut. 10:17). In the bibical context, "mighty and awesome" refers to God's victorious power in history, which enables a prophet to defeat a Pharaoh, but Jeremiah and Daniel's experience of history did not correspond to the portrait of God's power given by Moses. This is how the Talmud explains why in *their* prayers we find God addressed only as "great and mighty" (Jer. 32:18) and "great and awesome" (Dan. 9:4). When they were unable to see God's might or awesomeness, they did not want to "ascribe false things to Him."[7] The men of the Great Assembly, on the other hand, demonstrated their greatness by finding a way of restoring the full Mosaic formula when they offered prayer at the renewal of the Sinai covenant. They were able to recognize the might and awesomeness of God in His ability to restrain Himself and *not* wrathfully strike down the oppressors of Israel.

The rabbis who were responsible for this articulation of the significance of Nehemiah 9:32ff were themselves living in a period of defeat and humiliation. Unable to exalt in God's victories, they were nevertheless able to maintain their loyalty to Him because they could perceive His power also in His acceptance of defeat. While retaining the same theological language that had developed in the early biblical experience, they were able to bear their own tragic circumstances and the gap between promise and reality, since they saw their God now manifesting His power through "mighty" patience and "awesome" compassion. With this bold and ingenious reinterpretation, they shifted the focus of the notion of divine power from external victorious power to the inner power of God's patience with human beings.

This shift in the notion of power was not restricted to the conception of divine power, but also affected the rabbinic understanding of human morality and conduct. The Mishnah quotes Ben Zoma as saying: "Who is mighty? He who subdues his [base] instinct, as it is said: 'He that is slow to anger is better than the mighty, and he that rules over his spirit than he that captures a city' [Prov. 16:33]" (*Avot* 4:1). The heroic virtue of human self-control and restraint despite provocation parallels divine forbearance toward the wicked. Inner discipline is the source of power and strength.

A New Celebration of Revelation

The new rabbinic understanding of God's activity in history is reflected in the greatly increased importance ascribed to the Book of Esther. In early rabbinic times, there was controversy over whether it was divinely inspired (*Megillah* 7a). Modern biblical scholars, Jewish as well as Christian, have also sometimes felt uneasiness over the Book of Esther.[8] In the talmudic period, however, there were those who placed it above the Prophets and the other Writings, ranking it together with the Five Books of Moses. The Jerusalem Talmud states: "The truth of the Book of Esther is like the truth of the Torah . . . just as the Torah requires interpretation, so does the Book of Esther" (*Megillah* 1:1). Indeed, Esther is the only part of the Bible outside the Torah that is a subject of commentary in the Mishnah and the Talmud. The Jerusalem Talmud goes on to say:

> The Book of Esther was given to Moses on Sinai, but since there is no chronological order in the Torah, it appears after the Five Books of

Moses. Rabbi Johanan said that the Prophets and the Writings will one day be annulled, but the words of the Torah will not. . . . Resh Lakish added that the Book of Esther will also never be invalidated. (*Megillah* 1:5)

In his *Mishneh Torah*, Maimonides ascribes the same degree of importance to Esther.

All the books of the Prophets and all the Writings will be annulled in the days of the Messiah, except for the Book of Esther. It will continue to be binding like the Five Books of Moses and the entire oral law, which will never be invalidated. (*Hilkhot Megillah* 2:18)

These comparisons between the Torah and Esther can be explained in a simple way: the former encapsulates the manner in which history impressed itself upon the early Israelite community, but the latter accords better with the Jewish experience of history in the talmudic period and afterward. Instead of the Torah's picture of God intervening directly in the historical process and guiding His covenantal partners, Esther depicts history as an absurd drama in which intrigue, manipulation, and pure chance apparently determine whether the Jewish people will be preserved or destroyed. In their Midrashic analysis of Esther, however, the rabbis were able to discern a providential drama operating behind the scenes.

"On that night, the king's sleep was shaken" [Esther 6:1]: heaven, the throne of the Supreme King of Kings, the Holy One, blessed be He, was shaken when He saw Israel in such distress. (*Esther Rabbah* 10:1)

Where others might see merely the foolish and jealous king of Persia unable to sleep, the rabbis perceived the miraculous awakening of God from His apparent slumber in order to save the Jews from destruction. Others might see merely the intrigues of the Persian court and Esther's sexual manipulations of Ahasuerus and Haman; the rabbis perceived the hidden hand of God working to turn the genocidal plan of Haman into a victory for the Jews over their enemies (*Megillah* 12a–17a). The absence of any direct reference to God in the Book of Esther, which is hardly accidental, made the book all the more relevant to the situation of the Jews in exile. Persons of mature covenantal faith, who could discover God's providential love in the story narrated, were able to feel God's commanding voice under all historical conditions. The spiritual power implicit in the Sinai covenant reached full expression when the Jewish community was able to trust in the covenantal promise despite the apparent arbitrariness of history. Accordingly, the rabbis taught that the acceptance of the covenant at Sinai was less strictly valid than its renewed assertion after the defeat of Haman, since in the latter circumstances there was no divine coercion.

> "And they stood under the mountain" [Exod. 19:17]. Rabbi Avdimi ben Hama ben Hasa said: "This teaches that the Holy One, blessed be He, overturned the mountain and suspended it upon them like a barrel and said to them: 'If you accept the Torah, well and good, but if not—there shall be your burial!' " Rabbi Aha ben Jacob observed: "This furnishes a strong protest against the Torah" [i.e., a blanket excuse for nonobservance of a covenant ratified under duress]. Said Rava: "Yet even so, they accepted it again in the days of Ahasuerus, for it is written: 'They confirmed and they assumed, the Jews, upon themselves' [Esther 9:27]; they ratified [with the institution of Purim] what they took upon them long before [at Sinai]." (*Shabbat* 88a)

The comment of Rabbi Avdimi captures the situation of the Israelites at Sinai: they were in the presence of a God Who had repeatedly manifested His ability to crush any number of those who opposed His will. In the exilic conditions of Esther, by contrast, it required a deep covenantal faith to perceive God's presence in history at all. The full ratification of the covenantal relationship between God and Israel was consummated when the rabbis could interpret the narrated actions of Mordecai, Esther, and Ahasuerus as manifestations of God's redemptive involvement in history. In its treatment of the Book of Esther, the Talmud achieved the same liberation of Judaism from literalism, the same transcendence of the written revealed word by the oral tradition, as it achieved in its Torah exegesis. What began at Sinai as an externally imposed system of norms had become a successful internalization of those norms when Purim was identified as the celebration of the free acceptance of the Torah.

The above contrast between Purim and Sinai is paralleled in the Babylonian Talmud by a contrast between Purim and the Exodus from Egypt. At Passover, which commemorates the Exodus, the ordinary prayers are augmented by the singing of the Hallel, the psalms of praise and thanksgiving, but this is not done at Purim.

> Rabbi Hiyya ben Avin said in the name of Rabbi Joshua ben Korha: "If for being delivered from slavery to freedom we chant a hymn of praise, should we not do so all the more for being delivered from death to life? If that is the reason [why we do it at Passover], we should say Hallel also [at Purim]." . . . Rabbi Nahman said: "The reading of the scroll [of Esther] is equivalent to Hallel." Rava said: "There is a good reason in that case [of the Exodus], because it says [in the Hallel]: 'Give praise, O ser-

vants of the Lord,' who are no longer servants of Pharaoh. But can we say in this case [of Purim]: 'Give praise, O servants of the Lord' and not servants of Ahasuerus? We are still servants of Ahasuerus!" (*Megillah* 14a)

Of the various answers given, the last is the one relevant to the new theology of history that emerged out of the rabbinic response to Purim. Rava was living in Babylonia, which was still ruled by Persia several centuries after the time of Esther. The existence of the Jewish community was still dependent upon the goodwill of the Persian court. Ahasuerus had initially agreed to the genocidal plan of Haman; if one of the successors of Ahasuerus should acquiesce in a similar scheme, who could be sure that he would also providentially have a Jewish wife? We celebrate Purim, but without singing the Hallel, because we are celebrating a reprieve from death in a world where murderous evil forces continue to be a threat.

Religious Immediacy and Anticipation

The ability of the rabbis to relate to God within the partial and incomplete conditions of unredeemed history is beautifully portrayed in the following *midrash*.

> The ministering angels said before the Holy One, blessed be He: "Sovereign of the Universe, it is written in Thy law: "[the great, the mighty, and the awesome God] Who is impartial and takes no bribe" [Deut. 10:17]. And art Thou not partial toward Israel, as it is written: "The Lord lift up His countenance upon you" [Num. 6:26]? He replied to them: "And shall I not lift up My countenance for Israel, seeing that I wrote for them in the Torah, 'And you shall eat and be satisfied and bless the Lord your God' [Deut. 8:10], and they are particular to say grace if the quantity is but an olive or an egg?" (*Berakhot* 20b)

Here the angels object to God's special love for Israel, since He is the Creator of all humankind and has pledged Himself to impartiality. God's answer to the charge of favoritism is to point out that Israel has decided, through its rabbinic leaders, to say grace after even the most meager of meals, although His Torah merely commands Israel to give thanks after eating to satisfaction. This contrast between a full and an incomplete meal can be seen as symbolizing the difference between the biblical covenantal promise and the reality of Jewish life in the rabbinic period. Whereas the Torah had promised an organic unity between observance of the *mitzvot* and the community's prosperity and political independence, the rabbis taught the community to experience God's love in the life of *mitzvah* even when the community was struggling to survive under foreign domination. What vindicated God's special love for Israel, the *midrash* suggests, was Israel's ability to rejoice in being God's people even when they were so deeply hungry to experience the full power of God's providential blessings. Israel in the rabbinic period had learned to be thankful for a merely fragmentary realization of the biblical promise.

If one can transcend picturing God exclusively as an overprotective parent, by viewing His love also in terms of a restraint that encourages human responsibility, then one can establish a covenantal understanding of God's relationship to history that is grounded in a mature feeling of autonomy rather than in childhood dependency. A childlike spiritual personality needs to believe in a God Who immediately crushes sinners and the enemies of Israel. Only a more mature appreciation of the intrinsic significance of the Torah could enable the community to affirm commitment to a God Who manifests His power by giving sinners time to repent and by giving Israel's enemies time to bring about their own ruin. This process of maturation allowed the spirit of the Sinai covenant to continue to grow even when the power of God was not visibly triumphant in human history. The men of the Great Assembly who initiated the second commonwealth created a culture that was able to survive without external confirmation of God's triumphant power, because the Sinai covenant became an internal force shaping the Jewish community's self-identity. External reality does not easily destroy a religious culture that has internalized the covenantal ideal.

For the rabbis who inherited biblical theism, the attempt to understand divine will and power mediated through nature and history was a matter of preserving the life-giving love relationship with God felt daily in studying the Torah and in the joy of observing the *mitzvot*. The strength of that love is reflected in the following lines from the evening prayer.

With everlasting love hast Thou loved the house of Israel Thy people. Thou hast taught us Thy Torah, its commandments, statutes, and ordinances. Therefore, Lord our God, for all time when we lie down and when we rise up we will speak of what Thou hast ordained, rejoicing with fervor in learning the words of Thy Torah and Thy commandments. For they are our life and our length of days, and on them we will meditate by day and night. Mayest Thou never take Thy love away from us. Blessed art Thou, Lord, Who loves His people Israel.

One can live with a God Whose power is expressed in self-restraint if the Sinai covenant and the gift of the *mitzvot* are made into a vital carrier of God's covenantal presence in history.

It is in this achievement of rabbinic Judaism, I believe, that one must see the source of the amazing resilience of the Jewish people during its many centuries of exile. Others have attributed that resilience to the deep-seated belief of the Jewish community in the coming of the Messiah, the resurrection of the dead, and the world to come. But I find it impossible to believe that a community can exist for long with any degree of vitality if its eyes are fixed exclusively on the distant future. Human beings live in the everyday. Admittedly, they may draw strength from giving their ancient memories and future hopes a place in their daily lives. But memory and anticipation, even when incorporated in the perception of current experience, are not a diet that can suffice alone to nourish a community in the present. People have psychological and social needs that demand gratification in the here and now.

What has just been said about human communities in general may be seen to apply also in the case of the Jewish community. Admittedly, intense hostility was always manifested in that community toward anyone who undermined belief in its eschatological expectations. Maimonides, the greatest medieval halakhist, was horror-struck to discover near the end of his life that all his work on behalf of the community was threatened by rumors that he denied the resurrection of the dead. He was obliged to rescue himself by writing a treatise devoted entirely to the defense of that basic Jewish belief. The same hostility fueled the recent campaigns of the ultra-Orthodox community in Israel against autopsies. The hope for a redeemed future is still a driving force in most varieties of Judaism. But if we look at the way in which the Jewish community actually lived in exile, we can observe that this hope was never the *exclusive* driving force, nor even the *main* one.

For Jews who organized their covenantal life around the framework of *mitzvah*, the living God was not only a memory and an anticipation, but also a present experience. Of this basic fact various examples can be given. For instance, when rabbis studied the Torah, it was treated not as a historical record of an encounter with God in the past, but as a means of discerning God's will in the present. In earlier chapters, we looked at aggadic passages that brought Moses into the academy of Rabbi Akiva and spoke of interaction between the heavenly academy chaired by God and the earthly academy of the rabbis. When Jews built their civilization around a sacred text, they viewed that text not as a closed and final word, but as a starting point for creative interpretation.

This dynamic encounter with scripture gave the community the sense that revelation was a present experience when scripture was read and studied. The custom of public readings from scripture on Saturdays, Mondays, and Thursdays was explained by comparing the Torah to water: just as a human being cannot live without water for more than three days, so also a Jew cannot live without the Torah. It is said that the holiday that celebrates the revelation at Sinai is called not "the time of the receiving of the Torah" (*zeman kabbalat ha-torah*), but "the time of the giving of the Torah" (*zeman matan ha-torah*), because the receiving of the Torah takes place anew in every generation.

In their daily life, too, Jews met the living God in present experiences, since sacredness was brought into that daily life and normal human experiences were endowed with transcendent significance. The Jew's sense of the ever-presence and constant activity of God is evident throughout the prayer liturgy, exemplified by the following passages:

> Truly He alone performs mighty acts, creates new things, conducts battles, sows justice, produces triumphs, creates healing, is revered in renown, is a Lord of wonders, Who in His goodness renews the creation every day constantly, as it is said: "To Him who makes the great lights, truly His mercy endures forever." (Ps. 136:7) . . .

> Our Father, merciful Father, Thou who art ever compassionate, have pity on us and inspire us to understand and discern, to perceive, learn and teach, to observe, do and fulfill gladly all the instructions of Thy Torah. Enlighten our eyes in Thy Torah, attach our heart to Thy commandments, unite our heart to love and reverence Thy name, so that we may never be put to shame. In Thy holy, great and revered name we trust; may we thrill with joy over Thy salvation.

One may say more: above, after "truly His mercy endures for ever," the congregation adds, "O cause a new light to shine upon Zion . . . ," and after "may we thrill with joy over Thy salvation," it adds, "O bring us home in peace from the four corners of the earth and make us walk upright to our land. . . . " That is, the hope for a restoration of Jewish rule in Zion and for the ingathering of exiles—events traditionally seen as belonging to the messianic era—is expressed in benedictions that vividly recall God's activity in the present life of the community.

Reflected in these passages is a sense of God's presence in every aspect of daily life and the cosmic order alike. Life itself was a miraculous gift, "renewed every day constantly." The functions of the human body were seen not as routine performances, but as carriers of God's abundant grace.[9] Those biological functions displayed the mystery and wisdom of God's creation. They united Jews with a larger natural drama that expressed the might and love of a "Beneficent One" Who created the world out of abundant kindness. All the participants in this drama, like the sun and stars, "extol the Almighty, they constantly recount God's glory and holiness." Through the act of living in accordance with the *mitzvot* given by their covenantal Partner, Jews joined the whole of nature in joyously obeying the wishes of their Creator.[10]

This perception already endowed the everyday life of Jews with significance. The acknowledgment of life as a gift "renewed every day" did not presuppose any eschatological expectation, but rather the latter presupposed the former. The blessings recited daily for the gifts of life, well-being, and the Torah do not center on anticipation of a blissful distant future, but express confirmation of the meaningfulness of the present. The election of Israel through love in the giving of the Torah is not merely a distant historical memory, but manifests itself in the everyday life of the Jew who is attentive to the words of the Torah. God's commanding presence is an immediate reality, since all of life is placed under the normative guidance of His *mitzvot*. Rabbinic Judaism extended the perceived range of God's authority by making His kingdom a kingdom of *halakhah:* God reigns in the world now even when we do not see Him defeating Israel's enemies, since He reigns through His Torah, which molds all facets of Jewish life.

The rabbinic elaboration of the covenantal vision offered Jews an all-embracing way of life, a system of actions and symbols touching upon nearly every aspect of human experience, and a body of authoritative texts that appealed to the literary and intellectual sensibilities of the various sections of the community, since they were texts encompassing law, theology, wisdom, poetry, and legend. A large range of immediately relevant experiences enabled Jews to feel that their present lives had significance and a sacred purpose. Only in situations of acute persecution and catastrophe might those experiences prove insufficient to ensure the adherence of Jews to their way of life. Then, indeed, the community might fall back upon desperate belief in the eventual coming of the Messiah and end of exile. But it would be a mistake to characterize Judaism in terms of factors that came to the fore only in times of crisis, rather than factors dominant in the typical circumstances of Jewish life. Typically, Jewish life might have been beset by petty humiliations of foreign rule, but tragedy on a personal or communal level— thank God—was not a daily occurrence. Israel's condition in exile was not only one of persecution, torture, and helplessness. Families were formed and children were brought up. Synagogues and schools were built and communities were established.

Halakhah *and Eschatology*

Even the eschatological hope itself was not left as purely a matter of the remote future, but it was brought into present life by way of the Jewish understanding of the Sabbath.[11] "A psalm, a song for the Sabbath day" (Ps. 92:1), says the additional prayer for the Sabbath, is to be understood as meaning: "A psalm, a song for the coming future, for a day that is wholly Sabbath and a rest for eternal life." For one day of the week, Jews lived with a foretaste of the world to come, a foretaste of a time when toil and strife would no longer oppress the human spirit. The Sabbath anticipated a time when the struggle for economic survival would no longer limit the ability of people to sing the praises of God, to study His Torah, and to enjoy their family life. On the Sabbath, accordingly, the central petitional section of the Amidah is omitted from the liturgy, leaving only the expressions of thanksgiving and praise. Petitional prayer, which expresses a psychology of crisis and deprivation, has no place on a day that celebrates peace among human beings and independence from economic concerns. This was another example of the rabbinic ability to teach the community to express gratitude to God even in the absence of the promised "full meal." The Sabbath gave concrete expression in the rhythm of the present to what would be realized in its totality only in the eschatological future. Here again we see the future hope issuing from the ability of the community to achieve part of that hope already in the present, rather than a converse dependence of the present upon the future.

It is a misconception, therefore, to imagine that Jews survived in exile only by the power of messianic faith and by their dream of a return to Zion. This misconception is partly due to a certain kind of socialist Zionist ideology, which sought thereby to relate itself to the Judaic tradition. It is also present in Gershom Scholem's essay "Toward an Understanding of the Messianic Idea in Judaism."

> The magnitude of the Messianic idea corresponds to the endless powerlessness in Jewish history during all the centuries of exile, when it was unprepared to come forward onto the plane of world history. There's something preliminary, something provisional about Jewish history; hence its inability to give of itself entirely. For the Messianic idea is not only consolation and hope. Every attempt to realize it tears open the

abysses which lead each of its manifestations *ad absurdum*. There is something grand about living in hope, but at the same time there is something
profoundly unreal about it. It diminishes the singular worth of the individual, and he can never fulfill himself, because the incompleteness of
his endeavors eliminates precisely what constitutes its highest value. Thus
in Judaism the Messianic idea has compelled a *life lived in deferment*, in
which nothing can be achieved definitely, nothing can be irrevocably
accomplished. One may say, perhaps, the Messianic idea is the real anti-
existentialist idea. Precisely understood, there is nothing concrete which
can be accomplished by the unredeemed. This makes for the greatness
of Messianism, but also for its constitutional weakness.[12]

The "life lived in deferment" is what Scholem characterizes as "the
price which the Jewish people has had to pay out of its own substance
for this idea which it handed over to the world" (ibid.). But this is an
incorrect description of the workings of the dialectical tension in Judaism between the hope for a "full meal" in the future and the gratitude
for a partial meal in the present. As shown by the following discussion
in the Babylonian Talmud, the rabbis knew how to prevent "hope de-
ferred" from damaging present life.

> Has not Rabbi Hiyya ben Abba said in the name of Rabbi Johanan: "If
> one prays long and looks for the fulfillment of his prayer, in the end he
> will have vexation of heart, as it says: 'Hope deferred makes the heart
> sick' [Prov. 13:12]"? What is his remedy? "Let him study the Torah. . . . "
> (*Berakhot* 32b)

Whereas the yearnings expressed in long prayer reflect living in anticipation, Torah study reflects the determination to live out *mitzvah* in
the present. The Jewish people in exile were not characterized exclusively by the framework of prayer, by worship in synagogues. They also
sought every opportunity to study the Torah and learn how to live by
it. While the memory of redemption provided the certainty of faith that
ultimately there would be a different future, the petitional prayer for
the restoration of Zion was always balanced by the striving to create
thriving communities organized according to the *halakhah*. When rabbinic authorities sought to control messianic speculation, in the manner
described by Scholem in his essay, they were not expressing merely an
establishment mentality that fears any threat to the status quo; they
were manifesting a healthy realism that knows that satisfaction must be
felt in the present in addition to the yearning for total redemption.
Messianism did not become an "anti-existentialist idea" in Judaism, be-

cause learning to live with the precariousness of existence and building significance into partial achievements reflected the existential involvement of the rabbis and their sober awareness that a "life lived in deferment" would have destroyed the soul of their nation.

The rabbinic internalization of the Sinai covenant could have totally neutralized the triumphant model of history born from the Exodus from Egypt. Yet the rabbis did not wholly abandon the Exodus model in favor of a Sinai model of history. They did not claim that God's power was to be identified exclusively with compassion and self-restraint. They did not wholly reinterpret the biblical notion of divine power, but instead added a dimension of meaning to it: power can mean self-restraint as well as victory. In the end of time, God will be victorious again. The hope for the eventual triumph of Judaism remained. The eschatological vision was not eliminated. The two views of divine power are found side by side in numerous Midrashic statements.

In the period of exilic history, Jews could live with their humiliating lack of political power when they recognized that God could manifest His power by holding His peace and restraining Himself until the time came for final victory over idolaters. On the one hand, they built in exile a culture that did not presuppose that nature and history must always be organically united with *mitzvah* in the manner of the biblical myth. On the other hand, they retained the certainty that the expectations contained in the myth would be realized at some time in the future. Talmudic Judaism, which validated the political decision of Nehemiah and Ezra to create a second commonwealth in far less than ideal conditions, did not thereby totally renounce the vision of redemption found in Jeremiah and Ezekiel.

The weakness of that blend of self-restraint and hope was that it was inherently unstable. One could never know when the sober realists who were reconciled to living with the incomplete might suddenly be sparked into enthusiastic hope that the Messiah had appeared or that his coming was imminent. Traditional Jewish society was always vulnerable to an explosion of its covert utopic myth. Despite the efforts of the rabbis to warn against false messiahs, explosions of messianic fervor occurred with tragic consequences from time to time throughout the centuries of exile.[13]

The memory of the triumphant victory of God in the Exodus story creates a permanent, potentially explosive tension between reality and aspiration. One never knows when new conditions in history will awaken a yearning to return to the biblical understanding of God's triumphant role in history. It is this vulnerable feature of the traditional outlook that I shall strive to confront in the remaining chapters, while remaining broadly within the rabbinic and especially the Maimonidean tradition. A different perspective is particularly needed in our time on account of the revived biblical perceptions of history that have accompanied the rebirth of Jewish political independence.

10

Two Competing
Covenantal Paradigms

EARLIER, WE SAW how the rabbis expanded the range of human responsibility in the covenantal relationship with God so as to involve the intellect as well as the moral will. For them, the autonomy of the human partner to the covenant was expressed by a twofold attitude of accepting the divine norm and creatively interpreting it. Such autonomy was made possible by God's readiness to limit His say in human decision making and to grant the Jewish community the right to decide for itself how it should understand the commandments that it had received from Him in the Torah. Human reason, employed in clarifying and elaborating the *halakhah*, was seen as sufficient for that, without any need for divine intervention. Human responsibility for the conditions of life, moreover, was not confined to the religious sphere in the narrow sense, but included mastering sciences and establishing institutional frameworks for alleviating disease, poverty, illiteracy, and other social evils.

> . . . it was taught in the school of Rabbi Ishmael: "[It is written:] 'He shall cause him to be thoroughly healed' [Exod. 21:19]; from this we learn that permission has been given to the physician to heal." (*Berakhot* 60a)

The permission granted to the physician to heal signifies the legitimacy and importance of acting to alleviate human suffering. The broad network of helping agencies that Jews created in the diaspora exemplifies how Judaism fostered a responsible orientation to personal and communal needs.

Whereas the rabbis felt that they had superseded the biblical prophets in their manner of regulating social behavior, the two preceding chapters have shown that ultimately they remained with the prophets in their outlook upon human history. They had eliminated the need for ongoing prophetic revelation in determining the *halakhah*, but they retained and even intensified the prophetic expectation of a "day of the Lord" in which the humiliating relationship between the Jewish people and their foreign rulers would be reversed.

Following the tragic failure of the Bar Kochba rebellion, rabbinic authorities discouraged all attempts by the Jewish people to regain their political independence by human means. The reestablishment of a Jewish polity in the ancient homeland had to await an act of massive divine intervention that would take place sometime in the indefinite future. In the meantime, the community could do nothing toward ending its exile beyond remaining loyal to the covenant and the life of *mitzvot* despite whatever it might suffer at the hands of the nations. It had to wait patiently until God decided that time was ripe for the advent of the Messiah.[1]

The paradigmatic model for redemption and providence in history became the Exodus from Egypt, whose theme is certainly not divine self-limitation for the sake of human responsibility, but rather the manifestation of overwhelming divine power, which rescues the Hebrew slaves from their helpless subjection to Pharaoh.[2] This model is found, for instance, in the Passover Haggadah.

> Blessed art Thou, O Lord our God, King of the Universe, Who redeemed us and redeemed our fathers from Egypt and Who has brought us to this night to eat therein unleavened bread and bitter herbs. So, O Lord our God and God of our fathers, bring us to other festivals and holy days that come toward us in peace, happy in the building of Thy city and joyous in Thy service.

Here the implication is that the rebuilding of Jerusalem depends upon divine intervention no less than did the Exodus. The memory of redemption in the past becomes in this prayer the ground of the certainty of future redemption.

In this chapter, I shall suggest that the Exodus from Egypt is not the only available Judaic paradigm for understanding how divine providence or the messianic hope operates in history. The covenantal moment of Sinai can also serve as a paradigm. This paradigm has the advantage that it enables one to find the same relationship between divine self-limitation and human responsibility in Jewish history as in the normative affairs of the Jewish community. It enables one to pass beyond the prophetic outlook equally in both areas.

The giving of the Torah at Sinai can be understood as constituting a radical shift in God's relationship to human history.[3] The Torah turned the mass of Hebrew slaves into a distinctive value community by providing them with a framework of communal organization. This may be seen as a shift by God away from influencing history through direct miraculous intervention, since He now began to influence it through the continuing historical existence of a normative community. Just as Maimonides considered that God founded the orderly processes of nature at the moment of creation and made them into a vehicle of His will, so too one may regard Sinai as the place where God made the Torah into a vehicle of His directive influence in history. God is present in the community as an active force because His Torah is a guiding influence in its way of life. Just as one is not committed to thinking of God's power in nature as a series of miracles produced by repeated acts of the divine will, since the one act of creation suffices to establish the course of nature, so too is one not committed to regarding the divine will as operating in history through repeated miraculous interventions, but can instead regard God as having assumed a permanent presence in history by the one act of establishing the eternal covenant of His Torah.

In contrasting this Sinai model for understanding God's relationship to history with the dominant Exodus model, I do not wish to imply that only the Sinai model can be a basis for an active participation of the Jewish people in history. At various times during the centuries of diaspora existence, the belief that the Messiah had arrived or would shortly appear impelled smaller or larger segments of the Jewish community to begin upon a return to the historical arena, because they assumed that God would ensure the ultimate success of their efforts. The difference between the two models is that the Exodus model makes Jewish activity in history dependent upon a perception of direct divine intervention, whereas the Sinai model holds that God has conferred responsibility upon the Jewish people to decide for themselves when they have found realistic opportunities for involvement in history—with all the risks involved. My reason for preferring the Sinai model is that

I do not wish to divide my world into two separate realms, one of which is characterized by autonomous action based upon human understanding of the divine norm and the other by anticipation of and dependence upon divine interventions. I prefer to see God's will for Jewish history, just like God's will for Jewish communal life, as channeled exclusively through the efforts of the Jewish community to achieve the aims of the Torah given at Sinai.

Mitzvah and Human Responsibility

The notion that the *mitzvot* given at Sinai represent divine self-limitation for the sake of expanding the range of human responsibility is given clear expression in Maimonides' profound and radical interpretation of the talmudic statement that "everything is in the hands of heaven except fear of heaven."[4] Although his examples—marriage and theft—are drawn from communal life, it will become clear that he applies the dictum to the course of history as well.

> The statement of the sages saying, "Everything is in the hands of heaven except fear of heaven," is correct and is similar to what we have discussed. However, people often err about it and think that a man is compelled to perform some actions which are in fact voluntary; for instance, marrying a certain woman or seizing a sum of money illegally. That is incorrect, because if someone takes a woman by a marriage contract and betrothal and she is permitted to him and he marries her to be fruitful and to multiply, then this is fulfilling a commandment; God does not preordain performing a commandment. I there were some wickedness in marrying her, it would be a transgression; God does not preordain a transgression. The same applies to a man who robs someone of his money, or steals it, or deceives him about it and denies it and swears an oath on him about his money. If God had preordained that this money would go from the possession of the latter to that of the former, He would have preordained a transgression. This is not the case. Rather, obedience and disobedience [to the law] can undoubtedly be found throughout man's voluntary actions. We have already explained in the second chapter that the commandments and prohibitions of the law concern actions which man can choose to do or not to do. "Fear of heaven is not in the hands of heaven," but in this [appetitive] part of the soul. Indeed, it is given over to man's choice, as we have explained. Thus, in saying "Everything [is in the hands of heaven]," they [the sages] mean the natural matters about which a man has no choice, such as his being tall or short, or a rainfall or drought, or the air being putrid or healthy—and so too with

respect to everything in the world, except for the movement and the rest of man. ("Eight Chapters," 8)

It is important to note that, according to Maimonides, the category "fear of heaven" includes more than those acts enjoined by the explicit norms of Judaism. The domain of "the fear of heaven" includes not only explicit divine commandments, but also a vast range of social and economic activities. Only those activities that human initiative and effort cannot in any way alter, such as a person's height or eye color, are "in the hands of heaven." Consequently, only those areas which do not undermine human freedom and initiative are subject to divine determination. Whereas the rabbinic statement seems at first sight to make "fear of heaven" a tiny exception from what is "in the hands of heaven," thereby restricting human freedom to a minimum, Maimonides packs all of human behavior into "fear of heaven" and thus turns the statement into a far-reaching affirmation of human free will.[5] Maimonides' treatment of the statement "All is in the hands of heaven except the fear of heaven" shows that *mitzvah* can be understood as God's way of expanding the range of human freedom and responsibility in relationship to divine power. The sphere of unilateral divine intervention, whether in the community or in history, therefore shrinks as the range of activities and areas of life subject to *mitzvah* increases. Jews can be encouraged and energized to act when they become conscious of the broad range of activities for which they are autonomously responsible by virtue of the Sinai covenant of *mitzvah*.

For Maimonides, belief in human freedom is the cornerstone of the Torah. A theology that would negate the significance of human freedom would in turn undermine the *mitzvot*, the Torah, and the *halakhah*.

> If a man's actions were done under compulsion, the commandments and prohibitions of the law would be nullified and they would all be absolutely in vain, since man would have no choice in what he does. . . .
>
> The truth about which there is no doubt is that all of man's actions are given over to him. If he wishes to act he does so, and if he does not wish to act he does not; there is no compulsion whatsoever upon him. Hence it necessarily follows that commands can be given. (Ibid.)

Maimonides is aware, however, that certain biblical texts seem to contradict his radical approach to human freedom. These are texts in which God announces the future course of human history as if it had already been decided. On the face of it, they suggest a theology of history that is incompatible with the view that human beings have a choice between doing good and evil. God's revelation to Abraham that his descendants would be enslaved and oppressed (Gen. 15:13) is an example, as Maimonides puts it (ibid.), of "verses that lead people to fancy that God preordained and compels disobedience." If the enslavement in Egypt was preordained by God and if, consequently, the Egyptians necessarily oppressed Abraham's descendants, then God's punishment of the Egyptians not only violates our basic intuitions about justice, but also contradicts Maimonides' claim that freedom is a necessary presupposition of the Torah. For Maimonides, a predictive necessitarian theory of history would destroy the normative framework of the Sinai covenant.

Maimonides resolves this apparent contradiction in the Bible by arguing that none of the predictions mentioned in the Torah entailed the necessity of the actions predicted. No individual was compelled to act in a particular way as a result of any of these predictions. While they are expressed as unconditional statements about what will inevitably occur in the future, they are logically no different from correct predictions based upon the moral habits of human beings.[6]

> The answer is that this is like the Exalted saying that some people born in the future will be sinful, some will be obedient, some virtuous, and some bad. Now this is correct, but it does not necessarily follow from this statement that a given bad man is bad without fail, nor that a given virtuous man is virtuous without fail. Rather, whoever is bad is so by his own choice. If he wishes to be virtuous, he can do so; there is nothing preventing him. Similarly, if any virtuous man wishes to, he can be bad; there is nothing preventing him. The prediction is not about a particular individual, so that he could say: "It has been preordained for me." Rather, it is stated in a general way, and each individual remains able to exercise his choice upon his original inborn disposition. . . .
>
> The existence of the judgment of death by stoning in the Torah does not make us say that the man who profaned the Sabbath is compelled to profane it, nor do the curses force us to say that those idol worshipers upon whom the curses fell were preordained to idol worship. Rather, everyone who worshiped [idols] did so by choice and punishment befell him. "Just as they have chosen their ways . . . I too shall choose, etc." [Isa. 66:3-4]. (Ibid.)

Maimonides lumps God's prediction to Abraham that Israel would be enslaved and oppressed in Egypt together with legal judgments conditional upon the violation of specific norms. Just as in the latter case there is no presumption that violations of the laws in question must occur necessarily, so too in the cases involving divine predictions there is no presumption that particular individuals must necessarily act in predetermined ways. The crucial point of this argument is that predictive judgments concerning human behavior and divine predictions concerning the future course of history share a common logic. In neither case does necessity replace contingency. Regardless of the accuracy of the divine predictions related in the Torah, history remains within the domain of freedom and not "in the hands of heaven."

Because the Sinai covenant limits the scope of divine power in history, it also for Maimonides transforms and limits the concept of miracle as the way God relates to man.

> Though all miracles change the nature of some individual being, God does not change at all the nature of human individuals by means of miracles. Because of this great principle it says: "O that they had such an heart as this," and so on [Deut. 5:26]. It is because of this that there are commandments and prohibitions, rewards and punishments. We have already explained this fundamental principle by giving its proofs in a number of passages in our compilations. We do not say this because we believe that the changing of the nature of any human individual is difficult for Him, may He be exalted. Rather it is possible and fully within [His] capacity. But according to the foundations of the law, of the Torah, He has never willed to do it, nor shall He ever will it. For if it were His will that the nature of any human individual should be changed because of what He, may He be exalted, wills from that individual, sending of prophets and all giving of a law would have been useless. (*Guide* 3:32)

Here Maimonides is careful to distinguish between the claim that God *cannot* change human nature and the claim that he *does not* change it. Had he made the former claim, philosophers and theologians could have accused him of denying divine omnipotence. He makes instead the lesser claim that God's gift of the Torah presupposes that God has decided to act in history in ways that leave human nature unchanged. The fact that God gave the Israelite community *mitzvot* and prophets shows that He has decided to give human beings the opportunity to play an autonomous, responsible role in history. To obtain human obedience by miraculously changing someone's nature would be to take back the responsibility conferred upon Jews through the giving of the Torah and the sending of prophets.

Maimonides does not eliminate the category of miracle. As we saw in the opening chapter, he holds that the covenantal election and revelation at Sinai can be made intelligible only in terms of the freedom of God that was manifested in the act of creation. The Sinai covenant of *mitzvah* presupposes a divine miracle, but also implies limitations upon the subsequent occurrence of miracles in history. In granting that covenant, God chose to limit His infinite power of intervention in human affairs. Sinai marks a shift away from spontaneous divine miracles in history to an immanent structured communal framework that enables an orderly development of history based on the human freedom to act—with all the uncertainty that may result.[7]

Dependency and the Covenant

It is important to be aware, however, that Maimonides' understanding of the covenantal moment of Sinai and his neutralization of miracles did not go unchallenged. Nachmanides argued for an *undiminished* importance of miracle after Sinai.[8] Starting from the curses and blessings of Leviticus 26:3–45, where the Israelite community is told that the whole promised land will be fruitful if and only if it keeps the *mitzvot* faithfully, Nachmanides argues that the Sinai covenant implied that there would henceforth be a miraculous connection between the observation of the *mitzvot* and the processes of nature. The argument is presented in his commentary on Leviticus 26:11.

> Now we have already explained that all these blessings are miracles, for it is not natural that the rains should come [in their due season], and that we should have peace from our enemies, and that they should have faintness of heart so that a hundred of them flee before five, as a result of us observing the statutes and commandments of God, nor that everything should be the opposite because of us planting in the seventh year [which we are forbidden to do].

The same miraculous connection applies, he adds, in the case of the curses that fall upon the whole land and the whole community when the latter fails to observe the commandments. One such curse is sickness. Nachmanides therefore goes on to claim, in particular, that after Sinai Israel had no need of human medicine: the covenant implied that sickness was caused by iniquity, and the remedy for it was to have recourse not to physicians but to God.

Above I argued that the rabbinic statement that "permission has been given to the physician to heal" signifies that the *halakhah* encouraged human attempts to alleviate suffering. Nachmanides understands the statement quite differently: it makes, he argues, a magnanimous concession to those Jews whose reaction to sickness is to consult a physician. Since they have become accustomed to taking medicaments, the physician is permitted to treat them instead of simply telling them to reflect upon their iniquities and repent.

Nachmanides radically reinterprets the rabbinic dictum that "permission has been given to the physician to heal" so as to make it conform to the biblical worldview. He retains the prophetic outlook in cases where the rabbis had been prepared to pass beyond it. The dictum, he says, must be seen as merely a forced accommodation to existing circumstances: since people have become accustomed to consulting physicians, one allows the doctor to respond to their requests for healing. But this is not the ideal religious situation. Dependency of human beings upon doctors in the doctor-patient relationship undermines the total dependency that one should feel toward God. Trust in God implies placing oneself totally under His miraculous guidance and relying upon the promise that all who observe the Torah and follow its commandments will enjoy health and well-being. When Jews cannot turn to any source of help except prayer, are totally dependent upon the efficacy of the *mitzvah* to change the world, and have no autonomous power beyond obeying the will of God, they are in an ideal situation for covenantal spirituality.

What Maimonides thought of those who interpreted the dictum about the physician in the manner of Nachmanides may be seen from a passage in his *Commentary on the Mishnah*, where he discusses the putative reasons for a halakhic ban (mentioned in the Tosefta) on a certain "book of remedies" associated with King Hezekiah. He suggests two possible reasons. Either it was a book of talismans, which the author had intended as a theoretical study of that superstition, but which was banned after Jews began to use it to make talismans for themselves; or it was a book describing poisons and their antidotes, which was banned after murderers had consulted it to learn about poisons. Having offered these explanations, Maimonides goes on to castigate all those who see the ban on that particular book as extending to all kinds of recourse to medicine.[9]

> The reason I chose to comment at length on this matter is that I heard, and have had it explained to me, that Solomon composed a book of remedies, such that if anyone fell ill with any malady he could turn to it and do as it said and become healed; but that when Hezekiah saw that men did not trust in God to heal their sicknesses, but in that book, he hid it away. Aside from the utter nonsense of this explanation, and from its being utterly fantastic, it should be pointed out that those who hold it attribute to Hezekiah and his party an idiocy that should not be attributed except to the dregs of the masses. Now then, according to their stupid and corrupt fantasy, if someone suffers from hunger and turns to bread and, by consuming it, heals himself from his great suffering—shall we say that he abandoned trust in God?! They should be

condemned as great fools! For, just as I thank God when I eat for his having provided something to satisfy my hunger and to give me life and sustain me, thus should I thank him for having provided a remedy that heals my sickness when I use it. Indeed, I would not have taken the trouble to contradict this base interpretation, were it not so widespread. (*Commentary on the Mishnah*, *Pesahim* 4:10)

Maimonides wholly rejects the view that Jews can experience God only in that which is extraordinary and outside of the patterns of the everyday. A recurring feature of Maimonidean religious sensibility is the awareness that divine power manifests itself within the orderly structures of reality.[10] From a Maimonidean viewpoint, faith in God should not be an excuse for Jews to break with structure and necessity. Religion should rivet them back into a world where natural causality has to be taken seriously.[11] It is not a flight into fantasy, into "All is possible." Maimonides does not see God's providence in the strange and the unpredictable. He repeatedly tells his readers to perceive God's mercy, justice, and graciousness within the processes of nature. He also insists that the prophets knew and accepted the principle of causality, seeing it as an intermediary of God's will.

Know that all proximate causes through which is produced in time that which is produced in time, regardless of whether these causes are essential and natural, or voluntary, or accidental and fortuitous—I mean by the voluntary cause of that particular thing produced in time, the free choice of a man—and even if the cause consists in the volition of an animal other than man: that all these causes are ascribed in the books of the prophets to God, may He be exalted. And according to their manner of expressing themselves, it is said of such and such an act that God did it or commanded it or said it. (*Guide* 2:48)

In speaking of God's judgment and God's commanding will, one need not therefore presuppose a universe without order and causal pattern. The prophets' references to God's will were not meant to deny the causal empirical structure of reality. For Maimonides, the prophets only omit intermediate causality. They see all events, both in nature and in history, in their immediate direct relationship to divinity. The biblical language of reward and punishment need not be understood as a miraculous response by God to human actions, but rather as a description of the sufferings and benefits that are intrinsic to human behavior.

To give an example in the spirit of Maimonides, whoever cheats or steals or lies sets into motion a breakdown of human trust, and as a result human suffering will be inevitable. The punishment that God speaks of for lying and cheating and violence is therefore intrinsic to the norms of the Torah.[12] If God promises reward for virtuous actions, it is because virtuous actions are contagious and they set examples for imitation by others. Whoever performs a good act elicits good behavior on the part of other people and therefore benefits by contributing to a decent human world. The promise of reward for practicing virtue is thus intrinsic to the very activity.

God and the Ordered Patterns of Reality

In the thought of Maimonides, creation is a founding moment that has permanent consequences. Once established, the world is subject to its own causal structure.[13] Where there is no notion of necessity nor serious appreciation for the normal patterns of nature and history, religious hope can indulge itself in every fantasy (*Guide* 2:29). One of Maimonides' major achievements was the restoration to covenantal Judaism of a respectful appreciation for natural causality and for what empirical observation of reality suggests is possible.

Implicit in the religious anthropology behind Maimonides' thinking there is a suggestion that the development of human responsibility, the expansion of intellectual understanding of the world, the ability to cope with unpredictable features of reality, the sense of personal adequacy to handle one's environment, do not weaken covenantal religious consciousness, but rather express its fullest sense. It is not in self-negation, in feeling crushed, in denying oneself any worth, that a human being can truly grasp the redeeming power of God. For a Maimonidean religious sensibility, the giving of the *mitzvot* implies not that their observance is the only means that Jews have of controlling their environment, but that Jews are encouraged to employ all rational means of control that are consistent with the teachings and spirit of the *mitzvot*.

It is on these grounds that Maimonides censured the Jewish leaders of the second-temple period in his *Letter on Astrology*; the Jewish people were defeated because those leaders based their expectance of victory upon mythical and unempirical frameworks and did not learn the art of war. He might have claimed that the only reason for their defeat was that they did not study Torah, did not perform *mitzvot*.[14] Instead, he emphasized a very simple consideration of realpolitik: If you wish to maintain the independence of your nation, then you must not neglect the art of war. In no way did Maimonides feel that by urging the Jewish community to be awake to natural explanations of political reality he was weakening covenantal loyalty. As he implicitly pointed out in his justification of recourse to medicine quoted above, when Jews offer thanks to God for the bread they eat, they do not feel that they lost trust in God because the food for which they are blessing God required planting, irrigation, and other human initiatives.

Accordingly, Maimonides denies that there is any antipathy between Torah and *halakhah*, on the one hand, and natural science and philosophy, on the other; rather they are united in seeking to overcome the painful ignorance and pathetic gullibility that make human beings fall victim to every kind of superstitious belief and abhorrent idolatrous practice. His position may be contrasted with that of Nachmanides, who saw the Torah as standing alone against *both* superstition *and* human wisdom. We saw how Maimonides took the dictum "permission has been given to the physician to heal" to affirm the utility of the medical art, whereas Nachmanides interpreted it as making a concession to those whose faith was too weak to allow them to entrust their health to God alone. The difference between their two positions is also manifest in their understanding of the biblical prohibition against consulting sorcerers and diviners. In his commentary on Deuteronomy 18:9ff, Nachmanides describes sorcerers and diviners as people who have genuinely effective knowledge. Their powers are "matters publicly demonstrated before the eyes of witnesses," even though they are people "whose words are not all true and who do not provide all necessary information." The Israelite community would have "had complaint" about the prohibition against consulting them, were it not that God had provided it with alternative and more reliable sources of information in the prophets and in the Urim and Thummim, the device used in temple days for obtaining oracles.

For Nachmanides, the biblical verse "You shall be faultless with the Lord your God" (Deut. 18:13) demands of the community that they should rely only on God's direct providential guidance. Means of acquiring knowledge possessed by other peoples (e.g., astrology) therefore cannot be used by Israel, because the future of Israel is determined by the degree to which it approximates to faultless service of God, understood as living exclusively by direct dependence upon God's revealed instructions. The election of Israel creates a unique ontological structure; it creates a community with its own God-given ways of coping with reality. It is a community that is cut off from the universal rhythms of reasonableness found in those who do not live by the covenant. In that sense, the position of Nachmanides is similar to Soloveitchik's claim that the logos of the lonely community of faith is unique and can only be understood by those committed to the covenantal faith structure.

Maimonides, discussing the same passage from Deuteronomy in his *Mishneh Torah*, adopts a thoroughly different view of the powers of sorcerers and diviners.

> These things are all false and deceptive and they are what the ancient idolaters used to mislead the peoples of the countries and to deceive them into following them. And it is not proper for Israel, who are wise among the wise, to be attracted to those inanities or to imagine that there is any profit in them. . . . Whoever believes in these things and in their like and considers in his heart that they are true and pertain to wisdom, but that the Torah has forbidden them, is nothing but a fool, deficient in understanding. . . . But wise people of faultless understanding will know by clear proofs that all these things which the Torah has prohibited do not pertain to wisdom but are worthless and inane; the deficient in understanding are those who are attracted by them and abandon the ways of truth on their account. Therefore the Torah, in warning us against all these inanities, has said: "You shall be faultless with the Lord your God" [Deut. 18:13]. (MT *Hilkhot Avodah Zarah* 11:16)

According to this explanation, Israel was forbidden to consult sorcerers and diviners, not in order to emphasize its subjection to God, but in order to free it from inanities that have no basis in reality. The Torah seeks not to increase the dependency of Israel upon God by depriving it of useful knowledge, but rather to liberate Israel from pseudosciences that in point of fact cannot serve the true needs of humanity. Observance of the *mitzvot* goes hand in hand with the rational thought employed by the philosopher and with the genuine empirical observation underlying medicine. Jews can be "faultless with the Lord your God" when they understand the connection between the purpose of the law and the structure of reality, when they recognize the harmony between reality and the teleological framework of revelation. In living by the *mitzvot*, they are not living outside of the empirical structure of the world, but rather are getting closer through practice to the essential nature of reality.

Maimonides held that the rabbis of the talmudic period shared his view that observance of the *mitzvot* in no way obliges one to ignore proven knowledge available to all human beings. This is how he explains the ruling of Rabbi Meir that permits one to cure sleeping problems by hanging a fox's tooth over the bed or to assuage inflammations and fevers by applying a nail taken from the stake of a crucified criminal

(*Shabbat* 6:10). Although these practices smack of sorcery, Rabbi Meir had permitted them, Maimonides claims, because experience seemed to confirm their efficacy and therefore sorcery could not be involved.

> You must not consider as a difficulty certain things that they have permitted, as for instance the nail of one who is crucified and a fox's tooth. For in those times, these things were considered to derive from experience and accordingly pertained to medicine and entered into the same class as the hanging of a peony upon an epileptic and the giving of a dog's excrements in cases of the swelling of the throat and fumigation with vinegar and marcasite in cases of hard swellings of the tendons. For it is allowed to use all remedies similar to these that experience has shown to be valid, even if reasoning does not require them. For they pertain to medicine, and their efficacy may be ranged together with the purgative action of aperient medicines. (*Guide* 3:37)

The community is permitted by Maimonides to utilize any means that enlarge its ability to deal with disease and overcome insecurity. Its commitment to the *mitzvot* does not exempt it from utilizing any knowledge regardless of its source. Israel should not view *mitzvot* as a substitute for experience. A keen respect for reality as experienced by all human beings goes hand in hand with the covenantal community's faith allegiance to God in history. The more Jews through their own efforts are able to banish uncertainty and unpredictability in their lives, the more they unite the guidance of the Torah with the wisdom of God as implanted within reality. Revelation does not excuse Jews from the need to learn from practical experience, nor does it make unnecessary all knowledge gained through human reflection.

In the religious awareness of Nachmanides, by contrast, the Maimonidean God Who is revealed through the regularities of nature is replaced by the free power of God to operate independently of the structures and patterns of the world. The divine principle is a principle of spontaneity that breaks with regularity; it encourages Jews to feel free from the given framework of experience and orderly patterns of observed regularity in nature.

It is therefore understandable why miracle plays such an essential role in Nachmanides' understanding of *mitzvah*, why the Exodus from Egypt in his paradigmatic example for the religious consciousness of the covenantal Jew.[15] The Exodus from Egypt mirrors divine power and providence, the ability of God to transform the world in order to fulfill His promises to His elect people. The election of Israel is grounded in a metanatural category, a new power in the universe that should in no way be defined by what the Jew sees happening to other nations and to the surrounding world.

Crisis, Prayer, and Renewal

The differences we have distinguished in Maimonides' and Nachmanides' respective approaches to the covenant can also be seen in their approaches to prayer. Nachmanides sharply disagreed with Maimonides' ruling that daily prayer is a commandment deriving from the Torah. He held that if any kind of prayer is commanded, it is only that which issues from situations of national crisis. For Nachmanides, prayer in situations of national crisis is obligatory because it has the educative function of making the community realize that its survival in history depends exclusively on God's providential guidance.[16] Maimonides, however, ascribes a completely different function to crisis prayer. For him, crisis is not an occasion that highlights dependency on God, but exclusively an occasion for *teshuvah* (repentence and return to God). The community should always react to times of trouble by examining its own past moral failures so as to rectify them.

> A positive scriptural commandment prescribes prayer and the sounding of an alarm with trumpets whenever trouble befalls the community . . . be it famine, pestilence, locusts, or the like.
> This procedure is one of the roads to repentance, for as the community cries out in prayer and sounds an alarm when overtaken by trouble, everyone is bound to realize that evil has come upon them as a consequence of their own evil deeds . . . and that their repentance will cause the trouble to be removed from them. (MT *Hilkhot Ta'anit* 1:1–2)

The point of crying out in prayer in times of trouble is not merely to petition for divine grace, but also to create awareness of the relationship between the moral level of the community and the conditions of its history. Such prayer is "one of the roads to repentance" because it reaffirms belief in the connection between the well-being of the community and adherence to the covenant of *mitzvah*. The course of a fast day must therefore combine supplications to God with a determined attempt to remedy social injustices.

> On each feast day undertaken by a community beset by troubles, the court and the elders should remain in session at the synagogue from the end of the morning service until midday, to examine into the conduct

of the citizens and to remove the obstacles to righteous living provided by transgressions. They should carefully search and inquire after those guilty of extortion and similar crimes, in order to set them apart, and those who act high-handedly, in order to humble them, and after other such matters. . . . For the third quarter of the day, the scriptural blessings and imprecations [for observance and nonobservance of the commandments] should be read. . . . During the last quarter of the day, the afternoon service should be held and everyone, to the best of his ability, should recite supplications, cry out in prayer, and confess his sins. (Ibid., 1:17)

If the community cannot, through its own efforts, end a famine or ward off a foreign army, it can at least correct those features of its social life that fall short of its covenantal obligations. Tragedy and terror are to be met not with resignation and paralysis, but with an energetic process of seeking out and uprooting all forms of evil that members of the community have inflicted on one another.

While most of *Hilkhot Ta'anit* concerns the special fast days proclaimed in situations of communal crisis, the last chapter deals with the five fixed fast days, which are the anniversaries of past national traumas such as the destruction of the two temples. Here again, Maimonides channels the whole significance of the day of prayer and fasting into the need to "open roads to repentance."

There are days which are observed by all Israel as fasts because tragic events happened on them, the object being to stir the hearts to open roads to repentance, and to remind us of our own evil deeds, and of our fathers' deeds which were like ours, as a consequence of which these tragic afflictions came upon them and upon us. For as we remember these things, we ought to repent and do good. . . . (Ibid., 5:1)

"The World Pursues Its Normal Course"

In the rabbinic tradition, it is also possible to understand the national fast days primarily or simply as commemorations of past sufferings. The memory of those tragedies may seem reason enough for spending a day in mourning and dejection. But Maimonides mentions the commemorative aspect only to subordinate it immediately to the purifying influence of repentance. His main concern is not to recall past sufferings, but actively to reshape the present. The action of declaring a public fast in times of calamity is indeed placed by Maimonides in the class of commandments that promote correct opinions and belief in the Torah.

. . . the commandment given us to call upon Him, may He be exalted, in every calamity . . . likewise belongs to this class. For it is an action through which the correct opinion is firmly established that He, may He be exalted, apprehends our situations and that it depends upon Him to improve them, if we obey, and to make them ruinous, if we disobey; we should not believe that such things are fortuitous and happen by chance. . . . For their belief that this is chance contributes to necessitating their persistence in their corrupt opinions and unrighteous actions, so that they do not turn away from them. . . . (*Guide* 3:36)

A community that describes calamities as pure chance, that misses the opportunity for scrutinizing its past ways and repenting, lacks an important means of combatting moral decay within its midst. As Maimonides puts it in the *Mishneh Torah*, such a community will set itself on "a cruel path" when disasters happen.

If, on the other hand, the people do not cry out in prayer and do not sound an alarm, but merely say that it is the normal course of the world for such a thing to happen to them, and that their trouble is a matter of pure chance, they have chosen a cruel path which will cause them to persevere in their evil deeds and thus bring additional troubles upon them. (*MT Hilkhot Ta'anit* 1:3)

By "the normal course of the world"—*minhago shel olam*—Maimonides means the ordinary course of human experience, which includes our familiarity with orderly patterns in the world, such as the seasons of the year and the growth of children to adulthood, but also our familiarity with unpredictable disasters, whether occurring in nature or inflicted by other human beings. Maimonides does not deny that unseasonal drought, premature death, and invading armies belong to the normal course of the world. What he objects to is the further inference that they are "a matter of pure chance" without moral implications. As another section of the *Mishneh Torah* shows, Maimonides commends those who have no illusions about "the normal course of the world," whereas "cruelty" consists in a false reaction to its impact upon our lives. Human death is part of the way of the world. The bereaved are cruel if they refuse to recognize that the laws of mourning are meant to stimulate them to reconsider their own way of life.

One should not indulge in excessive grief over one's dead, for it is said: "Weep not for the dead, neither bemoan him" [Jer. 23:10], that is to say, [weep not] too much, for that is the normal course of the world, and he who frets over the normal course of the world is a fool. . . .
Whoever does not mourn the dead in the manner enjoined by the

rabbis is cruel. One should be apprehensive, troubled, investigate his
conduct, and return to repentance. . . . During the first three days the
mourner should think of himself as if a sword is resting upon his neck,
from the third to the seventh day as if it is lying in the corner, thereafter
as if it is moving toward him in the street.

Reflections of this nature will put him on his mettle, he will bestir
himself and repent, for it is written: "Thou hast stricken them, but they
were not affected" [Jer. 5:3]. He should therefore be wide awake and
deeply moved. (MT *Hilkhot Evel* 13:11–12)

With the two questions from Jeremiah, Maimonides implies that it
is also the message of the biblical prophet that God's providence is mediated through the normal course of the world. Much of the above
passage is taken directly from the Babylonian Talmud, where it is immediately preceded by an admonitory story about excessive mourning.

There was a certain woman who lived in the neighborhood of Rabbi
Huna. She had seven sons, one of whom died; she wept for him rather
excessively. Rabbi Huna sent word to her: "Act not thus." She did not
heed him. He sent word to her: "If you heed my word it is well; but if
not, are you anxious to make provision for yet another?" [Another son]
died and they all died. In the end he said to her: "Are you fumbling
with provision for yourself?" And she died. (*Moed Katan* 27b)

Obviously, Maimonides was aware of the story when he wrote his
own censure of excessive mourning. But his manner of censure is different from that of the Talmud. When the Talmud goes on to prescribe
"Three days for weeping, seven for lamenting." and so on, it adds:
"Therefore the Holy One, blessed be He, says: 'You are not more compassionate toward [the deceased] than I' " (ibid.). People who mourn
excessively are implying that God is not compassionate enough. They
are questioning the divine decree that allowed someone's death. In their
behavior, as the Talmud sees it, they purport to contrast the sensitive
compassion of human beings toward their beloved with the harsh rule
of God's justice for His creatures. God's patience with such blasphemy
is not unending. When the woman ignored repeated warnings, she was
punished by seeing all her other sons die and eventually by dying her-
self. Maimonides, however, would see the woman's fault quite differently. He would agree with the Talmud that her excessive mourning
mirrors a mistaken attitude to divine providence. But he would censure
her not for being a blasphemer who denies God's compassion and justice, but as "a fool who frets over the normal course of the world." To
be human is to be subject to mortality. The *halakhah*, with its fixed
periods of mourning and its urging to repentance, provides a disciplined

and constructive way to respond to the death of a loved one. Those who reject the guidance of the *halakhah* have a mistaken appreciation of reality and so will bring unnecessary sufferings upon themselves.

For Maimonides, excessive mourning is not so much a sin against God as it is a foolish error. The Talmud describes death as resulting from divine judgment. Maimonides is able to translate that theological language into a framework of the normal course of the world, as he does in the *Guide* when he translates the prophetic language of will into the ordered patterns of causal regularity within nature. In *Hilkhot Avelut* he cites Jeremiah's declaration "Thou hast striken them, but they were not affected," because death, although it is part of the normal course of the world, can nevertheless mediate the call to repent. One who does not mourn as the rabbis commanded is cruel, since that person has not utilized death and suffering as an opportunity to investigate his or her conduct. The cruelty referred to in this context is similar to the cruel path taken by those who did not respond to all forms of crisis with repentance as described in *Hilkhot Ta'anit*.

Providence and Moral Responsibility

Maimonides' rejection of Aristotle's position on providence is based on the fact that Aristotle cannot educate a community to respond in any meaningful way to seemingly unexpected intrusions of suffering in human life. It is not necessarily the daily hardships and suffering that weaken the will and numb one into moral passivity as much as it is the invasions of unanticipated suffering. One's initiative and moral will can be sapped of all vitality by unanticipated tragedy. Events such as the sudden death of a child often crush the will of a human being to build for the future. The unanticipated mocks the seriousness of one's moral aspirations.

To Maimonides, it would appear that for such occurrences not to create a mood of dejection and moral disillusionment, they must in some way be absorbed and integrated within a covenantal perception of life. To Aristotle, the predictable mediates divinity; the unpredictable, however, cannot be absorbed within a providential picture of God's relationship to being. A disastrous earthquake and the foundering of a ship at sea that takes the lives of hundreds of people remain for Aristotle unintelligible features of reality that we must learn to live with.

> . . . if a hurricane or a wind of less than hurricane force should blow,
> it would indubitably bring some leaves of this particular tree to fall, break

a branch of another tree, topple a stone from a certain fence, raise up the dust so that it covers a certain plant and causes its destruction, and agitate great waves in the water so that a ship that is there would founder and so that all the people that are on board, or at least some of them, would be drowned. Consequently, according to him, there is no difference between the fall of a leaf and the fall of the stone, on the one hand, or the drowning of the excellent and superior men that were on board the ship, on the other. Similarly, he does not differentiate between an ox that defecates upon a host of ants so that they die, or a building whose foundations are shaken upon all the people at their prayers who are found in it so that they die. And there is no difference, according to him, between a cat coming across a mouse and devouring it or a spider devouring a fly, on the one hand, or a ravenous lion meeting a prophet and devouring him, on the other. (*Guide* 3:17)

Through these repeated vivid examples of how the life of a human being appears to be of minimal significance, Maimonides tries to bring home to the reader the important fact that unless human suffering is placed in some intelligible framework, the grounds for taking human communal and moral action seriously will be undermined. He believes that "the ruin of order in human existence and the obliteration of all good qualities in man, both the moral and the rational" is brought about by "the opinion of those who abolish providence with respect to human individuals, putting the latter on a par with the individuals of the other species of animals" (ibid.).

Maimonides considers that if we look upon human suffering and death in the same way as we view the death of flies, then ultimately the seriousness with which the community takes moral norms will be undermined. If the community is to be influenced to build human life on the principles of the Torah, a way must be found to relate these occurrences of suffering to a larger scheme of justice. For moral reasons, therefore, Maimonides is prepared to utilize the model of reward and punishment, while admitting at the same time that he is unable to understand how this justice model of reward and punishment in fact works.[17]

But whereas [Aristotle] states that the foundering of a ship and the drowning of those who were in it . . . are due to pure chance, the fact that the people in the ship went on board . . . is not due to chance, according to our opinion, but to divine will in accordance with the deserts of those people as determined in His judgments, the rule of which cannot be attained by our intellects. (Ibid.)

Ignorance of the workings of the divine mind need not undermine belief in order or disturb an orientation to existence organized around the call to restore the proper moral balance to one's actions. Living permanently under the rule of divine judgment moves one to live continuously with the challenge of self-renewal. Aristotle's notion of necessity leaves us no alternative but to adjust to the fact that there will be occasions in human life when a mouse or a fly appears no different from a saintly man engaged in devout prayer. A prophet can be subject to the same indignities as an ant. This, for Maimonides, will bring havoc to the moral life of the community. The biblical notion of God's free will, however, enables invasions of the arbitrary, irrational, and fortuitous to be brought into a justice model that establishes the theme of repentance as a guiding principle in the life of community.

Aristotle's and Maimonides' distinct pictures of providence reflect two different political judgments as to how one is to build a society. Maimonides, in contrast to Aristotle, is able to build a total culture in which the orienting principle that guides its response to all the vicissitudes of human life is the theme of *teshuvah*. He agrees with Aristotle that providence is manifested in the ordered framework of causality and necessity, such as the motions of the heavenly bodies. At the same time, he realizes that it is crucial for a religious moral political order that the community remain firm in its belief that all human suffering occurs within the framework of divine judgment. Without that belief, the loyalty of the individual and the community to the Torah could be undermined. With that belief, on the other hand, the community can even be strengthened by tragedy, since it will react to disasters with repentance and moral self-renewal.

Messianic Hope in Maimonides and Nachmanides

The fundamental question separating a Maimonidean religious anthropology from a Nachmanidean one is: what is the most authentic way of keeping alive the living relationship with God that grows from the biblical tradition? Both inherit covenantal immediacy from the Judaic tradition. The question is then: can the vividness and vitality of the theistic passion of the biblical tradition be preserved only through a category of miracle in which God remains independent of order and structure? Must a religious vision that sees the divine will present in the autonomous structure and order of the world spell a weakening of the vitality of the personal God of the Bible? Must one mythologize the world by believing that *mitzvah* has cosmic powers in order to create an appreciation of the seriousness of the divine word?[18]

It is not my concern at this moment to judge whether Maimonides or Nachmanides was more successful in molding and strengthening the Jewish religious community. What I am concerned about showing is that there is a tradition of Jewish thought that understood divine providence and the implications of the covenantal principle within categories that neutralize the need for unilateral divine action and for the ongoing biblical mythologization of reality.

Maimonides, to whom the Jewish community gave such great authority to define its halakhic life that he may be said to have shaped the development of Jewish behavior for the last eight hundred years, believed that the theistic vision intrinsic to Judaism can be absorbed within a philosophy that recognizes the will of God in the ordered regularities of the world of nature. It is unimportant whether the Aristotelian philosophical and scientific conceptions embraced by Maimonides are seen as valid today. What is important is that here is a master authority of the Judaic normative tradition who struggled to give vitality to covenantal *halakhah* through a perception of the world that does not restrict divine immediacy to the miraculous. In this respect, therefore, Maimonides provides a more than adequate precedent in the Judaic tradition for seeing the Sinai covenant as an operative model for understanding God's action in history.

The contrast that I have drawn between Maimonides and Nachmanides, however, would be incomplete if I did not also consider their differing approaches to the Jewish messianic hope. For whereas the Nachmanidean emphasis on miracle might seem implausible in the conditions of Jewish exile, when there was little sign of miraculous divine intervention in history, it is more obviously appropriate to the messianic era, which Jews traditionally expected to be characterized by miracles of many kinds.

In other words, do traditional Jewish beliefs about the coming of the Messiah oblige even a Maimonides to resort to the model of history suggested by the miraculous redemption from Egyptian bondage? I believe that the interpretation of messianism which one finds in Maimonides shows that here, too, the philosophical worldview of Maimonides deliberately eschews the category of miracle. His understanding even of messianic hope is controlled by the category of the covenant at Sinai rather than by the concept of the miraculous divine intervention in the Exodus from Egypt.[19]

The framework in which Maimonides locates messianism is his description of the ideal political kingdom, which forms the climax of his discussion of the laws applying to kings. He conceived of the messianic kingdom as a social-political reality that, unlike the conditions of his own time, would permit Jews to give full expression to their commitment to *mitzvah*. Maimonides completely rejects the view that some of the *mitzvot* may be modified or abrogated in the messianic world. His rejection is not motivated by any polemical struggle with Christianity.[20] Rather, he sees the whole messianic hope as springing from the frustration felt by Jews whose economic and political situation prevents them from implementing the Torah in all its fullness. It is the eternal binding quality of *mitzvah* that creates the impetus to struggle to create a society that will wholly exemplify the covenantal ideal.

For Maimonides, therefore, messianism is a covenantal category motivated by the urge to keep the *mitzvot* given at Sinai; it is not a redemptive category presupposing a radical transformation of history. There is no qualitative break in the reality of the world when the Messiah appears. Messianism does not involve the creation of a "new man," since human nature, according to Maimonides, does not change. The basic human capacity for evil is constant. We can only aspire to inhibit the expression of evil by creating the best political society that we can. The ideal political society for Maimonides was a society constituted by the rule of Torah. If the Torah is to reign fully in a Jewish polity, moreover, one must establish a world political order from which exploitation and war have been banned, since otherwise the Jewish polity will be too preoccupied with its own survival.

Maimonides thus agrees with the Jewish tradition that the messianic era will be a world order of a kind never seen in the past. Nonetheless, implicit in the Maimonidean messianic idea is a realistic evaluation of the potential for evil to resurge again. In building a messianic society and world, one will not have eliminated the problems of the human condition. One will only have created an order that is capable of dealing adequately with those problems. It will be the optimal reality for the implementation of the Sinai covenant, but human nature itself will not have been redeemed. The potential for evil and sin will not have been eliminated. Human freedom, with the consequent possibility of choosing evil, will remain as operative in the messianic era as in the premessianic ages. The difference is merely that the range of opportunities for expressing human powers of love will have been greatly expanded because the majority of human energies will not be exhausted in the battle to survive.

In Maimonides, messianism is a normative category of history. It is the category that characterizes the ideal model of a society that is capable of realizing the fullness of the covenantal challenge. The principle of hope that is essential to Maimonides' understanding of Judaism springs from the desire to be loyal to the covenant of Sinai. Hope grows from a commitment to responsibility, not from a yearning for ultimate peace and resolution. There is a heroic impulse in the messianic conception of Maimonides, since he rejected all dreams portraying the messianic era as a time of miraculously guaranteed ease and comfort.[21]

Maimonides welcomed all attempts to build toward a messianic reality, provided that those attempts were realistic. Although he denounced messianic pretenders whose baseless fanaticism merely imperiled the Jewish community, he regarded the Bar Kochba rebellion as a risk that had been worth taking. He envisaged that there might be several more justified but failed attempts to establish a messianic kingdom in the land of Israel. His only criterion for identifying some individual as the Messiah was practical success: if there arose a Jewish king who succeeded in creating a polity satisfying the definition of a messianic kingdom, he would be the Messiah; if he failed somewhere on the way, he would not be, though he might nonetheless be a great Jewish king.

Messianism in Maimonides is therefore simultaneously a heroic and a realistic principle of hope anchored in the eternal covenant of Sinai. It is important for him because it does not allow Judaism to become merely a private existential experience. Messianism counteracts the heresy of turning Judaism into a faith for isolated human individuals. It springs from the essential concern of Judaism with the sociopolitical drama of the community. It also expresses the dimension of Judaism that goes beyond the tribal and national framework, since it makes the Jewish community aware that Judaism's fullest expression requires a changed world order if there is to be a reign of peace.

Nachmanides, on the other hand, uncompromisingly embraced the assumption that Maimonides resolutely sought to eliminate: in the messianic era human nature will be changed. It will be redeemed such that human freedom will no longer lead to sin, as his commentary on Deuteronomy 30:6 argues.

> But in the days of the Messiah, the choice of their good will be natural; the heart will not desire the improper and it will have no craving whatever for it. This is the "circumcision" mentioned here, for lust and desire are the "foreskin" of the heart, and circumcision of the heart means that it will not covet or desire evil. Man will return at that time to what he was before the sin of Adam, when by his nature he did what should properly be done, and there were no conflicting desires in his will. . . .

In the continuation of this passage, Nachmanides quotes Jeremiah and Ezekiel to the same effect. Clearly, for him the messianic age will be characterized by a fundamental transformation of human nature. The problematics of human freedom will be overcome, as all will then yearn to live always in accordance with the will of God. Since Nachmanides, as we saw, also held that the course of nature is influenced by the observance of *mitzvah*, a fundamental change of human nature implies for him a correspondingly fundamental change in the world as a whole. When "man returns to what he was before the sin of Adam," it is implied that the world will become a new Garden of Eden.

The messianic age envisaged by Nachmanides is thus the culmination of his conception of the *mitzvot*. The unity between the natural and the historical, between the powers manifested in nature and the powers contained in *mitzvah*, will have achieved its ultimate redemptive goal. The final age of history must make God's presence in the world fully visible, as the culmination of the process that began when the liberation from Egypt first made God's power visible in the history of the people of Israel. Therefore Nachmanides' controlling model for the messianic era is the Exodus from Egypt. His controlling category for messianic hope is openly a new liberation, a new creation, a new unity between nature and history, a new human being who is not troubled and threatened by his evil instinct (*yetzer ha-ra*), by the powers of imagination that lead to sin.

In Maimonides, by contrast, I suggest that the controlling category for messianic hope is the eternal covenant of Sinai, which demands of Jews that they seek to create a society that will enable them to be loyal to the total covenant of Judaism. Since the covenant of Judaism does not only deal with the individual in personal and family life, but with the individual in a total community, hope is manifested by a readiness to resume the struggle toward a messianic society whenever historical conditions permit.

The messianic vision, as formulated in the *Guide of the Perplexed*, is fully compatible with a perception of God's relationship to the world in terms of the principle of *olam ke-minhago noheg*, "the world pursues its normal course."

> These great evils that come about between the human individuals who inflict them upon one another because of purposes, desires, opinions and beliefs, are all of them likewise consequent upon privation. For all of them derive from ignorance, I mean from a privation of knowledge. . . . For through cognition of the truth, enmity and hatred are removed and the inflicting of harm by people on one another is abolished. It holds out this promise, saying: "And the wolf shall dwell with the lamb, and the leopard shall lie down with the kid, and so on. And the

cow and the bear shall feed, and so on. And the sucking child shall play, and so on" [Isa. 11:6-8]. Then it gives the reason for this, saying that the cause of the abolition of these enmities, these discords and these tyrannies, will be the knowledge that men will then have concerning the true reality of the deity. For it says: "They shall not hurt nor destroy in all My holy mountain; for the earth shall be full of the knowledge of the Lord, as the waters cover the sea" [Isa. 11:9]. (Guide 3:11)

If violence is seen as stemming from a privation of knowledge, then the movement in history from a world dominated by violence, war, and exploitation to one in which mutual understanding, the pursuit of justice, and the love of God prevail need not be based on a theology whereby God breaks into history and brings about the messianic reality. Reason, the image of God in every human being and the ground for the individual's love of God, can also serve as the ground of the hope of establishing a community whose central political focus will be the growth of the knowledge of God. Through that knowledge, human violent tendencies will be controlled.

It is not my concern here to determine whether Maimonides' understanding of violence is naive or possibly even utopian. What is important for my purposes is that this leading halakhic thinker perceived messianism in a way that does not require one to adopt the Exodus model of divine intervention in order to aspire to radical changes in human history. Maimonides taught his reader to see God's gracious power in history in the natural powers of human beings. He provides a precedent in the Judaic tradition for not allowing even messianic hope to force us to adopt a model of history that presupposes unilateral grace and a return to direct divine miraculous action. As I shall show in the remaining chapters, messianism is the spirit of Maimonides provides a viable way of understanding the modern national renaissance of the Jewish people. It enables Jews to attach a religious significance to their national renaissance in Israel without reverting to the biblical emphasis on miracle and eschatology.

To prevent misunderstandings, I must emphasize again that I am not claiming that Maimonides provides the *only* possible way whereby an observant Jew can participate in a return of the Jewish people to history such as has occurred in modern Israel. I do not wish to be identified with the socialist Zionist critique of traditional Judaism, according to which the attitude of waiting for the Messiah necessarily prevented the religious Jewish community from undertaking any activity in history. Although there are times when Nachmanidean Jews wait passively and Maimonideans decide to act, the converse may happen. If the Nachmanideans believe that the hour of redemption is close and that God has now decreed irresistible triumph for the Jewish people, they may hurl themselves into an activism that the Maimonideans would reject as imprudent. Similarly, Marxist revolutionary activism has its source in the belief that the hour is close for the inevitable triumph of the working class in history. The activism inspired by a mythic appreciation of the *mitzvot* is exemplified by those religious groups in Israel whose current eagerness to fulfill the *mitzvah* of settling the land brooks no objections on political, economic, or demographic grounds.

My interest in the Maimonidean model of history is motivated not by concern to promote political activism as such, but by the wish to demythologize the biblical perception of history and to develop a Judaic appreciation of history that is grounded in a serious respect for empirical considerations. We have already seen how rabbinic Judaism was able to neutralize the Exodus model as an operative daily category for the community, while retaining it as the basis of messianic hope. My aim has been to show that the autonomous spirit of the talmudic sage can pass beyond the biblical prophet also in the shaping of Jewish history. The living God of Judaism can be experienced in a world in which His providential love and guidance are discovered and felt as "the world pursues its normal course."

11

The Celebration of Finitude

Many religious thinkers, both Jewish and non-Jewish, have regarded the yearning for eternal life and redemption from the imperfect conditions of this world as essential to theistic belief.[1] It would be pointless to believe in a personal God, it is claimed, if that belief could not give us hope of transcending human finitude and witnessing the final resolution of human suffering and tragedy in history. In respect specifically to Judaism, it is argued that belief in God as the One Who created the universe and Who revealed His personal will at Sinai must lead to belief that God will eventually redeem His creation from the bane of evil through bringing about a final realization of His vision for human history. Creation and revelation necessarily lead on to redemption.[2]

This chapter will present an understanding of creation and revelation such that redemption and resolution need not be a necessary component of covenantal theism based on *mitzvah*. In the spirit of Maimonides' description of Job and his interpretation of "the world pursues its normal course," as we encountered them in earlier chapters, it will be shown possible to affirm the God of the covenant even though uncertainty, pain, and tragedy remain permanent possibilities in history. Maimonides' description of Job suggests that we are not obliged to interpret all events in history as exemplifying divine justice. His insistence that human nature will never change, not even in the era of a messianic king, suggests that the high aspirations embodied in the covenant of *mitzvah* can seek to find their realization without the presupposition of a·transformed and redeemed humanity.

It has been claimed against Maimonides that his ideal of contemplative love of God minimizes the religious significance of history and the community.[3] His emphasis on the individualistic and ahistorical moment of contemplative love, it is alleged, implies a depreciation of the value ascribed by Judaism to *mitzvah* as the basis of communal life and action in history. This claim will also be shown to be mistaken. The love awakened in us through our experience of a personal God in the life of *mitzvah* is certainly different from the contemplative love described by Maimonides, but the two kinds of love will be seen not to be mutually exclusive.

Notwithstanding, then, that hope for the messianic era has played such a prominent role in the Judaic tradition, I shall argue that the vitality of the covenant does not presuppose belief in messianic redemption, the immortality of the soul, or the resurrection of the dead. I am not claiming or implying that belief in a future radical transformation of history is naive, childish, escapist, or illogical. Far be it from me to deny the ability of God to act in such ways. I am merely claiming that those eschatological beliefs are not constitutive of the Sinai covenant and that, consequently, the covenant can retain its vitality even when those beliefs are not adduced in its support or when they are given a demythologizing reinterpretation.

The modern-day recognition of the human sources that influence religious outlooks on life—a particular community, particular teachers, a specific family tradition—prevents us from giving convictions of faith an absolute epistemological status like that ascribed by Maimonides to statements about God's existence, unity, and incorporeality, with regard to which he said, "perfect certainty is obtained" (*Guide* 1:71). Accordingly, I do not regard those with different understandings of the meaning of human existence—including atheists—as affected by hubris or malice that prevents them from seeing what is obviously the truth. Nor do I share Leibowitz's judgment of faith in the biblical promise as egocentric and narcissistic. Those who live with this faith are not shallow and naive or victims of confused thought. The behavioral consequences of their faith—the moral and political decisions they make on its basis— ought to be clarified, and the risks to which their vision is exposed can be pointed out. However, the "maturity" of their vision is not for me to decide.[4]

I cherish the epistemological humility commended by William James.

> Neither the whole of truth nor the whole of good is revealed to any single observer although each observer gains a partial superiority of insight from the particular position in which he stands. Even prisons and sick rooms have their special revelations. It is enough to ask of each of us that he should be faithful to his own opportunities and to make the most of his own blessings without presuming to regulate the rest of the vast field.[5]

It is in that spirit that I approach the issue of the claimed necessity of a messianic faith for covenantal theism.

Creation and the Dignity of Human Finitude

As earlier chapters have shown, there is in the Judaic tradition a religious perspective from which death and suffering are understood to result from our sins.[6] Sin has led to a disruption of the unity between morality and human happiness, but this is a state of affairs that can be remedied: a life led in accordance with Torah is the opportunity God has given us to restore that unity. Even the body's vulnerability to disease will ultimately be eliminated. The seriousness of our attitude toward the *mitzvot* and our concern with the elaborate details of the *halakhah* assume heightened spiritual significance from this perspective because it is believed that observance of the *mitzvot* unleashes forces in history and nature leading to the restoration of that unity.[7] In this view of covenantal faith, which is essentially a protest against the world as presently constituted, human beings are strangers wandering in an unredeemed world that awaits the realization of the eschatological vision. This is the perception according to which creation and the revelation embodied in the Sinai covenant necessarily imply a third category, redemption.

This view shares with pantheistic metaphysics a deprecation of human finitude, freedom, and uncertainty, all of which are considered part of the fallen human state and will eventually be overcome. The longing to overcome them is in fact a central impulse of this view. Pantheism suggests that the only reality of value is God. All of life is endowed with significance in that it participates in, expresses, and above all is identified with the divine reality. In a pantheistic perspective, our sense of human finitude and separateness results from our estrangement from our true self. We discover our true identity when we understand how we participate in and are one with the infinite divine life.[8]

There is also, however, a very different view of our relationship with God in which our finitude is appreciated for its own intrinsic value. This view willingly accepts the permanent difference between us creatures and our Creator. It is the development of this metaphysical picture of reality that allows us to value the covenant even without the certainty of eschatological redemption.

Creation involves an irreducible separation between the world and God. It encourages us to take both God and the world with extreme seriousness in their radical separateness. In the biblical story of creation, God confirms and legitimizes finitude: "And God saw all that He had made, and it was very good" (Gen. 1:31). If existence in its otherness from God is pronounced good, then our finitude has intrinsic dignity and significance.

As finitude is willed by God, death need not be viewed as punishment for sin. The human being as a biological organism is subject to the laws and rhythms of life, which include growth, suffering, and death. Acknowledging the dignity of finitude, one learns to accept death as a permanent feature of the human condition. This appreciation of creation is antipathetic to the mystic longing to get beyond finitude. It holds that our consciousness of our finitude is not an estrangement from our true being and that we do not need to anchor our existence in the eternal before we can discover authenticity, legitimacy, or "redeemedness." In the Genesis story, human finitude does not appear to be a source of embarrassment, crying out for redemption through absorption into an eternal realm. Belief in the immorality of the soul or the physical resurrection of the dead, and the mystical longing to be absorbed in eternity, are therefore not essential for us to stand as dignified finite creatures before our Creator. Finite human beings who accept their creatureliness know that they remain separate from their Creator. They know that eternity and necessity are qualities exclusive to God.

The Acceptance of Human Limitations

In medieval philosophical discussions, finitude and human limitation were often identified with corporeality, whereas the intellect alone might be immortal. From the viewpoint of Genesis, however, the whole human being—intellect as well as body—is anchored to finitude and temporality. God in creation wills both intellect and body, which form an organic biological unity. As a biological creature, the human being does not inhabit the world of eternity. Our biology is a constant reminder of our finitude and limitations. Yet the intellect, when not heedful of the body's message of finite human existence, may be tempted to believe that it can totally transcend temporality and context, be freed from finitude, and think the thoughts of God. That illusion has produced dogmatisms and even set off wars in the name of truth. An intellect conscious of its connection to the body, on the other hand, is always anchored to particular temporal moments in history. Rooted in our bodies, we are always reminded of the limited, fragile, but dignified quality of human finitude.

Our love for and feeling of acceptance by a Creator Who willed creation in its fullness and otherness is expressed in the variety of blessings (berakhot) that are recited before eating and drinking and upon witnessing manifestations of God's wisdom and power in nature and history. The blessings before eating (birkhot ha-nehenin) need not be understood as an expression of a fearful creature seeking permission from the Lord of Creation to enjoy what is His exclusive property.[9] Rather, they express our recognition that our enjoyment of the world must be accompanied by an awareness of ourselves as creatures of God. Our natural aesthetic and bodily joys need not be accompanied by a sense of guilt. They are willed by God, provided that we never forget our finitude and delude ourselves that we are the absolute masters of nature. "And God saw all that He had made, and it was very good" (Gen. 1:31). The finitude of God's creatures does not require sanctification, and nature as a creation of God is not in need of redemption. Human existence has intrinsic justification.

This joyous affirmation of human finitude is confirmed by the halakhic teaching that one may suspend all the laws of the Sabbath if their observance threatens an individual's physical existence. The halakhic demands of the Sabbath, which express the respect due to the infinite Creator Who Himself rested on the seventh day, are overruled by the value of a single created finite human life.[10] The Sabbath, which has played such a central role as a symbolic sign and carrier of the covenantal relationship between God and Israel, therefore exemplifies both the anthropocentric and the theocentric poles of Judaism. On the Sabbath, Jews celebrate God as the Creator. They abstain from many activities in recognition that they and the world result from the act of creation. Awe, wonder, and humility are expressed by giving up mastery and control over the world for a day. Nature is not our absolute possession. We are allowed and indeed commanded, however, to resume control temporarily as soon as human life itself is threatened. The Sabbath, therefore, does not force us to choose between a theocentric focus on the world and the dignity and significance of human existence. The vitality of the covenantal spirit demands that one maintain both poles with extreme seriousness. A religious humanism that ignores the religious vitality and power of awe and reverence before the infinite power and mystery of divinity violates the theocentric pole of Judaism. At the other extreme, a yearning to get beyond finitude and inhabit eternity is a violation of the dignity of human freedom and responsibility found in the covenantal concern for history.

Eschatological redemption, then, is not implicit in the notion of creation. But neither is it presupposed in the divine revelation that established the covenant at Sinai. On the contrary, the covenant reaffirms the dignity conferred upon human existence by creation. It does not aim to redeem the creature from creaturely finitude, nor does it point to an existence not shot through by the problematics of human freedom and temporality. As it is described in Exodus and Deuteronomy,[11] the covenant does not suggest any promise of resolution for the finite human condition. Rather, it teaches the community how to be responsible for its social and political existence even within the uncertain and possibly tragic conditions of history and even though many events are beyond human control.

In calling upon the community to implement the covenantal norm, the God of Sinai does not promise that history will be secure against the misuse of human freedom. Failure, uncertainty, and unpredictability are permanent features of life under the covenant, since human freedom is constitutive of the covenantal relationship. Nor does the covenant promise that God will unilaterally redeem history irrespective of human actions. In the modern situation, for instance, it does not rule out the possibility of total nuclear destruction. That risk is part of the open drama in which the covenant sets one as a participant. We are admonished: "Behold, I have set before you this day life and good, and death and evil; . . . therefore choose life" (Deut. 30:15,19). The human species may choose death and destruction. Theism mediated by the covenantal moment of Sinai does not free us from the terror of this possibility, regardless of what we do with our freedom and power. That is the burden of responsibility one carries when one lives only with the covenantal demand and not with the certainty of eschatological resolution.

It is significant that the Bible's account of the covenantal election of Israel in the desert is followed directly by a story of the community's rebellion. The presentation of the story of the golden calf right after the moment of election may be understood as a reminder that the covenantal community is always liable to fail in its task, for idolatry has a great and persistent seductive power. A *midrash* states (*Berakhot* 8b) that the broken first tablets of the Lord were placed in the ark of the covenant alongside the second set of tablets brought down from the mountain by Moses—as if to say that God's reconfirmation of the covenant after the incident of the golden calf created a memory and awareness that human failure and rebellion are permanent possibilities of the covenantal relationship between God and the community.

The biblical story of God's election of Israel does not permit illusions about the spiritual powers of God's covenantal community. Its account of the repeated testing of God by the children of Israel and their endless dissatisfaction with and rebellion against the leadership of Moses does not support Judah Halevi's claims about the spiritual genius and ontological uniqueness of Israel. They were a difficult community. Whenever they felt threatened, lacked water, or were tired of their daily food rations, they longed to return to Egypt. When they encountered difficulties, they fled from freedom and responsibility. When they met danger, they cried to Moses: "Was it for want of graves in Egypt that you brought us to die in the wilderness?" (Exod. 14:11). In hearing Israel's response to God in the desert, we recognize that a community always has the option of balking at the burden and risk that freedom and responsibility bring. The biblical description of Israel in the desert is a reminder not only of how vulnerable human beings are to idolatry, but also of how willing they are to succumb to the attractions of slavery.

In entering into the covenant, we are not freed from the limitations of the human condition, nor is promise held out to us that someday we will be freed from them. This is underscored by the covenantal election's taking place in the desert. The desert, bare of the veneers of civilization, exposes human weakness and elemental hungers, fears and terrors. It brings into sharp relief the fact that God's covenant is not made with intellectual or spiritual geniuses or with persons of exceedingly great moral capacity, but with persons who are prepared to ignore God's scheme for history when their fundamental biological needs are not satisfied. The desert location of the covenant demonstrates to Israel that the relationship with God can be reinstated despite weakness and vulnerability to sin. It teaches the community that it need not live with the terror that God will abandon it if it fails to maintain the elaborate norms of the *mitzvot*. It inspires the community to believe that the covenant is everlasting. The belief that God will not abandon Israel—which reflects His acceptance of human finitude and limitations—gives rise to a feeling that the road to renewal is never closed. While the covenant does not promise that the ambiguities of history resulting from human freedom will be eliminated or that we will overcome the limitations of our finitude, it does give us the courage to begin again, so that failure need never weaken our resolve to strive to reinstate the sanctifying power of the covenantal norm. Sinai teaches the power of the beginning and not the certainty of the end.

Both the story of creation and God's election of the community in the desert as His covenantal partner thus reflect God's acceptance of human beings with all their limitations. No spiritualization of our human nature nor any eschatological hope is needed to launch the covenant as an active force in human history. No category of ultimate total redemption is required from the outset in the biblical accounts of creation and the Sinai revelation.

Nonetheless, the bloodshed, violence, and suffering that fill the pages of human history can easily lead to disillusionment about the possibility of ever realizing the covenantal vision of life in the world as it is, so long as that vision depends on what human beings do with their freedom. Reflection on human puniness, moral shoddiness, proneness to violence, and thirst for revenge can lead to a desperate hedonism in which nothing has value except the individual's own immediate pleasures. Alternatively, it may induce people to see meaning only in activity within very narrow realms of existence—a small group or a limited range of human activities. Another possibility is to reinforce commitment to the covenant with the belief that we are not alone: God, too, participates in and is responsible for His demands on us in history. The conviction that God will achieve His predetermined aims in history irrespective of human actions can sustain the determination to live according to the covenant's demands even in the face of the failures of human efforts to bring about a just society. If a moral vision of history that relies only on finite humanity is dangerously fragile, faith in God's unilateral grace and spontaneous intervention in history can serve as a protective wall, shielding one from onslaughts of nihilistic despair.[12]

It is thus understandable that the eschatological visions of Jeremiah and Ezekiel assisted the people to maintain their commitment to the covenant. According to Ezekiel, God frequently resolved to wipe out the Israelite community on account of its failures to obey His commandments, but He always drew back because that would have contradicted His own purposes.

> So I resolved to pour out My wrath on them, to accomplish My anger against them in the wilderness. But I withdrew My hand and acted for the sake of My name, that it should not be profaned in the sight of the

nations, in whose sight I had brought them out [of Egypt]. (Ezek. 20:21–22)

The many failings of Israel recalled by Ezekiel in the same chapter lead him to a vision of history in which God acts independently of Israel's worthiness. God, to Ezekiel, has a stake in Israel's life. Even if the people of Israel are unworthy, even if they repeatedly rebel against His laws, He is nevertheless tied to them in ways that impel Him to act unilaterally. The covenant of mutuality, which presupposes human freedom and responsibility, is replaced by one in which God acts in a way that frees us of the burden of human choice. Ezekiel's vision, like that of Jeremiah, is of a covenant written directly onto human hearts. In that vision, obedience to God's Torah becomes an intrinsic feature of human nature. Finite human beings, susceptible to failure and rebellion, are transformed into creatures that necessarily mirror God's redemptive vision for history.[13]

The eschatological perspective of Jeremiah and Ezekiel is understandable, given the despair to which the spiritual aspiration of "You shall be a holy nation" can lead when it depends on human beings. Nevertheless, it is a radical departure from what is implicit in the Sinai covenant.

It is similarly understandable why certain rabbis in the Talmud taught that redemption will come about irrespective of Jewish efforts and worthiness. In a discussion between Rav and Samuel in *Sanhedrin* 97b, Rav declares: "All the appointed times [of redemption] are over, and the matter depends wholly upon repentance and good deeds." History will not be redeemed of necessity; redemption is contingent on human action and efforts. But Samuel states: "It is sufficient for a mourner to perform his mourning." It is enough for Israel to sustain itself in history; redemption is not dependent on successful moral renewal. The talmudic discussion then compares their views to those of two earlier teachers, Rabbi Eliezer ben Hyrcanus and Rabbi Joshua, both students of Rabbi Johanan ben Zakkai. Rabbi Eliezer says: "If Israel repent, they will be redeemed; if not, they will not be saved." Rabbi Joshua answers: "If they do not repent, they will not be redeemed?—But the Holy One, blessed be He, will set up a king over them, whose decrees will be as cruel as Haman's, and then Israel will engage in repentance." Rabbi Joshua argues here that God will not free Jews from the need to change, but He will create conditions compelling them to respond as He wishes.[14]

Although faith in the certainty of God's acting in history irrespective of human initiative and action is thus found in both the prophetic and rabbinic traditions, I have chosen to take up a different strand of the Judaic tradition and construct a covenantal anthropology in which the essential role of human freedom and responsibility in the realization of the covenantal vision of Judaism is never suspended or neutralized. I prefer to live without relying upon the hope expressed by Jeremiah and Ezekiel. For me, God's love is mediated not through a promise of eschatological redemption, but through the constant and ever-renewed covenantal *mitzvah*, which calls one to full responsibility and alerts one to the potential for spiritual renewal within *ongoing* history. God's love is felt in the fact that with all one's imperfections and limitations, one is fully accepted by God and commanded by Him to undertake a covenantal responsibility. Even as the founding moment of creation validates human finitude, otherness, and freedom, the covenantal moment of Sinai demonstrates God's love and willingness to build His vision of history with vulnerable human beings. These are permanent features of the challenge of living by the *mitzvot*.

God of Creation and God of the Covenant

Above I argued that, from the viewpoint of human finitude, the biblical accounts of the founding moment of creation and of the revelational moment of the Sinai covenant do not necessarily provide grounds for a utopian vision of historical redemption. Now I shall show that this vision is also not necessarily derivable from the viewpoint of infinite divine power. That is, we are not obliged to infer from God's omnipotence as Creator that He will certainly ensure the realization of all His plans for history, since it is possible to have an understanding of creation that does not make it *exclusively* a prologue to history.

As I view it, creation contains two distinct awarenesses of God. On the one hand, as was explained in the opening chapter of this book, the creation story told in Genesis points toward the covenant. In this story, God creates human beings in His image as dignified creatures aware of their otherness and freedom. This anthropocentric perception of creation is the prologue for the later moments in which God is understood within covenantal religious categories. Those moments, in which God as the source of reality becomes experienced as a personal being, climax in the revelation at Sinai. The covenantal perspective read back into creation thus unites the God of universal being with the personal God of the Torah. The full reality of God, however, is not encountered through the covenant. There is also a broader religious awareness of

God that is not reducible to theistic notions of covenantal mutuality. It is the awareness of God in the cosmic order, as discussed in Job's case in chapter 5. The divine self-limitation that allows for human freedom and dignity is a covenantal category, not a cosmic category, even though it first appears in the creation story. That self-limitation does not account for God's relationship to the *whole* of reality, but only for God's particular relationship to the human individual and community; it provides the ontological condition for the covenantal relationship with the community at Sinai, but only as part of a *broader* scheme of creation. It would be arrogant to presuppose that the whole scheme of creation exists merely for the sake of the relationship between God and humans.

When we follow Job and step out of our particular historical covenantal role as members of a specific community, where the social and political drama is central in mediating and nurturing our religious consciousness, a cosmic perception of divinity can surface. When we look at the universe in its impersonal fullness, we know that besides *mitzvah* and the covenantal structures of religious relationship with God, there is also a cosmic experience of God that is transethical and transpersonal. This religious reflection on the universe, which is at the source of Job's feeling overwhelmed by the mystery of existence, points to an awareness that God and creation are not exhausted by the relational intimacy of covenantal speech and *mitzvah*. There is also a larger cosmic, ahistorical, religious sense, what may be called an aesthetic dimension to religious consciousness, which responds to the broader mystery, power, and overwhelming beauty of existence. In the aesthetic, cosmic dimension of religious experience, being is celebrated not only from the perspective of the interest of our covenantal community, but also simply for its own sake. Our response in that dimension is awe and rapturous love for the divine Artist.

There are, then, two sources of love of God within Judaism. One is the love nurtured by the intimacy of the covenant, by the feeling of mutuality with the divine Partner, by the joy one experiences in the life of *mitzvah*. This love issues from the invitation we are given in the covenant to live with God through performance of His *mitzvot*. The other source of love for God is the one so ardently expressed by Maimonides. It reflects not a relational passion born from *mitzvah*, but the disinterested awe of a creature who feels blessed by the opportunity to reflect on God's power as mirrored in nature. This love is not covenantal but contemplative. In this love for God, I do not see myself as a being singled out and addressed by God.

When, however, *mitzvah* and the covenant are the sole framework in which divinity is perceived, the belief can arise that *all* of reality must express the personal will of a just God, that *all* events in history manifest a divine scheme and a rational purpose. It is that view which serves as the ground for the Judaic eschatological longing for redemption in history. Yet once it is recognized that God is not fully contained in the personal relationship between Him and us as mediated through *mitzvah*, once it is realized that experience of the God of being is not exhausted by notions of covenantal mutuality, it may be appreciated that belief in God as Creator of the Universe need not oblige us to believe that there is a divinely ordained ethical pattern in all events. It can be accepted that there is a divine drama independent of ourselves and not subject to our noblest aspirations for history.

I prefer, therefore, not to seek to discover God's personal will in all events of our experience, but only in such events as pertain to the normative framework of *mitzvah*. Since the Judaic tradition has provided me with this framework for understanding His will, I prefer to limit the quest for a divinely sanctioned ethical order to those aspects of life that can be brought into it. Within this framework, I encounter God as the personal will that spoke to me at Sinai. Outside it, I encounter Him simply as the Creator Who manifests His power in the world through *impersonal* patterns of order. In short, I apply a rabbinic dictum that held much significance for Maimonides, that "the world pursues its normal course," not merely to nature but also to human history.

Judaic thinkers who desired to recognize God's personal will outside the strict confines of the framework of *mitzvah*, because they felt that all of nature and history must mediate a just and loving personal God, were left with little choice but to struggle to find a way of making all events in human life fit into some larger, just and rational scheme. Although Maimonides and Soloveitchik evidently gave up hope of making sense of God's justice, their explanation of human history still operates with this model. While Soloveitchik does not suppose that we shall ever achieve a full rational comprehension of God's actions in history, he does believe that, in principle, were we able to look at the world from God's vantage point, we would understand how all of human suffering is compatible with the belief in God as a loving Creator and just Lord of History. He suggests that we respond to suffering as Job did, by becoming more sensitive, loving, and caring toward other human beings. That is for Soloveitchik not a theodicy but a way of redeeming suffering from its apparent meaninglessness. Nonetheless, believing in principle that events in history are the carriers of God's will, Soloveitchik looks forward to the eschatological moment of unity between nature and history, when the God of Creation will be manifestly mediated in His full loving justice in historical reality. In the meantime, however, the manner in which His justice operates is partly or largely inscrutable.

Against all attempts to retain divine justice by making it inscrutable, it may be argued that the God Who submits to the autonomy of human reason in the academy of Torah learning thereby invites the Judaic community to construct its covenantal relationship with God in categories that do not annul our human sense of justice. In chapter 1, we already met the paradigm of covenantal intelligibility in Abraham's challenge to God: "Shall not the Judge of all the earth deal justly?" (Gen. 18:25). Abraham speaks from a clear understanding of what "justice" implies. God does not tell Abraham in reply that His justice is in no way comprehensible to Abraham's limited human rational capacity. Instead, he agrees to spare Sodom if a few just men can be found within the city. This story clearly suggests that human beings are privy to God's criteria of what is considered justice. Were that not the case, the status of the individual as a rational moral being, which is implied by the notion of the covenant, would be denied.

I therefore do not accept that all of history embodies an inscrutable form of divine justice. The tragic is present in human life because contingency and the possibility of suffering are intrinsic to it. To reiterate Maimonides, it is "foolish" to imagine that one could be human and yet not be vulnerable to death and suffering. Undeserved suffering is a permanent possibility of life in this universe. In "pursuing its normal course," the world functions according to its own morally neutral pattern. It is therefore an error to try to explain such a world *in toto* by means of human ethical categories. Not everything that occurs in human history and in nature expresses the moral judgment of a personal God. Nor does the covenant of *mitzvah* offer a worldview that enables everything that occurs in the world to be placed within a larger, rational moral scheme—not now and equally not in an eschatological future. Rather, it provides a way for living in a universe shot through with the possibility of suffering.

The halakhic requirement that one recite the benediction "Blessed is the True Judge" on receiving bad tidings does not imply that it should be possible in principle to explain to the mourner why the death of a beloved parent or child was necessary to the divine plan and therefore ultimately rational and just. That death remains a violation of all one's longings for the reasonable and just within human life. Rather, the benediction can be seen as a means of affirming one's determination to continue to live by the covenant despite every disappointed expectation.[15] The same affirmation appears more fully in the Kaddish, which mourners pronounce at the graveside and repeatedly during their period of mourning.

> Magnified and exalted be His great name in the world which He has created according to His will. May He establish His kingdom during your life and during your days and during the life of all the house of Israel, even speedily and at a near time; and say "Amen." Let His great name be praised for ever and to all eternity. Blessed, praised and glorified, exalted, extolled and honored, magnified and lauded be the name of the Holy One, blessed be He, though He be high above all the benedictions and hymns, praises and consolations, which are uttered in the world; and say "Amen." May there be abundant peace from heaven, and life for us and for all Israel; and say "Amen." He who makes peace in His high places, may He make peace for us and for all Israel; and say "Amen."

This declaration of faith affirms that the tragic has not destroyed one's commitment to live by covenantal aspirations. It proclaims a resolve to maintain the struggle to bring the covenantal *mitzvah* to history despite the death and suffering that are ever-recurring features of the human condition. Not everything needs to be explicable, not even in principle, in order to live with faith in the covenant. The world pursuing its normal course is accepted as the world in which it is given us to live our short life, and in which we must decide either to live or not to live by the covenant of Torah.

The Significance of the Exodus

Against my claim that the biblical account of the Sinai revelation does not oblige us to anticipate future miraculous divine interventions and eschatological redemption, it may be urged that the first words of that revelation are "I am the Lord your God Who brought you out of the Land of Egypt, out of the house of bondage" (Exodus 20:2). Similar formulas of admonition accompany other *mitzvot* in the Torah. Evidently, the Torah does not regard the Exodus from Egypt as merely a past great kindness of God; we are required in some way to preserve the memory of the Exodus in our consciousness of the *mitzvot*. Does this justify the Nachmanidean view that our commitment to the *mitzvot* presupposes the expectation of ongoing divine miracles? Does it point to a time when we shall be redeemed not merely from the power of Pharaoh but also from the power of evil itself?

While the Nachmanidean view is one way of understanding "I am the Lord your God . . . ," it is by no means the only way. As we have seen, the rabbis of the talmudic period tended to direct consciousness of the miraculous power of God exclusively toward the eschatological future and to limit its application in ongoing daily experience. Life under oppressive foreign rule made them aware of the difficulties of incorporating an event-based theology within a disciplined *mitzvah* framework of theism; the one assumes an ongoing direct spontaneous activity of God, the other represents the way the tradition has mediated God's demands. The rabbinic tradition nonetheless sought to combine the two theistic models. God was seen both as the powerful Lord of History Who triumphs over His enemies and as the silent God Who has now temporarily withdrawn from history. The silent God has endowed the community with the means of autonomously discovering how He wishes them to live during this interim period of indefinite duration, but one day He will return and demonstrate His power in history. The rabbis thus maintained a delicate balance between the Torah and events in history as very different kinds of mediators of God's relationship to the community. That enabled them to reduce the significance of history in the present while retaining the model of the liberation from Egypt as a real possibility for the future.

Another way of viewing the significance of the Exodus is as a founding memory that creates the psychological grounds for a personalist theistic relationship. The Exodus is then comparable to early childhood experiences in which helpless children learn to trust their parents. The trust developed in early dependency relationships often serves as the psychological basis for mature love relationships entered into during adulthood, to which the Sinai covenant can be likened. The community's helplessness in Egypt could be remedied only through unilateral divine grace, which was manifested in the form of the Exodus. That dependence born of helplessness is ultimately transformed, by way of the covenant of *mitzvah*, into a dependence grounded in love. The Exodus as an early founding memory, which nurtures relational theism with the assistance of other stories of the living God Who acts in history, thus plays a central role in helping one build a theistic sensibility. The founding moment of theism is transcended, however, when theism is increasingly filtered through *mitzvah*. While the Exodus story is never negated or denied, it is now retained as a memory, like the memory of our early relational intimacy with our parents, which is fondly retained in later years as we build our life around mature friendships and voluntary commitments. Just as the memory of childhood dependence is imprinted in one's mature consciousness, so too can the Exodus from

Egypt remain a permanent memory for one who appropriates theism within the framework of *mitzvah*.

To this view of the Exodus as a psychological grounding memory for theism, I would add another approach, which absorbs the Exodus into the covenant as *complementary* rather than as merely *preliminary* to the experience of *mitzvah*. The story of the Exodus can be seen as signifying that the covenant of Sinai may be implemented in its fullness only if particular social and political conditions are met. Covenantal commitments require a social, economic, and political reality that creates room for us to apply our sense of freedom and dignity. Only after the slave-master's grip has been broken can the community be invited to participate in the covenantal drama. When the community is enslaved in Egypt, it is not yet challenged by God to become a holy people, it is not told that it has been entrusted with a creative responsible role in history. The language of *mitzvah* cannot be spoken to human beings whose social reality convinces them that they are merely objects for manipulation. The permanent significance of the Exodus from Egypt for the covenant of Sinai is thus that it prevents the misunderstanding of *mitzvah* as an inward spiritual category, unrelated to social and political conditions, which refers to the soul's longing for eternity and spiritual freedom. Our constant recall of the Exodus counteracts the temptation of escaping into otherworldliness because it anchors the covenant in history and in the social and political life of the community.[16]

Regarded in this last way, the Exodus story insists that the covenant can have meaning only to the degree that Jews enjoy freedom to organize their lives and believe they are capable of meeting the challenge placed before them at Sinai. As long as Jews lack social and political freedoms, they are under constraints that prevent them from obeying the rule of God. This is implicit in the Jerusalem Talmud's explanation for why the slave is exempt from the obligation of reciting the Shema. The Shema affirms one's allegiance to and faith in the rule of God, but, as the Jerusalem Talmud says (*Berakhot* 3:3), only a person who "has one master" can recite the declaration "Hear O Israel, the Lord our God, the Lord is One." Those whose life is tightly controlled and manipulated by human masters cannot in true conscience declare their allegiance to the rule of God, for they do not have the experience of living as free individuals under the guidance of God's *mitzvah*. The *mitzvot* are obligatory only when one is free. Thus, "I am the Lord thy God who brought you out of the land of Egypt, out of the house of bondage," can also be understood to mean that "I am the God who chooses to be loved and worshiped by a free people." Only free, dignified human beings can enter into the covenant. The Exodus, therefore, comple-ments the story of creation, which affirms that human beings are en-dowed with freedom. Taken together, the two stories show that only in a posture of human dignity and responsibility is a covenantal reality possible.

The stories in the Torah that tell of the community's recurrent desire to return to Egypt show that the community only gradually became prepared to undertake the risks and uncertainty of becoming a cove-nantal community. The forty years in the desert, as Maimonides taught (*Guide* 3:32), were meant not as a punishment for sin but as a training for the community, helping people to discover the adequacy that would enable them to accept the challenges of becoming a free nation. Rather than the Exodus from Egypt being a symbol of an ever-present need for miracles and unilateral grace, it describes how human beings are to be weaned from the helpless condition of slavery and their initial terror of freedom and uncertainty. The Exodus and the desert signify that only after the total need for unilateral grace and miracle has been *left behind* is the community ready to enter the Promised Land and begin to face the responsibility of building a covenantal society.

The Model of Mature Love

So far I have argued that the Sinai covenant can be understood and applied in the modern situation without a reliance on eschatological redemption. I do not deny that accepting the Sinai covenant without reliance on unilateral divine grace places a heavy and possibly oppres-sive burden on covenantal Jews. I have argued that the very fact that the covenant was made in the desert assures the community that the covenant is not based on illusions about their capacities and moral strength. The desert as the site of Israel's repeated rebellions against Moses and God is a permanent reminder that God is prepared to sustain a covenant with limited human beings. However, the memory of the desert is not the only source of the feeling of security that the covenant is eternal and not conditional.

One of the classic Judaic models for expressing the depth of the cov-enantal experience mediated through *mitzvah* is the marriage model that is found, for instance, in the prophet Hosea and in the rabbinic inter-pretation of the Song of Songs as an allegory of Israel's covenantal elec-tion at Sinai. An examination of this marriage and love model will help us to understand how the covenant can be appreciated and its power sustained without the certainty of God's unilateral redemptive grace.

At the beginning of married life, when one is in the first flush of love, the common feeling is that the love relationship will somehow compensate for everything lacking in one's previous experience. The feeling of many young lovers is that now that they have found each other, all will be well. Love can give a profound sense of security, of being free from the uncertainty and pain experienced when one lived as a single individual. In the early stages of their relationship, the lovers are usually not fully aware that separateness and otherness will always somehow remain permanent features of the love relationship. Early love has about it a quality of mystic union, a feeling that through love one has become whole and redeemed and that the problematics of the human condition have in some way been transcended. However, when the struggles of the real world impinge upon the consciousness of young lovers, they discover that love does not heal all.[17] They learn, often after many years of struggle, that love cannot compensate for human weaknesses and failures. Above all, they learn that neither partner in the relationship can redeem the other. They come to the hard-won realization that neither of them can single-handedly give dignity and a sense of wholeness and worth to the other. The feeling of personal integration and self-confidence that makes for dignity never comes exclusively as a gift from the other, but is always also the fruit of enormous personal effort.[18]

A mature relationship is based on respect for human frailty and weakness. The partners in such a relationship have been eased of any burden of guilt for not having redeemed their beloved from human failings. They appreciate the problematics of human finitude and the fact that separateness is a permanent feature of any love relationship. They thereby realize that they have no need to reject or be angry at their beloved because of the persistence of his or her "unredeemedness." When one learns to accept the implications of finitude, one discovers new sources of acceptance and love, which help in overcoming the anger and resentment that result from a false estimation of what a love relationship entails and can bring about. Maturity teaches one how to be kind, considerate, and seriously committed to the needs of the other, with the full awareness that one's love and care may not dispel the problems of the other. After the early mystic dimensions of love have receded, a new relationship develops, sustained by shared experiences and common memories of joy and suffering, and accompanied by the awareness that love expresses itself in the ability to accept the other fully in his or her limitedness. In such a relationship, mutuality is not made conditional upon judgmental scrutiny. Mature lovers no longer fear they will be condemned or rejected because of failures or mistakes.[19]

Let us see how this model of mature love parallels the relationship at the core of covenantal Judaic spirituality. Through the elaborate symbolic ritual structure constructed in the talmudic era, the covenantal community was given a way to internalize and feel secure about its relationship with God. Through the daily liturgy and the symbolic world of the annual festivals, Jews experience the repeated feeling that the relationship is too firm to admit the possibility of its termination. The covenant is certain. Specific actions may be judged, but not the vitality and significance of the relationship itself. The biblical descriptions of the covenant, by contrast, have many features that do suggest conditionality. Those can be seen, however, as reflecting the early appropriation of the relationship. As shaped by rabbinic Judaism, the covenantal marriage appears to exclude the possibility of divorce. Existence independent of it accordingly becomes unimaginable. Jewish spiritual history transforms biblical conditionality into a secure, nonjudgmental framework. Both God and Israel have invested too much in the relationship to terminate it. There is nothing Israel can do that would shock God into reconsidering His relationship with it. The truthfulness with which Israel's failures in the desert are portrayed, rather than warning of the limits of God's patience, has become a source of reassurance that God's covenant with Israel is not exclusively based on the passion of romantic love. The memory of renewed acceptance after the tablets had been broken, represented by Moses' second ascent of Sinai and encounter with God, is an assurance of God's ever-renewed love. Strengthened with this assurance, we can gladly embrace the life of covenantal norms even without the hope that history is guaranteed ultimate resolution and redemption.

The relationship between Israel and God in the early biblical period, over which a spirit of conditionality prevails, can be characterized as rule-dominated. It recalls the way young married couples work out the details of mutual obligations so as to build security and reliable anticipations into their relationship. However, when the relationship matures on the basis of years of shared struggle, concern, and memory, its organization goes beyond explicit rules. Similarly, talmudic Judaism's expansion of the halakhic framework of the mitzvot takes place within a relationship that has withstood the test of much suffering and numerous failures. The halakhic absorbs the aggadic portrayal of the mutual love of God and Israel for each other. An outside observer may see only rules. One who lives within the covenantal framework of *halakhah* understands, however, that the multiplying details of the law and the fascination to conceive of every possibility through which *halakhah* may be applied do not reflect an obsessive insecurity that the relationship may not survive without more and more rules. On the contrary, they reflect the passion of a lover who seeks to be accompanied by consciousness of the beloved always and everywhere. They reflect a longing to bring the God of Sinai into any number of personal living encounters by giving so many aspects of reality the possibility of reflecting our hearing of God through *mitzvah*. If no domain of life is devoid of the possibility of halakhic guidance, then there is no moment or place in reality that is not open to the passion of covenantal theism. To characterize rabbinic Judaism as pure legalism is thus profoundly to misunderstand its spiritual worldview.[20]

Underlying the covenantal anthropology presented here is a belief that it is possible to build a relationship to God and His *mitzvah* based on this model of mature love. This understanding of covenantal love is what enables me to give up the model of unilateral divine grace as the principal source sustaining the vitality of the covenantal relationship. The joy of mature love for God ensures covenantal significance in the midst of every uncertainty.[21]

Hope with Uncertainty

One can live in an open universe filled with uncertainty and yet retain the depth of commitment for the God Who is mediated by the drama of creation. History need not exhaust the plenitude of the divine reality, nor need the cosmic consciousness neutralize the significance of human history. Creation and the Sinai covenant can live in mutual interaction without either pole neutralizing and absorbing the other. A human being can yearn for the triumph of justice in history and yet know that the human world is shot through with contingency, uncertainty, and possible destruction.

From this perspective, in contrast to rabbinic thought, not all that occurs in history and nature expresses the moral judgment of God. The biblical and rabbinic concern with God's presence in history need not entail that history must express the full reality and power of divinity.

One can embrace the life of the covenantal community knowing full well that history and the community do not exhaust the fullness of the religious quest for God.

We are instructed by the rabbinic tradition to admit to the notion of divine justice and yet at the same time to resign ourselves to the fact that we shall never be able, from our own limited viewpoint, to see how God's judgment can be fully understood by human reason. As was pointed out in previous chapters, belief that nature and history must mediate a personal, just, and loving God leaves one with little choice but to struggle to find a way of making all events in human life fit into some larger, rational, just scheme. When this becomes extremely difficult, the only response can be silence and resignation before the mysterious will of God. God is proclaimed a truthful and just Lord of History, although His ways are unfathomable.[22]

The attempt to allege God's mysterious activity in history in order to explain suffering is, in my judgment, self-defeating. Although in both the rabbinic and the Maimonidean tradition there was a genuine practical impulse motivating attempts to offer judgmental models of response to suffering, that approach suffered from a basic weakness. The human will to act, which is a fundamental presupposition of the covenant, can be undermined by building a notion of justice that in no way fits what we know about ourselves in reality. The covenantal call to become active and responsible for the totality of human life is too great a burden to bear if it means walking around with a sense that at any moment one can be judged guilty and severely punished. If we are to uphold the dignity implied by the notion of the covenant, with its full respect for ourselves as rational and moral beings, we must reject attempts to see all of nature and history as mediating God's personal will.

When the occurrence of events patterned after the biblical description of miracle is made the normative criterion of what constitutes God's personal love for us, a built-in sense of guilt is imposed upon us. If the triumphant victory over Pharaoh and the miraculous activities of God in the desert are made to serve as the paradigmatic vehicles of the theistic vision, then Jews of all later ages who examine their own historical experiences are condemned to live with a sense of unworthiness in comparison with that generation which witnessed God's miraculous intervention in history. The very fact of being born later and living under historical conditions that in no way mirror the Exodus story from Egypt is then enough to demonstrate one's unworthiness, sinfulness, and guilt.

Refusing to make all events in history and nature the vehicle of theism frees us from the enormous burden of feeling spiritually inadequate simply because we were born in the age of Auschwitz. Since Jews are invited to renew the vitality of the covenant of Sinai in each generation, no intrinsic qualitative distinction in religious dignity and creativity should be made between the community of the biblical and rabbinic periods and those who live in the present world. Jewish history should not be seen from a theological viewpoint that creates an automatic permanent sense of personal guilt and inadequacy. We cannot decide which generation God loved more or less by considering who was the recipient of greater miracles. The eternal covenant invites all who are prepared to live by the *mitzvot* to see their own history and religious reality as filled with the same potential vitality as any other period in Jewish history.

I therefore disagree with George Steiner's assertions that "tragedy is alien to the Judaic sense of the world" and "the Judaic spirit is vehement in its conviction that the order of the universe and of man's estate is accessible to reason."[23] Judaism need not be seen to offer a worldview through which all that occurs in the world could be placed within a larger, moral, rational scheme. Love for the *mitzvah* given at Sinai inspires one with the courage to live responsibly and heroically in spite of the fact that so much of human effort is frustrated by the invasion of unexpected and undeserved suffering. The significance Jews find in their way of life and the compelling spiritual power of the Torah can act as a counterbalance to despair, enabling us to live by the covenant despite the pain of tragedy. Our covenantal anthropology thus allows an individual to satisfy the passion for theism within partial frameworks of intelligibility, to hope without the certainty of redemption.

12

The Third Jewish Commonwealth

THE REBIRTH OF ISRAEL and the ingathering of many Jews from the four corners of the globe has awakened new biblical religious passions within the Jewish community. Jerusalem is no longer a dream, an anticipation, a prayer for the future, but a living, vibrant reality. The Six-Day War further encouraged the belief that Israel is moving toward the fulfillment of the biblical promise. A deep sense of messianic grandeur fills the hearts of many young enthusiasts who feel called upon to settle in every corner of the biblical boundaries of the land of Israel in order to realize the prophetic promise of redemption.

It is not my concern in this chapter to deal with the moral and political difficulties that this messianic fervor generates. I wish rather to consider (1) how the rebirth of Israel can be given religious significance without having to make the bold theological claim that it is a manifestation of God's final redemptive action in history; (2) how the Maimonidean perspective on messianism can provide new normative directions for Israeli society; and (3) how the challenges that Israeli society must face create a new moral and spiritual agenda for Jews throughout the world.

The Religious Significance of Israel

Most Jewish religious responses to the rebirth of the state of Israel do see in it God's providential hand.[1] Two major halakhic thinkers who have taken such a view are Rabbis Kook and Soloveitchik. Kook, the first Ashkenazi chief rabbi of Israel in the Mandate period, viewed the Zionist revolution as part of God's redemptive scheme in history. He attributed profound religious significance to the Zionist revolution—despite its antireligious origins and manifestations—with the help of a dialectical perspective on history: Judaism's development in exile had caused the repression of vital spiritual forces in the Jewish people, and only by the overthrow of much of traditional Judaism would new, healthy forces and energies within the Jewish people be released. The Zionist activist concern for restoring the Jewish people to its homeland would unleash new messianic redemptive forces.[2] It was Kook's deepest conviction that ultimately the new energies brought forth by the revolution would be integrated with the covenantal Torah spirit in a higher religious synthesis. He looked forward to a new unity between the larger prophetic passion for history found in the Bible and the sober concern for details that characterizes talmudic Judaism.[3] Most religious Zionist youths in Israel are taught to perceive the state from this messianic perspective.

Soloveitchik, too, embraces the state of Israel, but without a messianic dialectic. In *Reflections of the Rav*, Soloveitchik characterizes the period of the Holocaust as the state of *hester panim*, a "hiding of the divine face," a state when God turned His back, as it were, chaos ruled, and human beings had no sense of the divine presence in the world. Israel's rebirth represents *middat ha-din*, the "attribute of God's judgment," which gives human life a sense that there is some divine order, justice, and structure in the world, that the world is not entirely under the sway of barbaric chaotic forces.

> We cannot explain the Holocaust but we can, at least, classify it theologically, characterize it, even if we have no answer to the question, "why?" The unbounded horrors represented the *tohu vavohu* anarchy of the pre-*yetzirah* state. This is how the world appears when God's moderating surveillance is suspended. The State of Israel, however, reflects God's return to active providence, the termination of *Hester Panim*.
>
> That Israel is being subjected to severe trials in its formative years does not negate the miraculous manifestations of Divine favor which have

been showered upon the State. Clearly, this is *Middat Hadin*, not *Hester Panim*. (p. 37)

In his essay "Kol dodi dofek" ("The voice of my beloved knocks"),[4] Soloveitchik utilizes the Purim story, in which natural events are appreciated as expressions of God's providential design, for understanding the theological significance of contemporary events. Just as the tradition understood that God worked His redemption for Israel through the actions of King Ahasuerus, so too we can sense God acting once again in history through the United Nations decision on the partition of Mandatory Palestine. Soloveitchik once again hears the voice of his beloved God in the events of contemporary Jewish history that have changed the social and political condition of the Jewish people. For Soloveitchik, the state of Israel has made Jews less vulnerable to physical persecution. It has also aroused a new sense of Jewish identity among Jews who were being carried along on a strong current of assimilation. The rebirth of the state of Israel has shattered the Christian theological claim of God's rejection of the Jewish people as witnessed by their endless suffering and wandering. These and other factors are strong indications for Soloveitchik of God's providential involvement in contemporary Jewish history. Soloveitchik pleads with the community to see in the rebirth of Israel an invitation by God to a new and deeper relationship of love. We must "open the door" to go out to meet our Beloved. We begin to demonstrate our responsiveness to God's invitation to renew the love affair between Israel and God by settling the land and by becoming responsible for the political and economic development of the Jewish state.

For Soloveitchik, the shared suffering and common historical fate of the Jewish people represent what he calls *brit goral*, a covenant of destiny, which is the foundation for the important halakhic category of collective responsibility (*kol Yisrael arevim zeh la-zeh*).[5] Care for others, feelings of empathy, and a sense of solidarity are not secular categories in Soloveitchik's appreciation of halakhic Judaism. Indeed, the covenant of Sinai requires that the covenantal community have a deep sense of solidarity. Political action that seeks to achieve a secure home for the Jews, thereby giving dignity and new vitality to Jewish communal life and identity, thus acquires religious significance and can be understood as mirroring God's providential love for Israel. Soloveitchik's hope is that the community in Israel will find the way to move from a shared covenant of destiny to a shared covenant of meaning, *brit ye'ud*, based on the halakhic framework of Torah.

Soloveitchik and Kook have provided conceptual frameworks within

which religious Jews can attribute religious significance to the rebirth of
Israel initiated by people in revolt against their tradition. Soloveitchik's
framework assumes the halakhic significance of a shared covenant of
destiny and adopts the model of Purim in which God can manifest Himself through the natural unfolding of historical events. Kook's offers a
dialectic messianic understanding of Jewish history and of Zionism.

As I have already stated, I do not interpret current events in nature
and history as direct expressions of God's will or design. I look exclusively to the Torah and *mitzvot* as mediators of the personal God of the
covenant. That, however, does not mean that I must adopt Leibowitz's
position and ascribe no religious significance to the rebirth of Israel.[6]
From my perspective, the religious meaning one gives to events relates
not to their divine origin but to their possible influence on the life of
Torah. If an event in history can be a catalyst for a new perception of
the scope of Torah, if it widens the range of halakhic action and responsibility, if it provides greater opportunities for hearing God's *mitzvot*, then this already suffices to endow the event with religious
significance, for it intensifies and widens the way God can be present
in the daily life of the individual and the community. One can religiously embrace modern Israel not through a judgment about God's
actions in history but through an understanding of the centrality of
Israel for the fullest actualization of the world of *mitzvot*. This covenantal appreciation of history dispenses with the impossible task of reconciling God's loving redemptive actions in the rebirth of Israel with
His total withdrawal from and indifference to our tragic suffering in
Auschwitz. Soloveitchik's conceptual distinction between *hester panim*
(hiding of the divine face) and *middat ha-din* (attribute of God's judgment) only underlines the impossibility of that task, since we are left
paralyzed by the prospect that the loving personal God of *middat ha-
din* can withdraw into *hester panim* and allow the triumph of such demonic evil in the Holocaust.

My position regarding the centrality of modern Israel for the full
realization of the Torah as a way of life is in sharp opposition to those
religious trends in Judaism which regard the Zionist quest for normalcy
as a revolt against the Torah. For certain schools within Judaism, the
paradigm of Jewish spirituality is God's miraculous providential guidance in the desert. Freedom from the normal burden of natural existence is perceived by them as a necessary condition for the full appreciation and realization of the Torah.[7] This view is reflected in the
talmudic tradition by Rabbi Simeon ben Yohai,[8] for whom the Torah
can be adequately studied only by those in a condition of total grace

as symbolized by the manna in the desert or under messianic utopian conditions where the Jewish community will not have to be responsible for its economic well-being.

> Rabbi Simeon ben Yohai used to say: "Only to those who have manna to eat is it given to study the Torah. For behold, how can a man be sitting and studying when he does not know where his food and drink will come from, nor where he can get his clothes and coverings? Hence, only to those who have manna to eat is it given to study the Torah." (*Mekhilta de-Rabbi Ishmael, va-yassa* 3)

> Our rabbis taught: " 'And you shall gather in your corn' [Deut. 11:14]. What is to be learnt from these words? Since it says, 'This book of the law shall not depart out of your mouth' [Josh. 1:8], I might think that this injunction is to be taken literally. Therefore it says, 'And you shall gather in your corn,' which implies that you are to combine the study of Torah with a worldly occupation." This is the view of Rabbi Ishmael. But Rabbi Simeon ben Yohai says: "Is that possible? If a man plows in the plowing season, and sows in the sowing season, and reaps in the reaping season, and threshes in the threshing season, and winnows in the season of wind, what is to become of the Torah? No; but when Israel perform the will of the Omnipresent, their work is performed by others, as it says, 'And strangers shall stand and feed your flocks, etc.' [Isa. 61:5], and when Israel do not perform the will of the Omnipresent their work is carried out by themselves, as it says, 'And you shall gather in your corn.' " (*Berakhot* 35b)

For Rabbi Simeon ben Yohai, the political conditions under which the Torah can reach its fullness are met only when Jews do not have to participate in the normal functioning of everyday society. The passion for learning cannot be realized if the community is preoccupied with the normal, everyday problems of survival. God could not have demanded that the community be so wholly engaged in studying the Torah and yet burden us with those problems.

From this perspective, the covenant was made in the desert to teach that only under conditions of total supernatural grace can the Torah be fully actualized within the life of the community of Israel. For me, however, the separation of learning from the normal concerns of daily life is a distortion and abrogation of the covenantal spirit of Judaism. I give preference to *midrashim* that imply that the covenant was made in the desert to teach the community that Judaism as a way of life was not exclusively a function of political sovereignty.[9] We were born as a people within the desert in order to understand that the land must always be perceived as an instrumental and never as an absolute value. The memory that the covenant was made in the desert prevents us from falling victim to the idolatry of state power. The desert, however, was not meant to serve as a paradigm for the life of *mitzvot*. The desert is the founding moment of covenantal consciousness, but never the controlling feature of its development. It was a prelude pointing to the land, where the covenantal challenge received at Sinai was meant to be realized. The centrality of the land in Judaism teaches us that *mitzvah* must not remain an aspiration, a utopian hope to be realized in messianic conditions of history, but must be tested and concretized within the normal, everyday conditions of human existence. Whereas the desert is a moment of withdrawal and concentration, what is received in that moment has to be transformed into a way of life. The land exposes the Jewish people and the Torah to the test of reality.

The Jewish society that we build in Israel has to validate the claim made in the Jewish tradition regarding how a Torah way of life creates a holy community, "a kingdom of priests and a holy nation" (Exod. 19:6). If the Torah is truly capable of sanctifying every aspect of human reality, if it is capable of giving new moral and spiritual dimensions to politics, if "its ways are ways of pleasantness and all its paths are peace" (Prov. 3:17), if the Torah scholar is a paradigm of the builder of peace, this must be seen and confirmed through the way we live our daily lives and not only proclaimed in our prayers.

A community that defines itself by learning and prayer is liable to be deceived by the richness of its powers of linguistic expression when evaluating its own moral and religious integrity. The existence of the state of Israel prevents Judaism from being defined exclusively as a culture of learning and prayer. Here Judaism must draw its pathos also from the exigencies of the concrete needs of life. "Not the learning is essential but the doing" then becomes constitutive of Torah study. Learning that excuses one from responsibility for the physical well-being of a nation, that provides a conceptual framework with its own inner coherence but whose correspondence to what actually takes place in reality is never tested, may have compelling logical vigor and be intellectually fascinating, but it has lost the sanctity of Torah, since it has become irrelevant to life itself.

If the desert is an instrument, a preparation, but never a substitute for what living is all about, then the land of Israel represents the intrusion of the normal into the desert covenantal consciousness. When the nation enters the land of Israel, the manna ceases to be the source of their economic sustenance.[10] In the land of Israel, the community must face the challenge of planting trees and harvesting crops, of exposure to economic hardships, of building a national political reality in a world that does not necessarily share or appreciate God's "dream" that Israel become a holy nation. The Torah was not given at Sinai for a messianic society; it was meant to be implemented and developed within an unredeemed world.[11] The dangers and seductions of pagan culture did not disappear when the Israelites entered the land of Israel. The concrete concern with military security did not stop with the conquests of Joshua. The need to build institutional frameworks of power and yet retain the covenantal ideal of a holy nation accompanied the community throughout the building of the first Jewish commonwealth. The same unredeemed world was the context for the renewal of the covenant by Ezra and Nehemiah in the second commonwealth and must be faced with courage by Jews as we build the third commonwealth under similar nonmessianic historical conditions.[12]

The normalization of Jewish consciousness that comes from living in the land of Israel is therefore not antithetical to covenantal consciousness, but is a necessary condition for its full realization. The land of Israel is holy from the covenantal perspective because it invites *greater* responsibility and initiative on the part of the community. It is the framework in which ways must be found to make the Torah a viable way of life for a community.

A radically different view of the centrality of the land of Israel for Judaism is taken by Nachmanides, commenting on Leviticus 18:25ff. For Nachmanides the land of Israel is holy because of its unique ontological relationship to God.

> But the Land of Israel, which is in the middle of the inhabited earth, is the inheritance of the Lord, designated to His Name. He has placed none of the angels as chief, observer, or ruler over it, since He gave it as a heritage to His people who declare the unity of His Name.

The land of Israel vomits out its sinful inhabitants (Lev. 18:28), continued Nachmanides, because only in this land does one live under God's direct providence. Since there is this unique ontological relationship between God and the land, Jews in the diaspora live as if they have no direct relationship to God and perform *mitzvot* only in preparation for their return to the land of Israel.[13]

In contrast to Nachmanides and in the spirit of Maimonides, I regard the land of Israel as central to the *mitzvot* because it invites greater initiative and gives the community a wider range to express its normative consciousness.[14] The land of Israel represents the freeing of Jews from the direct and total dependence on grace experienced in the desert and signifies the movement toward human initiative and responsibility as the defining feature of the covenantal community. Whereas Nachmanides believed that greater self-reliance undermines the full flowering of the covenant, my claim is that God is present in the land of Israel because there Jews are not frightened to be independent and responsible for a total society.

I view the Zionist revolution as a rejection of the view of Rabbi Simeon ben Yohai regarding the utopian conditions required for Israel to fulfill its covenantal destiny in history. I understand Zionism as a rejection of the theological claim that a unique providential relationship to Israel frees the Jews from having to be concerned with the ways in which nations seek to ensure their survival. In its profoundest sense, Zionism is the total demythologization of that Jewish historical covenantal consciousness which is represented by the spirit of Nachmanides.[15] As my covenantal anthropology has sought to demonstrate, we can build a new Jewish society within the framework of a tradition that places *mitzvah* at the center of its perception of the meaning of Jewish existence. By infusing Torah with the original Zionist passion for Jewish responsibility, we can renew the Sinai covenant once again in the conditions of modern Israel.

Although one can understand the Zionist quest for normalcy within covenantal categories, it is nevertheless true that the major trend of secular Zionism sought to replace the covenantal identity of the Jew with a secular political national identity. Though distinctive elements of Zionism indicate its continuity with traditional Judaism, such as the centrality of peoplehood, identification with biblical history, and, most important, the significance of the land of Israel for the political rebirth of the Jewish people, nevertheless Zionism is generally regarded as a departure from the covenantal tradition. Not only did its adherents repudiate the traditional posture of waiting for the messianic redemption and of avoiding active intervention in the political arena of history, but Zionists often viewed traditional Judaism as an obstacle in the path of Jewish national political rebirth.

For many centuries before Zionism, Judaic religious consciousness had been characterized by the sense that the everyday world was a preparation for a future messianic reality. It was felt that the temporal world does not reflect the full power of God as Creator and Lord of History, nor can it contain the reward promised to the community for allegiance to the covenant. Jewish teachings about the immortality of the soul and the resurrection of the dead and Jewish utopian messianism reflected this deep Judaic belief in a future world that would be in harmony with our most cherished aspirations.

For traditional religious Jews, the instruments for affecting history were prayer, observance of the *mitzvot*, and Torah study. The covenantal community was not to sully its hands with the uncertainties and political and moral ambiguities of modern nationalism. Judaism was secure if it was able to build healthy families, if it could have vibrant schools and synagogues. The Jewish covenantal community could leave responsibility for a total social and political order to the nations of the world, while it lived in anticipation of the ultimate triumph of Judaism in the messianic reality.

Scholem was correct in a certain sense in his observation that there is a conservative instinct within the halakhic temperament. Halakhic Jews were afraid to expose their dreams of history to the test of reality. The fate of the first and second commonwealths, Bar Kochba's abortive revolt against Rome, and the tragic failures of all messianic movements in Jewish history created in religious Jews a prudent, conservative instinct not to hope for too much in terms of their national political existence. The central significance attached to the land of Israel, Jerusalem, and the ingathering of the exiles was expressed with passion daily in the life of prayer, but was to be realized only in a messianic kingdom. History had taught the Jews not to attempt to translate those prayers into a program of action.

Jewish hope was nurtured by the belief that the third Jewish commonwealth would not in any way share the vulnerabilities of the previous attempts to build a Jewish society in the Holy Land. Rabbinic *midrashim* taught that the third commonwealth would last forever.[16] It would be free of all the tragic features of human history. It would usher in a historical period in which humanity would be liberated from sin and suffering would be abolished from human life. In that time, the community would no longer be burdened by the haunting and problematic features of freedom, contingency, and the human propensity for evil.

As long as the Judaic hope for the third commonwealth reflected such a longing for certainty, Zionism could not emerge as an effective political movement. Zionism had therefore to define itself as a movement seeking to overthrow the traditional religious sensibility. If the community was to learn to act effectively in history, Jewish historical consciousness had to be radically transformed. And indeed, the quest for normalcy, initiative, and responsibility was in fact pursued through a revolt against Judaic covenantal faith. The house of learning and the synagogue were deemed enemies of the revolution. Prayer was perceived as escapism and as bad faith. Only by a complete overthrow of everything the tradition cherished could the revolution succeed. The pious student of Torah had to be derided, rejected, and replaced by the pioneer. Secular Zionism ushered in a passionate yearning for new anthropological models that celebrated the dignity of human physical power. Jewish historical figures who demonstrated heroism in battle were held in high esteem. The new leadership of the community were those whose eyes were anchored to the everyday and who sought pragmatic solutions to the pressing problems of the third commonwealth.

For many Jews, Israel has become the new substitute for traditional Judaism. Israel is possibly the last haven in the world for Jewish secularism. Israeli "normalcy" enables many to assimilate and be like all the nations of the world without feeling guilty for having abandoned their ancestors. With all the risks that Israel poses to the future of covenantal Judaism, I am nonetheless prepared to build my hopes for Judaism's future on this new reality. For, as the tradition teaches, where there is a potential for desecration, there is also a potential for sanctification.

I live with the guarded hope that out of this complex and vibrant new Jewish reality will emerge new spiritual directions for the way Judaism will be lived in the modern world. Israel expands the possible range of halakhic involvement in human affairs beyond the circumscribed borders of home and synagogue to the public domain. Jews in Israel are given the opportunity to bring economic, social, and political issues into the center of their religious consciousness. The moral quality of the army, social and economic disparities and deprivations, the exercise of power moderated by moral sensitivity—all these are realms that may engage halakhic responsibility. From this perspective, the fact that Israel enables us to make the whole of life the carrier of the covenant is in itself sufficient to ascribe profound religious significance to the secular revolt that led to Israel's rebirth. I celebrate Israel's Independence Day with the recitation of the Hallel psalms, thus expressing gratitude to God for having been given the opportunity to renew the full scope of the covenantal spirit of Judaism. My religious celebration is not a judgment on God's activity, but only on the opportunity that Israel makes possible. The opportunity may be missed. But that does not in any way detract from the religious possibilities created by the event. The recitation of psalms of thanksgiving on Independence Day does not entail any divine guarantee regarding the successful realization of those opportunities.[17]

A Messianic Appreciation of Israel

Although, as I have shown, the vitality of Judaism does not depend on belief in the messianic resolution of history, and although I do not require the messianic notion to give religious significance to the rebirth of Israel, I am nonetheless prepared to consider how Israel's rebirth can be appreciated within messianic categories. For some time, I have had an ambivalent attitude toward the messianic vision of history. On the one hand, whenever Jews sought to act on the basis of their messianic hope, the result was invariably catastrophic. Furthermore, when messianism gains dominance, the community may find the gap between the imperfect present and their messianic vision so great that contemporary reality is considered an unsuitable arena for the larger normative vision contained in the Torah. When this happens, messianism may lead the Jew into a posture of passive anticipation.

On the other hand, if the messianic vision is abandoned, the resultant anchorage exclusively in the world of immediacy and everyday concerns may lead to cynicism or despair regarding the possibility of achieving anything radical in human history and may discourage responsible action by the halakhic community. A present that is not open to some larger vision of the future may turn sour and be drained of vitality. Wherever one turns, either toward or away from the messianic idea, there are dangerous risks, but presumably also new spiritual opportunities. I am prepared to take the risks of messianism because of the influence messianism can possibly have on moving the community toward a different appreciation of Israel and Judaism.[18]

Moreover, it seems to be the case that the majority of the religious Zionist community in Israel perceives Israel within a messianic redemptive scheme of history. To ignore or argue against messianism in this context would be to isolate oneself from effective discussion with this community regarding the spiritual and political direction of Israeli society. It is, I believe, politically essential to develop a shared language between Jews who look forward to the unfolding of a redemptive process in Jewish history and those whose religious response to Israel is grounded in the concern with the renewal of the covenant of Sinai.[19] I believe that Maimonides' portrayal of messianism can serve as the basis for such a shared language.

I have shown that one's religious interpretation of events does not presuppose knowledge of how God acts in history. Furthermore we have seen that messianic hope is fully compatible with the principle of *olam ke-minhago noheg*, "the world pursues its normal course." In light of Maimonides' understanding of messianism, I believe that it is possible to have a messianic appreciation of Israel without making factual claims that this or that event in the history of Israel is a providential redemptive divine act. Messianism can instead be understood as a *normative category* by which we evaluate the quality of life in the present reality of Israel. For religious Zionists who in their prayers refer to Israel as the beginning of redemption, *hathalta de-geulah*, messianism must make a difference in the way we conduct our economic, social, and political affairs. The commitment to Israel as initiating the process of redemption requires of Jews a significant reorientation in the way Judaism is understood and practiced. It would be short-sighted to manifest the messianic spirit only in the reclaiming and the rebuilding of the land. Any messianic appreciation of Israel worthy of the name must seek to discern the fulfillment of the biblical promise in the widening of the Jewish people's capacity for love. It is in a changed people and not only in a changed landscape that one must channel the messianic passion for the rebirth of Israel.

The longing for a messianic reality, in Maimonidean terms, expresses the community's love for and commitment to *mitzvah*. As I understand this, one who longs for the day when the full scope of the Torah can be reinstituted regards *mitzvah* as a joyful expression of living before God as a responsible normative agent in history. Messianism in this spirit reflects a triumph over any Pauline critique of *halakhah*. It regards *mitzvah* as a source not of guilt but of joy. A normative existence is not antithetical to human freedom, spontaneity, and passion, nor need the *mitzvot* and their materialization in *halakhah* be an oppressive force estranging us from our own individuality. *Halakhah* can be an expressive educational system, reflective of the richness of the individual's and the community's longing for God.[20]

Messianism not only expresses the love for and joy in *mitzvah* but equally gives us direction for the way halakhic jurists must apply *halakhah* to society. An essential feature of messianism is the ingathering of the exiles and the return of the entire community to its biblical homeland. The messianic emphasis upon the ingathering should direct contemporary halakhic jurists to develop Jewish law in ways that would reflect the spirit of the Kantian categorical imperative: shape Jewish law in a way that makes it a viable option for the *whole* Jewish community gathered together as an independent polity in the present era. Such an orientation toward the halakhic system would be guided by the aspiration to allow all Jews to share in the appreciation of *mitzvah*. In that situation, one does not render halakhic decisions that require that there be nonobservant Jews in the community in order for the society to function. Given this perspective, it would be counter to the very spirit of the Torah to bring about legislation in the Knesset excusing religious women from army service out of a concern to protect their modesty and their loyalty to Judaism, while ignoring the needs of women who come from nonreligious families. Nor would Sabbath regulations be developed that rely on there being nonobservant Jews in the community. One has to envision what is needed for a police force, fire patrol, army, foreign service, and international communication network to function within a society loyal to the Torah.[21] Contemporary halakhic thinking needs to be infused with the messianic spirit of responsibility and love for the *total* community. If one thinks of halakhic norms in terms of the survival and advantage of a particular religious group, one's thinking is anti-messianic and reflects the sectarianism of an exilic perspective on Judaism.[22]

The spirit of Judaism in exile reflects the concern of a community living in a hostile environment to survive and not be swallowed up by its alien surroundings. Not surprisingly, then, the religious conscious-ness of exilic Judaism puts great emphasis on the *mitzvot* that separate Jews from their alien environment. Under such circumstances, the holy often becomes defined by what separates Israel from the nations. For that reason, Sabbath observance in the home, *kashrut* laws, and similar *mitzvot* that set Jews apart from their environment became the focus of the covenantal passion. However, when Judaism becomes a total way of life of a reborn nation, the covenantal passion cannot be poured only into those *mitzvot* which separate Israel from the rest of humanity. When Jews live in their own environment and are responsible for the unfolding of the spirit of Judaism in a total society, they must also link their cov-enantal religious identity to the *mitzvot* through which they share in the universal struggle to uphold human dignity. The normalization of the Jewish people brought about by Zionism makes possible a new ap-preciation of the *mitzvot*, whereby the social, ethical, and political attain their full covenantal place.

In the messianic society, a total way of life and the society's entire social and economic structure have to mirror God's covenantal judg-ment. When that is so, the social, moral, and political status of the society becomes a religious issue. The Sabbath in a messianic society is not only the Sabbath of the seven-day week but also the Sabbatical and Jubilee years. The egalitarian spirit of the laws of those years should move the society and its political leaders to a concern with greater de-grees of social and economic equality. How the laws of the Sabbatical and Jubilee years can be expressed in a modern economic system is a serious halakhic question that many have tried to answer in different ways. One thing, however, is clear. Something radical will happen to Judaism when we are challenged to have our economic and social order mirror the Sabbath's celebration of the world as a creation and of human beings as creatures and not absolute masters over nature or other human beings.[23]

A Maimonidean messianic consciousness does not seek to build a Jewish state that compensates for past exilic powerlessness, deprivation, and abuse.

> The sages and prophets did not long for the days of the Messiah that Israel might exercise dominion over the world, or rule over the heathens, or be exalted by the nations, or that it might eat and drink and rejoice. Their aspiration was that Israel be free to devote itself to the law and its wisdom, with no one to oppress or disturb it, and thus be worthy of life in the world to come. (MT *Hilkhot Melakhim* 12:4)

Messianism for Maimonides is a liberation from and a complete victory over a triumphalist power-seeking nationalism. A messianic society's guiding principle is to seek to expand the powers of knowledge, wisdom, and love. Exilic religious consciousness has been dominated by fear, estrangement, and questions of communal survival. The psychology of religious persons in a premessianic reality is often the psychology of alienated persons who do not trust the world and therefore cannot open themselves fully to it. One whose self-identity is dominated by this sense of estrangement and fear cannot become a lover of God. Love becomes a potent possibility in our spiritual life when the problems of physical survival do not dominate our existence and when the political reality is not seen as oppressive or as harboring the dangers of aggression, war, and violence. The passion of love can begin to emerge when we derive from our polis the ability to feel at home in the universe. The more fear and estrangement are overcome, the more God and the Torah can be perceived in terms of love, and the more one can liberate oneself from seeing God in terms of reward and punishment or a nationalist triumphalist vision.

I am fully aware of the extreme difficulty of bringing this messianic appreciation of the third Jewish commonwealth to the social and political reality of Israel. We are still very worried about national survival. The atmosphere of war is not conducive to the creation of conditions that encourage the expansion of powers of love. The Zionist revolution has been enacted in a vulnerable reality in which there is no telling when wars will end and suffering will cease. There is therefore an understandable fear of the stranger in the land. Nevertheless, in spite of the imperfect conditions of Israel, and in spite of the enormous energies that have to be expended on survival, I believe that there is a heroic

spirit in this society that is capable of accepting messianism as a normative challenge. The courageous covenantal spirit of the new Israeli
Jew, which was revealed to me with immense power and tenderness by
my son-in-law, Aharon Katz, of blessed memory, has led me to believe
that there may be tremendous spiritual forces within Israeli society that
have not yet been fully tapped.

We have developed a new heroic type capable of enormous sacrifice
and dedication to the security of our society. Given our long exilic history, it is truly remarkable that we have developed a new human type
that has given up fear. Its heroism, which has been abundantly demonstrated on the field of battle and in the rebuilding of the land, can
equally be channeled to give expression to other features of the heroic
ideal in Judaism.

Maimonides taught that *kiddush ha-shem*, sanctification of the name
of God, is manifested on three levels. The first is the courage to stand
in opposition to religious oppression, the willingness to die to defend
one's loyalty to Torah and *mitzvot*. That is the heroism of the martyr
who is prepared to give up life for what is seen to be the essential spiritual vision of the nation. However, Maimonides believes that Jewish
spiritual heroism not only is the willingness to die, but also shows itself
in a second form when one is able to overcome the motives of fear and
reward as a ground for worship.

> Whoever abstains from a transgression or fulfills a commandment not
> from any personal motive nor induced thereto by fear and apprehension
> or by the desire for honor but solely for the sake of the Creator, blessed
> be He, sanctifies the name of God. (MT *Hilkhot Yesodei ha-Torah* 5:10)

Heroism is not only shown in the courage to transcend the normal
instinct of self-preservation, but is also reflected in the ability to transcend the motives of self-interest in one's appreciation of Judaism. To
be directed by the passion of love is for Maimonides to live a heroic
existence.

But there is also a third heroic ideal. It is the actions of the *hasid*, of
the pious individual whose behavior is a compelling example encouraging people to take the Torah and God seriously. The *hasid*'s example
makes God's name beloved and sought after; it opens the hearts and
souls of others to the living waters of the Torah. This kind of heroism
is not only heroism in opposition to an alien environment, but also a
demonstration of the strength and integrity of Judaism as a total way
of life.

> And if a man has been scrupulous in his conduct, gentle in his conver-
> sation, pleasant toward his fellow creatures, affable in manner when re-

ceiving them, not retorting even when affronted, but showing courtesy
to all, even to those who treat him with disdain, conducting his com-
mercial affairs with integrity . . . and doing more than his duty in all
things, such a man . . . has sanctified God and concerning him scripture
says: "And he said to me, 'You are my servant, O Israel, in whom I will
be glorified' [Isa. 49:3]." (Ibid., 5:11)

The task of covenantal Jews now is to show that we can build a
Judaic society not by resorting to dogmatism and legal coercion, but,
like the *hasid*, by means of the compelling example of the way we live
our daily lives. We must avail ourselves of the opportunities given to us
through education and must not deceive ourselves that religious legislation can in any significant way alter the character structure of a people. If we learn to appreciate the power of love and personal example,
we may be able to walk in the covenantal path of Abraham, who made
God beloved through the compelling power of his own actions.[24]

Israel and the New Jewish Agenda

So far I have described, from a covenantal perspective, the new opportunities provided by the rebirth of Israel. It is hardly less necessary, however, to be aware of the new risks that have arisen simultaneously.
Opportunities and risks alike owe their origin to the fact that the creation of the third Jewish commonwealth confronts Judaism and the Jewish people with a new moral and political agenda, whose implications
go beyond the strict geographical confines of the Jewish state. For a long
time in history, we did not have to deal with questions that touch upon
the relationship between *halakhah* and political power, since we were a
powerless community. Especially from the emancipation period onward,
Judaism was not involved with the public domain of power and politics.
Judaism gave meaning to the individual. It taught Jews how to conduct
their family life. It provided frameworks for the celebration of the holy.
It provided a structure that kept alive the major historical moments that
shaped the community's spiritual self-understanding. Judaism, however,
did not have to deal with those agonizing moral questions that confront
a nation that has military and political power. In the political sphere,
our activity was limited to the fight for minority rights, religious tolerance, and freedom of conscience in countries where we were an oppressed or vulnerable minority. As a result of the rebirth of Israel, our
political situation has dramatically changed. In Israel, religious and nonreligious Jews have a new sense of power and belonging that they have
rarely felt throughout their long sojourn in the diaspora.

Israel, however, not only allows us to give expression to what is most noble in the Jewish tradition, but it also readily exposes moral and spiritual inadequacies in that tradition. Israel therefore provides unique conditions for a serious critique of Judaism as it is practiced by committed halakhic Jews. In Israel there is no external non-Jewish world to inhibit the tradition's full self-expression. Moral attitudes that one never expected to characterize Jewish behavior can surface in this uninhibited, passionate, and complex Jewish reality. Triumphalist nationalism, lack of tolerance for other faith communities, indifference, and often an open disregard for the liberal values of freedom of the individual, human dignity, and freedom of conscience can be found articulated by would-be religious leaders in Israeli society. A mature appreciation of our liberation struggle requires that we recognize the mixed blessings that freedom and power bring to Jewish living.

Although Israel resulted from a profound revolt against the tradition, this revolution was materialized in a land that makes Jews aware of being attached to the three-thousand-year drama of their people. The Zionists did not leave their historical family when they undertook to revolt against the tradition. I would compare the Zionist revolt to a young person who loses patience with his parents, announces he is leaving home, goes to the door, slams it in great anger, but fails to leave the house.[25] The Zionists' radical revolution, after all, was realized in a land that forces a confrontation with different aspirations that have been part of the Jewish historical tradition. In deliberately choosing to materialize the Zionist revolution in the land of the covenant, secular Zionists make the claim that they have truly fulfilled the Jewish aspirations in history. Their claim invites severe criticism from other groups in the Jewish world who do not perceive the secular Zionist revolution as much of a fulfillment of the prophetic tradition. Mystics and sober halakhists who believe that the political task of the Jewish people is to wait patiently for God's final redemptive action in history, messianic religious activists who understand the Zionist revolution as the way God has utilized the secular forces in history for the sake of the realization of Torah—these people will never sit by idly and allow the secular Zionist dream of normalization to take root in the biblical land of Israel. Each one claims the whole field. The very fact that the revolution is realized in the land of Jewish historical aspiration forces a confrontation with all who claim to be the authentic carriers of Jewish tradition.

In Israel, intense ideological passions surface daily and confront one another in the public arena of our shared communal life. Major governmental decisions are influenced by the different Jewish dreams that inspired our national rebirth. Messianic religious visions collide with a socialist secular understanding of the significance of the Jewish state. This is what results from Jews feeling at home. Each group believes this is its own home. This feeling is often translated into a paternalistic attempt to have everyone share one's appreciation of how a Jewish national home should look. In Israel, therefore, religious and secular Jews try to influence the public domain so that it might mirror their understanding of how Jews should live. Paradoxically, Israel, which unites Jews from the four corners of the world, is the most vivid demonstration of how divided and estranged from one another we are. We prayed to be reunited with our scattered brethren—without realizing how different we had become from one another. Our sense of unity currently results more from the enemies who seek to destroy us than from an internal consensus as to how we believe the Jewish people should live in the modern world.

How do you build a Jewish society when there is no significant consensus as to what is normative in Jewish history nor any agreement about the sources out of which to build new norms? Can *halakhah* accommodate itself to the modern values of tolerance and freedom of conscience? Is there a way of sustaining the intense passion for Judaism and monotheism and yet appreciating the important modern value of religious pluralism? Does liberalism, with its concern for freedom of conscience, undermine the *halakhah*'s uncompromising rejection of idolatry? Should secular Zionism, which makes perpetuation of the nation the ultimate value of the Jewish people, be identified as a modern form of idolatry? The question of tolerance and pluralism refers not only to Judaism's relationship to other faith communities but above all to how Jews live among themselves. Halakhic thinkers must grapple with the fact that many Jews do not perceive *halakhah* and the talmudic tradition as normatively binding. There are many Israelis who are prepared to study Torah but will resist to the end the imposition of halakhic practices that clash with their own sense of personal freedom and conscience. What are the limits of tolerance for other Jews that could be acceptable to a halakhic community? What happens when religious Jews seek the legislative power of the state to impose halakhic practices on the community? Does this not invite the same corruption that has characterized the fate of other religions when they used political power to promote their vision of life? It is morally disastrous and religiously arrogant to claim that we have nothing to learn from the mistakes of other religions regarding the use of political power for the implementation of religious values.

It is not a simple task to translate a biblical perception of reality into the conditions of a modern democratic society. The way Joshua entered the land is hardly a paradigm for learning how to tolerate different faith communities and for allowing different groups the freedom to express their own particularity.[26] The separation of church and state and the American appreciation for pluralism are not yet firmly established in the Israeli political imagination. In contrast to the Western Jewish diaspora, Israel does not provide for a neutral or secular political public arena in which to orchestrate the different competing ideologies present in contemporary Jewish living. The diaspora allows different religious groupings to form their own synagogues. Each can have its own "four cubits of the law" in a way that does not impinge upon the life of the total Jewish community. In the diaspora, Jews live their public life under the protective umbrella of the larger non-Jewish political order and express their personal Jewish identity within their respective schools, synagogues, and community centers. The diaspora, in contrast to Israel, does not force the confrontation between religious and secular Jews or between the different ideological branches of Judaism to develop into overt conflict. Pluralism, therefore, does not surface as an urgent issue in the diaspora.

A long and arduous path must be traveled before we can create a healthy bridge between the needs of a modern democratic liberal society and the biblical and talmudic understanding of Jewish politics. On the one hand, Judaism is a repudiation of any spiritual vision that is related exclusively to the private and intimate domains of the personal life. Yet, on the other hand, if Judaism seeks expression in the communal political domain, does it not expose itself to the very corruptions that have characterized theocratic states in history? It will not be easy, therefore, to bring John Stuart Mill's advocacy of civil liberty and Isaiah Berlin's appreciation of pluralism into a serious and fruitful discussion with Maimonides and the talmudic tradition's understanding of how a halakhic polity should conduct its daily life.[27] What makes for the spiritual vitality of our third Jewish commonwealth is the fact that we cannot ignore these new fundamental issues.

The Zionist quest for normalcy should free the Jewish people of any myth about the unique moral and spiritual powers of the Jewish soul. In taking upon ourselves responsibility for a total society, we must allow ourselves to be judged by the same standards as we have judged others.[28] The Torah challenges us to become a holy people. It does not tell us that we are immune from the moral weaknesses and failures that affect every human being. The Jewish nation is not free from the same potential corruptions that affect any human community that has taken upon itself the bold challenge of living with power. Our newly gained sense of belonging and power enables us to look critically and honestly both at ourselves and at the halakhic tradition without the apologetic stance so characteristic of a community that saw itself as a persecuted and vulnerable minority. A community that feels dignified and secure in its identity and place in the world can allow itself the mature activity of honest critical self-appraisal.

To the degree that we can look at ourselves in a nonapologetic light, to that degree will we demonstrate our liberation from an exilic consciousness that is fundamentally timid, frightened, and outer-directed. We are free now to ask what we think of ourselves without being overly concerned with the way others will listen and respond to our agonizing self-appraisal. Because of our "role" as the suffering stranger in history, many have perceived the Jew as the moral conscience and critic of social and political injustice.[29] In building the third Jewish commonwealth, our role must shift from moral criticism of others to self-judgment. In coming home, the task before us is to clean up our own house.

If a moral message will emanate from Jerusalem, it will result not from what we say but from what we do. For the covenant to be renewed in its full power and vitality, Jews must be willing to face the serious moral and religious problems that arise when they seek to participate fully in modern society. This challenge faces Jews in both Israel and the diaspora, but it arises in its most acute and total form in Israel. The quality of life that we build in Israel will accordingly be paradigmatic for and influence the manner in which Judaism develops everywhere in the modern world. For wherever Jews live, they must bring the passion of their faith commitment to the moral and political concerns of their society. Torah is not, as Spinoza claimed, merely the political constitution of a nation with its own political sovereignty. Torah is a way of life not circumscribed by geographic boundaries. The rabbis taught in the Talmud that the mitzvot must be observed wherever a Jew is called upon to do battle against the false gods of history (Kiddushin 37a). It is the destiny of Jews wherever they may be to say no to all modern forms of idolatry.[30]

The significance of the rebirth of Israel cannot be circumscribed to those who live in Israel. The endless Zionist discussions regarding the relationship of Israel to the diaspora are usually futile. I reject the radical Zionist claim that a vibrant Jewish life is impossible in the diaspora. It is a total evasion of our larger responsibility to the Jewish people if we offer the diaspora only one message: "Come to Israel in order to safeguard your grandchildren from assimilation." Israel should not be understood merely as a haven for the persecuted and the wandering Jew or as a guarantee against assimilation. It is short-sighted to use the Holocaust as a justification for the need for a Jewish national home. Israel from my perspective provides a new direction for Judaism's confrontation with modernity. It opens up the possibility of renewing the covenantal drama of Sinai in a vital new way. The rebirth of Israel marks the repudiation of the halakhic ghetto as the means for guarding Jewish survival in history. Israel not only argues against the ghettoization of Judaism, but is also a rejection of the mistaken universalism that characterized the assimilationist tendencies that affected many Jews as a result of the breakdown of the ghetto. The birth of the third Jewish commonwealth teaches all of Jewry that being rooted in a particular history and tradition need not be antithetical to involvement and concern with the larger issues affecting the human world.

It would have been understandable if in response to the tragic suffering of the Jewish people in this century, and their profound disillusionment with Western values, Jews would have restricted their visibility in and concern for history. However, the covenant of Sinai teaches the Jew to trust and be open to the world again. The Sinai covenant does not allow Jews to adopt a spiritual orientation that gives up on history and emphasizes the inner life of the soul. To be a covenantal Jew is to share in Moses' understanding of God's dream for Israel and history. Moses is the paradigm of the way a Jew is to hear the significance of mitzvah in his or her life. Moses knew that he must leave the contemplative spiritual bliss that he discovered on the peak of Mount Sinai and enter into the struggle of history down below. Moses demonstrated that love of God must be found within the context of community. The heavy responsibility of implementing the Sinai covenant in the third Jewish commonwealth can be borne with dignity and joy because Judaism has always taught that in the eyes of God the doors of renewal are never closed.

Ben-Gurion and many Zionists believed that to build a healthy third commonwealth, it was necessary to leap back beyond the talmudic period, go back to the Bible, and reject much that exilic Jewish history gave to the Jewish world. I believe that they were mistaken. Estrangement from the postbiblical history of Judaism deprives the community of the important perspectives and values initiated by Ezra and Nehemiah and developed by rabbinic teachers in the talmudic tradition. Jeremiah and Ezekiel offered the community a utopian vision, but Ezra and Nehemiah rebuilt the community within imperfect historical conditions. They taught the Jewish people that the Sinai covenant could be renewed in spite of the gap between prophetic hope and reality. The rabbinic tradition has taught us to say grace over an incomplete meal. Rabbinic Jews can find spiritual meaning even though all their deepest hungers and longings are not fully gratified. It is to the rabbinic tradition that we must turn to learn how the prosaic details of daily life can be made the carriers of the larger covenantal prophetic vision of history. The third Jewish commonwealth can be enriched by the passionate sobriety of the covenantal tradition that places the hearing of *mitzvah* at the center of its conception of God and the world.

The Lord spoke to you out of the fire; you heard the sound of words but perceived no shape—nothing but a voice. (Deut. 4:12)

Postscript

A
LTHOUGH MAIMONIDES has been the major philosophical influence on my reflections on Judaism, the orientation to Judaism suggested in this work represents a serious departure from the way Maimonides believed one should speak about Judaism to the community. *Treatise on Resurrection*, Maimonides' final work, emphasizes belief in miracle, reward and punishment, and resurrection of the dead as central for maintaining belief in the living God of Judaism. He believed that the tradition would be endangered if the community were taught that God should not be served for the sake of receiving a reward. He therefore was very cautious in teaching the way of love of God to the community. Have I not by contrast been too bold? Do I not potentially weaken the hold of the covenant on the community by organizing the practice of Judaism exclusively around the motif of love? Can one disregard fear of God's power to punish and his promises of future reward and still believe that the community will practice the *mitzvot*?

In doing without eschatological beliefs, in emphasizing the power of the beginning rather than the promise of the end, in standing resolute at the mountain of Sinai and joyfully accepting the demands of becoming a holy people without any assurance that God's vision for Israel will necessarily be realized in history, have I not weakened the appeal of

Judaism to the wider community? I cannot conclude this work without some explanation for this departure from Maimonides, especially at a time when I claim that, as a result of the rebirth of Israel, Jewish philosophy must move from the existentialist concern with the "lonely man of faith" to a focus on the political and communal dimensions of halakhic Judaism.

Maimonides taught that one is led to love of God through the disciplined study of physics and metaphysics. He believed that passionate love for God is nurtured by the philosophical quest. I do not share his emphasis on physics and metaphysics and therefore do not subscribe to his belief that love of God is necessarily restricted to individuals gifted by God or nature with the intellectual endowments for becoming philosophic lovers of God. I believe, rather, that the capacity of love is related to the psychological maturity that comes with accepting one's finitude and self-limitation and to the productive use we make of this awareness in our interpersonal relationships. Although this type of maturity is a difficult achievement, it is not necessarily restricted to the few.

I also do not share Maimonides' concern with freeing halakhic Jews from their anthropomorphic understanding of God. I do not consider mistaken conceptions of God the highest form of idolatry. In a certain sense, therefore, I am closer to those Jewish theologians who placed greater emphasis on practice than on correct knowledge of God. I am concerned with the way our covenantal perception of divinity influences the way we live by the *halakhah*. For Maimonides, belief in the unity of God entailed belief in the noncorporeality of God. He therefore felt compelled to reinterpret biblical descriptions of God that suggest divine corporeality. For Maimonides, it made sense to educate toward the observance of *mitzvot* only if the human mind was first healed of the grievous sin of attributing any semblance of human feeling to God. For myself, belief in the unity of God requires that one learn to appreciate the way every human being reflects the divine image. The unity of God is a challenge to find a shared moral and spiritual language between different faith communities. The declaration of Judaic faith, "Hear, O Israel, the Lord is our God, the Lord is One," must lead a Jew to relate the profound sense of the particular and intimate relationship of Israel to God ("The Lord is our God") to an appreciation of the way God is manifested in the variety of spiritual cultures existing throughout the world ("The Lord is One"). Whereas for Maimonides, correct reasoning provides the healing powers that make belief in the unity of God possible, from my perspective the power to appreciate the other, the overcoming of individual or communal narcissism, is essential if we are to act in a way that reflects belief in the unity of God.

This focus on the behavioral and characterological consequences of religious belief shows itself in the way I differ from Maimonides in understanding the significance of the story of creation in Genesis and its relationship to revelation. Maimonides sees that story as underscoring the importance of the knowledge of physics for the proper understanding of God; I see it as teaching us to accept our finitude. For him, belief in creation provides the metaphysical foundation for ascribing will and spontaneous action to God. For me, creation provides the foundation for the covenant of Sinai by establishing the dignity of human freedom and otherness from God.

Besides our different approaches to love of God, there is also a reluctance on my part to speak about Judaism from a framework of reward and punishment. When Maimonides wrote, there was a sociocultural ambience that supported belief in miracle and divine reward and punishment. Theodicies that presupposed belief in the resurrection of the dead were then a reasonable way for making sense of human suffering. The fears of hell and anticipation of the joys of heaven were part of the way one experienced God's providential relationship to the community. This way of experiencing God is not a live and significant option for myself or many other modern Jews. It is not that I consider the *Treatise on Resurrection* false or childish or contrary to scientific enlightenment. Rather, it is not the way I experience Judaism as a living faith. It therefore would be inauthentic for me to articulate a philosophy of Judaism in the spirit of that treatise.

I am grateful that the secular spirit of the modern world has made the medieval option of fear of God's punishment spiritually irrelevant. I felt dignified and challenged as a teacher of Torah in not having the support of God's punitive powers as a fallback for awakening interest in Torah. In my experiences as a teacher, I never saw Judaism as necessarily weakened by the modern emphasis on the significance of the present or by people's indifference to or distaste for the terrifying descriptions of divine retribution awaiting the sinner found in the liturgy and rabbinic *midrashim*.

I am fully cognizant that the concern with immediacy in the modern world often finds expression in a compulsive need to deny all limitations and to relate to the world in the spirit of Kohelet: "I withheld from my eyes nothing I ached for and denied myself no enjoyment" (Eccles. 1:10). Nonetheless, despite the negative and often frightening manifestations of the celebration of the present, I believe there are features of this spirit that can help enrich Judaism in the modern world. I religiously embrace this spirit of modernity because it forces me to choose Judaism only on the basis of love. There is something profoundly religious about a culture that challenges one to find a way to God without being intimidated by His power. Those images of God in the tradition that portray Him as teacher and lover are most appreciated for those who share this religious sensibility.

Besides the above reasons for departing from the Maimonidean tradition, there is also a political urgency that leads me to emphasize the joy of *mitzvah* and the mature love of God as the key orienting framework for the practice of Judaism. I am deeply frightened by the growth of religious dogmatism and intolerance in many parts of the world, including Israel. I believe that a relationship to God based on fear of punishment, excessive repression, and fear of natural joy and spontaneity contributes to the growth of religious dogmatism and fanaticism. The practice of the *mitzvot* in the spirit of "The reward of *mitzvah* is *mitzvah*" helps one not to be threatened by human beings with different convictions. It allows one to feel secure and dignified in what one is doing without having to claim the whole field. Serving God with joy psychologically prepares one for the exciting possibilities of religious pluralism. An appreciation of the human being as a creature who is "condemned," or "blessed," to be other than God may offer us a biblical foundation for making pluralism a part of our religious sensibility and epistemology.

The existence of value disagreements does not necessarily reflect a fallen state of humanity that in principle can and must be overcome. A mature recognition of the implications of human finitude may help us to understand that different and often conflicting views on what makes a human life significant are intrinsic to our human condition. The emphasis on universalizing a particular way of life, which was so dominant in earlier centuries, is not a sign of moral and psychological maturity. There is no denying that this universalizing tendency has been influenced to a great extent by the biblical portrayal of a God Who accepts only one son of Abraham and one son of Isaac, while Ishmael and Esau are rejected. History has been haunted by the concern with identifying the true inheritor of the covenant of Abraham. Who is the carrier of God's redemptive scheme for history? Through whose ideology will all the nations be blessed? Implicit in such questions is the supposition that there is only one true perception of divine revelation and redemption in history. In the long run, I see no future for humanity so long as this perception of God and history defines our understanding of human existence. Judaism's passion for particularity, as witnessed in

our return to the third Jewish commonwealth and its appreciation of
the dignity of finitude and human limitation, may in the long run provide a key orienting framework for moving away from the dangerously
arrogant notion that there is one redemptive scheme for all humanity.

The return of Judaism to the realm of the concrete and the acceptance of the challenge to embody its spiritual vision within everyday
reality should engender a new perception of the relationships between
Judaism, Christianity, and Islam. Israel's return to history as a political
community constitutes a proclamation to the world that Judaism and
the Jewish people cannot be reduced to a spiritual abstraction. When
Judaism manifests itself as the way of life of a particular historical people,
as it can do in Israel today, it is a permanent obstacle to any theological
view that perceives Judaism as the superseded forerunner of the universalist conceptions of Christian and Islamic monotheism.

Our return to particularity in a concrete historical context does not
mean that Jews must turn their back on the universalist concerns that
engaged Jewish thinking throughout history, but rather entails a sober
rethinking for Jews of the significance and implications of those universal aspirations. What is normative for covenantal Jews is not only
the universalist vision of the prophets or the formal legal framework of
halakhah, but also the lived history of the community. We cannot ignore
what we have learned in history: Jews so often suffered tragically when
individuals, nations, or religious faiths attempted to force upon the
world their particular understanding of what makes life significant. The
prophetic Jewish dream of a world united under the kingdom of God
has to be rethought in light of the historical experiences of the Jewish
people. History has taught us that when people ignore the intrinsic dignity of particularity or forget their own human limitations and speak
as if they were the mouthpiece of the universal, they unleash new forces
of barbarism destructive of human dignity. Our return to nationhood
and particularity is therefore not an abandonment of the universal, but
a new opportunity to locate the universalist aspirations of Judaism within
a framework that allows us to give expression to the dignity and significance of particularity.

Notes

I N ORDER TO MINIMIZE the use of notes, references to rabbinic sources and to the writings of Maimonides, Joseph Soloveitchik, and Yeshayahu Leibowitz have been given in the text as far as possible. "The Talmud" means the Babylonian Talmud (London: Soncino Press, 1938) except where the Jerusalem Talmud is explicitly mentioned. The writings of Maimonides most frequently quoted are the *Guide of the Perplexed* (*Guide*)—from Shlomo Pines's translation (Chicago: University of Chicago Press, 1963)—and the *Mishneh Torah* (MT) in the Yale Judaica Series (*The Code of Maimonides*, vol. III, 1949, and vol. XIV, 1961 [New Haven and London: Yale University Press]) and from the translation by Moses Hyamson (Jerusalem: Boys Town Jerusalem Publishers, 1965). Maimonides' "Eight Chapters" is from Raymond L. Weiss and Charles E. Butterworth, eds., *Ethical Writings of Maimonides* (New York: New York University Press, 1975).

Nachmanides is quoted from his *Commentary on the Torah*, translated by C. B. Chavel (New York: Shilo Publishing House, 1971–1976). Unless otherwise stated, Leibowitz is quoted from the collection of his essays in Hebrew: *Yahadut, am yehudi u-medinat Yisrael* (Tel Aviv: Schocken, 1975). The following works of Soloveitchik are referred to:

"Ish ha-halakhah," published in Hebrew in *Talpiot* (New York) 1: 3–4 (1944), quoted from the English translation by Lawrence Kaplan: *Halakhic Man* (Philadelphia: Jewish Publication Society, 1983)

"Confrontation," *Tradition* 6:2 (Spring 1964), 5–29

"The Lonely Man of Faith," *Tradition* 7:2 (Summer 1965), 5–67

"Majesty and Humility," *Tradition* 17:2 (Spring 1978), 25–37 (based on a lecture from April 1973)

"Catharsis," *Tradition* 17:2 (Spring 1978), 38–54 (based on a lecture from November 1962)

"Redemption, Prayer, Talmud Torah," *Tradition* 17:2 (Spring 1978), 55–72

"Ra'ayonot al ha-tefillah," *Hadarom* (New York) 47 (Tishri 5739/October 1978), 84–106

Reflections of the Rav (Jerusalem: Jewish Agency, 1979), edited by Rabbi A. R. Besdin from oral expositions

Introduction

1. For Kant's criticism, see N. Rotenstreich, *The Recurring Pattern* (New York: Horizon, 1963), pp. 23–47; E. L. Fackenheim, *Encounters Between Judaism and Modern Philosophy* (New York: Basic Books, 1973), pp. 31–77; Y. Yovel, *Kant and the Philosophy of History* (Princeton: Princeton University Press, 1980), pp. 206–214.

2. For instance, R. Bultmann, "Prophecy and Fulfillment," in C. Westermann, ed., *Essays on Old Testament Hermeneutics* (Atlanta: John Knox, 1963), pp. 50–75; also his *Primitive Christianity in Its Contemporary Setting* (New York: Collins, 1956), pp. 59–71.

3. Compare S. Pines, "Spinoza's *Tractatus Theologico-Politicus*, Maimonides and Kant," *Scripta Hierosolymitica* 20 (1968), 3–54; L. Strauss, *Spinoza's Critique of Religion* (New York: Schocken, 1965), especially pp. 1–31.

4. For a vehement expression of this attitude, see Haim Hazaz, "The Sermon," in R. Alter, ed., *Modern Hebrew Literature* (New York: Behrman, 1975), pp. 271–287.

5. See D. J. McCarthy, *Old Testament Covenant* (Oxford: Blackwell, 1973); D. R. Hillers, *Covenant: The History of a Biblical Idea* (Baltimore: John Hopkins, 1969).

6. Besides many passages in rabbinic literature, the metaphor appears in the morning prayers: "Blessed art Thou, O Lord, who teachest the Torah to Thy people Israel."

7. As against G. Scholem, *The Messianic Idea in Judaism* (New York: Schocken, 1971), pp. 282–303.

8. Compare M. Buber, *Moses* (New York: Harper, 1958), pp. 39–55; M. Greenberg, *Understanding Exodus*, vol. 2 (New York: Behrman, 1969), pp. 78–84.

9. Spinoza's arguments in *Tractatus* 7 are discussed by W. Z. Harvey, "A Por-

trait of Spinoza as a Maimonidean," *Journal of the History of Philosophy* 19 (1981), 151–172.

10. The existence and normative significance of an oral tradition in Judaism are what enable Maimonides to legitimate the use of philosophy in *halakhah* and even to place its study under the rubric of the study of Talmud: MT *Hilkhot Talmud Torah* 1:11–12, *Guide* 1:71.

11. The concept of an ongoing conversation is put to fruitful use in P. M. van Buren, *Discerning the Way* (New York: Seabury, 1980).

Chapter 1. Fundamentals of a Covenantal Anthropology

1. Compare Maimonides, *Guide* 3:50; A. J. Heschel, *God in Search of Man* (New York: Farrar, Straus and Cudahy, 1955), pp. 320–335; E. E. Urbach, *The Sages* (Jerusalem: Magnes, 1979), pp. 315–317.

2. See Y. Kaufmann, *The Religion of Israel* (Chicago: University of Chicago Press, 1960), chap. 3; N. M. Sarna, *Understanding Genesis* (New York: McGraw-Hill, 1966), chap. 1.

3. See *Guide* 2: 19–25; J. Guttmann, *Philosophies of Judaism* (New York: Holt, Rinehart and Winston, 1964), pp. 165–170; H. Davidson, "Maimonides' Secret Position on Creation," in I. Twersky, ed., *Studies in Medieval Jewish History and Literature* (Cambridge: Harvard University Press, 1979), pp. 16–56. There is, however, a certain ambiguity on this point in the *Guide*, which can also be read as allowing that even the Aristotelian view is compatible with the life of *mitzvah*. If Maimonides nonetheless rejects Aristotle's arguments for eternal necessity, it may be because he regards belief in creation as a sounder basis for combating idolatry and educating toward belief in God. See *Guide* 2:31, 3:29, and 3:41; also Pines's introduction to his translation of the *Guide* (Chicago: University of Chicago Press, 1963), pp. cxxviii–cxxxi; L. Kaplan, "Maimonides on the Miraculous Element in Prophecy," *Harvard Theological Review* 70 (1977), 233–256; and W. Z. Harvey, "A Third Approach to Maimonides' Cosmogony—Prophetology Puzzle," *Harvard Theological Review* 74 (1981), 287–301.

4. Compare *Yevamot* 61b–65b; Maimonides, *Sefer ha-mitzvot, mitzvah* 212; *Sefer ha-hinukh, mitzvah* 1. The nonapplicability of this norm to women and non-Jews is morally problematic; see *Sanhedrin* 59a–b and D. M. Feldman, *Marital Relations, Birth Control and Abortion in Jewish Law* (New York: Schocken, 1974), pp. 53–59.

5. See G. Scholem, *Kabbalah* (New York: Quadrangle, 1974), pp. 128–135.

6. Compare Scholem, *"Devekut,* or Communion with God," *The Messianic*

Idea in Judaism, pp. 203–227; E. Simon, "Law and Observance in Jewish Experience," in A. Jospe, ed., *Essays on Jewish Thought and Life* (New York: B'nai Brith, 1970), p. 222.

7. Profound expression is given to this feature of Judaism in Heschel's writings.

8. Compare N. Leibowitz, *Studies in the Book of Genesis* (Jerusalem: World Zionist Organization, 1972), pp. 59–66. A contrary view is given in Hillers, *Covenant*, pp. 101–105, 158–166.

9. The concept of a covenant is not needed in order to make sense of the doctrine of the seven Noahidic commandments; see S. S. Schwarzschild, "Do Noachites Have to Believe in Revelation?" *Jewish Quarterly Review* 52 (1962), 297–365; A. Kirschenbaum," The Noahide Covenant as Contrasted with the Covenant at Sinai," *Dine Israel* 6 (1975), 31–48.

10. See *responsum* 293 of Maimonides to Ovadiah the proselyte, in I. Twersky, *A Maimonides Reader* (New York: Behrman, 1972), pp. 475–476.

11. See further E. Berkovits, *Not in Heaven* (New York: Ktav, 1983).

12. See my *Maimonides: Torah and Philosophic Quest* (Philadelphia, Jewish Publication Society, 1976), pp. 108–122.

13. *Sanhedrin* 99a and Maimonides, MT *Hilkhot Teshuvah* 3:8.

14. E. Fromm, *You Shall Be as Gods* (Greenwich, Conn.: Fawcett, 1966), chap. 3, and *Psychoanalysis and Religion* (New Haven: Yale University Press, 1950), pp. 34–55.

15. Urbach, *The Sages*, p. 18.

16. Ibid., pp. 317–330.

Chapter 2. Assertion Versus Submission: The Tension Within Judaism

1. See Gen. *Rab.* 55:5–56:11; also G. Outka, "Religious and Moral Duty: Notes on *Fear and Trembling*," in G. Outka and J. P. Reeder, Jr., eds., *Religion and Morality* (New York: Anchor, 1973), pp. 209–254. Whereas for Kierkegaard, Abraham's experience is incommunicable, the Midrash emphasizes Isaac's willing cooperation in a shared experience.

2. Compare Kaufmann, *The Religion of Israel*, pp. 74–77; W. Eichrodt, *Theology of the Old Testament* (Philadelphia: Westminster, 1961), vol. 1, pp. 271–276, and vol. 2, pp. 269–272 and 427. Eichrodt seeks to make unpredictable terrifying events constitutive of the covenantal relationship with God, an approach that this book rejects.

3. See Y. Muffs, "His Majesty's Loyal Opposition," *Conservative Judaism* 33:3 (Spring 1980), 25–37, and "Between Justice and Mercy" (in Hebrew), in A. Shapiro, ed., *Torah Nidreshet* (Tel Aviv: Am Oved, 1984), pp. 42–44.

Chapter 3. "Halakhic Man": Soloveitchik's Synthesis

1. Fromm, *You Shall Be as Gods*.
2. W. Kaufmann, *Critique of Religion and Philosophy* (New York: Anchor, 1961), pp. 335–339.
3. *Sifre, ekev* 49; *Sotah* 14a; *Guide* 1:54.
4. *Kiddushin* 40b.
5. See N. Lamm, *Torah lishmah* (Jerusalem: Mosad Harav Kook, 1972; in Hebrew).
6. W. Jaeger, *Aristotle*, 2nd ed. (Oxford: Oxford University Press, 1948), appendix II.
7. *Moed Katan* 19b–20a contradicts Soloveitchik's claim that the *halakhah* commands feelings as well as actions, since it allows the public to comfort mourners during festivals. See also Rashi on *Sukkah* 25a (mourning is *tirda di-reshut*).

Chapter 4. Ethics and Halakhah

1. See the discussion of the reasons for the *mitzvot* in Maimonides given by I. Twersky, *Introduction to the Code of Maimonides* (New Haven: Yale University Press, 1980), pp. 374–447.
2. E.g., Judah Halevi, *Kuzari* translated by H. Hirshfeld (New York: Schocken, 1964), 1:95.
3. See the promises of reward made by Abraham in *Guide* 3:29.
4. E.g., *Kuzari* 1:99, 2:26, 3:7, and 3:53.
5. Thus also Nachmanides commenting on Genesis 6:2 and 6:13, Leviticus 19:2 ("You shall be holy") and Deuteronomy 6:18 ("You shall do what is right and good in the sight of the Lord"). Compare M. Greenberg, "Mankind, Israel and the Nations in the Hebraic Heritage," in J. R. Nelson, ed., *No Man Is an Alien* (Leiden: Brill, 1971), especially pp. 19–20.
6. This statement should not be taken to imply that moral reasoning can have the same certainty as that claimed by Maimonides for truths of logic and physics. The absence of such certainty, however, does not exclude ethical considerations from playing a role in legal discussions. See, e.g., Ch. Perelman, *Justic, Law and Argument* (Dordrecht: Reidel, 1980). How contemporary ethical thinking should enter into the detailed application of *halakhah* is a subject for a future work. For a Reform theologian's concern with this issue, see E. B. Borowitz, "The Autonomous Jewish Self," *Modern Judaism* 4(1984), 39–56.
7. Maimonides begins *Hilkhot Deot* with a discussion of general (i.e., Aristotelian) psychology, thus establishing various values before introducing the category of *mitzvah*. A completely different view appears in M. Fox,

"The Doctrine of the Mean in Aristotle and Maimonides," in S. Stein and R. Loewe, eds., *Studies in Jewish Religion and Intellectual History Presented to Alexander Altmann* (Tuscaloosa: University of Alabama Press, 1979), pp. 93–120. But see the criticism of his view in n. 65 of S. S. Schwarzschild, "Moral Radicalism and 'Middleness' in the Ethics of Maimonides," *Studies in Medieval Culture* 11(1978), 65–94; also my *Maimonides*, n. 38 on p. 260.

8. Alasdair MacIntyre, *Short History of Ethics* (New York: Macmillan, 1966).

9. This is well illustrated by Leviticus 19.

10. "The gap of uniqueness is too wide to be bridged. Indeed, it is not a gap, it is an abyss" ("Confrontation," p. 15). So deep is the abyss that "The great encounter between God and man . . . is . . . incomprehensible . . . even to a brother of the same faith community" (p. 24). One wonders, indeed, how even self-understanding in language is possible if the faith experience is so unique.

11. See K. R. Popper, "Truth, Rationality and the Growth of Knowledge," in *Conjectures and Refutations* (New York: Harper, 1968), pp. 215–250.

12. See *Eduyot* 1:5 on "Why do they record the opinion of the individual against the majority?"

13. See my *Maimonides*, chap. 2.

14. "Marvel exceedingly at the wisdom of His commandments, may He be exalted, just as you should marvel at the wisdom manifested in the things He has made" (*Guide* 3:49).

15. In relating the patterns of the law to the patterns of nature, Maimonides remarks: "Indeed, all things proceed from one deity and one agent, and 'have been given from one shepherd' [Eccles. 12:11]" (*Guide* 3:34).

16. This readiness is exemplified for me by the writings of Paul van Buren, among others, and by his fruitful contribution to theological studies at the Shalom Hartman Institute.

17. One senses this fear in Soloveitchik's contrasts between "the community of the many" and "the community of the few" in "Confrontation."

Chapter 5. Human Beings in the Presence of God

1. Y. Leibowitz's review in *Petahim* (Jerusalem) 45–46 (Adar 5739/March 1979), 82–88.

2. Leibowitz's claim is discussed in the articles of A. Kasher and A. Margalit in A. Kasher and Y. Levinger, eds., *Sefer Yeshayahu Leibowitz* (Tel Aviv: University Students' Union, 1977).

3. E. L. Fackenheim, *The Jewish Return to History* (New York: Schocken, 1978).

4. *Berakhot* 17a, *Pesahim* 50b, and *Nazir* 23b.

5. Compare W. Z. Harvey, "The Return of Maimonideanism," *Jewish Social Studies* 42 (1980), 249–268.

6. See Leibowitz's essay on the Shema in *Emunah, historiyah va-arakhim* (Jerusalem: Akademon, 1982).

7. Leibowitz, *The Faith of Maimonides* (Tel Aviv: Ministry of Defense, 1980; in Hebrew), pp. 16–17 and 28–29.

8. My book *Maimonides* did not give sufficient weight to this feature. I would now say that Maimonides seeks not a harmonious integration of *halakhah* and philosophy at the end of the *Guide*, but rather to maintain a tension between the two. For Maimonides, the philosophic passion for God must have its own life independent of the *halakhah*; Soloveitchik integrates it into the halakhic framework; Leibowitz reduces it to the observance of *mitzvah*. See Maimonides' proof of the existence and unity of God in MT *Hilkhot Yesodei ha-Torah* 1:1–8 and *Guide* 1:71.

9. *Kuzari* 1:1–27.

10. *Guide* 1:63 and 2:39; MT *Hilkhot Avodah Zarah*, chap. 2; also the discussion in my *Maimonides*, pp. 56–62.

11. *Guide* 1:54, discussed in L. V. Berman, "The Political Interpretation of the Maxim: The Purpose of Philosophy Is the Imitation of God," *Studia Islamica* 15 (1962), 53–63.

12. See *Guide* 3:8–14.

13. See my *Maimonides*, chap. 5. Contrast A. Altmann, "Maimonides' 'Four Perfections,' " *Essays in Jewish Intellectual History* (Hanover, N.H.: University Press of New England, 1981), especially p. 73, and J. Guttmann, *Maimonides: The Guide of the Perplexed* (New York: Hebrew Publishing Company, 1947), pp. 29–36.

14. MT *Hilkhot Yesodei ha-Torah* 4:12–13. The views expressed here aroused great anger among those who believed that the *halakhah* was sufficient for the spiritual life.

15. See *Guide* 2:36 and my *Maimonides*, pp. 197–200. Maimonides' insistence that the philosopher-prophet must have an anchor point outside the communal framework is strikingly reminiscent of Plato, *Republic* 520e–521b. Common to Plato and Maimonides is the view that political power should be entrusted only to those whose sense of dignity and self-esteem does not derive from their position in the community.

Chapter 6. The Spirit of Judaic Prayer

1. As in Maimonides, MT *Hilkhot Yesodei ha-Torah* 7:2,6.

2. See A. J. Heschel, *The Prophets* (New York: Harper, 1962) pp. 355–366.

3. For medieval philosophers, the problem seen here was quite different: how is a divine response to prayer compatible with the Aristotelian conception of the immutability of God? Modern thinkers influenced by existentialism have shifted the focus to the subjective experience of the worshiper.

4. This is a good example of how Soloveitchik solves a halakhic problem in terms of his experiential understanding of the religious. In contrast is the solution of *Tosafot* on *Berakhot* 40b; kingship is presupposed in the words "the God of Abraham," since Abraham brought God's kingdom to the world. A view closer to *Tosafot* is expressed by Soloveitchik in "The Lonely Man of Faith," note on p. 35.

5. Fundamental to Soloveitchik's thought is the theme that the community has collectively a spiritual power that is not available to the individual. It appears, for instance, in his approach to repentance; see P. H. Peli, *On Repentance in the Thought and Oral Discourses of Rabbi Joseph B. Soloveitchik* (Jerusalem: Oroth, 1980), pp. 109–137.

6. M. Greenberg, *Biblical Prose Prayer* (Berkeley: University of California Press, 1983), shows how biblical prayer is rooted not exclusively in moments of ecstasy or terror, but rather in the everyday experience of members of the community. It is "the popular life of prayer" that enables the community to be receptive to the prophetic message (p. 57).

7. That prayer is a supplication for mercy was also used by medieval commentaries to explain why there is no *tefillat nedavah* on the Sabbath. Since the thirteen petitional benedictions are omitted on that day from the Amidah, the only themes of prayer are then praise and thanksgiving, whereas *tefillat nedavah* is a petition for mercy. See Rabad on MT *Hilkhot Tefillah* 1:10; Rabbenu Jonah on *Berakhot* 21a.

8. That the rabbis, on the contrary, encourage Jews always to bring their smallest needs to God is shown by J. Heinemann, *Prayer in the Period of the Tann-a'im and the Amora'im* (Jerusalem: Magnes, 1966; in Hebrew), p. 20.

9. See MT *Hilkhot Tefillah* 10:6 and the comments of Rabad. This ruling in formal legal terms leaves open the question of whether obligatory and voluntary prayer are also *experientially* incompatible. Do they presuppose two distinct kinds of consciousness of God? Among Soloveitchik's important contributions to *halakhah* is that he has taken such questions seriously, realizing that legal distinctions that do not point to experiential distinctions are verbal and not substantial. The magnitude of the step taken by Soloveitchik can be seen by comparison with his grandfather's statements in *Hiddushei R. Hayyim Halevi, Hilkhot Tefillah.* Soloveitchik has applied this approach especially to prayer, mourning, repentance, and charity. See, for example, Peli, *On Repentance*, pp. 58–60, 63–66.

Chapter 7. Individual and Community in Prayer

1. Heschel's work on prayer grapples with this problem. He is concerned not only with conceptual issues but with rehabilitating the Jew's religious sensibility, which accounts for his constant use of evocative language. His writ-

ings express anguish over the alienation of many Jews from their spiritual roots. See his *Man's Quest for God* (New York: Scribner, 1954). Further, see the volume of essays on prayer by the research fellows of the Shalom Hartman Institute, *Prayer to the Living God* (Tel Aviv: Schocken, 1985; in Hebrew).

2. See Soloveitchik, "Lonely Man of Faith," note on pp. 34–35. Among the medieval commentators, see Meiri and Rashba on *Berakhot* 13a and the latter's *responsum* 344.

3. Rashi, Rabbenu Jonah, and Meiri on *Berakhot* 4b.

4. Jerusalem Talmud, *Berakhot* 1:5, and Babylonian Talmud, *Berakhot* 12a. The former asserts that the Shema in any case implies the content of the Ten Commandments. See M. Kadushin, *Worship and Ethics* (Evanston, Ill.: Northwestern University Press, 1964), pp. 78–89.

5. For Soloveitchik, "Prayer . . . consists not only of an awareness of the presence of God, but of an act of committing oneself to God and accepting His ethico-moral authority," and therefore the Amidah is preceded by the Shema ("Lonely Man of Faith," pp. 40–41). I have no difficulty with this idea, but disagree sharply when he adds that there should be a sudden change in the worshiper's experience when passing from the Shema to the Amidah, since in contrast to the Shema awareness, the Amidah awareness "negates the legitimacy and worth of human existence" (ibid.). Note that the different approaches of Hillel and Shammai to the Shema reflect two distinct theological understandings: a posture of God's acceptance of our humanity and a posture of awe and trembling respectively; see I. Knoll, "Parashah she-yesh bah kibbul malkhut shamayyim," *Tarbiz* 53 (1984), 11–31.

6. See the sources mentioned in note 2 above.

7. See *Avodah Zarah* 8a.

8. *Hayyei Adam, kelal* 27:17.

9. See *Tur, Hilkhot Tefillah* 98 and 101; *Shulhan Arukh, Hilkhot Tefillah* 98:2 and 101:1; also Meiri on *Berakhot* 30b and Ritva on *Eruvin* 65a.

10. E.g., *Tur, Hilkhot Tefillah* 98; *Shulkhan Arukh, Hilkhot Tefillah* 98:1–5, 101:1 and 107:4; *Hayyei Adam, kelal* 22:11.

11. Maimonides, MT *Hilkhot Tefillah* 4:15, 4:20, and 10:1. It is instructive to contrast MT *Hilkhot Tefillah* 6:8 with *Shulhan Arukh, Hilkhot Tefillah* 106:3; the subtle difference in wording reflects two markedly different attitudes.

12. Compare Leo Strauss's introduction to Pines's translation of the *Guide*, pp. xli–xlii. See also Maimonides' *Treatise on Resurrection* for his explanation of why Moses did not teach the doctrine of resurrection in the Torah: the generation of Sinai was not ready for it. Similarly, his explanation of the sacrifices in *Guide* 3:32 implies that the Judaic community can grow spiritually in history.

13. Hasidic prayer, which was mediated to me through my father's joy in prayer, moves in this direction.

14. Petitional prayer is for Maimonides an imperfect and incomplete mode of relating to God. Those whose worship of God is exclusively anchored in petitional prayer worship Him out of fear, since the essential framework of their relationship to God is grounded in terms of the divine power to reward. Those who relate to other human beings from a sense of deprivation often fail to perceive the intrinsic significance of their relational partner.

Need relationships are also inherently unstable, since they are threatened the moment that someone appears who seems to offer more than the current relational partner. When the relationship with God centers on petitional prayer, there will always be the temptation to turn to any substitute deity that seems to promise more. When people's interest in God is motivated by their deprived condition and sense of helpless dependency, then idolatry under many different forms remains a permanent possibility. Scrupulous observance of the *halakhah* is insufficient for overcoming the inherent religious instability of worship based upon fear. To ensure unshakable fidelity to God, Maimonides believed it was necessary to combine the practice of the *mitzvot* with fascination with and love for the reality of divinity for its own sake. As long as the battle against idolatry is conducted with the weapons of fear—reward and punishment—any victory is precarious. Depending upon who makes the most enticing promises and the most persuasive threats, the community could oscillate between God and idolatry. Although the rabbis of the talmudic period believed that they had won a lasting victory against idolatry, I believe it would be correct in Maimonidean terms to claim that their achievement was incomplete. Only when one is drawn to worship by the objective reality of God or by love for the *mitzvot* can one finally overcome the temptations of idolatry.

15. Since Maimonides believed that people cannot worship God out of love without developing an understanding and appreciation of the object of their love, he would have rejected the existentialist outlook that judges love by the subjective sincerity and intensity of the lover. For Maimonides, authentic love has to be grounded in fascination with the object of love and in a sense of the beloved's intrinsic worth. Contrast S. Kierkegaard, *Concluding Unscientific Postscript* (Princeton: Princeton University Press, 1941), pp. 178–182).

16. Unlike many modern thinkers, Maimonides does not see the peak of personal achievement in the self-realization of the human being as a unique individual, but sees it in transcending the preoccupation with individual self-consciousness. When one is absorbed with rapt attention in the otherness of God, it is the principle of universal intelligibility that fills one's consciousness. The human individual becomes in some way part of this universal framework of knowledge. When reality in its full objectivity and necessity invades the religious consciousness of the halakhist and awakens

the passion for divinity, then one has finally been freed from the tyranny of subjectivity that dominates those whose worship reflects concern with divine reward and punishment. The "I" and its individual experiences cease to be significant concerns when one is enraptured by the objective beauty of reality and fascinated with the radical otherness of divinity. Maimonides' stress upon objectivity in worship permits a more wholehearted devotion to the divine "Thou" and a less insistent residual concern with the human "I" than do modern existentialist subjective analyses of the "I and Thou." There is more room for the other in Maimonides' portrayal of the love relationship based upon knowledge than in a focus on the subjective mode of experience. This applies also to interhuman relationships. Contrast M. Buber, *Israel and the World* (New York: Schocken, 1948), p. 13.

Chapter 8. Rabbinic Responses to Suffering

1. For example, G. Scholem, "Reflections on Jewish Theology," in *On Jews and Judaism in Crisis* (New York: Schocken, 1976), pp. 261–297.

2. E.g., *Deut. Rab.* 2:12; similarly *Peah* 1:1 in the Jerusalem Talmud; see also MT *Hilkhot Teshuvah* 3:14.

3. See the section on the ten martyrs in the *musaf* service for Yom Kippur; also Urbach, *The Sages*, pp. 520–523.

4. As in *Sukkah* 2:9.

5. See, e.g., J. L. Mackie, *The Miracle of Theism* (Oxford: Oxford University Press, 1982), pp. 150–176. Mackie's discussion of divine omnipotence, however, does not take account of that divine self-limitation which is implied in the notion of the Sinai covenant. Compare Rashi on Lamentations 3:48.

6. Among others who have discussed the rabbinic approach to this issue are A. Büchler, *Studies in Sin and Atonement* (London: Jews College, 1928), pp. 163–211; A. J. Heschel, *Theology of Ancient Judaism* (London and New York: Soncino, 1962; in Hebrew), pp. 93–116; Urbach, *The Sages*, pp. 268–273, 284, 436–448.

7. On the one hand, Rabbi Akiva is reported as describing providence in the manner of the cited *baraita*.

   "Thy righteousness is like the mighty mountains [Thy judgments are like the great deep; man and beast Thou savest, O Lord]" [Ps. 36:7]. Rabbi Ishmael says: "To the righteous who perform the *mitzvot* of the Torah that was given from the mighty mountains, the Holy One, blessed be He, shows charity that is like the mighty mountains, but with the wicked who do not perform the *mitzvot* of the Torah that was given from the mighty mountains, the Holy One, blessed be He, deals strictly even as far as the great deep." Rabbi Akiva says: "He is strict with the former as well as with the latter. From the righteous He collects payment in this world for the modicum of misdeeds which they have committed, in order to give them a good reward in the world to come, while He gives abundant peace to the wicked in this world, paying them for the modicum of good deeds which they have done, so as to inflict punishment upon them in the world to come." (*Lev. Rab.* 27:1)

On the other hand, besides instances in which Akiva pronounced in the spirit of the *baraita*, there are several reports of him interpreting providence in the manner of the this-worldly statement in the Mishnah.

Rabbi Akiva said: "Whoever does not occupy himself with the Torah causes poverty to come upon his children. What should a man do so that his children shall grow rich and flourish? Let him fulfill the will of God and the wishes of his wife. This is the will of God: let him freely distribute his money to the poor, as it is stated: 'He has scattered abroad, he has given to the needy; his righteousness endures for ever' [Ps. 112:9]." (*Kallah* 51a)

This passage is followed by a story of how Akiva, using that same biblical verse, persuaded Rabbi Tarfon to give alms in proportion to his riches. Elsewhere (*Shabbat* 156b), it is recounted that Rabbi Akiva lectured on Proverbs 10:2 ("Charity delivers from death") when his daughter had a remarkable escape from death by snakebite on her wedding night shortly after she had given her portion of the wedding feast to a poor man who had come to the door. In a third report (*Avot de-Rabbi Nathan* 3), Akiva sees a man renowned for his charity miraculously saved from drowning and again cites Proverbs 10:2 and also, very aptly, Ecclesiastes 11:1 ("Cast your bread upon the waters, for you shall find it after many days"). All these stories indicate that on suitable occasions Akiva was ready to teach those bibilical verses in the spirit of biblical optimism.

Heschel (see note 6) seeks to represent Akiva as one who consistently maintained a next-worldly viewpoint.

8. Urbach ascribes a completely different significance to Akiva's death: this was a major turning point after which many rabbis could no longer maintain any necessary connection between suffering and sin (*The Sages*, pp. 442–444). If Ben Azzai, Akiva's pupil, also expressed contradictory views about providence on separate occasions, it was because he taught one doctrine of providence in public—that is, that there is reward for the community in this world—but maintained a different one in the esoteric circle of the intellectual elite. It was the "real" Ben Azzai (according to Urbach) who said: "*Mitzvah* leads to *mitzvah* and transgression to transgression. For the reward of a *mitzvah* is a *mitzvah* and the reward of a transgression is a transgression" (*Avot* 4:2). Urbach takes him to mean that "in this world there is no reward except that which inheres in the actual observance" of the *mitzvot* (pp. 268–270).

Urbach's explanation is not convincing. Those sayings that Urbach ascribes to the esoteric teachings of Ben Azzai are ones that we can easily imagine him teaching in public on appropriate occasions. For instance, the context of his insistence that "the reward of a *mitzvah* is a *mitzvah*" could have been occasions when he wished to teach the public the importance of appreciating the intrinsic significance of doing *mitzvot*. With this saying, Ben Azzai shifted the perception of religious life away from an outer-directed anticipation of reward to an inner-directed appreciation of the significance of the act itself.

One who believes that virtue is its own reward need not therefore give up the hope and longing for long life or the desire to see his or her children healthy. Ben Azzai, like his teacher Akiva, could have celebrated moments of good fortune as gracious personal gifts of God's love without in any way implying that he had lost appreciation for the intrinsic significance of the *mitzvot*. This is because in relationships with a personal God, as with human beings, one does not focus constantly only on one perspective or on one need. The same complexity of needs that is present in human relationships can also be seen in the way people relate personally to God. Even if to Ben Azzai the dominant and central organizing perspective for the performance of *mitzvah* was that "the reward of a *mitzvah* is a *mitzvah*," this does not mean that he did not feel other needs in specific situations.

A young man may visit his father because he is in a specific crisis situation and turns to him for help. The father may wonder: "Is the child interested in me or only in what he can get from me? Does my son love me for my own sake or because I support him as he studies in university?" Parents make terrible mistakes in relating to children with this either/or orientation. Children can enjoy simply meeting and being in the presence of their father, and yet at the same time feel no contradiction in bringing their dependency needs to him. One can ask a friend for help without minimizing the appreciation and love one may feel for him or her. Bringing dependency needs to a relationship and seeking to gratify some of one's hungers does not imply that the only ground of the relationship is self-interest. Human beings bring their total selves and needs to a relationship; this includes not only the joy and appreciation of the intrinsic significance of one's father or friend, but also the pains and fears and hungers that one experiences in life and the hope that the father or friend will in some way respond. Rabbinic teachers could therefore enjoy the presence of God and feel the joy of simply fulfilling the *mitzvot*, yet also allow themselves to anticipate from God that He would be responsive to their hungers and needs. Ben Azzai strove to serve God out of love, yet at the same time he could be hopeful that God would reveal His providential concern.

It is not that Ben Azzai personally utterly rejected the doctrine of reward and punishment, as Urbach claims; rather he sought to prevent obsession with that concern. Although it is not essential for one who learns to love God to anticipate divine promises of reward, one's dependency upon God and need for His response may surface at specific times, given the loneliness and pain that may always assail an individual.

9. In this light it will be instructive to consider the statements in rabbinic literature about the death of two other martyrs, Rabbi Ishmael and his pupil Rabbi Simeon.

"You shall not afflict any widow or fatherless child. If you indeed afflict. . . . "
[Exod. 22:21–22]—whether by a severe affliction or a light affliction. . . . At the
time when Rabbi Simeon and Rabbi Ishmael were led out to be killed, Rabbi Simeon said to Rabbi Ishmael: "Master, my heart fails me, for I do not know why
I am to be killed." Rabbi Ishmael said to him: "Did it never happen in your life
that a man came to you for a judgment or with a question and you let him wait
until you had sipped your cup or had tied your sandals or had put on your cloak?
And the Torah has said: 'If you indeed afflict . . . '—whether it be a severe affliction
or a light affliction." Whereupon Rabbi Simeon said to him: "You have comforted
me, master." (*Mekhilta, nezikin* 18)

In other versions of this story (*Avot de-Rabbi Nathan*, 1st version, 38, and
2nd version, 41; *Semahot* 8), Rabbi Ishmael asks Rabbi Simeon about other
possible minor lapses in his past. Had he been eating and failed to invite
poor men in to eat with him when they appeared at his door? Had he been
expounding the Torah before a great multitude and felt arrogantly elated?
Had he let his secretary keep a woman waiting for a while when she urgently needed his advice on a matter of Jewish law that was affecting her
marital relationship?

It would be strange to try to understand these questions of Rabbi Ishmael
only in terms of theodicy. One of the reasons why many accuse rabbinic
Judaism of "legalism" is that they totally misunderstand texts like these.
Rabbi Ishmael does not mean that God is a severe judge waiting to strike
down the righteous for the slightest infraction of His commands. As the
end of the story shows, Rabbi Ishmael is above all concerned with comforting Rabbi Simeon and healing in some way the intense bitterness felt
by his pupil.

By responding in this way, the rabbis turned even their own suffering
into an occasion for a deeper appreciation of the *mitzvot*. The stories of
sufferings and martyrdom then themselves function as Torah lessons "as
they are told among the faithful." Accordingly I do not find plausible Büchler's strong emphasis (*Studies in Sin and Atonement*, e.g., p. 191) upon theodicy in the story of Rabbi Ishmael and Rabbi Simeon.

10. Soloveitchik takes this approach in "Kol dodi dofek," *The Man of Faith*
(Jerusalem: Mossad Harav Kook, 1968; in Hebrew), pp. 65–106.

11. See M. Greenberg, introduction to *The Book of Job* (Philadelphia: Jewish
Publication Society, 1980), p. xxiii.

12. This is Flew's question in A. Flew and A. MacIntyre, eds., *New Essays in
Philosophical Theology* (London: Student Christian Movement, 1955), p. 90.
Of the responses to Flew there, that of Mitchell (pp. 103–105) is somewhat
similar to mine. As a parable for the relationship between the believer and
God, he describes a partisan, fighting against a foreign occupying power,
who meets a mysterious Stranger. The latter deeply impresses the partisan
and convinces him that he is on his side. Subsequently, however, the behavior of the Stranger becomes ambiguous. When the partisan asks him

for help, the request is sometimes granted and sometimes refused. Some-times the Stranger gives assistance to other partisans, but at other times he is seen in the uniform of the police, handing them over to the occupying power. In this baffling situation, the partisan persists in believing that "the Stranger knows best," because he retains the memory of that impressive original meeting.

There are, however, features of the covenantal Jewish form of theism that have no counterpart in the parable. One is that the commitment to Judaism is based not *only* on the memory of an impressive original meeting centuries ago and on subsequent divine interventions in history, but also— as chapter 9 points out—on the felt presence of God in the daily life of *mitzvah*. Another is the limitation on divine omnipotence that is implicit in covenantal human autonomy: it would be absurd to suggest that the Stranger withheld help and assisted the enemy in order to encourage the partisans to play a dignified autonomous role.

13. Compare R. B. Braithwaite, "An Empiricist's View of the Nature of Re-ligious Belief," in B. Mitchell, ed., *The Philosophy of Religion* (Oxford: Ox-ford University Press, 1971), pp. 72-91, and D. Z. Phillips, *Religion Without Explanation* (Oxford: Blackwell, 1976); also the critique of both in Mackie, *The Miracle of Theism*, chap. 12.

14. W. James, *Essays on Faith and Morals* (New York: Meridian, 1962), p. 284.

Chapter 9. The Rabbinic Renewal of the Covenant

1. See R. C. Zaehner, "Religious Truth," in J. Hick, ed., *Truth and Dialogue* (London: Sheldon, 1974), especially p. 6.

2. See J. Bright, *Covenant and Promise* (Philadelphia: Westminster, 1976), p. 188.

3. Compare S. Liebermann, *Hellenism in Jewish Palestine* (New York: Jewish Theological Seminary, 1950), pp. 115-127; E. E. Urbach, "The Rabbinical Laws of Idolatry," *Israel Exploration Journal* 9 (1959), 149-165 and 229-245; D. Flusser, "Paganism in Palestine," in S. Safrai and M. Stern, eds., *The Jewish People in the First Century* (Assen: Van Gorcum, 1976), pp. 1065-1100.

4. Compare Urbach, *The Sages*, pp. 260-261.

5. Compare Bright, *Covenant and Promise*, pp. 194-198; G. von Rad, *Old Tes-tament Theology* (Edinburgh: Oliver and Boyd, 1965), vol. 2, pp. 213-217; Kaufmann, *The Religion of Israel*, pp. 425-426 and 441-443.

6. Compare my *Joy and Responsibility* (Jerusalem: Ben Zvi Posner, 1978), p. 198.

7. Compare my *Joy and Responsibility*, pp. 184-187, on the significance of si-

lence when there is a gap between present experience and an authoritarian tradition.

8. See E. Bickermann, *Four Strange Books in the Bible* (New York: Schocken, 1967), pp. 211–218; H. L. Ginsberg, *The Five Megilloth and Jonah* (Philadelphia: Jewish Publication Society, 1969), pp. 82–88; G. Cohen, *Five Megilloth* (Jerusalem: Mossad Harav Kook, 1973; in Hebrew), pp. 3–22; S. Talmon, " 'Wisdom' in the Book of Esther," *Vetus Testamentum* 13 (1963), 419–455.

9. See *Berakhot* 60b and MT *Hilkhot Tefillah* 7:1–9.

10. For example, Psalm 19, used in the morning service for the Sabbath.

11. Compare A. J. Heschel, *The Earth Is the Lord's and the Sabbath* (Philadelphia: Jewish Publication Society, 1962), chap. 8 of the second essay.

12. Scholem, *The Messianic Idea in Judaism*, p. 35.

13. See A. H. Silver, *A History of Messianic Speculation in Israel* (New York: Macmillan, 1927). Also Scholem, *The Messianic Idea in Judaism*, p. 21, describing messianism as "a kind of anarchic breeze" that blows into the "well-ordered house" of the *halakhah*. Behind the sobriety of halakhic practice lies a repressed world of religious fantasy. Maimonides' antipathy to that fantasy is indicated at the beginning of his introduction to *Helek*.

Chapter 10. Two Competing Covenantal Paradigms

1. See especially *Ketubbot* 110b–111b. This text serves as an ideological foundation for anti-Zionist ultra-Orthodox Jewish groups. Also *Sanhedrin* 97a–99a.

2. See Bright, *Covenant and Promise*, pp. 28–29, 46–48; J. L. McKenzie, *A Theology of the Old Testament* (New York: Image, 1976), p. 150.

3. See the suggestive statement of Rabbi Joshua ben Levi in *Pesahim* 118a and compare Urbach, *The Sages*, pp. 303–304.

4. *Berakhot* 33b and *Niddah* 16b; also *Tosafot* on the latter.

5. Compare Altmann, *Essays in Jewish Intellectual History*, pp. 47–59.

6. Contrast Maimonides' approach with that of Nachmanides commenting on Gen. 15:13.

7. Maimonides insists that belief in creation is a foundation of the entire law, but that belief that this world will come to an end is not (*Guide* 2:27).

8. Compare D. Berger, "Miracles and the Natural Order in Nachmanides," in I. Twersky, ed., *Rabbi Moses Nahmanides (Ramban): Explorations in His Religious and Literary Virtuosity* (Cambridge: Harvard University Press, 1983), pp. 107–128. Also C. Henoch, *Nachmanides: Philosopher and Mystic* (Jerusalem: Torah Laam, 1978; in Hebrew), pp. 53–62.

9. The view denounced by Maimonides is found in Rashi on *Pesahim* 56a.

The attempt of Soloveitchik to harmonize Rashi, Maimonides, and Nach-manides ("Lonely Man of Faith," p. 53) cannot be maintained.

10. See my *Maimonides*, pp. 149–160.

11. See Maimonides' criticism of the *mutakallimun* in *Guide* 1:71.

12. Compare Maimonides, *Commentary on the Mishnah*, *Avot* 2:7 and *Peah* 1:1.

13. Compare Strauss's introduction to Pines's translation of the *Guide*, p. liii; A. Nuriel, *Ha-ratzon ha-elohi be-More Nevukhim*, *Tarbiz* 29 (1970), 39–61.

14. As in JT *Hagigah* 1:7; *Mekhilta*, *be-shallah* 3 (2 in some editions); *Sanhedrin* 44a–b, and *Bava Batra* 76a–b.

15. See especially his commentary on Exodus 13:16 and 20:2. Also Henoch, *Nachmanides*, pp. 107–113.

16. In his *Book of Commandments*, Maimonides lists obligatory prayer fifth in his enumeration of the positive commandments.

> ... we are commanded to serve God, exalted be He. This commandment is re-peated several times in Scripture, e.g., "And you shall serve the Lord your God" [Exod. 23:25], "And Him shall you [pl.] serve" [Deut. 13:5], and "And Him shall you [sing.] serve" [ibid., 6:13], "And to serve Him" [ibid., 11:13].

The injunction to serve God, Maimonides goes on to explain, is not itself one of the 613 commandments, but rather a general charge that covers the whole body of commandments of the Torah. Nonetheless, he adds, it does imply specifically one of those commandments, namely, that of prayer, as we may see from what the *midrash Sifre* says about the last of the four verses just quoted.

> ... it nevertheless imposes a specific duty, namely, that of prayer. *Sifre* says: " 'to serve Him' [Deut. 11:13] means prayer."

Nachmanides, in his commentary on the *Book of Commandments* (ad loc.), sharply disagreed with Maimonides.

> But certainly the whole matter of prayer is not obligatory at all. Rather, it belongs to God's grace toward us that He hears and responds whenever we call out to Him. And what was learnt by the rabbis in *Sifre*—" 'to serve Him' means prayer"—is but an *asmakhta* [textual support]; or perhaps it is to teach that included in our service to Him is that we should study His Torah, pray to Him in times of trouble, and turn our eyes and our hearts toward Him "as the eyes of servants toward the hand of their masters" [Ps. 123:2].

For Nachmanides, to treat daily prayer as a commandment from the Torah would be to do violence to the essential grace quality of prayer. If any kind of prayer is commanded, he continues, it cannot be the daily prayer exemplified by the Amidah, but only crying out to God for help in times of trouble.

Soloveitchik maintains that there is a common denominator between Maimonides' and Nachmanides' approaches to prayer. In *Reflections of the Rav*, he suggests that both Maimonides and Nachmanides relate prayer to *tzarah* (crisis, distress), only they concern themselves with two distinct kinds of *tzarah* that arise in human life.

The views of Maimonides and Nachmanides can be reconciled. Both regarded prayer as meaningful only if it is derived from a sense of *tzarah*. They differ in their understanding of the word. Maimonides regarded daily life itself as being existentially in straits, inducing in the sensitive person feelings of despair, a brooding sense of life's meaninglessness, absurdity, lack of fulfillment. It is a persistent *tzarah*, which exists *bekhol yom*, daily. The word *tzarah* connotes more than external trouble; it suggests an emotional and intellectual condition in which man sees himself as hopelessly trapped in a vast, impersonal universe. . . .

. . . Thus while Nachmanides dealt only with "surface crisis," public distress, *tzarot tzibbur*, Maimonides regarded all life as a "depth crisis," a *tzarat yahid*. (pp. 80–81)

"Surface crisis," Soloveitchik adds, is an external crisis which may be experienced by anyone, such as poverty, illness, famine, war or death. "Depth crisis," on the other hand, is experienced only by those sensitive and intelligent people who are prepared to face it and even to seek it out, whereas superficial people evade it. Unlike "surface crisis," which may be overcome by social, political, or economic means, there is no way of combating "depth crisis" except by prayer.

According to Soloveitchik, then, Maimonides made prayer into a daily obligation because intelligent and perceptive people daily encounter the situation of existential crisis. The crisis can be alleviated by daily repetition of the Amidah in the spirit demanded by Soloveitchik: the spirit of insignificance, helplessness, and self-sacrifice. Such a prayer experience gives expression to the worshiper's sense of metaphysical unworthiness. It enables one to find an anchor point in eternity and provides the cathartic release that liberates sensitive human beings from their finite existential condition.

While Soloveitchik is correct in his claim that crisis plays an essential role in Nachmanides' approach to prayer, existential "crisis" is not what moved Maimonides to make prayer so central to his halakhic and philosophical works. As I have shown in chapter 7, he saw daily prayer as an essential means by which the Torah would achieve its purpose of educating individuals and the community toward love of God.

17. The same view is implied in MT *Hilkhot Teshuvah* 3:2: it is "the omniscient God" Who "alone knows how to set off merit against iniquities." Compare H. M. Schulweiss, *Evil and the Morality of God* (Cincinnati: Hebrew Union College, 1984), chap. 3, especially pp. 46–47.

18. Compare G. Scholem, *Major Trends in Jewish Mysticism* (New York: Schocken, 1941), chap. 1.

19. For a detailed discussion of Maimonides on messianism, see my *Leadership and Crisis: Three Epistles of Maimonides* (Philadelphia: Jewish Publication Society, 1985).

20. As against the view of A. M. Herschman, "Textual Problems of Book Fourteen of the Mishne Torah," *Jewish Quarterly Review* 40 (1950), 401–412.

21. See Aviezer Ravitzky, "Kefi koah ha-adam," in Tzevi Bras, ed., *Meshihiyut ve-eskhatologiyah* (Jerusalem: Merkaz Zalman Shazar, 1984), pp. 191–220.

Chapter 11. The Celebration of Finitude

1. Succinctly put in L. Kolakowski, *Religion* (Glasgow: Fontana, 1982), p. 158: "if nothing remains of human effort, if only God is real, and the world, after meeting its final fate, leaves its creator to the same void or plenitude He has always enjoyed, then truly it does not matter whether this hidden King exists at all."

2. This is a recurrent theme in Hermann Cohen, Rosenzweig, Buber, Heschel, Soloveitchik, and others. It is seen as the typically Jewish view by P. M. van Buren, *A Christian Theology of the People Israel* (New York: Seabury, 1983), pp. 69–70.

3. E.g., Guttmann, *Philosophies of Judaism*, pp. 171–182; I. Husik, *A History of Mediaeval Jewish Philosophy* (New York: Meridian, 1958), p. 300. Similar criticism of Maimonides was expressed by Samson Raphael Hirsch; see N. H. Rosenbloom, *Tradition in an Age of Reform* (Philadelphia: Jewish Publication Society, 1976), pp. 128–133.

4. See Mackie, *The Miracle of Theism*, pp. 261–262.

5. James, *Essays on Faith and Morals*, p. 284.

6. See also *Shabbat* 31a–34a and 55a–b; Urbach, *The Sages*, pp. 265–266 and n. 39 thereto.

7. See Scholem, "The Messianic Idea in Kabbalism," in *The Messianic Idea in Judaism*, pp. 37–48.

8. Compare R. Tucker, *Philosophy and Myth in Karl Marx* (Cambridge: Cambridge University Press, 1961), pp. 41–42 and 52–53 (in reference to Hegel).

9. There are many passages in Judaic sources that allow themselves to be understood in this sense. In case after case, however, one finds that the passages concerned can also be understood quite naturally in other ways, e.g., in *Berakhot* 35b: "To enjoy anything of this world without a benediction is like making personal use of things consecrated to heaven, since it says: 'The earth is the Lord's and the fullness thereof' [Ps. 24:1]." This may mean that such persons are arrogantly ignoring the fact that the world is God's creation. Compare other sayings there and in the Jerusalem Talmud, *Berakhot* 6:1; Midrash on Psalms 16:1; *Shabbat* 50b; Tosefta to *Berakhot* 4:1 and Liebermann's comments in *Tosefta Kifshuta* (New York: Jewish The-

ological Seminary, 1955), pp. 55–56. Similarly, biblical verses which assert that the Israelites are God's slaves and do not own the land they live on (Lev. 25:23 and 42) may be understood in context as warning against misuse of the land or of one's fellow Israelites (compare *Bava Metzia* 10a). The legal terminology describing God as Master and Israel as His slave requires careful rethinking when the covenant is understood in terms of the marriage metaphor. That terminology appears to reduce human beings to possessions of God, which violates the spirit of covenantal mutuality. Compare *Sifre, shelah* 115:

Why is the Exodus from Egypt mentioned in connection with every single commandment? The matter can be compared to a king, the son of whose friend was taken prisoner. The king ransomed him, not as a free man, but as a slave, so that, if he should at any time disobey the king, the latter could say: "You are my slave." So, when he came back, the king said: "Put on my sandals for me, take my clothes to the bath house." Then the son protested. The king took out the bill of sale, and said: "You are my slave." So when God redeemed the children of Abraham His friend, He redeemed them, not as children, but as slaves, so that if He imposed upon them decrees, and they obeyed not, He could say: "You are my slaves." When they went into the desert, He began to order them some light and some heavy commandments, e.g., Sabbath and incest commandments, fringes and phylacteries. They began to protest. Then God said: "You are may slaves. On this condition, I redeemed you, that I should decree and you should fulfill."

10. A classic text relates how several rabbis once debated the reason for this teaching, each offering a different justification. It ends:

Rav Judah said in the name of Samuel: "If I had been there, I should have told them something better than what they said: 'He shall live by them' [Lev. 18:5], but shall not die because of them." Rava said: "The exposition of all of them could be refuted, except that of Samuel, which cannot be refuted." (*Yoma* 85b)

While other rabbis applied their hermeneutic skills in an attempt to find legal precedents and analogies that would justify the suspension of the Sabbath laws, the irrefutable exposition is said to be Samuel's direct justification: the Torah's injunctions are given for us to live by them, not to die by them. The Torah is meant to serve life. Life has its own intrinsic justification regardless of whether or not it leads to the fulfillment of the *mitzvot*.

The *halakhah*'s concern for the dignity and sanctity of human life is brought into sharp focus in Maimonides' explanation of why the *halakhah* insists that saving a human life must take precedence over the laws prohibiting labor on the Sabbath.

. . . for scripture says: "Which if a man do, he shall live by them" [Lev. 18:5], that is to say, he shall not die by them. Hence you learn that the ordinances of the law were meant to bring upon the world not vengeance, but mercy, lovingkindness and peace. It is of heretics—who assert that this is nevertheless a violation of the Sabbath and therefore prohibited—that scripture says: "Wherefore I gave them also statutes that were not good, and ordinances whereby they should not live" [Ezek. 20:25]. (MT *Hilkhot Shabbat* 2:3)

The Lord of Creation is not an authoritarian God Who creates terror in the hearts of creatures. God did not give a law to demonstrate His mastery and lordship over Israel. Obedience to the law must not create a slave mentality. For Maimonides it is heresy for one to believe that the observance of the Sabbath laws prohibiting work should have a greater weight than a human life. Judaism's covenantal foundations are undermined if we are forced to choose between a total commitment to *mitzvah*, a reverential awe for the majestic Lord of Creation, and the intrinsic sacredness of human life.

See M. D. Herr, "Le-va'ayat hilkhot milhamah be-shabbat bi-yemei bayit sheni u-vi-tekufat ha-Mishnah ve-ha-Talmud," *Tarbiẓ* 30 (1961), 242–351.

11. See the interesting discussion in W. Zimmerli, *Man and His Hope in the Old Testament* (London: Student Christian Movement, 1971), especially p. 75–76.

12. Bright, *Covenant and Promise*, discusses the tension in biblical thought between the Mosaic covenant of *mitzvah* and the unconditional covenantal promises to Abraham and David. He argues that trust in those promises can readily "lapse into complacency" (p. 73), but that they were nonetheless essential because they assured Israel that "her future rested ultimately not in what she was—or had, or had not, done—but in the sure, immutable promises of God which nothing could cancel" (p. 196). Urbach, *The Sages*, pp. 496–504, discusses a similar tension in rabbinic thought. While recognizing the tension, I reject Bright's implication that *mitzvah* without the promise of redemption must create "despair, or a self-righteous legalism, an arid works-righteousness" (p. 198).

13. Ezekiel goes further: God did not intend the original covenant to be a success.

> "However, I swore to them in the wilderness that I would scatter them among the nations and disperse them through the lands, because they did not obey My rules, but rejected My laws, profaned My Sabbaths, and looked with longing to the fetishes of their fathers. Moreover, I gave them laws that were not good and rules by which they could not live. . . ." (Ezek. 20:23–25)

Compare M. Greenberg, *Ezekiel* (New York: Doubleday, 1983), ad loc. For Ezekiel, then, the repeated failures in the desert already show that the covenant based upon human freedom cannot succeed. The memory of failure induces despair, which is not total only because God's own glory is at stake in the history of Israel. I have pointed out above, however, that it is also possible for the memory of failure in the desert to encourage persistence in living by the covenant. There are elements in the tradition that regard it as a reassuring memory and not as one that leads to Ezekiel's despair.

14. See Urbach, *The Sages*, pp. 658–673.
15. See *Berakhot* 33b and 48b. Also the Jerusalem Talmud, *Berakhot* 9:5; MT *Hilkhot Berakhot* 10:3. Since Akiva is the paradigm, one can discern in these texts that the benediction expresses continuing love of God rather than a motif of justice. In *Avodah Zarah* 18a, however, the latter motif appears to dominate, as in *Sanhedrin* 6:10 in the Jerusalem Talmud.
16. M. Waltzer, *Exodus and Revolution* (New York: Basic Books, 1985), shows that there is a long political tradition, antecedent to current liberation theology, that treats the Exodus not merely as a memory but as a spur to revolution.
17. Elkanah had not yet learned this when he told his barren wife, Hannah: "Am I not better to you than ten sons?" (1 Sam. 1:8). He imagined that his love could compensate for whatever Hannah lacked. It is no wonder that Hannah left his question unanswered, since he could not grasp that the issue was not his love but her own self-fulfillment as a human being. See the rabbinic discussion of Hannah's prayer in chapter 2.
18. "For the verse 'No man can by any means redeem his brother' [Ps. 49:8] means that a man's brother cannot redeem him; if a man does no good in this world, he has no right to put his trust in the works of his forebears" (*Midrash on Psalms* 146:2). See also *Sifre* Deut. 329 and Urbach, *The Sages*, pp. 499–501.
19. For this understanding of the marriage metaphor, I am grateful to Dr. Emanuel Green and Mary Devor.
20. With increasing spiritual maturity, *mitzvah* can pass from being a duty to being also expressive of relationship to God. Duty and expressiveness are not, however, antithetical religious postures. The sense of duty, the seriousness with which one takes obligations, is needed at times when joy in the relationship is incapable of moving one to action.
21. I therefore prefer to emphasize the marriage model more than another one that features in the tradition: the model of father and child. It may be thought that the latter model has the advantage of expressing unconditionality from the outset, rather than only after a possibly prolonged period as in the marriage model. But note the view of Rabbi Judah in *Kiddushin* 36a: " 'You are sons of the Lord your God' [Deut. 14:1]: if you do not behave as sons, you are not designated sons." A father may also disown his children. The marriage model, grounded in freedom and choice, can provide as strong a sense of security as the biological model of father and child. Although the latter relationship can mature to the point where mutuality and friendship are prominent, I believe the feature of ontological dependency and the sense of gratitude for having been nurtured through one's helplessness continue to give this model a different coloring.
22. See Urbach, *The Sages*, pp. 511–523, especially p. 514.
23. G. Steiner, *The Death of Tragedy* (London: Faber and Faber, 1961), p. 4.

Chapter 12. The Third Jewish Commonwealth

1. Even anti-Zionist Satmar Hasidim and the Netorei Karta community of Meah Shearim view the state of Israel as God's providential act, though as a great and supreme trial rather than as a blessing. The rebirth of Israel, they claim, tests the community's loyalty to Torah and *mitzvah* by challenging it to await God's redemption *despite* the deceptive promises and successes of Zionism. Many more Jews, of course, see Israel's rebirth not as a trial but as a blessing bestowed by God upon the Jewish people. Belief in a personal God who acts in history can lead one to recite special prayers of joyful thanksgiving on Israel's Independence Day or to mourn the fact that the majority of Jews have succumbed to the seductions of a Zionist state that threatens the covenantal identity of the Jewish people. The attempt to understand the actions of a personal God in history is thus not an unambiguous enterprise.

   See Aviezer Ravitzky, "Ha-zafui ve-ha-reshut ha-netunah," in Aluf Har-Even ed., *Yisrael li-kerat ha-me'ah ha-21* (Jerusalem: Van Leer Foundation, 1984), pp. 135-197, especially pp. 140-146, noting a strong necessitarian perception of history of religious Zionists and anti-Zionists alike.

2. See A. I. Kook, *The Lights of Penitence* . . . (New York: Paulist Press, 1978), pp. 256-269, 282-302. Also S. Avineri, *The Making of Modern Zionism* (London: Weidenfeld and Nicholson, 1981), chap. 16.

3. Kook, *The Light of Penitence* . . . , pp. 196-199 and 253-255.

4. "Kol dodi dofek," pp. 77-82.

5. *Rosh ha-Shanah* 29a and *Shavuot* 39a.

6. See Y. Leibowitz, "Jewish Identity and Jewish Silence," in Ehud Ben Ezer, ed., *Unease in Zion* (New York: Quadrangle, 1974), pp. 177-200. Also his *Emunah, historiyah va-arakhim*, pp. 112-134.

7. Maimonides takes strong exception to this view: *Commentary to the Mishnah* on *Pirkei Avot* 4:7, MT *Hilkhot Talmud Torah* 3:1-11. The view is adopted, by contrast, in *Tur, Hilkhot Talmud Torah* 246.

8. See Urbach, *The Sages*, pp. 603-614.

9. E.g., *Mekhilta, ba-hodesh* 5:

   Why was the Torah not given in the land of Israel? . . . To avoid causing dissension among the tribes. Else one might have said: "In my territory the Torah was given." And the other might have said: "In my territory the Torah was given." Therefore, the Torah was given in the desert, publicly and openly, in a place belonging to no one. To three things the Torah is likened: to the desert, to fire, and to water. This is to tell you that just as these three things are free to all who come into the world, so also are the words of the Torah free to all who come into the world.

   See also S. Talmon, "The 'Desert Motif' in the Bible and in Qumran Literature," in A. Altmann, ed., *Biblical Motifs* (Cambridge: Harvard University Press, 1966), pp. 31-63.

10. *Lev. Rab.* 25:5.

11. This is the basis of my serious disagreement with Steven Schwarzschild, who understands *halakhah* and the Jewish people only within messianic categories. Israeli normalcy is for him therefore a paganization of the Jewish people. But Israeli normalcy need not mean, as in A. B. Yehoshua, *Between Right and Right* (New York: Doubleday, 1981), that whatever Jews do in Israel is by definition Jewish. I hold that living in Israel is not a substitute for the normative Jewish tradition, but a framework for its implementation.

12. See further my "Power and Responsibility," *Forum* 44 (Spring 1982), 53–58.

13. See also *Sifre* Deut. 43, quoted by Nachmanides in this context. Also Henoch, *Nachmanides*, pp. 141–159; D. Rapel, "Ha-Ramban al ha-galut ve-ha-geulah," in Y. Ben Sasson, ed., *Geulah u-medinah* (Jerusalem: Ministry of Education, 1979), pp. 79–109.

14. The holiness of the land of Israel consists in that certain *mitzvot* can be performed only there, according to MT *Hilkhot Beit ha-Behirah* 10:12–13 (following *Kelim* 1:6). See also the distinction between the holiness of Jerusalem, which derives from the divine presence, and that of the land of Israel, ibid. 6:14–16. Further, MT *Hilkhot Terumah* 1:2–6 (from 1:3 it would seem that the concept of the land is defined in juridical and political terms rather than in metaphysical or theological ones).

15. See N. Rotenstreich, "Dimensions of the Jewish Experience of Modernity," in *Essays on Zionism and the Contemporary Jewish Condition* (New York: Herzl Press, 1980), pp. 4–18, which brings out the shifts in historical consciousness that accompanied the emergence of Zionism. On the connection between messianism and Zionism, see J. Katz, "The Jewish National Movement," *Journal of World History* 11 (1968), 267–283.

16. Among many examples, see *Shevi'it* 6:1 and *Kiddushin* 1:8 in the Jerusalem Talmud; *Mekhilta, shirta* 1.

17. This is my answer to Leibowitz's criticism in his review of my *Joy and Responsibility* in *Petahim*. He claims that by my ascription of religious significance to the renewal of Jewish national independence, "Judaism is brought down to the level of the faith of the magicians in Egypt who saw the finger of God in particular events in human reality." As I have just pointed out, I make no judgment on God's activity but only on the new opportunities that Israel provides for living our Judaism. Regarding particular events, such as the Six-Day War, I claim only that they may influence individual Jews to feel greater commitment to the community and sensitize them to the historic dimension of Judaic spirituality that is fundamental for halakhic commitment.

    My position is also unaffected by Leibowitz's claim that "the mass movement of Jews away from Judaism has not been halted, nor has it even been slowed, under the influence of the national Jewish rebirth." I am not making an empirical statement about the actual return of Jews to the worship of God, but am merely speaking of opportunities. Israel can be a profound instrument serving the renewal of Jewish spirituality because it forces individual Jews to become responsible for a total way of life in a land that anchors them to their biblical and talmudic historical roots. That the covenantal community has not yet been renewed does not vitiate my argument. What I claim is only that in Israel there are unprecedented living conditions that may renew Jewish spiritual sensibilities. Apart from expanding the possible range of *mitzvah*, those conditions also highlight the notion of collectivity and act against the loss of historical memory. Israel as a political entity focuses attention on the inescapable fact that Jews share a common historical destiny. And Israel as a land acts against the propensity of modern technological society to create individuals who, in their concern for novelty and progress, tend to regard the ideas and visions of the past as backward and inapplicable to their own times and lives.

My disagreement with Leibowitz regarding the place of events generally—and of the rebirth of Israel in particular—in the building of one's religious consciousness thus reflects our respective anthropologies. I claim that Jews serve God with their total personality, which is embedded in historical and communal contexts. Leibowitz's man of faith, by contrast, is nurtured by an act of will irrespective of the sociopolitical conditions of history. Under any conditions, Leibowitz's halakhic individual is able to transcend his own human interest and the needs of the community in an Akedah-like act of unconditional surrender and affirm the dignity of religious worship. The absence in Leibowitz's philosophy of any relationship between *mitzvah* and the shaping of human character enables him to transcend the significance of historical contexts and events. Judaism as a total way of life for a whole society, however, cannot be built exclusively on an Akedah model of spirituality. The Zionist yearning for Jewish "normalcy" is a rejection of the Akedah consciousness as the definitive feature of Jewish spirituality.

18. Here I part ways completely with Leibowitz, for whom messianism is a menacing religious category that should be eliminated as totally and as quickly as possible. See his manner of understanding Maimonides on messianism in *Emunah, historiyah va-arakhim*, pp. 89–111.

19. I am grateful to the leadership of the Netivot Shalom movement for their role in bringing me to this realization.

20. It is a task for another work to spell out what it means to regard *halakhah* as both an educational and a legal system. Heschel's writings have made a beginning in this direction.

Compare *Pesikta de-Rav Kahana* 12:25:

"Moreover," said Rabbi Jose bar Rabbi Hanina, "the divine word spoke to each and every person according to his particular capacity. And do not wonder at this. For when manna came down for Israel, each and every person tasted it in keeping with his own capacity—infants in keeping with their capacity, young men in keeping with their capacity, and old men in keeping with their capacity. . . . Now if each and every person was enabled to taste the manna according to his particular capacity, how much more and more was each and every person enabled according to his particular capacity to hear the divine word. Thus David said: 'The voice of the Lord is in its strength' [Ps. 29:4]—not 'The voice of the Lord in His strength' but 'The voice of the Lord in its strength'—that is, in its strength to make itself heard and understood according to the capacity of each and every person who listens to the divine word."

This *midrash* indicates that *mitzvah* can be appropriated not merely as a formal duty but also as expressive of the particular individual's relationship to God. Accordingly, the statement that "He who is commanded and fulfills it is greater than he who fulfills it though not commanded" (*Kiddushin* 31a, etc.) does not oblige us to identify *halakhah* with acting out of a sense of duty. Compare, however, Rashi on *Rosh ha-Shanah* 28a: "They [the *mitzvot*] were not given to Israel for enjoyment, but as a yoke on their necks." Similarly, Rashi on *Berakhot* 33b.

21. Leibowitz was the first halakhic philosopher to realize, already in the late 1940s, that the creation of the state of Israel demands that the religious community face this fundamental challenge. As he expected no initiatives in this respect from the established halakhic jurists, he addressed his call directly to the religious community. His theory of halakhic change, which eliminates the necessity of precedent, sought to provide a basis for the community to accept the challenge. See Leibowitz, "Rashei perakim le-va'ayat dat Yisrael bi-medinat Yisrael," pp. 85–87; "Yemei Zikkaron," pp. 95–97; "Dat u-medinah," pp. 105–107; also *Emunah, historiyah va-arakhim*, pp. 71–74.

22. Soloveitchik has frequently deprecated self-righteous sectarian tendencies of this kind in modern orthodoxy.

23. One of the forthcoming publications of the research fellows of the Shalom Hartman Institute will be a collection of essays devoted to this topic.

24. See *Yoma* 86a and Maimonides, *Sefer ha-Mitzvot*, positive commandment 3.

25. As Scholem remarked in Ehud ben Ezer, ed., *Unease in Zion*, p. 273: "Zionism has never really known itself completely—whether it is a movement of continuation and continuity, or a movement of rebellion." Also Scholem, "Reflections on Jewish Theology," pp. 290–297. See H. Fisch, *The Zionist Revolution* (London: Weidenfeld and Nicholson, 1978), for a discussion of the paradox (chap. 1–2) and for a very different covenantal understanding of Zionism.

26. Neither are MT *Hilkhot Avodah Zarah* 7:1, 10:1, and 5–6 or MT *Hilkhot Melakhim* 5:1–6, 6:1–6, and 8:10.

27. Contrast Maimonides' advocacy of coercion in MT *Hilkhot Gerushin* 2:20

with Berlin's defense of negative liberty in *Four Essays on Liberty* (Oxford: Oxford University Press, 1969), chap. 3. The work of M. J. Sandel has an important bearing on how Judaism needs to deal with the question of liberalism; see, e.g., his *Liberalism and the Limits of Justice* (Cambridge: Cambridge University Press, 1982).

28. According to *Sanhedrin* 21a, a king cannot be a member of a court because "if they may not be judged, how could they judge?"

29. Hermann Cohen was a notable example who has been followed by various contemporary Jewish theologians who have serious difficulty in coming to terms with the power embodied in the state of Israel.

30. "Why was he [Mordecai] called 'a Jew' [Esther 2:5]? Because he repudiated idolatry. For anyone who repudiates idolatry is called a Jew . . ." (*Megillah* 13a). See my *Joy and Responsibility*, pp. 145–149.

General Index

NOTE: Further references to modern authors will be found in the Notes.

Aaron, 44–45, 86–87
Abraham, 9, 14, 27–32, 43–44, 52, 55, 61, 81–83, 87, 135, 144, 147, 206, 233–34, 268, 293, 303, 312
Adam, 78, 80, 134–35, 252–53
Aggadah, 106
Akedah, 14, 43–44
  as model of religious worship, 59, 62–63, 83, 88, 97, 103, 109–10, 114–16, 130, 132, 141, 151, 153, 156
Aknai, oven of, 32–33, 47, 52
Amidah (prayer), 131–32, 139–41, 143–44, 146, 151–52, 155, 160–63, 165–66, 168, 172, 225
  immutability of expressions in, 157–58
Aristotle (Aristotelian), 9–11, 22, 74, 84, 93, 98–99, 105, 121, 125, 127, 199, 208, 247–50, 307, 311
Asher ben Yehiel, 173
Auschwitz, 17, 202–203, 277, 281

Bar Kochba, 230, 252, 286
Ben Azzai, 316–17
Ben-Gurion, D., 298
Berlin, I., 296
Brit goral, 280

Brit ye'ud, 280
Buber, M., 7, 51, 64, 134

"Chastenings of love," 197–98
Christianity, 115, 206, 251, 304
Contemplative love of God, 119–20, 123–24, 127, 176–79, 257; *see also* Love of God
Covenant: *see also* Human adequacy; *Mitzvah*; Revelation
  with Abraham, 27–32
  and community, 4, 204–206, 280
  and God of Creation, 265–70
  and human freedom, 25–27, 319
  internalized, 219, 221, 227
  and mature love, 272–75
  and messianism, 249–53
  metaphors of, 4–6
  and miracle, 235–37, 249–50
  as model of divine presence in history, 231, 250
  and mutuality, 14, 24–25, 28–30, 43, 97, 324
  and mystic union, 24–25, 39–40
  with Noah, 27–31
  and race, 31–32
  renewal of, 9, 214
  sense of permanence of, 272–75, 325

Creation, 22–24, 65–66, 144, 259–61, 265–66, 302
Criticism, rational, 102–105

Daniel, 216
Desert, 262–63, 281–83
Divine-human interdependence, 25–27
Divine love, 24, 32–33, 79–80, 144, 148, 193, 197–98, 201–202, 220–22, 265
Divine power, 216–17, 221–22, 227, 238, 253, 265–66
Divine presence, 185, 222–24, 253, 319
  and ordered patterns of reality, 238–43
  Sinai model of, 230–32
Divine providence, 75–76, 125, 188–94, 315–16
  Exodus model of, 230–32
  Maimonides' and Aristotle's views on compared, 247–49
  and normal course of the world, 245–47, 250, 253–55, 267
Divine self-limitation, 24, 32–33, 232–33, 266
Divine transcendence, 113
Divine will, 22–23, 148–49, 185–86, 193, 221–22, 232, 238, 266–67; see also Events in nature and history

Elijah, 33, 54–55
Esther, 217–20
Ethics
  and Halakhah, 89–90, 98–101
  and incomprehensibility of God's ways, 44–46
  and mitzvah, 96–101, 107–108, 110–11
  and revelation, 98–101
Eve, 78, 134–35
Events in nature and history
  as carriers of divine will, 16–17, 266–70, 275–77
  and communal self-perception, 204–206
  and divine promises, 184–86, 188–93, 204–28
  religious significance of, 281
Exodus, the, 4, 164, 186, 201, 219–20
  as model of divine providence, 227, 230–31, 242, 250, 253–55
  significance of, 269–72, 324
Ezekiel, 41, 213–15, 227, 252, 263–65, 298, 325
Ezra, 135, 139, 147, 156, 213–14, 216, 227, 284, 298

Fackenheim, E., 114
Fear of God, 300, 302, 314
"Fear of heaven," 232–33
Flood, the, 26–29
Fromm, E., 39, 60–62

Great Assembly, the, 135–36, 142, 147–48, 159, 214, 216, 221

Halakhah, 8, 10–12, 63, 177–79, 200, 224, 289, 293, 295, 324–25, 330; see also "Halakhic man"; Mitzvah
  and ethics, 89–90, 98–101
  and heroism, 85–86
  and philosophy, 120–24
  and prayer, 137, 146, 150–59, 162–63, 170
  submission to, 82–84, 88
"Halakhic man"
  activism of, 72–74
  and concrete world, 71–74
  and creation, 65–67, 74–77
  and "cognitive man," 64–65, 70
  and homo religiosus, 64–68, 71–72, 77
  intellectual dignity of, 63–71
  normative autonomy of, 68–69
  and Torah learning, 63–65, 67–74, 76–77
Hannah, 53–55, 326
Hayyei Adam, 171, 173
Heteronomy, 40, 66, 100; see also Mitzvah and human autonomy
Hezekiah ("book of remedies"), 237
Historical expectations: see also Events in nature and history
  and Book of Esther, 217–20
  and divine power, 215–17
  and messianism, 225–28
  and religious immediacy, 220–25
  and renewal of the covenant by Ezra and Nehemiah, 213–15
  and triumph of paganism, 207–12
History, 129–30; see also Events in nature and history
Hosea, 273
Hukkim, 57–59, 90–97, 106, 175
Human finitude
  and belief in redemption, 263–65
  and creation, 259–61
  and mature love, 273–74, 301
  and Sinai convenant, 261–63
Human freedom, 23–27, 39, 213–14, 233–36, 251–53, 261–65, 271–72
Humanism, 12, 61, 99, 183

Idolatry, 114–15, 207–12, 214–15, 301, 314
Ima Shalom, 49
Imitatio Dei, 65–66, 82, 99, 100
Isaac, 9, 32, 43–44, 61–62, 82–83, 87, 141, 144–45, 151, 303
Isaiah, 9
Islam, 206, 304
Israel, state of, 114, 293–97
  and convenantal tradition, 298–99
  and messianism, 287–93
  religious significance of, 17, 279–87, 327–29

Jacob, 9, 85, 144
James, W., 203, 258
Jeremiah, 6–7, 41, 213–16, 227, 246–47, 252, 263–65, 298

Job, 124–30, 186, 257, 266–67
Joshua, 34, 214, 284, 296
Judah Halevi, 93, 95, 122, 262

Kant (Kantian), 11, 14–15, 40, 64, 66–68, 71, 81, 87, 100, 115, 121, 166, 179, 186
Kaplan, M., 114
Karet, 50
Katz, J., 8
Kaufmann, W., 61
Kavvanah, 133, 160, 163, 165–68, 171–74
Kiddush ha-shem, 114, 292–93
Kierkegaard, S., 10, 81, 308, 314
Kook, A.I., 279–81

Legalism, 1, 109, 275, 318, 325
Leibowitz, Y., 10–11, 14–15, 44, 121, 124–26, 129–30, 165, 174, 257, 281, 311, 328–30
on ethics and Judaism, 61–62, 110–11
and human needs in worship, 109–15
on prayer, 132, 161–64, 170–71, 179
on stages in worship, 61–63, 109, 116–19
Li-shemah: see She-lo li-shemah
Literalism, 35, 40, 219
Love of God, 5, 38–39, 41, 89–91, 95, 103, 120–22, 195, 266, 275, 291, 300–301, 303, 314; *see also* Contemplative love of God

MacIntyre, A., 99–100
Maimonides, 9–11, 14, 16, 25, 36, 69, 74, 109, 113, 162, 222, 231, 256–57, 272, 284, 296, 300–303, 311, 314–15, 320, 324–25
anthropocentrism and theocentrism in, 120–22, 127–36
on creation, 22–23, 307
on extra-halakhic worship, 121–22
on heroism, 292–93
on highest form of worship, 117–20, 126
on human freedom, 233–35
on human insignificance, 124–26
on Job, 124–28
on miracle, 235–36
on messianism, 249–54, 288–91
on "normal course of the world," 245–47, 253–54, 266–68
on prayer, 155–57, 159, 174–75, 243–45, 314, 321–22
on rational control of environment, 237–42
on rationality of *mitzvot*, 90–96, 106
relation between philosophy and *halakhah* in, 98–99, 105–107, 120–24, 307, 311
stages of worship in, 175–79
Marx, K., 2
Messianism, 205, 222–28, 231, 257–58, 285–87, 320
Maimonides' view of, 249–54, 288–91
Nachmanides' view of, 249–53
Mill, J.S., 296
Miracle, 235–36, 242, 249–50, 276
and Torah study, 33

Mishpatim: see Hukkim
Mitzvah (mitzvot), 3, 14, 17, 79, 115, 122–23, 130, 140, 237, 251, 253, 270–71; *see also Halakhah; Hukkim; Kavvanah*
and ethics, 96–101, 107–108
and God's love, 5, 201, 221–22, 257, 265–66
and human autonomy, 40–41, 66–69, 81, 87, 100, 112, 115–16
and idolatry, 92–95
and land of Israel, 283–85
and prayer, 148–49, 156, 160, 162–63, 174, 178–79
and reason, 90–98, 105–107, 239–42
reasons for, 57–58, 116–19
and responsibility, 232–36
reward for observing, 184–94, 220–21, 315–17
and suffering, 267–69
and worship, 110–15, 119, 122
Moses, 9, 11, 34, 36–38, 44–47, 53–55, 62, 66, 83, 87, 94–95, 124, 136–37, 139, 141–42, 147–48, 154, 156, 158–59, 177, 202, 214, 216–18, 222, 262, 272, 274, 298

Nachmanides, 17, 150–51, 242–43, 284–85, 321–22
dependence on God in, 236–37, 240
on messianism, 249–53
Nehemiah, 135, 213–14, 216, 227, 284, 298
Nietzsche, F., 75
Noah, 21, 27–31, 37, 44

Otto, R., 11

Particularity, 3–4, 12, 96, 105, 108, 301–304
Paul, 184
Plato (Platonic), 9, 99, 186, 311
Pluralism, 17–18, 303
Pollock, R.C., 12
Prayer, 15, 311–12; *see also* Amidah; *Mitzvah* and prayer; Shema, the; *Tefillat nedavah*
assertiveness in, 53–55
communal dimension in, 137–38, 168–73
and covenant, 147–49, 164–65
and dead, 52–53, 55, 141–45
individual dimension in, 160–79
Kavvanah in, 160, 163, 165–68, 171–74
and love, 133–35
Maimonides' view of, 155–57, 159, 174–75, 243–45, 314, 321–22
and moral action, 138
Nachmanides' view of, 237, 243
and need, 131–32, 139, 151–53, 164, 314
and precedent, 145–47, 153–55, 159
and prophecy, 135–38, 141–42
and repentance, 243–44
and self-discovery, 138–40
and (self-) sacrifice, 132–33, 139–41, 145, 150–52

Prophecy, 34, 76–77; see also Prayer and prophecy
Purim, 50–51, 219–20, 280

Rabbi Akiva, 9, 36, 38–39, 46–47, 48, 69, 194–95, 211, 222, 315–17, 326
Rabbi Eleazar, 53–55, 155, 191–92, 198, 216
Rabbi Eliezer, 32–33, 47–49, 154, 166
Rabbi Gamaliel, 48–49, 210–11
Rabbi Hanina, 154, 158–59, 166, 198
Rabbi Ishmael, 229, 282, 318–19
Rabbi Jacob, 2, 189–91, 193–94
Rabbi Johanan, 6, 10, 30, 52, 154, 155, 197–98, 218, 226
Rabbi Joshua ben Levi, 50–51, 216
Rabbi Meir, 241–42
Rabbi Simeon ben Yohai, 282–83, 285
Rava, 37, 189, 212, 219, 220
Redemption, 115, 256–67, 269–70, 277, 325
Repentance: see Teshuvah
Revelation, 142, 144, 148, 164–65, 223, 265, 269
  and ethics, 98–101
  and human love, 133–34
  and intellectual autonomy, 32–41
  interpretation of, 6–11, 35–36, 114–16
  and redemption, 256–63, 269
Rosh ha-Shanah, 53, 56–57

Sabbath, 116–17, 225, 260–61, 290–91, 324–25
Saul, 51–52
Scholem, G., 64, 225–26, 286, 320
She-lo li-shemah, 61–62, 116–17, 119, 129
Shema, the, 39, 152, 163–68, 170–72, 184, 195
Shulhan Arukh, 11, 172
Solomon, 201, 206, 213, 237
Soleveitchik, J., 7–8, 10–11, 14–15, 89–91, 95, 97, 109, 123, 163, 267, 311–12, 321–22; see also "Halakhic man"

and "ethic of defeat," 81–84, 87
"Catharsis," 84–88
Jewish heroism, 85–86
loneliness of man of faith, 77–81, 100–107, 240
"Majesty and Humility," 81–84
on prayer, 132–59, 170–71, 174–79, 312–13
on religious significance of state of Israel, 279–81
Spinoza, B., 1–2, 9–11, 68–69, 179, 183, 297
Steiner, G., 277
Submissiveness, 13–14, 42–60, 133; see also Akedah
Suffering, 16–17, 267–69, 276–77
  and commitment to mitzvot,, 187–88, 190, 193–94, 198–203, 268–69
  rabbinic responses to, 188–201, 317–18
  and self-doubt, 186–87

Tefillat nedavah, 145–46, 153, 157–59, 170–73, 312
Teshuvah (repentance), 26, 75–76, 195–96, 243–47, 249
Theodicy, 187, 267, 318
Torah study, 3, 41, 63–65, 67–74, 76–77, 185, 221–23, 226, 282–83
Tur, 172
Tzelem elohim, 23
Tzimtzum, 24, 82

Uniqueness (Jewish), 3, 12, 102, 105, 107, 240–41, 262, 296; see also Particularity
Urbach, E., 39, 316–17

World to come, 188–90, 222

Yetzer ha-ra, 126, 214–15, 253
Yom Kippur, 53, 56, 110, 113

Index of Jewish Sources

The Bible

Genesis 1:5	152
1:27	23
1:28	23
1:31	259–60
2:18	78
6:6–8	26
6:9	30
7:7	30
8:20–21	28
9:8–17	27
9:9–11	27
9:16–17	31
12:2	43
12:7	43
15:13	234
17:1–14	27
17:1	30
17:5	29
17:7	147
18:1–4	31
18:13–25	30
18:17–19	28, 43
18:23–32	28
18:25	43, 268
24:2–3	29
24:7	29
32:24–32	85

| Exodus 2:23 | 139 |
| 3:14–15 | 9 |

14:11	262
15:2	8
19:6	283
19:17	219
20:2	269
20:18–19	142
21:19	229
22:21–22	318
23:2	33, 47
23:20	142
23:25	321
32:10	54
32:11–14	55
33:11	137
34:27	6

Leviticus 1:9	150
10:1–2, 6	44
18:4	58
18:5	324
18:25ff.	284
18:28	284
19:18	111
26:3–45	236
26:11	236

Numbers 5:28	53
6:26	220
18:20	121

| Deuteronomy 4:6 | 92, 106 |
| 4:12 | 25, 299 |

4:24	210
5:16	189
5:26	235
6:5	195
6:13	321
8:10	220
9:18	154
9:19	154
9:26	154
10:17	158, 216, 220
11:13–17	184
11:13	321
11:14	282
13:2	34
13:5	321
14:1	326
17:11	34
18:9ff.	240
18:13	240–41
21:1–9	51
22:7	189
23:3	59
25:3	50
28:9	65
29:13–14	148
30:6	252
30:12	33–34, 47
30:15, 19	261
30:20	38
33:10	121
33:11	121

Joshua 1:8	282

1 Samuel 1:8	326
1:11	53
1:13	54
6:19	45
15:1–35	51
22:18	52

2 Samuel 6:6	45

1 Kings 18:37	54

Isaiah 11:6–8	253–54
11:9	254
40:15	125
43:9	207
49:3	293
61:5	282
66:3–4	234

Jeremiah 5:3	246
9:23	123
12:2	118
23:10	245
31:30–32	213
32:18	216

Ezekiel 14:4–5	190
20:21–22	263–64

20:23–25	325
20:25	324–25
36:25–27	213

Micah 6:8	32

Haggai 2:3	213

Zechariah 5:8	215

Psalms 4:5	159
16:5	122
24:1	323
29:4	330
36:7	315
49:8	326
51:15	143
65:2	159
66:20	197
92:1	225
94:12	196–97
112:9	316
123:2	321
136:7	223

Proverbs 3:12	196–97
3:17	283
3:18	154
3:34	212
10:2	316
13:12	154, 226
16:33	217

Job 13:24	186

Lamentations 3:40	196

Ecclesiastes 1:10	302
4:1	58
7:16	52
7:17	52
11:1	316
12:11	310

Esther 2:5	331
6:1	218
9:27	51, 219

Daniel 9:4	216

Ezra 3:12	213

Nehemiah 8:6	216
9:1	215
9:4	214
9:32	158, 216–17
9:36–10:1	214

The Mishnah

Berakhot 2:5	167
2:8	167
3:3	152

5:1	53
5:3	157
9:5	158
Shabbat 6:10	241–42
Ta'anit 1:7	186
Kiddushin 1:10	188
Makkot 3:15	50
Eduyot 1:5	310
Avodah Zarah 4:7	209
Pirkei Avot 3:6	185
4:1	217
4:2	316
4:16	2

The Jerusalem Talmud

Berakhot 3:3	271
Rosh ha-Shanah 1:3	56–57
Megillah 1:1	217
1:5	217–18
Sotah 5:5	195

The Babylonian Talmud

Berakhot 5a	196–97
5b	198
8b	262
17b	171
20b	220
21a	153, 155
22a	185
26a	151–52
26b	151, 169
29b	154, 168
31b	53–54
32a	54
32b	153–54, 226
33b	157–58
34a	131
35b	282, 323
40b	312
60a	229
61b	39
Shabbat 88a	219
127a	31
156b	316
Eruvin 65a	166
Pesahim 22b	38

Yoma 22b	52
67b	58
69b	215–16
85b	324
Rosh ha-Shanah 32b	56
Megillah 7a	217
12a–17a	218
13a	331
14a	219–20
Moed Katan 27b	246
Nedarim 20b	68
Gittin 60b	6
Kiddushin 36a	326
37a	297
39b	188–91
57a	38
Bava Metzia 59b	33, 48–49
86b	36
Sanhedrin 59a–b	307
97b	264
Makkot 22b	37
23b	51
Avodah Zarah 2a–b	207–208
54b	209–10
55a	211–12
Avot de-Rabbi Nathan 3	316
38 (41)	318
Semahot 8	318
Kallah 51a	316
Menahot 29b	36, 46
Temurah 16a	34

Tosafot

on Berakhot 17b	171
on Berakhot 40b	312

The Midrash

Mekhilta,	
ba-hodesh 5	4–5, 327
va-yassa 3	282
nezikim 18	318
Sifre,	
shelah 115	324
ha'azinu 313	29

Genesis Rabbah 30:9   30
30:10   30
32:6   31
49:2   29

Leviticus Rabbah 22:1   36
24:10   58–59
27:1   315–16

Song of Songs Rabbah 1:2   34

Ecclesiastes Rabbah 7:16   52

Esther Rabbah 10:1   218

Midrash on Psalms 146:2   326

Pesikta de-Rav Kahana 12:25 329–30

Tanhuma, Genesis 1:11   21

Seder Eliyahu Zuta 2   35

Maimonides

Commentary on the Mishnah
  Pesahim 4:10   237–38

Eight Chapters
  Chap. 8   232–34

Book of Commandments
  Positive Commandment 5   321

Mishneh Torah
  Hilkhot Yesodei ha-Torah 124
    4:12
  5:10   292
  5:11   292–93
  Hilkhot Deot 1:5–6   99
  Hilkhot Avodah Zarah 11:16 241
  Hilkhot Tefillah 1:2–3   177
  1:3   156
  1:5–6   156
  1:11   155
  Hilkhot Shabbat 2:3   324–25
  Hilkhot Ta'anit 1:1–2   243
  1:3   245

1:17   242–43
5:1   244
Hilkhot Megillah 2:18   218
Hilkhot Shemitah
  ve-Yovel 13:12   121
  13:13   122–22
Hilkhot Tumat Tzara'at 2:9 36–37
Hilkhot Evel 13:11–12   245–46
Hilkhot Melakhim 12:4   291

Guide of the Perplexed
1:59   159
1:71   257
2:25   23, 98
2:29   239
2:48   238
3:11   253–54
3:13   125
3:17   200, 247–48
3:22–23   126–28
3:26   162
3:31   91–92
3:32   25, 175–76,
                            235, 272, 313
3:34   310
3:36   245
3:37   93, 242
3:45   95
3:51   117–18, 120,
                            124, 178
3:52   126
3:54   123

Nachmanides

Commentary on the Torah
  Leviticus 1:9   150–51
  18:25ff.   284
  26:11   236
  Deuteronomy 18:9ff.   240
  30:6   252

Commentary on Maimonides'
Book of Commandments
  Positive Commandment 5   321

ABOUT JEWISH LIGHTS PUBLISHING

People of all faiths and backgrounds yearn for books that attract, engage, educate and spiritually inspire.

Our books focus on the issue of the quest for the self, seeking meaning in life. They are books that help all people to better understand who they are and who they might become as a person who is part of a tradition that has its roots in the Judeo-Christian world. They deal with issues of personal growth. They deal with issues of religious inspiration.

We bring to you authors who are at the forefront of spiritual thought and experience. While each has something different to say, they all say it in a voice that you can hear.

Our books are designed to welcome you and then to engage, stimulate and inspire. We judge our success not only by whether or not our books are beautiful and commercially successful, but by whether or not they make a difference in your life.

We at Jewish Lights take great care to produce beautiful books that present meaningful spiritual content in a form that reflects the art of making high quality books. Therefore, we want to acknowledge those who contributed to the production of this book.

EDITORIAL & PROOFREADING
Richard Fumosa

PRODUCTION
Maria O'Donnell

COVER DESIGN
Glenn Suokko, Woodstock, Vermont

COVER PRINTING
John P. Pow Co., Inc.,
South Boston, Massachusetts

PRINTING AND BINDING
Royal Book, Norwich, Connecticut

Theology/Philosophy

A LIVING COVENANT
The Innovative Spirit in Traditional Judaism
by *David Hartman*

WINNER,
National Jewish
Book Award

The Judaic tradition is often seen as being more concerned with uncritical obedience to law than with individual freedom and responsibility. Hartman challenges this approach by revealing a Judaism grounded in a covenant—a relational framework—informed by the metaphor of marital love rather than that of parent-child dependency.

"Jews and non-Jews, liberals and traditionalists will see classic Judaism anew in these pages."
—*Dr. Eugene R. Borowitz, Hebrew-Union College–Jewish Institute of Religion*
6" x 9", 368 pp. Quality Paperback, ISBN 1-58023-011-3 **$18.95**

THE SPIRIT OF RENEWAL
Finding Faith after the Holocaust
by *Edward Feld*

Trying to understand the Holocaust and addressing the question of faith after the Holocaust, Rabbi Feld explores three key cycles of destruction and recovery in Jewish history, each of which radically reshaped Jewish understanding of God, people, and the world.

"A profound meditation on Jewish history [and the Holocaust]....Christians, as well as many others, need to share in this story."
—*The Rt. Rev. Frederick H. Borsch, Ph.D., Episcopal Bishop of L.A.*
6" x 9", 224 pp. Quality Paperback, ISBN 1-879045-40-0 **$16.95**

•AWARD WINNER•

SEEKING THE PATH TO LIFE
Theological Meditations On God
and the Nature of People, Love, Life and Death
by *Rabbi Ira F. Stone*

For people who never thought they would read a book of theology—let alone understand it, enjoy it, savor it and have it affect the way they think about their lives. In 45 intense meditations, each a page or two in length, Stone takes us on explorations of the most basic human struggles: Life and death, love and anger, peace and war, covenant and exile.

•AWARD WINNER•

"A bold book....The reader of any faith will be inspired...."
— *The Rev. Carla V. Berkedal, Episcopal Priest*

6" x 9", 132 pp. Quality Paperback, ISBN 1-879045-47-8 **$14.95** HC, ISBN-17-6 **$19.95**

THEOLOGY & PHILOSOPHY...Other books—Classic Reprints

Aspects of Rabbinic Theology by Solomon Schechter, with a new Introduction by Neil Gillman 6" x 9", 440 pp, Quality Paperback, ISBN 1-879045-24-9 **$18.95**

The Last Trial: On the Legends and Lore of the Command to Abraham to Offer Isaac as a Sacrifice by Shalom Spiegel, with a new Introduction by Judah Goldin 6" x 9", 208 pp, Quality Paperback, ISBN 1-879045-29-X **$17.95**

Judaism & Modern Man: An Interpretation of Jewish Religion by Will Herberg; new Introduction by Neil Gillman 5.5" x 8.5", 336 pp, Quality Paperback, ISBN 1-879045-87-7 **$18.95**

Tormented Master: The Life and Spiritual Quest of Rabbi Nahman of Bratslav by Arthur Green 6" x 9", 408 pp, Quality Paperback, ISBN 1-879045-11-7 **$18.95**

Your Word Is Fire Edited and translated with a new Introduction by Arthur Green and Barry W. Holtz 6" x 9", 152 pp, Quality Paperback, ISBN 1-879045-25-7 **$14.95**

CLASSICS BY ABRAHAM JOSHUA HESCHEL

The Earth Is the Lord's: The Inner World of the Jew in Eastern Europe
5 1/2" x 8", 112 pp, Quality Paperback, ISBN 1-879045-42-7 **$13.95**

Israel: An Echo of Eternity with new Introduction by Susannah Heschel
5 1/2" x 8", 272 pp, Quality Paperback, ISBN 1-879045-70-2 **$18.95**

A Passion for Truth: Despair and Hope in Hasidism
5 1/2" x 8", 352 pp, Quality Paperback, ISBN 1-879045-41-9 **$18.95**

Spirituality

MY PEOPLE'S PRAYER BOOK
Traditional Prayers, Modern Commentaries
Vol. 1—The Sh'ma and Its Blessings
Edited by *Rabbi Lawrence A. Hoffman*

Provides a diverse and exciting commentary to the traditional liturgy, written by 10 of today's most respected scholars and teachers from all perspectives of the Jewish world.

This groundbreaking first of seven volumes examines the oldest and best-known of Jewish prayers. Often the first prayer memorized by children and the last prayer recited on a deathbed, the *Sh'ma* frames a Jewish life.

7" x 10", 168 pp. HC, ISBN 1-879045-79-6 **$19.95**

FINDING JOY
A Practical Spiritual Guide to Happiness
by *Dannel I. Schwartz* with *Mark Hass*

Searching for happiness in our modern world of stress and struggle is common; *finding* it is more unusual. This guide explores and explains how to find joy through a time-honored, creative—and surprisingly practical—approach based **on the teachings of Jewish mysticism and Kabbalah.**

"Lovely, simple introduction to Kabbalah....a singular contribution...."
—*American Library Association's* Booklist

•AWARD WINNER•

6" x 9", 192 pp. HC, ISBN 1-879045-53-2 **$19.95**

THE DEATH OF DEATH
Resurrection and Immortality in Jewish Thought
by *Neil Gillman*

Noted theologian Neil Gillman explores the original and compelling argument that Judaism, a religion often thought to pay little attention to the afterlife, not only offers us rich ideas on the subject—but delivers a deathblow to death itself. By exploring Jewish thought about death and the afterlife, this fascinating work presents us with challenging new ideas about our lives.

"Enables us to recover our tradition's understanding of the afterlife and breaks through the silence of modern Jewish thought on immortality.... A work of major significance."
—*Rabbi Sheldon Zimmerman, President, Hebrew Union College–Jewish Institute of Religion*

6" x 9", 336 pp., HC, ISBN 1-879045-61-3 **$23.95**

THE EMPTY CHAIR: FINDING HOPE & JOY
Timeless Wisdom from a Hasidic Master,
Rebbe Nachman of Breslov
Adapted by Moshe Mykoff and the Breslov Research Institute

A "little treasure" of aphorisms and advice for living joyously and spiritually today, written 200 years ago, but startlingly fresh in meaning and use. Challenges and helps us to move from stress and sadness to hope and joy.

Teacher, guide and spiritual master—Rebbe Nachman provides vital words of inspiration and wisdom for life today for people of any faith, or of no faith.

•AWARD WINNER•

"For anyone of any faith, this is a book of healing and wholeness, of being alive!"
— *Bookviews*

4" x 6", 128 pp., 2-color text, Deluxe Paperback, ISBN 1-879045-67-2 **$9.95**

Spirituality

HOW TO BE A PERFECT STRANGER, In 2 Volumes
A Guide to Etiquette in Other People's Religious Ceremonies
Edited by *Stuart M. Matlins* & *Arthur J. Magida*

BEST REFERENCE BOOK OF THE YEAR

"A book that belongs in every living room, library and office!"

Explains the rituals and celebrations of America's major religions/denominations, helping an interested guest to feel comfortable, participate to the fullest extent possible, and avoid violating anyone's religious principles. Answers practical questions from the perspective of *any* other faith.

VOL. 1: America's Largest Faiths

VOL. 1 COVERS: Assemblies of God • Baptist • Buddhist • Christian Science • Churches of Christ • Disciples of Christ • Episcopalian • Greek Orthodox • Hindu • Islam • Jehovah's Witnesses • Jewish • Lutheran • Methodist • Mormon • Presbyterian • Quaker • Roman Catholic • Seventh-day Adventist • United Church of Christ

6" x 9", 432 pp. Hardcover, ISBN 1-879045-39-7 **$24.95**

VOL. 2: Other Faiths in America

VOL. 2 COVERS: African American Methodist Churches • Baha'i • Christian and Missionary Alliance • Christian Congregation • Church of the Brethren • Church of the Nazarene • Evangelical Free Church of America • International Church of the Foursquare Gospel • International Pentecostal Holiness Church • Mennonite/Amish • Native American • Orthodox Churches • Pentecostal Church of God • Reformed Church of America • Sikh • Unitarian Universalist • Wesleyan

6" x 9", 416 pp. HC, ISBN 1-879045-63-X **$24.95**

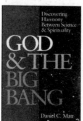

GOD & THE BIG BANG
Discovering Harmony Between Science & Spirituality
by *Daniel C. Matt*

Mysticism and science: What do they have in common? How can one enlighten the other? By drawing on modern cosmology and ancient Kabbalah, Matt shows how science and religion can together enrich our spiritual awareness and help us recover a sense of wonder and find our place in the universe.

"This poetic new book...helps us to understand the human meaning of creation."
—*Joel Primack, leading cosmologist, Professor of Physics, University of California, Santa Cruz*

6" x 9", 216 pp. Quality Paperback, ISBN 1-879045-89-3 **$16.95** HC, ISBN-48-6 **$21.95**

MINDING THE TEMPLE OF THE SOUL
Balancing Body, Mind, & Spirit through Traditional Jewish Prayer, Movement, & Meditation
by *Tamar Frankiel* and *Judy Greenfeld*

This new spiritual approach to physical health introduces readers to a spiritual tradition that affirms the body and enables them to reconceive their bodies in a more positive light. Relying on Kabbalistic teachings and other Jewish traditions, it shows us how to be more responsible for our own psychological and physical health. Focuses on the discipline of prayer, simple Tai Chi–like exercises and body positions, and guides the reader throughout, step by step, with diagrams, sketches and meditations.

7"x 10", 184 pp. Quality Paperback Original, illus., ISBN 1-879045-64-8 **$16.95**

Audiotape of the Prayers, Movements & Meditations (60-min. cassette) **$9.95**
Videotape of the Blessings & Meditations (46-min. VHS) **$20.00**

Art of Jewish Living Series for Holiday Observance

THE SHABBAT SEDER
by *Dr. Ron Wolfson*

A concise step-by-step guide designed to teach people the meaning and importance of this weekly celebration, as well as its practices.

Each chapter corresponds to one of ten steps which together comprise the Shabbat dinner ritual, and looks at the *concepts, objects,* and *meanings* behind the specific activity or ritual act. The blessings that accompany the meal are written in both Hebrew and English, and accompanied by English transliteration. Also included are craft projects, recipes, discussion ideas and other creative suggestions for enriching the Shabbat experience.

"A how-to book in the best sense...."
—*Dr. David Lieber, President, University of Judaism, Los Angeles*

7" x 9", 272 pp. Quality Paperback, ISBN 1-879045-90-7 **$16.95**

Also available are these helpful companions to *The Shabbat Seder*:	
•Booklet of the Blessings and Songs	ISBN 1-879045-91-5 $5.00
•Audiocassette of the Blessings	DNO3 $6.00
•Teacher's Guide	ISBN 1-879045-92-3 $4.95

HANUKKAH
by *Dr. Ron Wolfson*
Edited by *Joel Lurie Grishaver*

Designed to help celebrate and enrich the holiday season, *Hanukkah* discusses the holiday's origins, explores the reasons for the Hanukkah candles and customs, and provides everything from recipes to family activities.

There are songs, recipes, useful information on the arts and crafts of Hanukkah, the calendar and its relationship to Christmas time, and games played at Hanukkah. Putting the holiday in a larger, timely context, "December Dilemmas" deals with ways in which a Jewish family can cope with Christmas.

"Helpful for the family that strives to induct its members into the spirituality and joys of Jewishness and Judaism...a significant text in the neglected art of Jewish family education."
—*Rabbi Harold M. Schulweis, Cong. Valley Beth Shalom, Encino, CA*

7" x 9", 192 pp. Quality Paperback, ISBN 1-879045-97-4 **$16.95**

THE PASSOVER SEDER
by *Dr. Ron Wolfson*

Explains the concepts behind Passover ritual and ceremony in clear, easy-to-understand language, and offers step-by-step procedures for Passover observance and preparing the home for the holiday.

Easy-to-Follow Format: Using an innovative photo-documentary technique, real families describe in vivid images their own experiences with the Passover holiday. **Easy-to-Read Hebrew Texts:** The Haggadah texts in Hebrew, English, and transliteration are presented in a three-column format designed to help celebrants learn the meaning of the prayers and how to read them. **An Abundance of Useful Information:** A detailed description of how to perform the rituals is included, along with practical questions and answers, and imaginative ideas for Seder celebration.

"A creative 'how-to' for making the Seder a more meaningful experience."
—*Michael Strassfeld, co-author of* The Jewish Catalog

7" x 9", 336 pp. Quality Paperback, ISBN 1-879045-93-1 **$16.95**

Also available are these helpful companions to *The Passover Seder*:	
•Passover Workbook	ISBN 1-879045-94-X $6.95
•Audiocassette of the Blessings	DNO4 $6.00
•Teacher's Guide	ISBN 1-879045-95-8 $4.95

Spirituality—The Kushner Series

INVISIBLE LINES OF CONNECTION
Sacred Stories of the Ordinary
by *Lawrence Kushner*

Through his everyday encounters with family, friends, colleagues and strangers, Kushner takes us deeply into our lives, finding flashes of spiritual insight in the process. This is a book where literature meets spirituality, where the sacred meets the ordinary, and, above all, where people of all faiths, all backgrounds can meet one another and themselves.

"Does something both more and different than instruct—it inspirits. Wonderful stories, from the best storyteller I know."
— *David Mamet*

5 1/2" x 8 1/2", 160 pp. Quality Paperback, ISBN 1-879045-98-2 **$15.95** HC, -52-4 **$21.95**

HONEY FROM THE ROCK
An Easy Introduction to Jewish Mysticism
by *Lawrence Kushner*

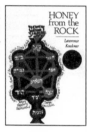

"Quite simply the easiest introduction to Jewish mysticism you can read."

An introduction to the ten gates of Jewish mysticism and how it applies to daily life.

"Captures the flavor and spark of Jewish mysticism. . . . Read it and be rewarded." —*Elie Wiesel*

6" x 9", 168 pp. Quality Paperback, ISBN 1-879045-02-8 **$14.95**

THE BOOK OF WORDS
Talking Spiritual Life, Living Spiritual Talk
by *Lawrence Kushner*

In the incomparable manner of his extraordinary *The Book of Letters*, Kushner now lifts up and shakes the dust off primary religious words we use to describe the spiritual dimension of life. For each word Kushner offers us a startling, moving and insightful explication, and pointed readings from classical Jewish sources that further illuminate the concept. He concludes with a short exercise that helps unite the spirit of the word with our actions in the world.

"This is a powerful and holy book."
—*M. Scott Peck, M.D., author of* The Road Less Traveled *and other books*

"What a delightful wholeness of intellectual vigor and meditative playfulness, and all in a tone of gentleness that speaks to this gentile."
—*Rt. Rev. Krister Stendahl, formerly Dean, Harvard Divinity School/Bishop of Stockholm*

6" x 9", 152 pp. HC, beautiful two-color text, ISBN 1-879045-35-4 **$21.95**

THE BOOK OF LETTERS
A Mystical Hebrew Alphabet
by *Rabbi Lawrence Kushner*

In calligraphy by the author. Folktales about and exploration of the mystical meanings of the Hebrew Alphabet. Open the old prayerbook-like pages of *The Book of Letters* and you will enter a special world of sacred tradition and religious feeling. Rabbi Kushner draws from ancient Judaic sources, weaving talmudic commentary, Hasidic folktales, and kabbalistic mysteries around the letters.

"A book which is in love with Jewish letters."
— *Isaac Bashevis Singer* (ז״ל)

• **Popular Hardcover Edition** 6"x 9", 80 pp. HC, two colors, inspiring new Foreword.
ISBN 1-879045-00-1 **$24.95**

• **Deluxe Gift Edition** 9"x 12", 80 pp. HC, four-color text, ornamentation, in a beautiful slipcase.
ISBN 1-879045-01-X **$79.95**

• **Collector's Limited Edition** 9"x 12", 80 pp. HC, gold-embossed pages, hand-assembled slipcase. With silkscreened print. **Limited to 500 signed and numbered copies.** ISBN 1-879045-04-4 $349.00

To see a sample page at no obligation, call us

Spirituality

GOD WAS IN THIS PLACE & I, i DID NOT KNOW
Finding Self, Spirituality & Ultimate Meaning
by Lawrence Kushner

Who am I? Who is God? Kushner creates inspiring interpretations of Jacob's dream in Genesis, opening a window into Jewish spirituality for people of all faiths and backgrounds.

In this fascinating blend of scholarship, imagination, psychology and history, seven Jewish spiritual masters ask and answer fundamental questions of human experience.

"Rich and intriguing."
—*M. Scott Peck, M.D., author of* The Road Less Traveled *and other books*

6" x 9", 192 pp. Quality Paperback, ISBN 1-879045-33-8 **$16.95**

THE RIVER OF LIGHT
Spirituality, Judaism, Consciousness
by Lawrence Kushner

A "manual" for all spiritual travelers who would attempt a spiritual journey in our times. Taking us step by step, Kushner allows us to discover the meaning of our own quest: "to allow the river of light—the deepest currents of consciousness—to rise to the surface and animate our lives."

"Philosophy and mystical fantasy....Anybody—Jewish, Christian, or otherwise...will find this book an intriguing experience."
—*Kirkus Reviews*

6" x 9", 180 pp. Quality Paperback, ISBN 1-879045-03-6 **$14.95**

GODWRESTLING—ROUND 2
Ancient Wisdom, Future Paths
by *Arthur Waskow*

BEST RELIGION BOOK OF THE YEAR

This 20th-anniversary sequel to a seminal book of the Jewish renewal movement deals with spirituality in relation to personal growth, marriage, ecology, feminism, politics, and more. Including new chapters on recent issues and concerns, Waskow outlines original ways to merge "religious" life and "personal" life in our society today.

"A delicious read and a soaring meditation."
—*Rabbi Zalman M. Schachter-Shalomi*

"Vivid as a novel, sharp, eccentric, loud....An important book for anyone who wants to bring Judaism alive."
—*Marge Piercy*

6" x 9", 352 pp. Quality Paperback, ISBN 1-879045-72-9 **$18.95** HC, ISBN-45-1 **$23.95**

BEING GOD'S PARTNER
How to Find the Hidden Link Between Spirituality and Your Work
by Jeffrey K. Salkin Introduction by *Norman Lear*

Will challenge people of every denomination to reconcile the cares of work and soul. A groundbreaking book about spirituality and the work world, from a Jewish perspective. Helps the reader find God in the ethical striving and search for meaning in the professions and in business and offers practical suggestions for balancing your professional life and spiritual self.

"This engaging meditation on the spirituality of work is grounded in Judaism but is relevant well beyond the boundaries of that tradition."
—Booklist *(American Library Association)*

6" x 9", 192 pp. Quality Paperback, ISBN 1-879045-65-6 **$16.95** HC, ISBN-37-0 **$19.95**

Healing/Recovery/Wellness

Experts Praise *Twelve Jewish Steps to Recovery*

"Recommended reading for people of all denominations."
—*Rabbi Abraham J. Twerski, M.D.*

TWELVE JEWISH STEPS TO RECOVERY
A Personal Guide to Turning from Alcoholism & Other Addictions...Drugs, Food, Gambling, Sex...

by *Rabbi Kerry M. Olitzky & Stuart A. Copans, M.D.*
Preface by *Abraham J. Twerski, M.D.*; Intro. by *Rabbi Sheldon Zimmerman*; "Getting Help" by *JACS Foundation*

A Jewish perspective on the Twelve Steps of addiction recovery programs with consolation, inspiration and motivation for recovery. It draws from traditional sources and quotes from what recovering Jewish people say about their experiences with addictions of all kinds. Inspiring illustrations of the twelve gates of the Old City of Jerusalem introduce each step.

6" x 9", 136 pp. Quality Paperback, ISBN 1-879045-09-5 **$13.95**

Recovery from Codependence: A Jewish Twelve Steps Guide to Healing Your Soul
by Dr. Kerry M. Olitzky

6" x 9", 160 pp. Quality Paperback Original, ISBN 1-879045-32-X **$13.95**   HC, ISBN-27-3 **$21.95**

Renewed Each Day: Daily Twelve Step Recovery Meditations Based on the Bible
by Dr. Kerry M. Olitzky & Aaron Z.

6" x 9", Quality Paperback Original,   **V. I**, 224 pp. **$12.95**   **V. II**, 280 pp. **$14.95**
Two-Volume Set ISBN 1-879045-21-4   **$27.90**

One Hundred Blessings Every Day: Daily Twelve Step Recovery Affirmations, Exercises for Personal Growth & Renewal Reflecting Seasons of the Jewish Year
by Dr. Kerry M. Olitzky

4 1/2" x 6 1/2", 432 pp. Quality Paperback Original, ISBN 1-879045-30-3   **$14.95**

HEALING OF SOUL, HEALING OF BODY
Spiritual Leaders Unfold the Strength and Solace in Psalms

Edited by *Rabbi Simkha Y. Weintraub, CSW, for The Jewish Healing Center*

A source of solace for those who are facing illness, as well as those who care for them. The ten Psalms which form the core of this healing resource were originally selected 200 years ago by Rabbi Nachman of Breslov as a "complete remedy." Today, for anyone coping with illness, they continue to provide a wellspring of strength. Each Psalm is newly translated, making it clear and accessible, and each one is introduced by an eminent rabbi, men and women reflecting different movements and backgrounds. To all who are living with the pain and uncertainty of illness, this spiritual resource offers an anchor of spiritual comfort.

"Will bring comfort to anyone fortunate enough to read it. This gentle book is a luminous gem of wisdom."
—*Larry Dossey, M.D., author of* Healing Words: The Power of Prayer & the Practice of Medicine

6" x 9", 128 pp. Quality Paperback Original, illus., 2-color text, ISBN 1-879045-31-1 **$14.95**

Spirituality

MEDITATION FROM THE HEART OF JUDAISM
Today's Teachers Share Their Practices, Techniques, and Faith
Edited by *Avram Davis*

A "how-to" guide for both beginning and experienced meditators, it will help you start meditating or help you enhance your practice.

Twenty-two masters of meditation explain why and how they meditate. *A detailed compendium of the experts' "Best Practices"* offers practical advice and starting points.

"A treasury of meditative insights and techniques....Each page is a meditative experience that brings you closer to God."
—*Rabbi Shoni Labowitz, author of* Miraculous Living: A Guided Journey in Kabbalah

6" x 9", 256 pp. Hardcover, ISBN 1-879045-77-X **$21.95**

SELF, STRUGGLE & CHANGE
Family Conflict Stories in Genesis and Their Healing Insights for Our Lives
by *Norman J. Cohen*

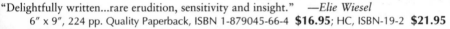

How do I find greater wholeness in my life and in my family's life?

The people described by the biblical writers of Genesis were in situations and relationships very much like our own. We identify with them. Their stories still speak to us because they are about the same problems we deal with every day. Here a modern master of biblical interpretation brings us greater understanding of the ancient text and of ourselves in this intriguing re-telling of conflict between husband and wife, father and son, brothers, and sisters.

"Delightfully written...rare erudition, sensitivity and insight." —*Elie Wiesel*
6" x 9", 224 pp. Quality Paperback, ISBN 1-879045-66-4 **$16.95**; HC, ISBN-19-2 **$21.95**

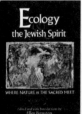

ECOLOGY & THE JEWISH SPIRIT
Where Nature & the Sacred Meet
Edited and with Introductions by *Ellen Bernstein*

What is nature's place in our spiritual lives?

A focus on nature is part of the fabric of Jewish thought. Here, experts bring us a richer understanding of the long-neglected themes of nature that are woven through the biblical creation story, ancient texts, traditional law, the holiday cycles, prayer, *mitzvot* (good deeds), and community.

For people of all faiths, all backgrounds, this book helps us to make nature a sacred, spiritual part of our own lives.

"A great resource for anyone seeking to explore the connection between their faith and caring for God's good creation, our environment."
—*Paul Gorman, Executive Director, National Religious Partnership for the Environment*

6" x 9", 288 pp. HC, ISBN 1-879045-88-5 **$23.95**

ISRAEL—A SPIRITUAL TRAVEL GUIDE
A Companion for the Modern Jewish Pilgrim
by *Rabbi Lawrence A. Hoffman*

Be spiritually prepared for your journey to Israel.

A Jewish spiritual travel guide to Israel, helping today's pilgrim tap into the deep spiritual meaning of the ancient—and modern—sites of the Holy Land. Combines in quick reference format ancient blessings, medieval prayers, biblical and historical references, and modern poetry. The only guidebook that helps readers to prepare spiritually for the occasion. More than a guide book: It is a spiritual map.

"At last, the missing guide book—one that can spiritually deepen any trip to Israel."
—*Rabbi Richard Jacobs, Westchester Reform Temple; member, Board of the New Israel Fund*

4 3/4" x 10 1/8", 192 pp. (est.) Quality Paperback Original, ISBN 1-879045-56-7 **$18.95**

Children's Spirituality

A PRAYER FOR THE EARTH
The Story of Naamah, Noah's Wife

For ages 4 and up

by *Sandy Eisenberg Sasso*
Full-color illustrations by *Bethanne Andersen*

NONDENOMINATIONAL, NONSECTARIAN

This new story, based on an ancient text, opens readers' religious imaginations to new ideas about the well-known story of the Flood. When God tells Noah to bring the animals of the world onto the ark, God *also* calls on Naamah, Noah's wife, to save each plant on Earth.

•AWARD WINNER•

"A lovely tale....Children of all ages should be drawn to this parable for our times."
—*Tomie dePaola, artist/author of books for children*

9" x 12", 32 pp. HC, Full-color illus., ISBN 1-879045-60-5 **$16.95**

THE 11TH COMMANDMENT
Wisdom from Our Children

For all ages

by The Children of America

MULTICULTURAL, NONDENOMINATIONAL, NONSECTARIAN

"If there were an Eleventh Commandment, what would it be?"

Children of many religious denominations across America answer this question—in their own drawings and words—in *The 11th Commandment*.

"Wonderful....This unusual book provides both food for thought and insight into the hopes and fears of today's young."
—*American Library Association's* Booklist

8" x 10", 48 pp. HC, Full-color illus., ISBN 1-879045-46-X **$16.95**

SHARING BLESSINGS
Children's Stories for Exploring the Spirit
of the Jewish Holidays

For ages 6 and up

by *Rahel Musleah* and *Rabbi Michael Klayman*
Full-color illustrations by *Mary O'Keefe Young*

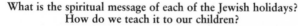

What is the spiritual message of each of the Jewish holidays? How do we teach it to our children?

Many books tell children about the historical significance and customs of the holidays. Now, through engaging, creative stories about one family's spiritual preparation, *Sharing Blessings* explores ways to get into the *spirit* of 13 different holidays.

"A beguiling introduction to important Jewish values by way of the holidays."
—*Rabbi Harold Kushner, author of* When Bad Things Happen to Good People *and* How Good Do We Have to Be?

7" x 10", 64 pp. HC, Full-color illus., ISBN 1-879045-71-0 **$18.95**

THE BOOK OF MIRACLES
A Young Person's Guide to Jewish Spiritual Awareness

For ages 9–13

by *Lawrence Kushner*

With a Special 10th Anniversary Introduction and all new illustrations by the author.

From the miracle at the Red Sea to the miracle of waking up this morning, this intriguing book introduces kids to a way of everyday spiritual thinking to last a lifetime. Kushner, whose award-winning books have brought spirituality to life for countless adults, now shows young people how to use Judaism as a foundation on which to build their lives.

6" x 9", 96 pp. HC, 2-color illus., ISBN 1-879045-78-8 **$16.95**

Children's Spirituality

For ages 8 and up

BUT GOD REMEMBERED
Stories of Women from Creation to the Promised Land
by *Sandy Eisenberg Sasso*
Full-color illustrations by *Bethanne Andersen*

NONDENOMINATIONAL, NONSECTARIAN

A fascinating collection of four different stories of women only briefly mentioned in biblical tradition and religious texts, but never before explored. Award-winning author Sasso brings to life the intriguing stories of Lilith, Serach, Bityah, and the Daughters of Z, courageous and strong women from ancient tradition. All teach important values through their faith and actions.

•AWARD WINNER•

"Exquisite....a book of beauty, strength and spirituality."
—*Association of Bible Teachers*

9" x 12", 32 pp. HC, Full-color illus., ISBN 1-879045-43-5 **$16.95**

IN GOD'S NAME
by *Sandy Eisenberg Sasso*
Full-color illustrations by *Phoebe Stone*

For ages 4 and up

MULTICULTURAL, NONDENOMINATIONAL, NONSECTARIAN

Like an ancient myth in its poetic text and vibrant illustrations, this modern fable about the search for God's name celebrates the diversity and, at the same time, the unity of all the people of the world. Each seeker claims he or she alone knows the answer. Finally, they come together and learn what God's name really is, sharing the ultimate harmony of belief in one God by people of all faiths, all backgrounds.

•AWARD WINNER•

"I got goose bumps when I read *In God's Name*, its language and illustrations are that moving. This is a book children will love and the whole family will cherish for its beauty and power."
—*Francine Klagsbrun, author of* Mixed Feelings: Love, Hate, Rivalry, and Reconciliation among Brothers and Sisters

"What a lovely, healing book!"
—*Madeleine L'Engle*

> Selected by
> Parent Council, Ltd.™

9" x 12", 32 pp. HC, Full color illus., ISBN 1-879045-26-5 **$16.95**

For ages 4 and up

GOD'S PAINTBRUSH
by *Sandy Eisenberg Sasso*
Full-color illustrations by *Annette Compton*

MULTICULTURAL, NONDENOMINATIONAL, NONSECTARIAN

Invites children of all faiths and backgrounds to encounter God openly in their own lives. Wonderfully interactive, provides questions adult and child can explore together at the end of each episode.

"An excellent way to honor the imaginative breadth and depth of the spiritual life of the young."
—*Dr. Robert Coles, Harvard University*

•AWARD WINNER•

11" x 8 1/2", 32 pp. HC, Full-color illus., ISBN 1-879045-22-2 **$16.95**

Also Available!
Teacher's Guide: A Guide for Jewish & Christian Educators and Parents
8 1/2" x 11", 32 pp. PB, ISBN 1-879045-57-5 **$6.95**

Life Cycle

GRIEF IN OUR SEASONS
A Mourner's Kaddish Companion
by *Rabbi Kerry Olitzky*

Strength from the Jewish tradition for the first year of mourning.

Provides a wise and inspiring selection of sacred Jewish writings and a simple, powerful ancient ritual for mourners to read each day, to help hold the memory of their loved ones in their hearts. It offers a comforting, step-by-step daily link to saying *Kaddish*.

"A hopeful, compassionate guide along the journey from grief to rebirth from mourning to a new mourning."
—*Rabbi Levi Meier, Ph.D., Chaplain, Cedars-Sinai Medical Center, Los Angeles*

4 1/2" x 6 1/2", 390 pp. (est.) Quality Paperback Original, ISBN 1-879045-55-9 **$15.95**

MOURNING & MITZVAH • WITH OVER 60 GUIDED EXERCISES •
A Guided Journal for Walking the Mourner's Path Through Grief to Healing
by *Anne Brener, L.C.S.W.*; Foreword by *Rabbi Jack Riemer;* Introduction by *Rabbi William Cutter*

"Fully engaging in mourning means you will be a different person than before you began." **For those who mourn a death, for those who would help them,** for those who face a loss of any kind, Brener teaches us the power and strength available to us in the fully experienced mourning process. Guided writing exercises help stimulate the processes of both conscious and unconscious healing.

"A stunning book! It offers an exploration in depth of the place where psychology and religious ritual intersect, and the name of that place is Truth."
—*Rabbi Harold Kushner, author of* When Bad Things Happen to Good People

7 1/2" x 9", 288 pp. Quality Paperback Original, ISBN 1-879045-23-0 **$19.95**

A TIME TO MOURN, A TIME TO COMFORT
A Guide to Jewish Bereavement and Comfort
by *Dr. Ron Wolfson*

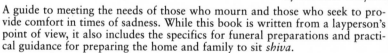

A guide to meeting the needs of those who mourn and those who seek to provide comfort in times of sadness. While this book is written from a layperson's point of view, it also includes the specifics for funeral preparations and practical guidance for preparing the home and family to sit *shiva*.

"A sensitive and perceptive guide to Jewish tradition. Both those who mourn and those who comfort will find it a map to accompany them through the whirlwind."
—*Deborah E. Lipstadt, Emory University*

7" x 9", 320 pp. Quality Paperback, ISBN 1-879045-96-6 **$16.95**

WHEN A GRANDPARENT DIES
A Kid's Own Remembering Workbook for Dealing with Shiva and the Year Beyond
by *Nechama Liss-Levinson, Ph.D.*

Drawing insights from both psychology and Jewish tradition, this workbook helps children participate in the process of mourning, offering guided exercises, rituals and places to write, draw, list, create and express their feelings.

"Will bring support, guidance, and understanding for countless children, teachers, and health professionals."
—*Rabbi Earl A. Grollman, D.D., author of* Talking about Death

8" x 10", 48 pp. HC, illus., 2-color text, ISBN 1-879045-44-3 **$15.95**

Life Cycle

A HEART OF WISDOM
Making the Jewish Journey from Midlife Through the Elder Years
Edited by *Susan Berrin*

We are all growing older. *A Heart of Wisdom* shows us how to understand our own process of aging—and the aging of those we care about—from a Jewish perspective, from midlife through the elder years.

How does Jewish tradition influence our own aging? How does living, thinking and worshipping as a Jew affect us as we age? How can Jewish tradition help us retain our dignity as we age? Offers insights and enlightenment from Jewish tradition.

"A thoughtfully orchestrated collection of pieces that deal candidly and compassionately with a period of growing concern to us all: midlife through old age."
—Chaim Potok

6" x 9", 384 pp. HC, ISBN 1-879045-73-7 **$24.95**

LIFECYCLES
V. 1: Jewish Women on Life Passages & Personal Milestones
Edited and with Introductions by *Rabbi Debra Orenstein*
V. 2: Jewish Women on Biblical Themes in Contemporary Life
Edited and with Introductions by
Rabbi Debra Orenstein and *Rabbi Jane Rachel Litman*

This unique multivolume collaboration brings together over one hundred women writers, rabbis, and scholars to create the first comprehensive work on Jewish life cycle that fully includes women's perspectives.

"Nothing is missing from this marvelous collection. You will turn to it for rituals and inspiration, prayer and poetry, comfort and community. *Lifecycles* is a gift to the Jewish woman in America."
—Letty Cottin Pogrebin, author of Deborah, Golda, and Me: Being Female and Jewish in America

V. 1: 6" x 9", 480 pp. HC, ISBN 1-879045-14-1, **$24.95**; V. 2: 6" x 9", 464 pp. HC, ISBN 1-879045-15-X, **$24.95**

LIFE CYCLE— The Art of Jewish Living Series for Holiday Observance
by Dr. Ron Wolfson

Hanukkah—7" x 9", 192 pp. Quality Paperback, ISBN 1-879045-97-4 **$16.95**

The Shabbat Seder—7" x 9", 272 pp. Quality Paperback, ISBN 1-879045-90-7 **$16.95**; Booklet of Blessings **$5.00**; Audiocassette of Blessings **$6.00**; Teacher's Guide **$4.95**

The Passover Seder—7" x 9", 336 pp. Quality Paperback, ISBN 1-879045-93-1 **$16.95**; Passover Workbook, **$6.95**; Audiocassette of Blessings, **$6.00**; Teacher's Guide, **$4.95**

LIFE CYCLE...Other Books

Bar/Bat Mitzvah Basics: A Practical Family Guide to Coming of Age Together
Ed. by Cantor Helen Leneman 6" x 9", 240 pp. Quality Paperback, ISBN 1-879045-54-0 **$16.95**

Embracing the Covenant: Converts to Judaism Talk About Why & How
Ed. and with Intros. by Rabbi Allan L. Berkowitz and Patti Moskovitz
6" x 9", 192 pp. Quality Paperback, ISBN 1-879045-50-8 **$15.95**

The New Jewish Baby Book: Names, Ceremonies, Customs—A Guide for Today's Families by Anita Diamant 6" x 9", 328 pp. Quality Paperback, ISBN 1-879045-28-1 **$16.95**

Putting God on the Guest List, 2nd Ed.: How to Reclaim the Spiritual Meaning of Your Child's Bar or Bat Mitzvah by Rabbi Jeffrey K. Salkin 6" x 9", 224 pp. Quality Paperback, ISBN 1-897045-59-1 **$16.95**; HC, ISBN 1-879045-58-3 **$24.95**

So That Your Values Live On: Ethical Wills & How to Prepare Them
Ed. by Rabbi Jack Riemer & Professor Nathaniel Stampfer
6" x 9", 272 pp. Quality Paperback, ISBN 1-879045-34-6 **$17.95**

AVAILABLE FROM BETTER BOOKSTORES.
TRY YOUR BOOKSTORE FIRST.

Order Information

# of Copies	Book Title / ISBN (Last 3 digits)	$ Amount
_____	_____	_____
_____	_____	_____
_____	_____	_____
_____	_____	_____
_____	_____	_____
_____	_____	_____
_____	_____	_____
_____	_____	_____
_____	_____	_____
_____	_____	_____
_____	_____	_____
_____	_____	_____
_____	_____	_____

For shipping/handling, add $3.50 for the first book, $2.00 each
add'l book (to a max of $15.00)   **$ S/H** _____

TOTAL _____

Check enclosed for $_____ *payable to:* JEWISH LIGHTS Publishing

Charge my credit card: ❏ MasterCard   ❏ Visa

Credit Card #_____Expires _____

Signature _____Phone (_____)_____

Your Name _____

Street_____

City / State / Zip _____

Ship To:

Name _____

Street_____

City / State / Zip _____

Phone, fax or mail to: **JEWISH LIGHTS Publishing**
P.O. Box 237 • Sunset Farm Offices, Route 4 • Woodstock, Vermont 05091
Tel (802) 457-4000   Fax (802) 457-4004   www.jewishlights.com
Credit card orders (800) 962-4544 (9AM–5PM ET Monday–Friday)
Generous discounts on quantity orders. SATISFACTION GUARANTEED. Prices subject to change.